The Religion
of Ancient Israel

LIBRARY OF ANCIENT ISRAEL

Douglas A. Knight, *General Editor*

The Religion
of Ancient Israel

PATRICK D. MILLER

SPCK
LONDON

WESTMINSTER JOHN KNOX PRESS
LOUISVILLE, KENTUCKY

First published in the United States in 2000 by
Westminster John Knox Press
100 Witherspoon Street
Louisville, KY 40202-1396

First published in Great Britain by
Society for Promoting Christian Knowledge
Holy Trinity Church
Marylebone Road
London NW1 4DU

© 2000 Patrick D. Miller

Book design by Publishers' WorkGroup
Cover design by Kim Wohlenhaus

This book is printed on acid-free paper that meets the American National Standards Institute Z39.48 standard. ∞

PRINTED IN THE UNITED STATES OF AMERICA
00 01 02 03 04 05 06 07 08 09 — 10 9 8 7 6 5 4 3 2 1

Library of Congress Cataloging-in-Publication Data

Miller, Patrick D.
    The religion of ancient Israel / Patrick D. Miller
        p. cm. — (Library of ancient Israel)
    Includes bibliographical references and index.
    ISBN 0-664-22145-9 (alk. paper)
    1. Bible. O.T.—Criticism, interpretation, etc. 2. Middle East—Religion. I. Title.
    II. Series.

BS1171.2 .M55 2000
296'.09'013—dc21   00-34978

British Cataloguing-in-Publication Data

A catalogue record of this book is available from the British Library.

ISBN 0-281-05381-2

To Frank Moore Cross
and my colleagues and friends in the
Colloquium for Biblical Research

Contents

Illustrations

Foreword

The historical and literary questions preoccupying biblical scholars since the Enlightenment have focused primarily on events and leaders in ancient Israel, the practices and beliefs of Yahwistic religion, and the oral and written stages in the development of the people's literature. Considering how little was known about Israel, and indeed the whole ancient Near East, just three centuries ago, the gains achieved to date have been extraordinary, due in no small part to the unanticipated discovery by archaeologists of innumerable texts and artifacts.

Recent years have witnessed a new turn in biblical studies, occasioned largely by a growing lack of confidence in the "assured results" of past generations of scholars. At the same time, an increased openness to the methods and issues of other disciplines such as anthropology, sociology, linguistics, and literary criticism has allowed new questions to be posed regarding the old materials. Social history, a well-established area within the field of historical studies, has proved especially fruitful as a means of analyzing specific segments of the society. Instead of concentrating predominantly on national events, leading individuals, political institutions, and "high culture," social historians attend to broader and more basic issues such as social organization, conditions in cities and villages, life stages, environmental contexts, power distribution according to class and status, and social stability and instability. To inquire into such matters regarding ancient Israel shifts the focus away from those with power and the events they instigated and onto the everyday realities and social subtleties experienced by the vast majority of the population. Such exploration has now gained new force with the application of various forms of ideological criticism and other methods designed to ferret out the political, economic, and social interests concealed in the sources.

This series represents a collaborative effort to investigate several specific topics—societal structure, politics, economics, religion, literature, material culture, law, intellectual leadership, ethnic identity, social marginalization, the international context, and canon formation—each in terms of its social dimensions and processes within ancient Israel. Some of these subjects have not been explored in depth until now; others are familiar areas currently in need of reexamination. While the sociohistorical approach provides the general perspective for most volumes of the series, each author has the latitude to determine the most appropriate means for dealing with the topic at hand. Individually and collectively, the volumes aim to expand our vision of the culture and society of ancient Israel and thereby generate new appreciation for its impact on subsequent history.

The present volume by Patrick D. Miller covers the wide expanse of religious practices and expressions that have been rediscovered or reconstructed for ancient Israel from the early Iron Age to the latter part of the Second Temple period. Organized topically rather than historically, the discussion presents a discerning portrait of an extremely complex subject, one that has been sketched in part and in full by many previous scholars. Miller draws judiciously on available sources—biblical texts, other literature from the region, inscriptions, artifacts, iconographic representations, comparative resources, as well as theoretical models. He remains sensitive to the limits of our knowledge with respect to dating and interpreting the evidence, but he does not refrain from making judgments as appropriate, acknowledging at the outset that he is presenting here not the ancient Israelite religion itself but a construct of that religion. He sets the social context for many of the details he describes, without attempting to press these details into an overall social history for which our evidence is often too sparse. Depicting the cultic practices and beliefs not as monolithic, orthodox entities but as variable and diverse forms allows for consideration of three basic religious types—family religion, customs in villages and towns, and official state religion. Against this background, Miller proceeds to three specific topics for further analysis—sacrifices and offerings, holiness and purity, and religious leadership and participation. The whole study conveys a deep appreciation for the complexities of Israel's religion, for the biblical renderings of religious thought and practices, and for their significance in subsequent traditions.

Douglas A. Knight
General Editor

Acknowledgments

This book has taken longer from its inception to its completion than it should have. Along the way, I have benefited from the help and support of many persons and some institutions. First and foremost my thanks goes to Princeton Theological Seminary, its Board of Trustees and particularly its President, Thomas Gillespie, and its Dean, James Armstrong. Both of these persons value the scholarly work of their faculty and undergird it in every way. In my case, that has meant support of varying sorts—personal interest, financial assistance, and released time for sabbaticals and leaves.

During two sabbaticals when parts of this book were being prepared or revised, the Association of Theological Schools provided grants to help fund the sabbatical time, in part through money provided by the Lilly Endowment. All of us in theological education are indebted to both of these institutions for their vigorous support of theological scholarship.

The early drafts of the book were written during a sabbatical spent at Clare Hall in Cambridge, England. I want to express my gratitude to the then President of the College and his wife, Anthony and Belle Low, as well as to the fellows of the College for their invitation to be a Visiting Fellow and for the warm reception they extended to me and my wife, Mary Ann. A special word of thanks is owed to Elizabeth Ramsden of the staff of the College for her continuing friendship. Through the years she has been a key person in making Visiting Fellows and their families at ease and at home at Clare Hall.

The final drafts of part of this book were written during a year's stay at the Center of Theological Inquiry. While this was not my main project during my time at the Center, it would not have been possible to complete the book by this time had the Center not provided both support and a congenial atmosphere for research and writing. I am indebted to the Director of the Center, Wallace M. Alston, and to Robert Jenson, Senior Scholar for Research. Under their leadership the Center has become a genuinely exciting "center" of theological discussion and inquiry.

Numerous individuals have helped me along the way by providing materials for study. I hope I have identified them at the appropriate places. Walter Brueggemann and Gerald Janzen read parts of the manuscript and made many helpful suggestions. I am particularly indebted to three other persons. Douglas Knight, the editor of the series to which this book belongs, not only extended the invitation to write this volume but patiently waited for its completion, always providing encouraging words. Bryan Bibb has quietly, diligently, and with great efficiency served as my research assistant during the past year as I have completed the book. I am especially grateful for his care in preparing the final manuscript for the publisher. Finally, on quite short notice and with a limited amount of time, my student Christine Thomas took time away from other responsibilities to prepare the drawings for the book. I am grateful to all of these persons for their different contributions.

Introduction

PERSPECTIVE

On its own terms, the religion of Iron Age Israel cannot help but interest, indeed fascinate, the student of the ancient world. In the midst of the much larger and equally fascinating empires of Mesopotamia, Anatolia, Syria, and Egypt, the small nation of Israel found itself at a crossroads of political, economic, and cultural life in the Fertile Crescent. Unlike most of the other political entities of the same age, the extant literary remains are almost entirely focused on the religious dimension of Israel's life and history. While information about other aspects of life in ancient Israel can be extracted from those remains, they stand as a testimony first of all about the religion of that people.

When one then takes account of the continuing impact of these literary remains, particularly and primarily the Bible, and the dependence of major contemporary religious communities upon the literature of that ancient religion, comprehending the religious life and faith of the people of Israel becomes a matter of heightened significance. The enterprise of uncovering the religion of Israel has a paradoxical effect upon contemporary readers who belong to the religious communities that still read the texts as religious documents and not simply as an antiquarian library. On the one hand, there is a distancing from the biblical texts as one discovers that much of the practice that is either central or undergirds the faith and the beliefs represented there is quite foreign and strange, and often unrelated to the practice of the communities that hold to the Bible as a religiously significant document, for example, the practice of sacrifice. On the other hand, however, the interplay between practice and literature that is everywhere evident means that the literature is illumined by the knowledge of religious practice even as one discerns much of the practice from the literature. So the student of the Bible, whether for academic or religious purposes, is led more deeply into the text and its meaning as one learns of the religious practices and institutions that the text reflects.

The pages that follow are an effort to comprehend and present the religion of this ancient people in behalf of a greater understanding of the "then"—an appropriate task in itself—and toward an understanding of the "then" in behalf of the "now." The word "effort" is used intentionally as an important qualifier. There is much that we do not know, much that we cannot know, and much that we probably misunderstand. The possible and highly variable interpretations of many key texts informing us about the religious life of Israel mean that misunderstanding is built into the process. The only thing one can do is make judgments as carefully and judiciously as possible, often finding oneself forced to choose among legitimate but differing interpretations of the data and often having to acknowledge the impossibility of making any kind of final decision.

What is true for the literary remains is equally the case for artifactual and iconographic evidence that is available to the contemporary scholar and interpreter as a result of the extensive archaeological work of the last century and more. The stones are not utterly mute and certainly the pictorial remains convey a great deal. But in both instances, the interpretive task is as large or larger than it is for the written remains. They can illumine one another, and in this work I have sought to draw upon the artifactual and the iconographic as well as the literary. But in the final analysis, much of our judgment about the artifactual comes from what we know of the literature, both biblical and extrabiblical. The responsibility of the student of Israel's religion is not one of choosing or emphasizing one body of evidence over another but the intermixing of data from literary (and epigraphic), iconographic, and artifactual remains that are neither literary nor pictorial. All of the evidence is subject to varying interpretations. One has only to look at the discussion of the inscriptions that refer to "Yahweh and his asherah," inscriptions that are quite legible and readable but evince a variety of interpretations of their significance for understanding the ancient religion of Israel, identified often in these pages—as elsewhere—by the term Yahwism (see chapter 1).

In addition to the openness arising out of the difficulties of interpretation and the many possibilities of interpretation often present with regard to any piece of evidence, there is the matter of how one weighs the data, what things are given primacy or emphasis, what matters are ignored. What follows here clearly represents some choices about what is to be examined, what topics are central, and what data are pertinent. The exponent of Israel's religion cannot avoid such choices and the risk of distortion that the choices inevitably create. When one then adds the difficulty of dating texts—less a problem though not altogether missing in dealing with the archaeological remains—and the question of the significance of the dating of the text for the dating of the information it contains, then the room for misunderstanding simply mushrooms.

In light of all these inhibiting factors blocking an accurate assessment of the religion of ancient Israel—to which one must add the perpetual difficulty of ever adequately understanding the culture of another people far distant in time—it is important to recognize that what follows is a construct of that religion, pieced together from a mass of data and an even larger mass of interpretive assessments of the data. The whole matter is like a picture puzzle, in a sense. The outcome, however, is not simply a puzzle with a lot of pieces missing; there are bound to be many pieces that have been put together wrongly, so that one ends up not only with holes in the picture but with all sorts of distortions. It is my hope that the construct presented here does not distort that picture too much.

It certainly does not look like everybody else's picture. But then that would be an impossible goal because it assumes a kind of consensus that does not exist. There are ways in which the presentation of the religion of Israel in these pages parts company with some rather dominant views, a few of which offer themselves as a premature consensus or as the assured results of archaeological and literary study. There are other places where I hope that the depiction will be widely acknowledged, for it often grows out of the capable work of other scholars in the field.

The influences on this work of certain leading figures will be evident. I first began the study of Israel's religion under the tutelage of Frank Moore Cross. Those who have studied with him and paid close attention to his careful mix of detailed study of biblical and extrabiblical texts with brilliant intuition and insight will not be surprised to find these pages often reflective of his deep study of Israel's religion in the light of its milieu. But I am heavily indebted to such scholars as Jacob Milgrom and Baruch Levine, Othmar Keel and Christoph Uehlinger, Phyllis Bird, Judith Hadley, and Rainer Albertz, and many other persons, some of whom I do not know but whose labors have made mine much lighter and have helped me see what I could not have seen without their assistance. No single scholarly enterprise that I have undertaken has involved as much research and reading as this one, and there is a large amount of still untouched richness of interpretation of Israel's religion of which I have not been able to avail myself, simply by the limits of time and endurance.

One of the aims of this series is to pay attention to social processes and settings as the context for understanding the material and the subject before us. That is certainly appropriate for the study of Israel's religion. I have sought to do that at a number of places and to read the religion of Israel in relation to the culture and the society of which it was a part. Two caveats, however, must be entered at the beginning. One is the recognition that I am not a sociologist or an anthropologist and my knowledge of the methods and conclusions of those and related disciplines is secondhand and thus limited. I have sought to pay attention to the literature and learn from it, but I have not tried to go beyond my competence, seeking simply to make careful judgments about the social dimensions and process where appropriate and accessible. The second caveat is my conviction that there is much in the sociohistorical study of Israel's religion that remains highly speculative. That is a danger for any kind of reconstruction, but comprehensive theories about various topics, such as sacrifice, holiness, aniconism, and the like often seem difficult to root in the text and therefore difficult to appropriate with any confidence. Reticence at this point may be a result of ignorance, but it is appropriate under the circumstances.

APPROACH

While what follows is a construct, that is, an effort to draw together in somewhat systematic fashion a picture of a whole—one that was never as systematic as this picture portrays it and that surely varied in certain ways from this and any construction of the religion—this does not mean that either the entity Israel or its religion are to be regarded as figments or largely fictive projections from a later time. The existence of "Israel" from the Late Bronze Age until the time of the latest documents of the Old Testament is a fact, attested as well from extrabiblical documents as from biblical ones.[1] The texts cover a wide range of that history and so bear witness to a complex phenomenon of practice and institutional setting, of liturgy and belief, about the god Yahweh and the proper and improper worship of him. The centrality of this deity at the heart of all the practices of Israelite religion, even when having to do with the worship of other gods, is also a fact, well attested from extrabiblical documents (see chapter 1).

The nature and character of this deity, in many respects a profile markedly like that of other Late Bronze Age/Iron Age gods, is so clearly at the heart of Israelite religion that it provides the starting point for a presentation of that religion. Sketching the profile of that deity and the divine world within which Yahweh was the center is the focus of chapter 1 of this book. As such, it is foundational for all that follows. The same is true of chapter 2, which is an extended attempt to describe forms or types of religious expression and practice that may be discerned from the various kinds of evidence about Israel's religion. At the heart of this analysis is a recognition especially of three fundamental types of Israelite religion: family religion, local cults, and official state religion. The reader familiar with Rainer Albertz's comprehensive two-volume study of the history of Israel's religion will not be surprised to encounter such a reconstruction of the religion of Israel. I am much indebted to Albertz, but in this regard more to his earlier monograph on official and popular religion than to his history, which had not appeared when the basic draft of chapter 2 was first written. By that time, however, a number of other works had appeared along with Albertz's monograph that helped us see in the biblical and artifactual evidence indications that the religious expression of the people of Israel had in fact taken different forms in different settings. That form-critical analogy has suggested the possibility of describing "types" of Israelite religion, and I have attempted that in chapter 2 from two different angles.

There is some sense in which these two chapters cover the whole of Israelite religion (and their length is the equivalent of a small monograph), but I have chosen to explicate three other topics in more detail, believing that while each of them is anticipated in the first two chapters, they are each more complex and so important for the religion of Israel that they warrant more extended treatments. These are sacrifice, holiness and purity, and the leadership and participation of persons in the practices of Israelite religion, particularly the more formal cult of the national expressions of that religion. Other topics could also justify a more developed approach, for example, the temple or the festivals, but they are treated at other points, and the limits of space prohibit a detailed examination of many different aspects of the religion of Israel. I hope that the first two chapters provide sufficient orientation and that the next three chapters will help the reader get at some of the more difficult and debated aspects of Israel's religion. I am not unaware that there has been a predisposition of Protestant interpreters to slough over sacrifice and for Christians in general to ignore the concerns for order, purity, and holiness that are represented especially in the priestly legislation. The choice of topics at that point reflects such awareness. At several points in the book, I lift up a more recent and much-debated topic of some contemporary interest and possible relevance: the role of women in Israelite religion. So the agenda of this view of Israelite religion is shaped in part by the materials and in part by the circumstances of its writing. In my judgment, such objective and subjective elements are nearly always present in our scholarly endeavors and often bring forth fruitful results.[2]

Most readers will note immediately that I have not taken the tack of

Albertz and many interpreters of Israelite religion, that is, a primarily historical approach. In that respect, this volume does not pose as a *history* of Israelite religion. Happily, the reader has access to Albertz's thoroughly historical approach if and when that is needed. I have sought to focus rather on significant dimensions or topics of Israelite religion, believing that getting a grasp on them in some depth will be of benefit to those who want a profile of the religious character of the people of Israel. At the same time, however, I have tried to be attentive to historical dimensions, to changes in the form and character of Israelite religion all along the way. Taking a more topical approach with attention to historical movement and change has the disadvantage of blurring many of the finer points of the history and of the developments in that history. It has the advantage of keeping certain key features front and center in a way that lets one get at them less spasmodically and atomistically. The more topical framework also manages better to avoid some of the inevitably speculative character of most historical approaches, which are forced to make decisions about dating of practices in relation to texts in a way that the material often resists.[3]

A feature missing from the book is any summary presentation of the history of the discipline or of the discussion of methodological issues involved in dealing with Israel's religion. I have dealt with those in part elsewhere, and there are accessible surveys of at least some of the more recent scholarly work on the religion of Israel.[4]

CHAPTER 1

God and the Gods

Deity and the Divine World in Ancient Israel

ISRAEL'S GOD

The center of ancient Israel's religion was the worship of a deity named Yahweh. Biblical, epigraphic, and archaeological evidence all confirm that fact.[1] For this reason, the religion of Israel is often referred to, not incorrectly, as Yahwism. That other deities were worshiped at different times or by different groups or that syncretistic movements took place from time to time cannot undermine the centrality of the worship of Yahweh throughout the course of ancient Israel's history.[2]

The origins of the worship of Yahweh are shrouded in mystery, but they reach back at least to the early Iron Age and apparently as far as the Late Bronze Age. The earliest known possible reference to the name of the deity occurs in an Egyptian toponym list from the time of Amenhotep III (c. 1400 B.C.E.), where a place called *Yhw* is associated with a nomadic group, the Shasu, whose location south of Palestine is indicated by other toponyms in the list. That is consistent with indications in the early poetry of Israel that Yahweh was a deity associated at the beginning with the South. Various places—Sinai, Seir, Edom, Paran, and Teman—are given as the places from which Yahweh marches or comes.[3] They identify the locus or abode of this deity with the region of Edom and Midian,[4] which also seems to be the area where Moses first encountered this deity at the "mountain of God" (Ex. 3:1–5).[5] That encounter, as well as the indication that Moses' father-in-law, Jethro, priest of Midian, may have been a worshiper of Yahweh (Ex. 18:9–12),[6] provides a plausible point of contact between the cult of Yahweh in the South and the Moses group or Proto-Israel.[7]

The name of the deity was a matter of some importance to the Israelite religious community, both for the way in which it identified the deity and also because of its character as a kind of theologumenon for him. The initial encounter between Moses and Yahweh in the biblical tradition focuses upon the name (Exodus 3–4). That is probably an accurate reflection of the significance the name came to have at an early stage in the tradition. While the vowels were lost and its pronunciation forgotten as a result of the later decision of the Jewish community not to pronounce the sacred name of God,[8] linguistic and transcriptional evidence indicates that the spelling of the divine name was in all likelihood *yahweh*.[9] That evidence also suggests that *yahweh* is "a shortened form of a sentence name taken from a cultic formula."[10] It is probably a causative form of the verb "to be," meaning "he causes to be," or "he creates." The name may have had an object after it at one point, the most likely being *Ṣĕbā'ôt,* "hosts," in light of the liturgical name of the ark, "Yahweh of hosts, enthroned on the cherubim," which refers to the cherub throne of the invisible God that was part of the iconography of the Yahweh shrine at Shiloh and later at Jerusalem. The name *Yahweh Ṣĕbā'ôt* would mean "He creates the hosts." The reference would be to the hosts of heaven who made up the coterie and military entourage of Yahweh marching forth alongside the armies of Israel in the holy war ideology of early Israel as reflected in its early poetry and other texts.[11] Creative activity, therefore, is not a late accretion to the mythology of Yahweh. Creation and procreation[12] of gods and human beings as well as of the natural order[13] was an aspect of the deity's activity, as was true of other high gods and especially of El, the Canaanite god with whom Yahweh was most closely associated (see below) and who was characterized as father of human beings and of the gods.

An object is not required for the verbal form *yahweh,* but it may have been a part of a longer sentence name, as reflected in Ex. 3:14, where the sentence *'ehyeh 'ăšer 'ehyeh* is given as the first answer to Moses' question about the name of the deity he encounters at Horeb/Sinai. Frank Cross has suggested quite plausibly that lying behind this sentence may have been the sentence name, *el dū yahwī (ṣaba'ôt),* "El who creates the hosts."[14] The god El is well known from the mythological and religious texts at Ugarit as the high god who was the head of the Canaanite pantheon (figs. 1 and 2). Genesis and Exodus 6 show indications of pre-Yahwistic worship by pre-Israelite clans as the worship of El and/or the clan deities, known as the gods of the fathers (see below). The Priestly stratum of the Pentateuch identifies an earlier stage (Ex. 6:3) of Israel's religion that centered on the worship of *El Shaddai* but maintains that this was a prior revelation of the god Yahweh. That judgment seems to be correct. *Yahweh* was probably originally a cultic name of El as worshiped in the South. In some fashion, unknown to us, it would have split off into the particular worship of Yahweh, but the association with El continued throughout the history of Israel's religion.[15] El's names, iconography, and characteristics were

Fig. 1. The so-called El stele from Ugarit, featuring a relief of what is probably the high god El on his throne. (*After* ANEP, *no. 493*)

always freely associated with Yahweh and without condemnation, a fact that seems not to have been true with regard to any other northwest Semitic god.[16]

The absence of any god but Yahweh from a central place in the course of Israel's religion is matched by the absence of Yahweh from any place in the pantheons or in the cultus of any other people of the ancient Near East. While it is possible that signs of such worship may yet turn up, that fact is rather remarkable, for there are many indications of the sharing of deities among the various groups of the Near East.[17] Besides the evidence for the essentially exclusive worship of Yahweh by Israel (there are, of course, exceptions to this) this association of Yahweh exclusively with Israel or pre-Israelite elements suggests an intimate relation between deity and people, which the biblical traditions tend to confirm in a variety of ways as they characterize Israel's god and that relationship.[18]

The early association of Yahweh with the desert or its fringes in southern Palestine and with what were probably seminomadic pastoralists probably

Fig. 2. Statuette of seated god El, bronze covered with gold, from Ugarit. (*After* ANEP, *no. 826*)

has something to do with the character of the deity and the relationship between the deity and his worshipers. Yahweh was not a god whose locus was the Canaanite city-states and their pantheons or triads of deities.[19] He was more the clan or patron god of a group that developed into a nation. It is not surprising that the closest analogies, sociopolitical and religious, may be found in the southern areas of Edom, Moab, and Ammon where, as in Israel, kingdoms developed late and league or patriarchal institutions centered around a patron deity, later the national god, rather than around a complex of deities.[20] The close relationship between deity and tribe or tribes was rooted in kinship relations and historical experience. It expressed itself in covenantal forms, at the heart of which was a binding together of the people in a sociopolitical relation with the deity that recognized the involvement of Yahweh in the guiding and protecting of the people and that obligated them to maintain allegiance to him, adhering to various stipulations that served to order their life and their relationship to other social groups or peoples.

The covenant forms of the league constitute an extended kinship
group, provide means for group action in war by the creation of a militia in times of crisis, [and] provide a limited judicial system for mediation of intertribal disputes.[21]

There does not seem to have been any period in Israel's religious
history where the specific recognition of the relation of deity and tribe or
people was not expressed in such a pact, though it took different forms
prior to the monarchy and during it and may have been understood or for-
mulated differently in the North and in the South. In its simplest form,
which is not necessarily the earliest, that covenantal bond rested in the rec-
iprocal claim and promise of Yahweh, "You are my people," and of Israel,
"You are my God" (Hos. 2:25[23]).[22] In its more complex form, the covenantal bond has been compared with international political treaties of the first
and second millennium that spelled out the way in which a great king (in
this case, Yahweh) had dealt beneficially with a vassal (in this case, Israel),
set forth stipulations that such benevolence placed upon the vassal, and
built in provisions for sanctions, witnesses, safekeeping of the treaty document, and its regular reading by the vassal.[23]

The covenantal structure assumes a theocratic model of rule mediated
through various officials and leaders, such as judges and elders, priests and
prophets. Its modes of power were ideological, coercive, and consensual.
The ideological dimension is seen in the degree to which the effectiveness
of the structure of covenant for Israel's religious and communal life
depended upon deference and allegiance to the deity, mutual recognition
between the two parties, deity and people, and the exclusiveness of the
relationship between them. That the exercise of power was by persuasion
and rhetoric is seen in the covenant document par excellence, Deuteronomy. It set up a structure for existence—social, political, economic, and
religious—that depended upon the willingness of the people to accede to
the demands of the covenant, a willingness that was elicited in large part
by preaching, testimony, self-understanding, and self-indictment through
song and instruction taught and learned by the people. At the same time,
this social structure was rooted in a consensual-coercive power reflected in
the people's acceptance of the requirements of obedience to the divine
command as well as the sanctions invoked for obedience and disobedience, sanctions that were spelled out in curses and blessings incorporated
into the covenant document, certainly at least in its first-millennium form.
To some extent, the economic mode of power in the social structure came
into play in that obedience to the covenant was presented as a necessary
prerequisite to the enjoyment of the good fruits of a good land.[24] When the

covenantal structure of Israel's life shifted to incorporate the kingship (at least in Judah), the ideological became rooted in a royal theology that claimed the king was the chosen of Yahweh, adopted as "my son" by the deity and beneficiary of a covenantal relationship requiring obedience and offering eternal dynastic rule. The ability of the kings of Judah to maintain control and power depended heavily upon this ideological component even as the coercive dimension increased with the power of the king and his military might to gain access to the means of economic production.[25] In the North, a less developed royal covenant and ideology contributed to a less stable royal control and dynasty.

The development of family religion alongside larger communal expressions of Yahwism and the melding of these, particularly in the Deuteronomic movement (see chapter 2) was surely aided by the fact that from the beginning the covenant between Yahweh and Israel was not only a political structure; it was also an expression of kinship relations. The kinship modes of Israel's life in the early period were precisely the context in which covenantal notions developed, both in interpersonal and intertribal relations and also in the relation between Yahweh and Israel. If relationships in ancient Israel were first of all governed by kinship (and that seems to have been the case), so that family and tribe were the central social units, then covenant was the legal way of effecting what Cross has called "kinship-in-law."[26] That is, covenant was the mode whereby someone or some group not a part of the kinship unit was brought into it, a legal means of creating a new kinship bond between persons—for example, David and Jonathan, who were not kin, but covenanted together as brothers (1 Sam. 18:1, 3; 20:17). This kinship relation through covenant placed law at its center; that is, it understood the law as the way of defining relationships within the family unit, relationships that included mutuality of treatment but also acts of love and loyalty (Lev. 19:17–18). So, while the obligation to love the Lord arose out of the suzerain relationship as governed in the treaty-covenant, the love of the neighbor/brother/sister was an obligation of the kinship relation and extended into other relationships by an act of covenant, a complex covenantal structure signaled in the simple but early designation of Israel as "the people of Yahweh."

Images of Yahweh

It is not surprising, in light of the above, that the chief images and metaphors by which ancient Israel characterized its God were heavily sociopolitical.[27] While the association of Yahweh with the natural world is clear, with the deity who claimed power over the forces of the storm (e.g.,

Psalm 29) and fertility (e.g., Hosea 2)[28] becoming apparently more associated with solar and lunar imagery in the late preexilic period,[29] the dominant and controlling images that Israel carried of its God were *warrior*, *judge*, and *king*.[30] Two of the earliest texts preserved in the Bible, Exodus 15 and Judges 5, are victory songs celebrating Yahweh's defeat of the enemies of Israel. In the former, the battle at the sea and the victory were understood to be entirely the deity's. The people were not involved except as the recipients of the divine act. The song concludes the complex account of the conflict between Hebrew slaves and an unnamed Egyptian king (Exodus 1–14) and claims to see in that conflict and its outcome the nature and character of the deity whose name was revealed in that context: Yahweh is a warrior; Yahweh is his name (v. 3). The establishment of Yahweh's sanctuary (v. 17) and kingship (v. 18) were confirmed in this victory, as Israel's historical experience was couched in part in the categories of myth where the deity defeats the powers of chaos, sea, and death, thereby winning the right to build an abode or palace and claim kingship over the gods.[31] In the Song of Deborah (Judges 5), the enemies (v. 31) and the victory (v. 11) are still Yahweh's. There is a more symbiotic involvement of the people, however, who were expected to come to the aid of Yahweh in the battle (v. 23).

The two songs are indicative of the sociopolitical character of the relation between Yahweh and Israel. The deity's name and character were revealed in a war of liberation, interpreted via the mythopoeic categories of Late Bronze Age Canaan (Exodus 15). The Israelites identified their deity as one who had brought them out of slavery in the defeat of the Egyptians, and that act shaped the perception of Yahweh's character and became indicative of how Israel was to treat slaves and other groups outside the fixed structures of power. In other words, the ethos of Israel, which manifested a perduring concern for the marginal and powerless—a concern reflected in legal collections, prophetic oracles, narratives, psalms, and wisdom sayings—was rooted in its earliest understanding of the revelation of Yahweh as the liberating warrior. The sociopolitical context of the revelation of the deity to the people in their suffering and liberation from slavery placed that same context as a controlling factor in their moral life[32] and their understanding of community.[33]

Judges 5 attests to the locus of this imagery of the divine warrior also within the early league traditions and covenantal obligations,[34] in which the tribes were understood to have mutual responsibilities for protection and support as a part of their obligation to Yahweh. The poem is a celebration (v. 3) of Yahweh's "triumphs" (*ṣidqôt*, v. 11), but they are also the "triumphs" of "his peasantry in Israel." The poem is as much a recounting of the participation of the tribes who are led by Yahweh as it is a recounting of Yahweh's might.[35] But throughout, the poem also deals with the issue of willing participation and acceptance of obligation on the part of the tribes who were bound together in responsibility for mutual defense and common allegiance to Yahweh.[36] The expression "people of Yahweh" (v. 13), one of the oldest characterizations of the Israelite community, probably was a designation of that group as a militia in service of the warrior God who protected them and led them in battle against their enemies and his (vv. 4–5, 31).[37] At its conclusion, this ancient text pronounces doom on all Yahweh's enemies and blessing on "his friends," literally, "those who love him," or keep the covenant obligations of allegiance and social solidarity within the "people of Yahweh."

The image of Yahweh as divine warrior, reflected in early poems such as these as well as in the epithet "Yahweh of Hosts" continued to play a major role throughout the history of Israel's religion. The story of the battle of Ebenezer and the loss of the ark on that occasion in 1 Samuel 4–5 attests to the assumptions on the part of Israelites and Philistines alike that the ark was the palladium of the God or gods of Israel and its presence assured the power or "hand" of the Israelite deity against the enemy.[38] That the battle seems to deny such power should not mislead one. The Philistines are defeated ultimately by the "hand" of Yahweh, and the turning point is a quite specific, if narratively veiled, account of Yahweh's battle with and defeat of the Philistine god Dagon (1 Sam. 5:1–5).[39] One encounters the imagery of Yahweh the warrior in a major way in the oracles of the prophets from the ninth century onward, and the prophetic function to be the herald or announcer of Yahweh's interventions in war is rooted in this conception of the deity.[40] Two things particularly are noticeable. One is a popular belief, shared by prophetic figures, that the Day of Yahweh was a time when their God would destroy their enemies (Amos 5:18–20). This "Day of Yahweh," which was rooted in the early notions of Yahweh as warrior and in the recollection of the early wars of Yahweh, became one of the prime categories for Israelite eschatology and apocalyptic, as official and popular theology anticipated the march of Yahweh and his armies against the armies of the nations and the forces of darkness.[41] Both the earlier wars of Yahweh and the anticipated Day of Yahweh were celebrated in the festivals of the Israelite cultus, where Yahweh's victories were recalled cultically in recollection of Israel's liberation and occupation of their land and also in commemoration of Yahweh's kingship established in these victories. The other dimension in the prophetic presentation of the divine warrior is the claim that the activity of the warrior deity could and would be against Israel itself when it failed to live by the religious and social obligations to which it was bound by covenantal agreement (e.g., Amos 5:18–20; Isaiah 10). The religious ideology that centered in a mythohistorical perception of Yahweh as the warrior in behalf of Israel's need for liberation and preservation as well as for land and space to settle and live thus carried within itself the seeds of its own undoing in prophetic critique as well as the elements by which a rationalization of the fate of the people when defeated and sent into exile could be achieved.[42]

Closely allied to the imagery of God as warrior and sharing some of the social functions of that imagery was the conception of Yahweh as the righteous judge. Again, this imagery is present in archaic poetry, such as Deut. 32:4–5 and Ps. 68:6(5), where Yahweh is called "father of orphans" and "judge of widows," but it is pervasive in texts from different periods and settings within ancient Israel: ancient confessional statements (Ex. 34:6–7), sagas (Gen. 18:22–33), hymns (Psalms 96–99), legal codes (Ex. 21:6; 22:8–9, 11, 21–25), and prophetic lawsuits (Isa. 3:13–15; Micah 6:1–8) and judgment speeches (Amos 5:7, 10–11; Micah 2:1–5). In part, such imagery undergirded and provided religious or theological sanction for the administration of justice in the community of Israel. That is, the righteous Judge of Israel called for a righteousness and justice in the human community and pronounced judgment upon those who did not carry out explicit and implicit norms for justice. Indeed, the righteousness of Yahweh was whatever activity the deity carried out or required of others to establish and maintain.[43] The divine judge, therefore, like the divine warrior, was a powerful religious impetus—within the established procedures for the administration of justice (e.g., the legal statutes and processes) and through critical voices from outside (e.g., Amos)—for the maintenance of justice in the courts and the protection of the weaker elements in the society from exploitation and oppression. A particular ethos was effected and the order of society was enhanced. As with the imagery of warrior, however, the activity of the divine judge could be a polemical tool perceived by elements in the society as threatening social chaos (e.g., Amos 7:10–17) and also a means of rationalizing the chaos when it took place (e.g., Isa. 40:1–2).

There were further and significant political and religious effects of this divine imagery. The judgment of Yahweh extended over the nations, as one sees in texts such as Deuteronomy 32, where the judgment of the divine judge is carried out in his warrior role, and more generally in the prophetic oracles against the nations. But that judgment also extended over the divine realm. Psalm 82 is a surprising and somewhat unprecedented ancient Near

Eastern text recounting a judicial assembly of the gods in which Yahweh stands up to indict and pronounce judgment upon all the other gods of the cosmos for their failure to maintain justice for the weak. The justice of Yahweh and his role as judge (i.e., the one responsible for maintaining justice and the right of the innocent) was thus also a significant polemical weapon in the conflict with the gods of the nations. It is doubtful that one can necessarily read a stage in the history of Israel's religion in this text, but its testimony to the moral dimension at the center of the notion of the divine is clear.

The kingship of Yahweh is a feature of Israelite religion from early stages.[44] It is thematic in the earliest poetry. The Song of the Sea in Exodus 15 reaches its climax with the declaration that "Yahweh will reign forever and ever," and other archaic poetry speaks of Yahweh as king.[45] As a divine title or epithet, "king" originally meant one god as ruler over other gods. That was true in Ugarit, Egypt, and Mesopotamia. It had its roots significantly in the mythological pattern discerned in such texts as the Babylonian Creation Epic and the Baal-Anat cycle at Ugarit in which the god fought against hostile and chaotic forces (associated with sea or death), achieved victory, and was rewarded with the building of a house (temple/palace) as an eternal abode. The victory also brought about the declaration of the god's eternal rule or kingship.

This pattern had its impact on Israelite conceptions of Yahweh's nature and role but with significant modifications. The rule of God was seen and explicated primarily in terms of human communities, as, for example, in Exodus 15, while the cosmic rule of Yahweh was always affirmed.[46] The victory of Yahweh to bring about this divine rule took place primarily over the human forces of chaos, although mythopoeic categories were sometimes explicitly the vehicle for describing the battle and the victory (e.g., Isa. 51:9–11), and the defeat of the deity who led the opposing forces might be assumed (e.g., 1 Sam. 5:1–5). In the course of Israel's religion, the divine rule also came to be extended temporally and spatially without any limits and was understood to have its full manifestation in the future when victory over the hostile nations would be complete and all would acknowledge the universal reign of Yahweh.[47]

The images of Yahweh as warrior and king[48] were joined not only conceptually in the interpretation of historical experience with the language and clothing of myth but also in the cultus, where the procession of the Divine Warrior into the sanctuary was a celebration of Yahweh's kingship, a rule demonstrated in the victory over Israel's enemies. While there is much that we do not know about the cultic enactments of the major festivals, there are indirect indications in such texts as Psalm 24 and 132 as well as Joshua 3–5 that in the premonarchical and monarchical periods the central act was the procession of the ark, on which was enthroned "the King of glory," into the temple. Such celebration of Yahweh's victory and rule, which would have been characteristic of the earliest spring festival ritual at Gilgal,[49] also served to confirm and validate the establishment of Zion as the dwelling of Yahweh and the Davidic king as the anointed agent of Yahweh's rule (see chapters 2 and 5).[50]

The close connections between the rule of Yahweh and the warrior imagery carry over into the juridical imagery. That is, the provision for justice was a function of the ruler, and the enthronement psalms, which are among the primary declarations of Yahweh's kingship, specifically couch that reign or dominion frequently in judging language and assert the rule of Yahweh as a righteous and just rule (Pss. 96:10–13; 98:7–9; 99:4).

The kingship of Yahweh seems at all times to have served both to undergird the existing sociopolitical structure and to challenge its manifestations.[51] While that is especially true of the monarchical period, it seems also to have been the case in the less-ordered earlier period of the league of tribes, although the data there are less clear. Yahweh's rule as king over Israel in a theocratic structure was conducive to a system of tribal life and community that lacked a central government and permanent controls over clan and personal behavior and that left kinship and regional groups with a fair amount of freedom and flexibility of action.[52] The book of Judges in its earliest levels is an account of the somewhat chaotic sociopolitical situation of premonarchic Israel with Yahweh as its only permanent king. Efforts to fix permanent rule or control in an individual were resisted in different ways, as the stories of the judges also indicate. The kingship of Yahweh was thus a part of the implicit resistance to the monarchical political structure of Late Bronze Age city-states.[53] At the same time, the rule of Yahweh without permanent human leadership and structures meant that the Israelite components were vulnerable both to dissatisfaction on the part of the divine ruler and to the claims and attacks of forces and powers of more structured political organizations among their neighbors. The claim of Yahweh to be king over Israel as well as over the gods thus meant there was a religious element within the sociopolitical structure that exercised both stabilizing and destabilizing functions within it.[54]

The same is true of the even more elaborated conception of Yahweh as king in the monarchical era. As noted above, the cultic procession into the temple of the victorious deity enthroned on the ark served to undergird and support the claims of the Davidic dynasty and Jerusalem to having been chosen by Yahweh. The real king was still the deity. The human ruler was the regent or representative of Yahweh.[55] The divine ruler, therefore, stood behind the human king and served as a guarantor of the human throne.[56] Enthroned now permanently in the temple at Zion, Yahweh also was a guarantor and validator of the national capital and national shrine, Jerusalem. The radical move to kingship in the sociopolitical sphere thus acquired legitimation by the same conceptuality that also lay behind and was at work in earlier social structures.[57]

Again, however, the functionality of divine rule could be destabilizing and critical. This is found particularly in the figure of the prophet as the agent of the divine rule who had responsibility for designating the one chosen by Yahweh as ruler as well as for pronouncing "judgment on the king, the forfeit of kingship for breach of law or covenant, as well as the death of the king for like reasons."[58] In like manner, the national shrine was not only guaranteed but also threatened by Yahweh's rule, as demonstrated by the oracles of Amos in the North and those of Micah, Jeremiah, and Ezekiel in the South.[59] Furthermore, the rule of Yahweh on Zion and through Yahweh's anointed became one of the primary carriers in Israel's religion of a vision of social and political harmony, peace, and justice.[60]

Characteristics of Yahweh

In all this imagery of Yahweh there were significant lines of continuity between Yahweh and the gods of Canaan. In many respects Yahweh was a typical Late Bronze/Early Iron Age deity. The sociopolitical metaphors for expressing the relation of deity and people were present in the worship of other gods in Syria-Palestine.[61] The close association with El, the high god of the Canaanite pantheon, which was manifest in the acceptance of the El name as a Yahweh epithet, is reflected also in the assimilation of El characteristics by Yahweh. We have already noted the reflection of such characteristics in the understanding of Yahweh as creator and father. Like El, the Israelite deity was also patriarchal in other ways, such as being old or eternal, wise, and compassionate.[62] The last attribute is lifted up by its being a part of an ancient Israelite liturgical or cultic formula that appears frequently in biblical texts and is also found in extrabiblical inscriptions.[63] It represents one of the most persistent and apparently widespread characterizations of Yahweh in Israelite religion.[64] In Ex. 34:6–7, we find the following self-disclosure or proclamation by Yahweh to Moses on Sinai:

> The LORD passed before him, and proclaimed,
>
> > "The LORD, the LORD,
> > *a God merciful and gracious,*

> *slow to anger*
> *and abounding in steadfast love* and faithfulness,
> keeping steadfast love for the thousandth generation,
> forgiving iniquity and transgression and sin,
> yet by no means clearing the guilty,
> but visiting the iniquity of the parents
> upon the children
> and the children's children,
> to the third and the fourth generation."[65]

The text sets this self-disclosure in the context of the name (v. 5). It is already anticipated in the preceding chapter, again in the context of the revelation of the name (Ex. 33:18–19):

> Moses said, "Show me your glory, I pray." And he said, "I will make all my goodness pass before you, and will proclaim before you the name, 'The LORD'; and I will be gracious to whom I will be gracious and will show mercy on whom I will show mercy."

Both of these texts characterize the deity in a fundamental way as gracious and merciful, abounding in steadfast love and faithfulness. While the text in Exodus 34 makes it very clear that such a picture of the deity is not to be set over against Yahweh's function as judge who acts in behalf of justice and exercises judgment against sin, these repeated characterizations of Yahweh as merciful and gracious ('ēl raḥûm wĕḥannûn) and acting in steadfast love define this deity in a way that lifts up mercy alongside justice as indicating the particular "bent" of the God of Israel.[66] While there may be some tension between the divine judgment and the divine mercy, that tension is indicative of Yahweh's character. The cultic formula is cited explicitly in other contexts[67] and is alluded to elsewhere.[68] The language of the formula even appears in an inscribed prayer from the seventh or sixth century found on the wall of a cave at Khirbet Beit Lei in which Yahweh is called 'l ḥnn, "gracious God," and the petitioner asks the deity as yh 'l ḥnn, "Yah(weh), gracious God," to "absolve" or "clear" (nqh) him or her.[69] The ancient blessing of Num. 6:24–26, also a text that is both echoed throughout the biblical literature[70] and known from an early sixth-century inscription on two silver amulets found outside Jerusalem (plate 9, page 166), calls for Yahweh to "be gracious" (ḥnn).[71] Further, the attributing to Yahweh of "steadfast love" (ḥesed) is ubiquitous throughout the biblical texts and frequently the ground of prayer to the deity.[72]

Two other characteristics of the Israelite deity that affected the religious expressions and convictions of the people need to be mentioned in particular. The conviction that Yahweh was *holy* permeated the religion of Israel.

It is most noticeable and emphasized in the prophets and the cultic legislation. The older poetic texts do not lift up this feature as an aspect of the
character of Yahweh in a sharp way, but it is explicitly stated in the Song
of Hannah (1 Sam. 2:2): "There is no Holy One like the LORD." The epithet
"Holy One of Israel" or even just "Holy One" came to be one of the most
common of all appellations of the deity especially in the Isaianic traditions,[73] where the theophanic context of Isaiah's call is a vision of the
enthroned Yahweh Sebaot, the King, with the angelic attendants crying out,
"Holy, holy, holy is the LORD of hosts" (Isa. 6:3). From the references to
Yahweh's holiness or Yahweh as holy, it is clear that the notion denoted
separateness and transcendence and also moral purity and right. The holiness of Yahweh was not separated from the deity's righteousness,[74] but it
was not exhausted in moral categories. It identified Yahweh as belonging
to a sphere apart from everything else in the universe, except as other
places, acts, words, and people were drawn into that sphere by association
with the deity.[75] The overlap with the notion of Yahweh as righteous is seen
in the fact that Yahweh's holiness served to define the order of the universe, which included both the moral sphere and the cultic sphere. These
could not be separated, and the claim that Yahweh was holy and required
holiness—a requirement spelled out extensively in the cultic legislation of
Leviticus, Numbers, and Ezekiel 40–48 but also claimed by the prophets as
a way of speaking about Yahweh's dealings with Israel and their
response[76]—incorporated moral and cultic claims in the broadest sense.
Increasingly in Israel's religion, the definition of the holiness that reflected
Yahweh's holiness (order and righteousness) was articulated and elaborated in cultic regulations. This seems to have been exacerbated by the
experience of judgment for sin in the destruction of Jerusalem and the exile
to Babylon and in the demands of survival in the postexilic era as an identifiable Yahwistic community without political sovereignty and in the midst
of other groups. The focus upon order and purity in the Priestly legislation
was not only a symbolic expression but a real effort to actualize the holiness of the people under a holy God.

Related to the holiness of Yahweh but standing in close textual and conceptual relation to the grace and mercy of God (Exodus 34) and the
demand for Israel's exclusive worship of Yahweh was the claim of Yahweh
to be *jealous*, an epithet that is probably quite ancient in Israel's religion
and closely associated with the covenantal relationship.[77] The jealousy of
Yahweh was a theological form of the prohibition of the worship of other
gods[78] and was a way of expressing the mutual commitment of people to
deity[79] and deity to people.[80]

While in origin the jealousy of Yahweh may have been primarily associated with the exclusive worship of Yahweh, it came to be associated also
with the prohibition of making and worshiping images.[81] Here we come
upon one of the distinctive features of the worship of Yahweh in ancient
Israel—its aniconic character.[82] The absence of images of the deity and the
concomitant prohibition against representation of deity in any form of
image[83] is anomalous in the ancient Near East.[84] The creation and use of
images in the cultus was ubiquitous in the religions of that time and place
(fig. 3).[85] For the most part in Israel, they were not present and were officially inveighed against. Three questions about this unusual phenomenon
are the subject of considerable debate: (1) Was the prohibition of images
directed primarily toward images of Yahweh or images of other gods? (2)
When did the prohibition against images actually begin? Was there a time
when images were permissible in the worship of Yahweh? (3) What was
the function or meaning of this aniconic feature? Why were images not
used and not permitted? An attempt to answer these questions will uncover
at least some of the dimensions of this rather unique feature of Yahwism.

The close tie between the commandment against images and the prior
commandment against the worship of other gods in the Decalogue (Ex.

Fig. 3. Image of a god, head covered with gold
and body with silver. From Syria. (*After* ANEP,
no. 481)

20:3–6) suggests that the veto of images was directed toward any image that might be construed as an idol or cult artifact of another deity. While the prohibition in its earliest form may have been simply, "You shall not make for yourself images," the addition of the words "or any likeness of anything that is in the heaven above, or that is on the earth beneath, or that is in the water under the earth," and the reference to bowing down and serving them, which originally had in mind the other gods of the previous commandment, serves to make a sweeping exclusion of any image of any deity. The elaboration of this prohibition in Deut. 4:16–19 confirms that as at least the eventual understanding of the prohibition. Indeed, the comprehensiveness of these formulations tended to make any kind of image, whether for purposes of worship or not, questionable.

In light of the strong resistance to the worship of other gods in the official cult of Yahweh, such an understanding is to be expected. But it is likely that at an earlier time, the prohibition was specifically directed toward the exclusion of *Yahweh* images. Deuteronomy 4, itself a late text, suggests as much when it prohibits images on the grounds that at Sinai the people saw no form when the Lord spoke to them (v. 15). The likelihood that the prohibition against images was separate from that against other gods tends to confirm this understanding. If other gods are ruled out, obviously their images are also. The imageless character of the cult of Yahweh also supports this understanding. The deity was represented by a cherubim throne upon the moveable ark (fig. 4). When the ark was carried into battle, the people and their enemies believed that Yahweh was present. But there was no statue or image of the deity. Rather, Yahweh was enthroned *invisibly* upon the cherubim. Later, in the Deuteronomic theology, the ark came to be understood as the container of the torah, or law. As such, it still represented the deity's presence, only now in the torah rather than upon an invisible throne.

The question of the antiquity of the aniconic tendency in Yahwism is more uncertain and much debated in contemporary scholarship, with views ranging from the earliest period of Israel's history to the Hasmonean period at the end of the first millennium.[86] The weight of textual and archaeological evidence suggests that it belongs to the earliest stages of Israelite religion, at least within the more official cultus of Yahweh found at the central sanctuary or sanctuaries.[87] While the dating of the decalogical prohibition of images (Ex. 20:4; Deut. 5:8) is difficult, and the formulation may have been articulated fairly late in the history of Israel,[88] the ubiquity of the prohibition in the legal collections is matched by the absence of Yahweh images or those of other male deities from Israelite sites to weight the

Fig. 4. Phoenician king Ahiram seated on a sphinx or cherubim type of throne. From Ahiram's sarcophagus. (*After* ANEP, *no. 458*)

evidence toward the assumption that the aniconic tendency was an early phenomenon in ancient Israel.[89] There is a marked contrast in the movement from Late Bronze Age sites (plate 1), where male and female images are common, to Iron Age strata in Israelite sites, where hardly any male images have been found and only one or two that might be serious candidates as an Israelite divine image (figs. 5 and 6).[90]

In his important study of Israelite aniconism, Tryggve Mettinger has suggested that one may distinguish between a de facto aniconism and a programmatic aniconism, the former being fairly tolerant, the latter moving toward a rigorous iconoclasm but developing out of the aniconic tendency of an earlier time.[91] By the former, he means either the use of aniconic symbols, such as a stone or a stela, or empty space, such as an empty throne. The programmatic aniconism represents the development from a generally assumed use of empty space or certain symbols to a very explicit stand against any possible iconography to represent the deity. Thus, Mettinger concludes that "the Yahwistic cult was aniconic from the very beginning," but such aniconism included cults with aniconic symbols, specifically, standing stones. "Standing stone aniconism" was widespread in the West Semitic region and not distinctive to Israelite religion.[92] But within Israelite religion, de facto aniconism in the state cults (see chapter 2) was represented by the empty cherubim throne and possibly Jeroboam's bulls.[93]

Mettinger does not try to say when a more programmatic aniconism developed in Israelite religion, one that rejected even the standing stones

Plate 1. Late Bronze Age Shrine of the Stelae at Hazor. (*Collection of the Israel Antiquities Authority*)

within the cult, but he rightly calls attention to the signs of such a move in the account of the conflict between the Israelite ark and the Philistine Dagon statue in 1 Sam. 5:1–5, though he acknowledges that the issue is more the conflict among the gods than a stance on divine images.[94]

Fig. 5. Seated bronze figure from eleventh-century Hazor that may be an image of a male deity. (*After Hendel, in* The Image and the Book, *p. 213, fig. 1*)

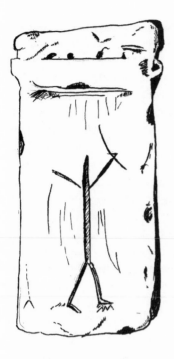

Fig 6. Possible divine stick figure carved into a miniature limestone altar from tenth-century Gezer. (*After Dever et al.*, Gezer II, *pls. 41 and 75*)

In this plausible construction, de facto aniconism was not one of the differentiating features of Israelite religion, but programmatic aniconism was. Consistent with this reading are the data from archaeological and iconographic investigations, particularly the indications that by the seventh century the Judean name seals show a clear tendency toward aniconicity, a tendency that is not exclusive but begins even further back and then becomes quite pronounced.[95]

The primary challenge to this picture is not from archaeology but from the biblical texts themselves. There are three cases of image-making by Israelites in the premonarchical period that either receive no condemnation or the condemnation comes from a later period. One is the bronze serpent Moses made in the wilderness, upon which those bitten by poisonous snakes could look that they might live. It is not depicted as an image of Yahweh; in fact, Yahweh commands Moses to make it. Later, however, it became an object of worship and persisted as such for some time until it was finally broken up by Hezekiah in his reform (2 Kings 18:4). Gideon made an ephod, whose character is unclear. But a later Deuteronomic voice regarded it as some kind of divine image and condemned the people for prostituting themselves to it (Judg. 8:27). The clearest case of making an image of Yahweh is in Judg. 17:2–3, where the mother of Micah (a good

Yahwistic name) gives him silver that she has dedicated to Yahweh to make an image (*pesel*, the same term used in the aniconic prohibition of the Decalogue), which he sets up in a domestic shrine. There is no condemnation of this in the text except for a Deuteronomistic note in verse 6.[96]

Perhaps the best explanation of the textual and archaeological data is that the aniconic tendency was dominant and gained weight in the course of Israel's history, but was not totally uniform. From earliest times, the main or official cult of Yahweh, as represented in its leaders and in its main sanctuaries, was largely aniconic, particularly with regard to representation of Israel's God.[97] Other cultic paraphernalia that were eventually regarded as images were tolerated in the earlier stages, but by the time of the Deuteronomic movement in the eighth and seventh centuries they were condemned, at least by major elements of Yahwistic leadership.[98] At the same time, there may have been domestic and extramural shrines that were more generally open to iconography and, in some instances, images of the deity. There is textual (Judges 17) and archaeological evidence indicating this.[99]

The cult of Jeroboam, attested to in 1 Kings 12:25–33 and reflected in the story of the making of the golden calf in Exodus 32, was, in origin, probably an imageless Yahwistic cultic movement set up as a counter to the cult of Yahweh in Jerusalem. There, however, are indications that, early on, the bulls of Jeroboam came to be understood not just as pedestals for the invisible God (fig. 7) as they were probably intended (and as the ark was in Judah), but images to be worshiped.[100] The absence of any condemnation of the bulls from prophets such as Elijah, Elisha, and Amos, as well as Jehu's not removing them in his drastic purge of Baalistic elements in the North (2 Kings 10:29) suggest that they were not regarded as Yahweh images initially. Hosea, however, condemned them on exactly those grounds in the eighth century (see plate 2).

The meaning and function of the absence of images is less certain. The tradition itself gives some indications that should be taken seriously. The attachment of the prohibition against images to the prohibition of the worship of other gods (Ex. 20:3–6 // Deut. 5:7–10; cf. Ex. 20:23; 34:11–17; Deut. 4:15–31) suggests that at least one function of the aniconic requirement was to safeguard the exclusive worship of the Lord of Israel. The association of the gods of the neighboring peoples with images meant that a representation of deity could always be potentially another deity. The aniconic tendency was, therefore, a feature of the conflict—divergence and differentiation of Yahweh vis-à-vis other deities.

The Deuteronomic tradition, however, also claimed that the resistance to images was a safeguard of the transcendence of Yahweh as well as of the

Fig. 7. Reliefs of storm god standing on a bull pedestal. (*After* ANEP, *nos. 500 and 501*)

proper form of God's immanence in the world. Deuteronomy 4:9–31, which is an extended sermon on this prohibition, presents it as a resistance to the worship of other gods. But it also sets imaging God over against the voice from the fire that has no form, is fluid, intangible, and potent (v. 15),[101] and prohibits the making of an image in the form of anything in the whole creation (vv. 16–18). God's abode is in heaven; on earth there is only the voice from the fire, the word (v. 36). The interpretation of the prohibition in this text is consistent with the Deuteronomic understanding of the ark as the receptacle of the torah, that is, the words of Yahweh, through which the deity is present among the people (Deut. 10:1–5).[102]

It is possible, however, that the prohibition had other functions than safeguarding the exclusive worship of Yahweh and his transcendence. There are some indications that the aniconic insistence was also closely related to sociopolitical and economic realities. The close association of conceptions of kingship and of deity in the ancient world, in Egypt and Mesopotamia, for example, may have been a factor in the early appearance of the aniconic tendency. The clearest analogies to the cherub throne upon the ark are iconic representations of kings on cherub thrones.[103] As R. S. Hendel has noted,

> The close relationship between the image of the god and the image of the king is an important part of the ideology of kingship in the ancient

Plate 2. Small bronze statuette of a bull that may have been an object of worship. Found in northern Samaria at what some believe was a cultic site. From the twelfth century. (*Collection of the Israel Antiquities Authority*)

> Near East. The king was regarded as the earthly representative of the gods, and as such the image of the god was a symbol of the legitimacy of the earthly king. The divine image was pictured and was treated as a king, therefore serving as a reminder of the divine authority of the king.[104]

The resistance to divine images may, therefore, have been linked to a distinctive feature of early Israelite social structure, the resistance to kingship. As such, it would have been a reflection on the iconographic level of "the early Israelite bias against the institution and ideology of kingship."[105] The images on thrones were gods and kings. The physical image of Yahweh on a throne could have served to suggest and legitimate a mode of leadership foreign to Israel's early social structure. If this hypothesis about the social function of the aniconic requirement is at all correct, it does not mean that the other functions identified in the tradition were not also a part of its rationale at one time or another. It does mean, however, that the prohibition, or at least the creation of an imageless divine throne at the center of the cultus, would have belonged to the early stages of Israelite religion, prior to the beginnings of kingship.

W. Brueggemann has called attention to several instances in the biblical texts where the iconic tendency is closely associated with gold and wealth.[106] These include the use of the gold rings of the Israelites to build the golden calf in the wilderness, gold that Brueggemann associates with the plundering of silver and jewelry from the Egyptians, noting that "confiscated gold is evidence of an economic surplus," and that Gideon made an "ephod" (image? cf. Judg. 17:5) out of golden earrings taken from the Midianites (Judg. 8:22–28), as earlier Hebrews had plundered the Egyptians.[107] The prophets inveigh often against idols made of silver and gold (figs. 2 and 3),[108] and Deuteronomy warns against coveting the silver and gold on the idols (7:25). The temple in Jerusalem is another indication of the move toward the iconic in a situation of settled and secure affluence.[109] There is a puzzling incongruity between the heavily iconographic and affluent character of the temple, built with much precious or fine metal and rich imagery (not images) and the aniconic character of the excavated "establishment" sanctuaries of Iron Age Judah.[110] Rest and riches, booty and plunder, seem to some degree to go hand in hand with the iconic tendency.

THE DIVINE WORLD

The place of Yahweh vis-à-vis other gods, or vice versa, remained an issue of Israelite religion throughout its course. That is no surprise in light of the continuing impetus toward the exclusive worship of Yahweh by Israel. The existence of a divine world, "peopled" with divine and semidivine beings, some named and others not, was a common feature of Near Eastern mythology and was reflected in their religious conceptions and practices. In each society, the relationships among such divine figures was varied and complex. There were pantheons in which gods figured in familial relationships and/or in conflictual ones. They interacted in some instances as groups in making decisions. They might have individual shrines or shrines in which more than one deity could be worshiped. Some deities acted as mediaries between human beings and other deities. Some were recognized as demonic figures who could and did afflict human beings. Many were associated with particular aspects of nature, while others were primarily national deities. In the case of deities such as Marduk and Ashur, the national gods of Babylon and Assyria, there was a tendency to absorb various features often associated with other individual deities.

In such a varied, complex, and polytheistic world, Israel worshiped the god Yahweh. Yahwism was a part of that world but had its own particularities and mutations. While there are varying ways and varying opinions about how Israelite religion understood the relation of Yahweh to other deities, there are certain aspects of that relationship that are clearly indicated. Yahweh came into existence as a worshiped deity out of the world of the gods with discernable antecedents, so we may speak of Yahweh as coming out of the gods and the divine world of Canaan. It is also the case, however, that the divine world, that is, characteristic central features of other deities, seem to be a part of Yahweh's profile as a deity; so we may also recognize that the gods are present in Yahweh. But one of the most obvious features of the presentation of that divine world in biblical literature is the conflictual relation between Yahweh and the gods, so that it is necessary also to speak of Yahweh against the gods as a dimension of the relationship. Each of these aspects of Yahweh's involvement with the divine world, then, may be illustrated as follows.[111]

Yahweh out of the Gods

Various kinds of evidence from biblical and extrabiblical sources attest to the fact that the god Yahweh had roots and origins among the high gods of Canaanite religion and the tutelary or clan deities of patriarchal family religion. The most plausible reconstruction of those origins of Yahweh, in my judgment, is that of Cross.[112] Building on the work of Albrecht Alt, he notes that in the patriarchal traditions in the Pentateuch, the god worshiped by a patriarch and his family is identified by the patriarch's name, for example, "the god of Abraham" or "the bull of Jacob." Such a deity, "the god of the father/ancestor," was not a local god but the patron of the clan or social group, existing in a kinship or covenantal relation with it, responsible for assisting and guiding the clan in its movements and its conflicts in matters of family and generational need. The special relationship to the social group and the "historical" character of the deity's activities anticipated traits and "characteristics of the religion of Yahweh, the lord of covenant and community."[113] Such clan deities, however, were not nameless and without identity apart from the clan. They were high gods, easily identified by common traits or cognate names with the gods of the Canaanite or Amorite pantheon.[114]

The other element identified by Alt, Cross, and others as present in pre-Yahwistic patriarchal religion was the worship of the high god El as indicated in the divine names in Genesis, such as El Olam and El Shaddai (figs. 1 and 2). These were titles of the high god of the Canaanite pantheon, a patriarchal figure, head of the assembly of the gods, primordial father of gods and human beings. He was a social god both in reference to the family of gods as well as to human beings. He frequently played the role of "god of the father/ancestor," the social deity bound to tribe or king with kinship or covenant ties, guiding or leading them. The epic materials from

Ugarit regularly show El answering, helping, directing the royal figures. In addition, El was the transcendent creator God. As the Genesis narratives reveal, the gods of the ancestors were identified with Canaanite El who bore in his character traits that made the identification natural, particularly in light of the fact that the god of the ancestor—of Abraham, Jacob, and the like—may have been Amorite Ilu or El.[115]

As we have already noted, Yahweh appeared on the scene probably as a cultic name of El and would have split off as a separate deity in the differentiation of Yahweh's cultus in south Canaan, an area where the worship of El was popular. Yahweh was thus, in origin, an El figure, as Ex. 6:2–3 suggests rather directly in identifying the pre-Mosaic manifestation of Yahweh as El Shaddai,[116] and the various El names continued throughout the history of Israel's religion to be acceptable titles for Yahweh. The roots of Yahweh, therefore, are to be traced back far (historically) and broadly (geographically) into the religious world of the ancient Near East, and particularly Syria-Palestine. Clan religion, Amorite religion, Canaanite religion—these formed the matrix out of which the worship of Yahweh came. It is not simply a matter of a few similarities between Yahweh and these other divine figures. Virtually all of the characteristics of the God of Israel are present in the early stages of Yahwism, and most of them reach back beyond Israel's earliest stage, wherever that is placed, to pre-Israelite religious developments.

The Gods in Yahweh

It is equally the case that the gods of the ancient world, particularly Syria-Palestine, were to be found in Yahweh. That is, their character and mythology were reflected in various ways in the character and mythology of Yahweh. If Yahweh was in origin a split-off from El, El features were part of the character of Yahweh—El's compassion and wisdom, being divine judge and head of the divine council as well as creator and father, El's kingship, his tent and cherubim throne, to name some of the major shared elements. So also were fundamental dimensions of the god Baal basic to Yahweh. The patterns and motifs of Baal as storm god who rides the clouds and whose theophany has such powerful effects on the natural world were present in the numerous hymnic and prose traditions of the theophany of Yahweh. The imagery of Yahweh as the divine warrior reflected the character of El and other gods and goddesses but most particularly Baal, who was frequently depicted both in his march accompanied by his entourage to battle the enemy and in his return from battle to take his place in his new temple on his holy mountain.

Paul Riemann has drawn upon the work of Thorkild Jacobsen to make the cogent proposal that there was a centralization or integration of divine power and authority, perceived as the supremacy of one single deity to whom all other divine beings are subordinate, a tendency discernable in first-millennium Mesopotamian religion in the rise to supreme power in the divine realm of the two national gods, Marduk of Babylon and Ashur of Assyria.[117] Other gods acted as agents or intercessors. There was a strong feeling of unified central power in the divine world. Various gods were seen as in essence one, with aspects of a supreme god. Enlil, for example, was Marduk (as god) of lordship and council. The gods were either identified with the supreme god (as in the ascription of fifty divine names to Marduk in the Creation epic) or reinterpreted as manifestations of the supreme god. The polytheistic framework was never abandoned in Mesopotamia. But "the emphasis had subtly shifted; power and decision were now centered in Marduk or in Ashur," national and political deities closely tied to their people, divine powers active in human affairs as well as nature. Looking at this effective integration of divine power, Jacobsen concludes, "There is a recognizable drive to see the forces that govern the cosmos as basically one and unified."[118]

One cannot transfer the process that led to this point in Babylonia and Assyria directly to Israel. Yet it may be that this integrative dimension, this drive to see the cosmic forces as unified, was reflected in Yahweh and is one way of comprehending the monotheistic tendency that was always present in Yahwism. A number of Yahwistic factors make sense on analogy with the Mesopotamian development.[119] One is the difficulty of articulating a peculiar character to Yahweh as a deity. In origin, Yahweh has been seen as a mountain god, a sky god, a storm god, a national god, and so forth. But none of these was the case and all of them were. The forces and aspects of the cosmos were all caught up in Yahweh, and the characterization of deity in its manifold possibilities—as portrayed in Near Eastern religion and mythology—were present in Yahweh.[120]

While there are some fragmentary mythological pieces in the Old Testament, the general absence of myth is probably also a reflection of this centralization of divine authority and rule. Riemann notes, "The radical subordination of all other divine powers has radically reduced the role of the heavenly realm as the locus of drama and conflict."[121]

The integration of the divine world is probably reflected best in the numerous biblical references and allusions to the divine council or heavenly assembly, a mythological phenomenon ubiquitous in the polytheistic world of ancient Near Eastern religions.[122] Yahweh was envisioned seated on a throne in his temple or palace surrounded by a nameless host of divine beings who rendered service to the enthroned deity (1 Kings 22:19; Isa. 6:1–4). Yahweh took counsel with them and commissioned them with tasks. They sat as a court to judge a case and pronounce a verdict. The gods went from the assembly to accompany Yahweh into battle. In all of this activity, the members of the divine assembly had no autonomy or independence apart from the word and action of Yahweh. They remained essentially nameless, without personality or profile. Unlike Ugaritic or Babylonian mythology, for example, there was no conflict over power in the world of the gods that was brought before this assembly except for one quasi-mythological text, Psalm 82, whose point is precisely Yahweh's claim to rule as judge over the divine world. In that psalm, Yahweh condemns all the gods to death for their failure to maintain justice on earth and takes over the total rule of the divine world. It is, in effect, a story of the radical integration of deity in one god—Yahweh.

The divine assembly, therefore, was a manifestation of the integration of divine power while it also maintained its social character.

> [The] complexity and plurality of the universe was not lost but ruled. The plurality and diversity of experiences and phenomena that make up the creation point to a complex cosmos that is allowed both its complexity and its ordered direction by a fully integrated divine world whose rule by one is as clear as its social character.[123]

This means, therefore, that the mythopoeic symbol of the divine assembly not only served the radical integration of the divine world in the figure of Yahweh, but also gave to the reality of the divine a highly political shape. The assembly was understood as the machinery by which the just rule of Yahweh was effective in the universe. It is no accident that central to the conception of Israelite prophecy was the notion that the prophet was the herald from the council of Yahweh. Yahweh's rule took place in the activity of the divine assembly where the decrees of Yahweh directing the human community and the divine world were set forth and through which they were communicated or enacted.[124]

The absence of demons as a significant force in Israelite religion and in its conception of divine powers may be accounted for in a similar way. Such a proposal was put forth long ago by Paul Volz, who saw in the many manifestations of the terrifying, the uncanny, the pernicious, and the hostile in the activity of Yahweh signs of the demonic, a dimension of deity that represented an absorption of the demonic forces of the divine world that were well-known from other religions of the ancient Near East.[125] These are reflected in the biblical literature not only in such strange episodes as the "bloody bridegroom" of Ex. 4:24–26, the death of Uzzah upon touching the ark (2 Samuel 6), and the anger of Yahweh inciting David to take the census of Israel and Judah (2 Sam. 14:1–9), but also in the many images of Yahweh as wild animal or natural force that breaks out into terrifying acts.[126]

At the same time, it is this dimension that points to an eventual partial breakdown of the integration of the divine powers in Yahweh. The Chronicler attributes the incitement of David's census to *śāṭān,* whose appearance as *haśśāṭān,* "the adversary" or "the accuser," in Job 1–2 and Zech. 5:1–5 reflects an incipient opposing force to the power of the deity. While not in the biblical literature reflective of a forthright dualism, such a move sowed the seeds of dualistic thinking within Israelite religion in the postexilic period. It is likely, as the story of the census and the book of Job suggest, that such a move toward a subdued dualism was rooted in the community's attempt to deal with the problem of evil and the fact that the reality of human sin and divine judgment could not alone carry the moral burden of accounting for all the evil that happened.[127] The conflict between the "children of light" and the "children of darkness" in apocalyptic thinking was a further indication of an incipient dualistic way of thinking that served to undermine the integration of divine power in Yahweh of Israel without, however, fully undoing it.

Yahweh against the Gods

The conception of Yahweh over against or in conflict with the gods of the Near Eastern religions permeates much of biblical literature. The God of Israel, who came out of the gods and in whom the world of the gods can be discerned, stood over against all other gods, claiming a unity and exclusiveness that ruled them out. Such a claim carried with it a theological perspective on the nature of the divine reality that was of far-reaching significance in the history of Israelite religion.[128]

Psalm 82 is an explicit and possibly early manifestation of this opposition. While the gods who are gathered in the "council of El" or "divine council" (v. 1) are unnamed and do not speak, Yahweh stands up in their midst and condemns them all to death, in effect taking over all power, indeed all claim to deity, in the divine realm. The encounter with the Philistines described in 1 Samuel 4–6 contains a veiled allusion to the conflict, even battle, with the Philistine deity Dagon.[129] The places at which this conflict was made definitional are the commandments of the Decalogue forbidding the worship of other gods and the making of divine images (Ex. 20:3–6; Deut. 5:7–10) and the Shema of Deut. 6:4–5, requiring Israel's full allegiance to Yahweh alone, as well as the insistence on Yahweh's jealousy (Ex. 20:5; Deut. 5:9).

The temporal point at which the conflictual relationship between Yahweh and other deities began is much debated. It may reach back to premonarchical times, though some interpreters of Israel's religion would place it later. There may well have been elements within the community open to the worship of other deities, while a more orthodox Yahwism prohibited such worship.[130] The clearest indicators of that conflict appear first in the ninth century, especially in Elijah's opposition to the worship of the Canaanite deity Baal.[131] The issue was not that Yahweh could be forgotten or ignored, but that the deity would become simply another god alongside the great gods and goddesses of Canaanite religion. The high point of the ninth-century conflict was the contest between Elijah and the prophets of Baal on Mount Carmel and its sequel in Yahweh's revelation to Elijah at Horeb (1 Kings 18–19). Not only was Baal defeated in the contest, but the appearance of Yahweh to Elijah at Horeb, not in the wind or earthquake or fire but in the sound of a low whisper, was clearly a polemic against the storm god Baal. Imagery and mode of revelation from the world of Canaanite religion that were once acceptable as a vehicle for Yahweh are here rejected.[132]

In an almost reverse manner, the prophecy of Hosea in the eighth century set forth the polemic against Baal in terms, not of Yahweh's rejection of Baal's imagery, but the deity's appropriation, in transformed fashion, of Canaanite language and thought. Yahweh preempted the role of Baal by promising to bestow fertility upon a faithful people and their land. The socioeconomic dimensions of the conflict appear especially here.

THE FEMININE DIMENSION
AND THE QUESTION OF THE GODDESS

Other ways of describing the relation of Yahweh to other gods can be set forth with plausibility. But some such dynamic as is laid out in this framework would seem to be necessary to account for the data. In the next chapter, we will seek to show that matters are even more complex than presented here. One further matter requires some attention, however, in sketching a picture of Israel's God. That is the question of the feminine dimension and the presence or absence of the goddess or goddesses, who played a significant part generally in the surrounding religious systems.[133] With the appearance of inscriptions referring to "Yahweh and his asherah," the latter word a term that customarily referred to or was the same as the name of one of the most prominent Canaanite goddesses, this question has come more to the fore. In the scholarly literature there are increasing claims Yahweh had a consort.

Here it is proposed that the extreme integration of divine characteristics, roles, and powers in Yahweh carried with it an absorption of the feminine dimension in deity represented in ancient Near Eastern religions by the worship of a goddess.[134] That would mean, in effect, its disappearance as a separately identifiable dimension because the characteristics of goddesses in the ancient Near East were shared by male deities also, except for child-bearing, and even there procreative activities were carried on by both gods and goddesses.

Again, the Mesopotamian situation may give us some analogies. The god list AN = *Anu ša amēli* gives the various names of the sky god or god of heaven, Anu. The last name of Anu given there is Uraš, "earth," who else-where is Anu's spouse.[135] The female counterpart in the divine world is here specifically identified with or merged into the male deity. The name is pre-served in the list, but integration and absorption take place.

That process may go a step further in a text referred to by both Jacob-sen and Lambert in their discussion of integration, merger, or absorption in the Mesopotamian pantheon.[136] In CT 24 No. 50, in which the major gods of the pantheon are identified with Marduk, Lambert observes that the only exclusions from the list of deities are demons and goddesses and suggests that "presumably the compiler of this list would not have denied the exis-tence of Zarpanitum, spouse of Marduk in his temple in Babylon," and so the monotheism of the text would have to be qualified by allowing for the existence of one god *and his spouse*.[137] The presumption may be correct. It is what one would expect. At the same time, one has to admit that the text as a whole is not exactly what one would normally expect in a polytheis-tic context, and it may be that Zarpanitum is either absorbed implicitly as Uraš with Anu or is simply outside the picture. No goddesses are named. The elevation of the male deity to position as "the sole possessor of power in the universe" involves the integration of all the divine roles and powers associated with male deities and the absence or disappearance of the female deities. Whatever the structural process involved in such a move, the end result is clear: The goddesses are not present.

Much the same seems to be the case with Yahweh in Israelite religion.[138] Either the feminine deity was implicitly absorbed in Yahweh from the beginning along with all other divine powers and so had no independent existence or character, or the radical integration of divine powers in the male deity Yahweh effectively excluded the goddess(es), as seems to be the case with CT 24 No. 50 in Mesopotamia. There is some evidence that suggests that absorption and integration of the goddess into the character and indeed the cult of Yahweh was what took place and at an early stage, though the nature and character of that process and the extent to which there is evidence of a separate goddess alongside Yahweh at any stage in Israelite religion is a matter of much debate. At a minimum, the data—biblical and extrabiblical, literary and artifactual—suggest the possibility that the feminine dimension did not disappear altogether.

Inscriptions from the ruins of a ninth to eighth century caravanserai or way station at Kuntillet 'Ajrud, which was visited by Israelites and Judeans, record blessings "by Yahweh of Samaria/Teman[139] and by his asherah" invoked by an individual on others, all of whom have good Yahwistic names. The expression "Yahweh and his asherah" occurs also in an inscription from a tomb in Judah, probably to be translated as follows (fig. 8):

> (For) Uriyahu the rich: his inscription.
> > (Or: has written it.)
> Blessed is Uriyahu by Yahweh;
> Yea from his adversaries by his asherah he has saved him.
> (Written) by Oniyahu
> > (. . . ?) and by his asherah.[140]

The occurrence of the word "asherah," well known from the Bible as either a goddess or a cult object and usually condemned as contrary to appropriate worship of Yahweh,[141] in the formulation "Yahweh and his asherah" is obviously of some moment for an understanding of Israel's God and the

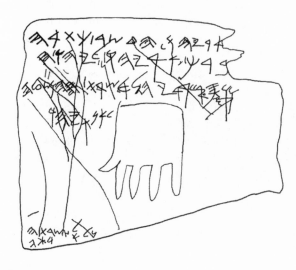

Fig. 8. Tomb inscription referring to "yahweh" on the left side of the second line and "his asherah" in the middle of the third line and at the bottom left. (*After Hadley,* Vetus Testamentum *37 [1987], p. 52*)

cultus associated with his worship.[142] But what exactly the phrase means or refers to is a matter of much debate.[143]

There is no question that the term "asherah" can refer to a cult object of some sort, apparently wooden, though whether it is a tree or a crafted wooden object is not altogether clear (fig. 9 and the second register from the top of Taanach cult stand, plates 3 and 4). Both possibilities are indicated in different texts. In the biblical texts, the word "asherah" occurs most often with the definite article, "*the* asherah," but also in an indefinite singular as well as a number of times in the plural. Several times it occurs alongside other cult objects, such as high place (*bāmâ*), pillar (*maṣṣēbâ*), altar (*mizbēaḥ*), incense altar (*ḥammān*), and image (*pesel*).[144] The asherah stood alongside an altar. Together with the pillar, these made up a shrine, whether a high place or a temple (plate 1).[145]

While some interpreters would see at least some of the references to "asherah" as referring to a goddess of that name, in continuity with the well-known Aṯirat associated with El in Ugaritic mythology, that is less clear. The reference to worshiping "the Baals and the Asherahs" in Judg. 3:17 probably is an error for "the Baals and the Ashtaroth," referring to the well-known second-millennium goddess Astarte alongside the male deity Baal.[146] The allusion to "the four hundred prophets of Asherah" in 1 Kings 18:19 is also a suspect text and probably a secondary gloss.[147] In several instances, a clear distinction is made between "making" an asherah or asherahs and "bowing down to" or "worshiping" and "serving" Baal and the host of heaven.[148] That is, Baal and the host of heaven are frequently treated in the text as objects of worship, using exactly the vocabulary for worship that appears in the commandments prohibiting worship of other gods and images, while the asherah is not.[149] The strongest suggestion of a goddess Asherah is to be found in 2 Kings 23:4, where it is reported that Josiah had

Fig. 9. Ibexes feeding on a tree that may have symbolized the goddess Asherah. (*After Beck,* Tel Aviv *9 [1982], fig. 4*)

Plate 3. Tenth-century cult stand from Taanach (front view). (*Courtesy of Nancy Lapp*)

Plate 4. Tenth-century cult stand from Taanach (side view). (*Courtesy of Nancy Lapp*)

brought out of the temple "all the vessels made for the baal, for the asherah, and for all the host of heaven." Inasmuch as Baal and the host of heaven are elsewhere worshiped as deities, the same might be suggested here. But it cannot be excluded that this is again a cult symbol. Immediately after this, in verses 6–7, the asherah is treated differently and the "vessels made for the asherah" may refer to the "houses" the women wove for the asherah.[150]

In short, the many references to the asherah associate it frequently with nondivinized cult objects and dissociate it from verbs of worship and service applied customarily to deities while also associating it with deities in a way that was not true of any other cult object. The silence concerning Asherah (goddess) on the part of prophets such as Elijah and Elisha who condemned so vigorously the worship of Baal and other gods,[151] as well as the fact that the asherah erected in Samaria survived the radical and bloody purge of Baalism, its adherents, and its cultic objects by Jehu under the auspices of Elijah and Elisha (2 Kings 9–10), suggest both that there was no worship of a separate goddess Asherah in Israel and that the asherah in some fashion could be acceptable to a radical Yahwist like Jehu.[152]

The inscriptions speaking of "Yahweh and his asherah" may be a clue to what is going on here (fig. 8). They occur in a context that is otherwise Yahwistic.[153] At a minimum one must recognize here a cult object of Yahweh marking his presence, in other words, a form of hypostatization of Yahweh.[154] How far that hypostatization has taken place in these inscriptions is not altogether clear. A number of scholars argue that the presence of asherah as a consort of Yahweh may be inferred from them.[155] The presence, however, of the possessive "*his* asherah" and the use of singular verbs with the expression "*yhwh . . . wl'šrth*" at both Kuntillet 'Ajrud and Khirbet el-Qom inhibit a simple reading of this as referring to a goddess with some separate identity.[156] The term "asherah" does not have to be understood as referring to the cult symbol of the goddess Asherah. Other names for deities are also common nouns, the most obvious being *baal* ("lord") itself, which does not always refer to a deity and can be used in reference to Yahweh.[157] In their extended treatment of the inscriptional and iconographic evidence, particularly the stylized tree that is associated with asherah/Asherah, Keel and Uehlinger have made a cogent proposal: "The iconographically important evidence, referring transparently to the goddess by means of a stylized tree, but which even more frequently represents a gender-neutral symbol of numinous power, can best be understood if we interpret the Iron Age IIB *asherah* as a *mediating entity* associated with Yahweh, rather than as a personal, independently active, female deity."[158]

Having said that, one must also recognize that the blessing formulas in which the expression "Yahweh and his asherah" occurs at Kuntillet 'Ajrud usually list only deities as the source of blessings and that the separation at Khirbet el-Qom of *l'šrth* from *yhwh* in a kind of poetic parallelism (the word also is written separately on the stone) suggests some kind of separate identity, related to Yahweh, of the asherah referred to in these texts. That separate identity does not have to be the goddess Asherah or even the goddess's cult symbol.[159] But to the extent that a goddess named Asherah was worshiped in Iron Age Syria-Palestine,[160] there was always the possibility that the asherah of Yahweh could be identified with that goddess. Its feminine character is clear linguistically. The fears of the Deuteronomists were well founded (see Deut. 7:5–6; 16:21–22). The setting up of an asherah in the temple of Yahweh, whether in the Northern Kingdom or in Judah, was not necessarily indicative of the worship of a separate goddess. It may have been a cult object of Yahweh, but, if so, it was one that could be understood separately from Yahweh[161]—and thus, potentially at least, as the consort of Israel's God—which along with him could be the source of blessing (Kuntillet 'Ajrud) or salvation (Khirbet el-Qom).[162] The history of Israel's religion, therefore, would represent in the asherah a move toward hypostatization of the feminine dimension of deity—a move that was suppressed in the activities of the reforming kings and the Deuteronomistic supporters—what one scholar has described as "an aspect of the divine . . . becoming concretized or reified."[163] Other forms of such hypostatization, or at least personification, occurred in late biblical and postbiblical times. Divine characteristics that were feminine in linguistic form, such as *ḥokmâ*, "Wisdom," and *šĕkînâ*, "Presence," were seen to have a kind of reality subordinate to and representative of Yahweh. In Proverbs 8 and elsewhere, Lady Wisdom is described as the first of God's creative acts and a participant with Yahweh in the creation of the universe.[164]

If one could establish clearly that Asherah was worshiped in Israel at an early time as a separate deity and consort of Yahweh,[165] then it would be necessary to think of the process leading to the inscriptional formula "Yahweh and his asherah" and to the Deuteronomists' condemnation of the asherah in a reverse manner to that suggested above, that is, as a gradual absorption of the goddess and her characteristic features into the character of Yahweh *within the course of Israel's history*. What we find in the Old Testament and in the epigraphic sources would represent a subordination of the goddess into a cult object belonging to the worship of Yahweh, in effect again a kind of hypostatization. This possibility has been set forth by J. Hadley as follows:

By Manasseh's time, it is possible that the asherah statue had lost enough of its "goddess background," and was considered more as an aspect of fertility, so that the image was allowed to stand until Josiah's reform. . . .

If it is indeed true that Israel was gradually losing the identity of the goddess Asherah as a fertility goddess, one must look for ways in which this need continued to be met. As a male deity, Yahweh needed to be able, in some capacity, to take over some of these fertility aspects. . . . It may be that he has absorbed the earlier Canaanite fertility goddesses into his cult, and the statues which were formerly dedicated solely to the goddess Asherah have now become part of Yahweh's cultic paraphernalia. The asherah pole may have even become a hypostatization of Yahweh's fertility aspects. . . . By the time of the deuteronomistic compilers, the distinction between Asherah the goddess and asherah the wooden cultic symbol had perhaps become totally obscured, hence the tendency to pluralize asherah.[166]

Another example of the presence of the feminine dimension in Israelite religion is the number of female figurines that have been found in domestic locations in Israel and Judah from different periods during the monarchical era (plate 5).[167] The function of these figurines is unclear. It is possible that they represent a goddess, Asherah or Astarte. One interpretation suggests that they "may be smaller copies of the asherah statue which stood in the local temple, or they may be a part of a separate form of domestic worship of the goddess."[168] Unfortunately, it is not possible to make a clear identification with any known goddess, which does not mean that they were not in fact so identified by those who possessed them. It is certainly possible, as many have suggested, that they were identified with the mother goddess and served some function in relation to fertility or were aids to childbirth and nurturing. The figures regularly are depicted holding their breasts. They may have been talismanic in character, "used in sympathetic magic to stimulate the reproductive processes."[169] That there tended to be only one figurine to a house or domestic site[170] would suggest a more specific identification and cultic function within family or domestic religious life.[171]

In the process of Yahweh's absorption or integration of the feminine dimension, specifically feminine characteristics and images were applied to Yahweh on occasion, for example, the imagery of Yahweh giving birth to the earth (Ps. 90:2) and to Israel (Deut. 32:18), or the comparison of the deity to a nursing mother (Isa. 49:15; cf. Num. 11:12) and a comforting mother (Isa. 66:13).

Before leaving the question of the feminine and the goddess in relation

Plate 5. Female figurines from Judah, eighth to sixth century. (*Collection of the Israel Antiquities Authority*)

to Yahweh, it should be noted that the cultus around the asherah, whether cult object of Yahweh or his consort Asherah, seems to have involved women particularly.[172] This is seen first of all in the roles of the queens or queen mothers who seem to have nurtured or been attentive to the asherah of Yahweh and were condemned for that in Deuteronomistic circles.[173] In 1 Kings 15:13, reference is made to the *mipleṣet*, "abomination," that the queen mother Maacah made for the asherah, which Asa then cut down and burned. It is impossible to tell what the *mipleṣet* is. The term may be simply a substitute word for what was actually made. Whatever its meaning, the queen mother was actively involved in supporting the cult of the asherah/Asherah. A more general indication of the involvement of women in the cult of asherah/Asherah is found in 2 Kings 23:7. There we are told that the women "wove houses for the asherah." Like the *mipleṣet* of 1 Kings 15:13, the "houses" or "coverings" here are enigmatic, and the text may be corrupt.[174] But the point that women were active in making things for the asherah/Asherah is clear in the text.[175]

Other indications may be set alongside these two explicit associations of women with the cult of Yahweh's asherah or the goddess Asherah, as the case may be. We have called attention to the suspect character of the textual reference to the "four hundred prophets of Asherah" in 1 Kings 18:19.

If that is not a gloss, however, it specifically identifies the Asherah prophets with Jezebel, at whose table they sat. That should come as no surprise, since Aṭirat in the second-millennium Ugaritic texts is identified with Tyre and Sidon, and Jezebel was the daughter of the king of Tyre and Sidon (1 Kings 16:31).[176] Judith Hadley has suggested that the devotion to the Sumerian and Babylonian god Tammuz reflected in the scene of the women weeping for Tammuz in Ezek. 8:14 may be viewed in this connection: "if the Israelites had 'lost' their fertility deity [i.e., Asherah], they may have then 'adopted' the popular Sumerian and Babylonian god Tammuz for this purpose."[177] More explicitly, women are seen as the primary or initiating participants in the cult of the Queen of Heaven as described in Jer. 7:17–18 and 44:15–25.[178]

The significance of the involvement of women in the activities around the asherah or around goddess worship, as the case may be, is not altogether clear. Two or three possibilities, not necessarily mutually exclusive, may be suggested in light of the place and role of women in ancient Israel. It may have been that they were generally marginalized in most of the formal cultic activities of orthodox and public Yahwism (see chapter 2) and so forced into marginally acceptable to unacceptable roles from that perspective (see chapter 5). One notes that the women weeping for Tammuz were at the gate of the temple forecourt and not inside it, in contrast to the men who are condemned in the following verses for abominable practices they perform within the inner court.[179] But one notices also in several of these cases that the women's cultic activities were of the sort that women customarily carried out in society and domestic life generally, for example, weaving and cooking. In both cases, the weaving for the asherah (or for Asherah) and the cooking of cakes for the Queen of Heaven, the usually domestic activities are explicitly cultic. The weaving took place in the temple; the making of special cakes was done along with the pouring out of the libations by the women, though the husbands joined in.[180] The domestic role of women is attested in these practices, but this role was brought into the cultic sphere. That suggests further that the cult of the goddess or the cult of the asherah, whether as a hypostatized or mediating dimension of Yahweh or as a goddess, was particularly open to the participation of women, and in a way that incorporated their customary activities as women into its ritual and cultic life. One notes further that while the women weeping for Tammuz were not involved in goddess worship, the deity in whose ritual support they participated was a vegetation and fertility deity, who—if Hadley's tentative suggestion is at all on the right track—may have taken the place of the worship of their "fertility" deity represented in Asherah or in the asherah of Yahweh. The weeping, again, is an activity with which women were often particularly associated, in the cult of Tammuz and more generally.

One must not assume, however, that participation in the cult of the goddess was automatically or always a positive and self-enhancing activity for women. If Georg Braulik's interpretation of Hos. 4:18 is correct, then we have there a reference in the eighth century to the cult of the goddess (mentioned obliquely in v. 18 as "[the goddess] whose shields are shame") that seems to put women in humiliating and exploited positions as sexual objects for men in alcoholic and orgiastic rites.[181]

The worship of Yahweh, therefore, stood at the center of Israel's religion. But, as we have seen, other currents and various ways of expressing that worship—or, indeed, modifying it—were present at nearly all times. In an effort to get a clearer grasp on those variations, we need to turn to an examination of the types of religion in ancient Israel.

EXCURSUS 1: YAHWEH IN ANCIENT ISRAEL

The biblical evidence for the centrality of Yahweh is so clear and obvious from even the most cursory reading that it need not be recounted. Where other gods are acknowledged as being worshiped, that activity is always condemned. The indications of syncretism, heterodoxy, and different types of religious expression in ancient Israel (see chapter 2) do not obviate the claims for the centrality of Yahweh.

Epigraphic data from Israelite and Judean sites during the eighth to sixth centuries confirm this fact. We now have over forty extrabiblical references to *yhwh* (including *yh* and *yhw*) in blessings, oaths, religious salutations, votive offerings, seals, prayers, and even an oracle of salvation. For a complete listing as of 1991, see the concordance in Graham I. Davies, *Ancient Hebrew Inscriptions* (Cambridge: Cambridge University Press, 1991). Davies lists 42 occurrences of the divine name. Two more have appeared on inscriptions published since 1991. For these, see Pierre Bordreuil, Felice Israel, and Dennis Pardee, "Deux ostraca paléo-hébreux de la Collection Sh. Moussaieff," *Sem* 46 (1996): 49–76; and Hershel Shanks, "Three Shekels for the Lord: Ancient Inscription Records Gift to Solomon's Temple," *BARev* 23 (1997): 28–32. The Mesha Stele, a ninth-century Moabite inscription recounting a Moabite victory over Israel, identifies Yahweh as the god of Israel. No clear reference to any other deity has been found except for possible references to "Asherah," a goddess. These are all associated with Yahweh (for example, "Yahweh and his asherah"), and are more probably to be understood as a reference to a cultic symbol of the deity Yahweh than to a goddess consort, though a number of scholars have so interpreted them and that possibility cannot be excluded. See below on this issue. On the attestations of Yahweh in the Hebrew inscriptions, see André Lemaire,

"Désses et dieux de Syrie-Palestine d'aprés les inscriptions (c. 1000–500 av. n. é.)," in *Ein Gott allein? JHWH-Verehrung und biblischer Monotheismus im Kontext der israelitischen und altorientalischen Religionsgeschichte*, ed. Walter Dietrich and Martin A. Klopfenstein, OBO 139 (Freiburg: Universitätsverlag, 1994), 147–49.

In addition, a hymnic fragment from Kuntillet 'Ajrud contains references to El and Baal. Written in Phoenician script, it may or may not be Israelite/Judean in origin. At the moment, this fragment contains the only divine names besides Yahweh—or El/Elohim in reference to Yahweh—from any site clearly occupied by Israelites or Judeans. Kyle McCarter has argued cogently that "baal" in this text is a title, an epithet meaning "lord," and that that epithet in early Israel, especially the early monarchy, was an acceptable title for Yahweh. Thus, he would see in the Kuntillet 'Ajrud plaster inscription an early extrabiblical account of Yahweh coming from the south as a warrior, comparable to some of the theophanic early biblical poetry. See P. Kyle McCarter, "The Origins of Israelite Religion," in *The Rise of Ancient Israel*, ed. Hershel Shanks (Washington, D.C.: Biblical Archaeology Society, 1992), 123–29. The claim that "baal" in the early part of Israel's history was an acceptable epithet of Yahweh and is reflected in the Baal proper names and place names of the Bible has been made by other scholars, most recently, for example, by Stig Norin, "Onomastik zwischen Linguistik und Geschichte" (paper delivered at the Congress of the International Organization for the Study of the Old Testament, Oslo, August 1998), forthcoming in the proceedings of the Congress in a volume of VTSup; and J. Andrew Dearman, "Baal in Israel: The Contribution of Some Place Names and Personal Names to an Understanding of Early Israelite Religion," in *History and Interpretation: Essays in Honour of John H. Hayes*, ed. Matt P. Graham, William P. Brown, and Jeffrey K. Kuan; JSOTSup 173 (Sheffield: JSOT Press, 1993), 173–91.

The name "Asherah," apparently the goddess by that name, appears on inscriptions from Ekron, but this is clearly a Philistine site, as is indicated by the royal dedicatory inscription found there with references to two known Philistine kings. See note 142 for further discussion and references.

Similarly, anepigraphic remains from Israelite excavations have included a number of female figurines, whose meaning and function are somewhat enigmatic. But male images that could represent another deity than Yahweh are absent, with one or two possible exceptions, Tel Dan and possibly a sanctuary at Megiddo. On the latter, see David Ussishkin, "Fresh Examination of Old Excavations: Sanctuaries in the First Temple Period," in *Biblical Archaeology Today, 1990: Proceedings of the Second International Congress on Biblical Archaeology, Jerusalem, June/July 1990*, ed. Avraham Biran (Jerusalem: Israel Exploration Society, 1993), 67–85. There is no archaeological evidence for a cult of a deity other than Yahweh, except possibly at eleventh century Hazor, and that is much debated. The image found there may represent the carryover of worship of one of the Canaanite deities from the Late Bronze period. See Ora Negbi, *Canaanite Gods in Metal* (Tel Aviv: Tel Aviv University, 1976), 138. William Dever does not think the context or the image is Israelite. See "Material Remains and the Cult in Ancient Israel: An Essay in Archaeological Systematics," in *The Word of the Lord Shall Go Forth: Essays in Honor of David Noel*

Freedman in Celebration of His Sixtieth Birthday, ed. Carol L. Meyers and Michael O'Connor (Philadelphia: American Schools of Oriental Research, 1983), 582–83 n. 12. Cf. Othmar Keel and Christoph Uehlinger, *Gods, Goddesses, and Images of God in Ancient Israel* (Minneapolis: Fortress Press, 1998), 118, 147–49. A tenth-century cultic stand from Taanach has Asherah imagery on it and may have Yahweh imagery as well, though some would see Baal there instead (see the discussion in excursus 2). There are cultic areas in domestic loci and elsewhere, unrelated to the main sanctuaries, that could represent a less "orthodox" form of religion (see chapter 2) that may have included goddess worship within an understood Yahwistic context. The very important study of the iconography of Canaan-Israel from the Middle Bronze Age on by Keel and Uehlinger tends to confirm the centrality and dominance of Yahweh, though it richly nuances it in relation to the symbolism and the way in which developments contributed to it, for example, the transformation of goddess images into icons of blessing associated purely with Yahweh (see Keel and Uehlinger, *Gods, Goddesses, and Images of God*, 233ff.) This is evident both from the iconography of Iron Age II, where there is a decrease in anthropomorphic representations of gods and goddesses and a substitution of symbols, and also from the tendency of Deuteronomy and other biblical writings to "de-deify" or "de-mystify" other gods and turn them into icons and things. See also Georg Braulik, "The Rejection of the Goddess Asherah in Israel: Was the Rejection as Late as Deuteronomistic and Did It Further the Oppression of Women in Israel?" in *The Theology of Deuteronomy: Collected Essays by Georg Braulik, O.S.B.* (North Richland Hills, Tex.: BIBAL Press, 1994), 176–78; Judith M. Hadley, "The Fertility of the Flock? The De-Personalization of Astarte in the Old Testament," in *On Reading Prophetic Texts: Gender-Specific and Related Studies in Memory of Fokkelien van Dijk-Hemmes*, ed. Bob Becking and Meindert Dijkstra; BibInt 18 (Leiden: E. J. Brill, 1996), 115–33; idem, "Chasing Shadows? The Quest for the Historical Goddess," in *Congress Volume, Cambridge 1995*, ed. John A. Emerton; VTSup 66 (Leiden: E. J. Brill, 1997), 169–84; and idem, "The De-deification of Deities in Deuteronomy" (paper presented at the Congress meeting of the International Organization for the Study of the Old Testament, Oslo, August 1998). I am indebted to Dr. Hadley for sharing her paper with me.

The evidence from personal names is consistent with all the above. In the monarchical period and later, there are so few non-Yahwistic personal names that those who had them were a very small minority and possibly foreigners. Out of nearly 600 theophoric names found on inscriptions from the ninth century on, six per cent or less are not Yahwistic (see Jeffrey Tigay, "Israelite Religion: The Onomastic and Epigraphic Evidence," in *Ancient Israelite Religion*: Essays in Honor of Frank Moore Cross, ed. Patrick D. Miller Jr., Paul D. Hanson, and S. Dean McBride [Philadelphia: Fortress Press, 1987], 194). Roughly the same percentages are to be found in the onomastica of the Bible itself for the same period. In the period from the time of settlement up to David, there may have been a preference for El names to Yahweh names (so de Moor), but the evidence is unclear at this point because different studies have come up with different results. The identification of El and Yahweh, however, is a feature of Israelite religion from the earliest period onward.

The onomastic evidence is presented and discussed by Tigay in the essay referred to above and more extensively in his book *You Shall Have No Other Gods: Israelite Religion in the Light of Hebrew Inscriptions* (Atlanta: Scholars Press, 1986). Cf. Jeaneane D. Fowler, *Theophoric Personal Names in Ancient Hebrew: A Comparative Study,* JSOTSup 49 (Sheffield: JSOT Press, 1988); Johannes C. de Moor, *The Rise of Yahwism: The Roots of Israelite Monotheism* (Louvain: Leuven University Press, 1990), 10–41; and the Stig Norin article referred to above. On the basis of a study of hypocoristic names in the biblical and epigraphic texts, Norin concludes that the veneration of Baal was a limited phenomenon associated with persons closely connected to the Northern Kingdom's central administration and so reflecting the after effects of the Phoenician cultus on the Omrides rather than a widespread popular religion. He also notes a close correlation in the results from studying biblical names and those from studying epigraphic names and that in both contexts *yhwh* names increased during the monarchy in the biblical material and in the datable inscriptional material. (I am indebted to the author for sharing his paper with me.)

This fairly exclusive worship of a national deity in Israel should not seem surprising. As André Lemaire has shown in the essay referred to above, in Moab fairly clearly and probably in Ammon and Edom as well, first-millennium inscriptions suggest that in the religions of these Transjordanian states, there was the cult of the national deity (Chemosh in Moab, Milcom/El in Ammon, and Qos in Edom) that was monolatrous or quasi-monolatrous in a way not greatly dissimilar to what was the case in Israel during the Iron Age.

EXCURSUS 2: TANAACH CULT STAND
(Plates 3 and 4)

One of the pieces of evidence for the possible worship of Asherah in ancient Israel is a tenth-century cult stand found at Taanach with four levels or registers containing a number of divine symbols. On the bottom register, or level four, there is a female figure with hands resting upon the heads of lions standing to either side. This presumably represents a goddess, either Asherah, Astarte, or Anat. The third register has two winged sphinx-type figures (female heads and lion bodies) with vacant space between them. The second level contains a sacred tree with two ibexes on hind legs standing against either side of the tree. Here one probably has an asherah or the symbol of the goddess Asherah. The first register shows a horse (?) with a sun disk above it.

It is likely that at least one of the levels represents Asherah or the asherah and possibly both levels two and four. J. Glen Taylor has suggested that that is the case and that levels one and three are representations of Yahweh, first with the symbol of horse and sun disk, reminiscent of "the horses that the kings of Judah had dedicated to the sun, at the entrance to the house of the Lord" (2 Kings 23:11), and then with the empty space between the sphinx/cherubim figures representing "Yahweh of Hosts who dwells (between) the cherubim." (See J. Glen Taylor, "The Two Earliest Known Representations of Yahweh," in *Ascribe to the Lord: Biblical and*

Other Studies in Memory of Peter C. Craigie, ed. Lyle M. Eslinger and J. Glen Taylor; JSOTSup 67 (Sheffield: JSOT Press, 1988), 557–66). Taylor's proposal was anticipated by Silva Schroer, *In Israel gab es Bilder: Nachrichten von darstellender Kunst im Alten Testament,* OBO 74 (Fribourg: Universitätsverlag, 1987), 39, and accepted by Judith M. Hadley, "Yahweh's Asherah in the Light of Recent Discovery" (Ph.D. diss., University of Cambridge, 1989), 216–23. A modification of that interpretation has been offered recently by David N. Freedman, who sees in the top two registers a bovine symbol for Yahweh representing the North Israelite bull iconography together with an Asherah-symbol sacred tree identifying Yahweh's northern consort and in the bottom two registers the cherubim iconography associated with Judah and a southern-oriented Astarte goddess representation. The proposal is ingenious but rather a lot to ask of a single tenth-century cult stand, that it offer a collection of some of the main orthodox and heterodox iconography of Israelite religion (Review of M. Smith, *The Early History of God* in *JBL* 110 (1991): 698). For a critique of Taylor's interpretation, especially of the empty space as a manifestation of the invisible Yahweh, see Othmar Keel and Christoph Uehlinger, *Gods, Goddesses, and Images of God in Ancient Israel* (Minneapolis: Fortress Press, 1998), 157–60. They note that the biblical expression refers to Yahweh's enthronement on the cherubim, not dwelling between them. They suggest that the cherubs are guarding an entrance.

If, however, the views of Taylor and others are on target and the stand belongs to an Israelite context, then we would have evidence for the first representation of Yahweh and probably of the existence of his consort Asherah in early Israel. The interpretation of the stand is sufficiently uncertain, as is the assigning of it to a clearly Israelite religious context, that one must be cautious in building much upon it. Ruth Hestrin has made the strongest case for seeing in the stand asherah as both an image of the sacred tree, that is, cult object, and as image of a naked woman, that is, goddess ("Understanding Asherah: Exploring Semitic Iconography," *BARev* 17 (Sept./Oct. 1991): 50–59).

It should be noted that the associations of Yahweh with El make it not implausible that a feminine divine figure associated with him would be the first-millennium form of the goddess Aṯirat, known in the second millennium as companion of El.

In this connection, one should recognize that while the figures on Pithos A from Kuntillet 'Ajrud may not give us a visual depiction of Yahweh and/or the goddess Asherah, there is a depiction of the ibexes standing against a sacred tree that is identical to the one on the second register of the Taanach stand. Judith M. Hadley has suggested plausibly that here one sees "the goddess Asherah (or at least her image)." The fact that the tree is drawn above an image of a striding lion, another symbol for the goddess Asherah, reinforces her conclusion ("Yahweh's Asherah," 200). Hadley's work and the study of the iconography in Keel and Uehlinger offer the most extensive collection of all the iconographic, artifactual, and epigraphic data pertaining to the interpretation of the expression "Yahweh and his asherah." Several seals from Israelite occupation levels and bearing a representation of a sacred tree with worshipers on either side perhaps should be included in the picture. See Karl Jaroš, "Die Motive der heiligen Bäume und der Schlange in Gen 2–3," *ZAW* 92

(1970): 204–15; and Schroer, *In Israel gab es Bilder*, 34. For an interpretation of the iconography associated with the inscriptions at Kuntillet 'Ajrud in the light of the broader iconographic evidence, see Keel and Uehlinger, *Gods, Goddesses, and Images of God*.

The interpretation of the Taanach cult stand by Taylor and others, if correct—and that remains rather dubious—would have a further implication for the history of Israelite religion. It would provide iconographic evidence for the antiquity of the aniconic dimension in Yahwism via a tenth-century representation of the invisible deity.

CHAPTER 2

Types of Religion in Ancient Israel

Any effort to describe the religion of ancient Israel comes up against clear indications that, as in most religious communities, there was not a single understanding or expression of what that religion was. Both biblical and extrabiblical evidence suggest a certain degree of pluralism, of multiformity rather than uniformity. At a minimum, that is suggested in the prophetic and Deuteronomistic attacks on the worship of Baal and the making of an asherah. But the diversity and complexity was more than simply a matter of the worship of Baal alongside or in preference to Yahweh, such worship being contrary to true Yahwism. The very effort to define Yahwism opens up a certain complexity within Israelite religion. Further, the distinction between what goes on in public worship and what happens of a religious nature outside the public and formal sphere, what is commonly called "popular religion," has been widely recognized as apropos of Israelite religion.

If, therefore, it is necessary to speak first of Israel's God in dealing with Israelite religion, one must then take some account of this multiformity that always makes the reality behind any presentation of that religion more complex than the presentation ever indicates, a state of affairs already indicated in the previous chapter. To that end, we will try to identify some of the types of religion found in ancient Israel. The term *types* may not be the best label. Some would say stages or levels, but such terms incorporate presuppositions about the relationship of these types to one another that are not necessarily appropriate. *Type* is a fairly neutral term, not unrelated to the use of *form, type,* or *genre* in form criticism to identify the different forms of speech in ancient Israel. Here the term is being used to identify different forms of religious practice and conceptuality, recognizing they may have had varying relationships to one another (e.g., outgrowth, independent simultaneity, conflict).

Two assumptions should be laid out at the beginning. One is that a particular type, as it is proposed here, could and often did overlap with another type. The other presupposition is that over a period of time, the description of a particular type might change so that what had been characteristic at one point was no longer the case, or a practice that seemed to fit in one type at one time became characteristic of another type at another time.

If there is an obvious danger in oversimplification, one also runs the risk of distorting the evidence in overcomplicating a religious phenomenon, breaking up into many pieces what was not perceived as such in practice. For this reason, it must be said that the types set forth here, while in no sense ideal, represent a reconstruction and a typology rather than a precise account of how the religion was actually practiced and experienced. Further, we are suggesting that different types may be identified around certain questions or perspectives. They will overlap with others or take different forms if the question is changed. In this instance, two different perspectives provide the categories or types to be discussed: (1) the question of orthodoxy, and (2) the form and character of the cult. Diachronic change and development make matters even more complex. That will be taken into account as much as possible even though the approach here as in the rest of this presentation of Israel's religion is not primarily historical or diachronic. No effort will be made to describe each type completely. The data do not even allow that. Rather, we will seek to be illustrative so that the reader may have a feel for the greater complexity of Israel's religion, especially when, in later chapters, it is necessary to state matters more simply for reasons of space and presentation.[1]

THE QUESTION OF ORTHODOXY

In any religious system, orthodoxy is a relatively slippery term, one practitioner's orthodoxy being another's heterodoxy and vice versa. Yet there is some justification for suggesting that the tradition that became the end point of Israelite religion, or more accurately, the character it had as it moved into its two primary and immediately continuing streams, Judaism and Christianity, serves to define—in retrospect—what was orthodox and normative. That character is probably best represented in the words of the prophets, the history as told by the Deuteronomists and the religious system by which they measured it, and the cultic establishment of the priestly elements and writers of exilic and postexilic Judah. There is, of course, much inconsistency in details among these perspectives. Significant dimensions of the Torah not immediately represented by these groups also

belong to this definition of orthodoxy, and its fundamental character is presupposed and may be discerned in the Psalms and the wisdom materials.
It happens that some of the epigraphic and anepigraphic data are consistent with these biblical materials, but that is not uniformly the case. In any
event, orthodoxy was not a fixed or unchanging reality in Israelite religion.

Orthodox Yahwism[2]

In the broadest of strokes, the following primary features of orthodox
Yahwism stand out.

First, exclusive worship of the deity Yahweh was expected. Yahweh was
understood as the sole divine power ultimately effective in the world even
if there was resistance or encroachment by other deities. The cult of Yahweh was without representation of the deity and the deity was without sexuality as a primary feature. The powers of blessing (fertility, continuity,
health, and wealth) and of salvation (forgiveness, victory, deliverance from
threat and oppression) resided fully in Yahweh.

Second, the will of the deity was conveyed by means of oracle inquiry
and prophetic audition or vision. Dreams, casting of lots within the sacral
assembly, and prophetic revelation were legitimate means of discerning the
divine will or direction. Divination, soothsaying, and necromancy, however, were prohibited.[3] That is, there were both prescribed and proscribed
techniques for consultation of the deity. The difference between the two is
not always easy to tell, although the tradition makes it a matter of what is
Yahwistic and what belongs to foreign cults. The individual or the community could cry out to Yahweh, either in the sanctuary or outside it, and
would receive a divine response, mediated by priestly or prophetic figures.
Whether such appeals for help on the part of the individual centered in cultic activities in a sanctuary or were more a part of ritual processes in the
family or clan circles is a matter of debate. They could have been both (see
below). Priestly instruction and direction of various sorts might be sought
or offered. Sorcery was prohibited, though it was legitimate to invoke
God's curse upon someone as much as to invoke blessing.

Third, sanctuaries were erected in various places (see example from
Arad, plate 6) for the expression of devotion to the deity by means of sacrifice, festival meals and celebrations, prayer and praise.[4] Some served as
major sanctuaries where the formal or public cult of Yahweh took place.
Toward the end of the seventh century in Judah, worship of Yahweh was
restricted to the temple in Jerusalem. After the split of the kingdom into two
parts, the major sanctuaries of the Northern Kingdom were Dan in the
north and especially Bethel in the south, near the border of the Southern

Plate 6. Altar, floor, and steps of "Holy of Holies" at shrine found at Arad (tenth to seventh centuries). (*Collection of the Israel Antiquities Authority*)

Kingdom.[5] The deity's presence was associated with the ark of the covenant, a moveable palladium, and the cherubim. In pre-Solomonic times, the ark moved about in different sanctuaries. With the building of the Jerusalem temple, it became lodged there.[6] While altars of different sorts, along with basins, chalices, and the like, were used for various kinds of libations and sacrifices, such as grain, meat, and incense, other cult objects such as pillars (*maṣṣēbôt*), sacred poles or trees (*'ăšērîm*),[7] and images (*pĕsîlîm*) were prohibited, as was anything that might be associated with the worship of another deity. The sacrifice of children, for example, was expressly forbidden.

Fourth, certain times were set for the gathering of the people to celebrate the gifts of Yahweh and the deity's acts of deliverance and redemption. Pilgrimage festivals involved the whole community of Israel celebrating at a major shrine. Partly agricultural in background, they came to represent thanksgiving on the part of the people for both the blessings of nature and the occasions of God's deliverance and provided the context for renewal of the covenant that bound together the tribes as well as Yahweh and the people (see below). The primary activities at such festivals were the presentation of sacrifices and offerings and the sharing of meals.[8] But central features of the community's historical experience of Yahweh's deliverance and rule were also celebrated, including, at different times and different festivals, the deliverance from Egypt and the coming into the land, the proclamation of the covenant law, and Yahweh's choice of David and Zion. Other special occasions were set during certain periods of Israel's history, some of which centered in the family, such as the Passover, and the Sabbath, a day of rest and remembrance. In the course of Israel's religion, other community-wide celebrations arose, for example, the Day of Atonement, and, in the late– and post–Old Testament period, Purim and Hanukkah.[9]

Fifth, the moral and ethical sphere was a matter of stress, with requirements and expectations about guarding the welfare of neighbors and providing for weaker members of society. Family relationships were protected by divine law. Purity of conduct, dress, food, bodily functions and characteristics, and other matters were regulated in different ways and different times. Everything in the moral and cultic realms was understood to be a part of the individual's and the community's relation to Yahweh, a manifestation of their holiness (see chapter 4).

Sixth, religious leadership resided especially in the various priests who were associated with the sanctuaries and were dependent upon sacrifice and offering for support, but also in prophets, who were bearers of divine oracles and operated both at the center of the religious life, sometimes in relation to the court and sometimes in relation to sanctuaries, and also on the periphery, without a religious or political base and exercising an ideological and rhetorical power apart from economic and coercive means. The king and his predecessor, the judge, were understood to be appointees and agents of Yahweh in the political sphere. On occasion they assumed responsibilities in the leadership or oversight of worship and the official religion, for example, Solomon at the dedication of the temple and Hezekiah and Josiah in their reform movements. Various other officials came to be associated with the temple or other sanctuaries. While women occasionally exercised positions of leadership, that customarily fell to males, the women being given positions of a more supportive and maintenance sort.[10]

It should be noted that some elements of Israelite religion seem to have moved in and out of favor with orthodox Yahwism as described here. The calves or bulls set up by Jeroboam in Bethel and Dan (1 Kings 12:25–33) may have been originally a quite acceptable form of iconography for the northern sanctuaries, only to become regarded as idolatrous, at least in the south, by the eighth century. The asherah also may have been acceptable in premonarchical and monarchical stages, particularly in the north, but it came to be regarded as a part of an unacceptable syncretism.

Heterodox Yahwism[11]

Heterodox Yahwism by definition was an amalgam of the above, together with particular practices that came into conflict with some of the facets of more orthodox Yahwism or were not customarily a part of it. Among those features that seem most indicative of a heterodox Yahwism are (1) the presence of cult objects rejected in more orthodox expressions, (2) the use of unacceptable procedures for discerning the divine will, and (3) veneration and consultation of the dead.

Among the cult objects that had a place in these less orthodox forms of Yahwism, the asherah stands out particularly. It seems to have been present in different forms throughout much of the divided monarchy and probably reaches back to an earlier time. The references to "Yahweh and his asherah" in inscriptions from two Judean sites in the eighth century is a good indication of the inclusion of the asherah of Yahweh in Yahwistic worship and piety. At Kuntillet 'Ajrud, the inscriptions seem to be quite Yahwistic in character but occur in a site of varying inhabitants and where an inscription about El and Baal appears that may or may not be Yahwistic.[12] The inscription of Uriyahu over his tomb, however, seems to be thoroughly Yahwistic in its character except for the reference to the asherah.[13]

When we hear of a blessing by "Yahweh of Samaria and by his asherah," as we do at Kuntillet 'Ajrud, and then read of the asherah at Samaria, which still stood past the anti-Baal purge of Jehu, there is reason to believe that a fairly widespread element in the north and the south[14]—and not just the general populace or common people[15]—regarded the asherah cult object as a legitimate part of Yahweh piety.

We may assume that the pillar (maṣṣēbâ), rejected in orthodox Yahwism, was also used in cultic centers on occasion. At least, objects that may represent such standing stones or pillars have been found in some excavated cultic sites (for earlier examples, see plate 1).[16] Further, while one may not be sure of the exact character of the asherah, figurines of various sorts—females (plate 5), horses and riders (fig. 10), animals/birds and the like—have been found in Israelite and Judean sites, with a greater number of them by far in those extramural sites Holladay has described as "nonconformist." The more heterodox forms of Yahwism seem to have incorporated both iconography and diverse cult objects into their cultic sites and activities to a greater degree than orthodox Yahwism thought appropriate, though we are not clear how they used these objects. The presence of such cult objects, it should be noted, is subject to considerable variation, both temporally and geographically. For example, the plaque-type figurines seem to have begun to disappear or go into eclipse in the ninth century and the "more fully formed figurines came into vogue at some time in the eighth century in the north and either the later eighth century or the middle years of the seventh century in the south" (see plate 5).[17] Further, the evidence of cultic activity in the more "nonconformist"[18] cult centers belongs to "surprisingly short periods."[19] The presence of figurines in domestic sites (see below on family religion) also varied in intensity in different periods and different places.[20]

In this connection, one should probably include also the calves or bulls of Jeroboam in the Northern Kingdom, which may have been acceptable to such orthodox Yahwistic prophets as Elijah and Elisha but clearly were regarded as anti-Yahwistic by Hosea and later figures. That is, what was probably originally a pedestal for the deity (fig. 7) came to be understood as a divine image itself, either of Yahweh or of Baal. The same was apparently true of Nehushtan, the bronze serpent of Moses that was a cult object to which offerings were made in the Jerusalem temple until Hezekiah in his reforming activities broke it up.

The "high place" (bāmâ) as a shrine also seems to have moved from an acceptable place within Yahwism to an increasingly condemned status in official and orthodox circles.[21] Samuel and Saul, both strong Yahwists,

Fig. 10. Horse and rider figurines. (*After Taylor,* Yahweh and the Sun, *pl. 7 and fig. 9*).

met at a *bāmâ* (1 Samuel 9). Solomon received a revelation from Yahweh in a dream at the great or principal high place at Gibeon. Even the Deuteronomistic Historian seems to have acknowledged the acceptability of the high places as sites for worship before the temple was built. The Historian notes their continuation as sites of sacrifice by the people and their continued construction by kings. Deuteronomy, which prohibits all sorts of cult objects because of their connection with Canaanite worship, says nothing about the *bāmâ*. Nor do the prophets have much to say about this, if one excludes the frequent inveighing against false worship "on every high hill and under every green tree." Hosea does explicitly condemn the high places of the Northern Kingdom as a sin (Hos. 10:8). One expects that the ambivalence about the high places was because they were acceptable places of sacrifice and worship in outlying areas, and therefore more connected to local cults (see below), but were less under control of the official Jerusalem cultus and therefore became places where heterodox and idolatrous practices were possible and in fact happened.[22] It is tempting to associate the "nonconformist" cultic areas described by Holladay with such high places, with their greater collection of heterogeneous and figurative cult objects. One notes that they were largely extramural, as seems to have been the case with at least some of the high places. But many of the high places at various towns may have been fairly orthodox in their activities of sacrifice and eating.[23]

Inquiry of the deity, or the effort to divine the future and the divine will, was another sphere in which there were religious practices that were frowned upon or condemned in the main traditions that articulated what we are calling orthodox Yahwism.[24] Even dreams, which were regularly a vehicle for Yahweh's authentic communication,[25] at times became suspect, usually because they were perceived as vehicles of lies.[26] Indeed, much of the prophetic condemnation of dreams, prophetic visions, and divination is less because of an inappropriate medium being used than because of its false product.[27] Saul's visit to the witch of Endor (1 Samuel 28) is indicative of the existence within early Israel of practices of divine consultation that were not acceptable but were nevertheless practiced. Saul's reform of such practices, their persistence despite the reforms, and his own resort to them despite being a strong Yahwist, all suggest that consultation of mediums, wizards, and diviners—clearly prohibited by Deuteronomy—took place within Yahwistic circles. Saul's act to cut off such practices on pain of death is indicative of either a changing assessment of their acceptability in the early monarchy or a more aggressive effort to maintain an ortho-dox stance on these matters. His use of what he condemned indicates its persistence. The tradition, at least, claims that the necromancy pro-duced a word from Yahweh. Furthermore, Samuel's spirit condemned Saul, not on religious or Yahwistic grounds, but because he disturbed Samuel's rest.

Resorting to proscribed means of divining the divine will or the future may have been prevalent as a way of gaining the necessary knowledge on the part of persons who did not have access to the acceptable means of oracle inquiry. There was also probably an economic factor involved in that divination has been practiced consistently as a profitable or remunerative activity, in ancient times as well as in the present.[28] Yahwism's denuncia-tion of traditional means of divination may have been as much an effort to control the avenues of access to the divine will as it was a reaction to foreign religious influences. Such divinatory practices competed with Yah-wistic prophecy for claims to divine revelation.[29]

Particularly in this case, one notes the practice of necromancy, the con-sultation of the dead Samuel.[30] The realm of the dead was always a "shad-owy" matter for Yahwism, but consultation of the dead here takes place by a strong Yahwist calling up the spirit of one of the most aggressive of Yah-wistic prophets, Samuel. Isaiah 8:19 suggests that such consultation was expected among the people but to be rejected as against the true word from Yahweh that was to be found in words and deeds of the Yahwistic prophet.[31] Other practices involving veneration of the dead or special mourning rites were apparently practiced but passed out of acceptability to orthodox Yahwism by the seventh century.[32] The Deuteronomic code prohibits some of these, suggesting, by inference, that they were popular at the time of its formulation. See, for example, "You must not lacerate yourselves or shave your forelocks for the dead" (Deut. 14:1).

The prophets of the eighth to the sixth centuries, however, did not generally criticize such actions and in some instances seemed to presuppose their acceptability (e.g., Jer. 16:1–9), and Schmidt's analyses of the Deuteronomic, Deuteronomistic, and prophetic texts urges caution about an interpretation of texts that may reflect patterns of mourning so that they are seen to be explicit religious rites having to do with venerated and/or deified ancestors.[33] At least one needs to take seriously his claim that such practices as consultation and veneration of the dead may have come in only in the Assyrian period and do not reflect long-standing Israelite practices.[34] Further, the conflicts between Deuteronomic and prophetic texts from approximately the same period in their attitude toward practices having to do with death and the dead indicate something of the fluidity between orthodoxy and heterodoxy or the different views on where that line was to be drawn.

In Mesopotamia and Syria, the cult of the ancestors or dead kin was a part of family religion, and to the extent that it may have existed in Israel it also belongs to that context (see below).[35] Again, Deuteronomy seems to be an implicit testimony to the veneration of the ancestors within Yahwism, but not as an acceptable practice for the form of Israelite religion that won out in the Deuteronomic and prophetic reforms. In the liturgy for the presentation of the tithe in Deut. 26:12–15, the one bringing the offering is required to testify that "I have not offered any of it to the dead" (v. 14).[36] The erection of a commemorative stele by Absalom because he had no son to do so (2 Sam. 18:18) may also be a reflection of the practice of a son honoring his father by setting up a funerary stele to the ancestral spirit of his father.[37] So also the reference to a *bêt marzē(a)ḥ* or "house of mourning" in Jer. 16:5 points to the existence of an institution and practice common to Syria-Palestine, a social association of revelry that may have involved commemoration of the dead.[38] The judgment pronounced on such "revelry" (*mirzaḥ*) in Amos 6:7 suggests that the *bêt marzē(a)ḥ* and its activities were seen as heterodox in some fashion.[39] Practices concerning the dead did not cease with the Deuteronomic movement but continued on in the postexilic age.[40]

A particularly sharp example of heterodox Yahwism in the early period, at least as judged by the main line of orthodox Yahwism articulated by prophets and Deuteronomists, is the account of a Yahwist named Micah, who set up a household shrine in Ephraim sometime in the premonarchical period (Judges 17–18).[41] The shrine (*bêt-'ĕlōhîm*, "house of God") contained an expensive image of cast silver,[42] an ephod, and (a) teraphim. The ephod functioned in Yahwism quite normally for the most part, but was at least ambiguous or condemned in some texts (e.g., Hos. 3:4; Judg. 8:27). Its character is somewhat unclear here, although it is plausible that, in conjunction with the teraphim, it was an instrument of divination or a divine representation of some sort. The teraphim, often regarded as household gods or idols but more plausibly interpreted as ancestor figurines used in necromancy,[43] were even more ambiguous and were a part of the "abominations" (*haššiqqusîm*) removed by Josiah in his reform (2 Kings 23:24). There are numerous indications that the shrine and the family that set it up were Yahwistic. The name of the owner, Micaiah/Micah (Judg. 17:4) is Yahwistic ("Who is like Yahweh?"). His mother blesses by Yahweh and consecrates the silver to Yahweh to make a cast metal image, surely of Yahweh (17:2–3). Micah understands his act as one that will gain the blessing of Yahweh (17:13). He pays a Levite to preside at the shrine, and the Levite later provides a word from Yahweh when an inquiry is made of him by some Danites. Here is no true syncretism, joining together specific elements from the cultus of different deities. The shrine of Micah was thoroughly Yahwistic and also clearly heterodox, initiated by a woman, as in the case of other heterodox activities, and supported by a person of considerable wealth, as was the case with the tomb of Uriyahu at Khirbet el-Qom. The iconic tendency is associated once again with affluence and made possible by it.[44]

If we ask what groups or communities were primarily responsible for the more heterodox elements of Yahwism, we may not be able to answer with much certainty. Indeed, there is no reason to assume that such heterodoxy as described above was peculiar to a particular element in Israelite society. The practices described above probably cut across economic strata. Some of them were associated with the family,[45] some were apparently carried on particularly by women (cf. chapter 1).[46] Both biblical and archaeological data indicate that heterodox elements of Yahwism could be found at cultic centers, such as Samaria and Jerusalem, as well as at more peripheral locations. The complexity of Yahwism in both orthodox and heterodox forms was not confined to a particular group or place.[47]

Syncretistic Yahwism

The term "syncretistic Yahwism" may be a complete misnomer in that there is some sense in which many of the most orthodox practices of Yahwism were known and shared by other religious communities and entered Israelite religion in the prolonged experience of intercommunal contact or were the result of the very heterogeneous character of the Israelite community and its being fully a part of the religio-cultural world in which it lived. One often encounters references to what Israel "borrowed" from Canaanite religion or other sources. In the minds of some interpreters, "syncretistic Yahwism" may be simply an alternative term for what is discussed above under the rubric "heterodox Yahwism."[48] Some, therefore, would lump together in one whole what we have separated under two rubrics. In this instance, however, we have in mind a distinction around the recognition that some practices did not seem to be a part of Yahwism until they were explicitly drawn into it out of the cults of other and specific deities. Such practices and related concepts were explicitly dependent upon the recognition of other deities and their worship and not generally a part of the religious activity and conceptuality of Yahwists except the particular individuals and groups who self-consciously appropriated and assimilated aspects of the worship of other deities. It may be that, in the end, some of these developments are to be regarded as simply another form or aspect of heterodox Yahwism as described above.

The most obvious indication of such explicit syncretism is in the several references to the worship of Baal, attested in the Deuteronomistic History and Hosea as a prominent religious feature of Israel from the ninth century onwards, but also present in Judah, as both the Deuteronomistic History and the prophets (Jeremiah, Ezekiel, and Zephaniah) indicate, as well as the worship of the heavenly bodies—sun, moon, and stars—possibly under Assyrian influence. The rise of Baalism among the Yahwists, especially in the Northern Kingdom but also in Judah, may have been under the influence of Jezebel and the Phoenician worship of Baal (see fig. 11). Biblical texts speak of a "temple of Baal" in Samaria (2 Kings 10:18–27) and Jerusalem (2 Kings 11:18), but no such clearly Baal cultic center has been excavated to this date. Israelite personal names on the Samaria Ostraca seem to confirm the presence of Baal worship in Samaria. These are the primary non-Yahwistic divine elements in Israelite proper names from epigraphic sources, and it is not altogether certain that they do not have Yahweh in mind. The low number of Baal names—or names of other deities

Fig. 11. Stele of deity, presumed to be Baal holding stylized lightning in his left hand, from second-millennium Ugarit in Syria. (*After* ANEP, *no. 490*).

for that matter—in the Israelite and Judean onomastica or in the inscriptions from the time of the Divided Monarchy require us not to exaggerate the degree of syncretism around the figure of Baal or the cosmic deities of Assyria.[49] Its presence may have been largely a matter of royal politico-religious policy whether by virtue of marriages with foreign wives, or for the purpose of coalition building, or under the influence and dominance of Assyrian power. The polemic of Deuteronomists and prophets suggests a greater prominence to such syncretistic influences in the general populace than the inscriptional and onomastic evidence indicates.[50]

The worship of the "Queen of Heaven" may have been a cult around either Canaanite-Phoenician Astarte or the Mesopotamian goddess Ishtar.[51] We only know of it as an Israelite religious phenomenon in the time of Jeremiah (7:18; 44:15–30) when there is a return to it among the general populace. But the Jewish refugees in Egypt who insist on making offerings to the Queen of Heaven speak of it as something that they and their ancestors used to do in Judah and Jerusalem, as if it were an old custom interrupted by the late monarchical religious reforms. Furthermore, in the context of divine speech, Jeremiah reports it as a widespread activity in Judah. In all likelihood, however, the cult of the Queen of Heaven, which was particularly associated with women or wives who made cakes stamped with the image of the goddess and offered them, together with libations, to her, was brought into Judean religious life during the time of the Divided Monarchy. While particularly nurtured by women, the cult of the Queen of Heaven was supported by the husbands and, according to Jer. 44:17 and 21, incorporated kings and other officials as well. Its restoration was associated with the claim that poverty, famine, and death had been the consequence of its abandonment. Here one may find a clue generally to the syncretistic impetus, a clue consistent with what we see in the worship of Baal, child sacrifice, and the women weeping for Tammuz (see below). Other gods were invoked and serviced in order to bring about help in time of need or blessing and provision for life when the worship of Yahweh seemed inadequate to such purposes.[52]

The practice of child sacrifice may have had some continuing place in heterodox Yahwism, but it seems to have been a genuinely syncretistic practice brought in from outside in the assimilation of cults of other deities to the worship of Yahweh.[53] If it could be demonstrated conclusively that the *molek* to whom children were sometimes dedicated in sacrifice[54] was a deity[55] and not a technical term for a type of sacrifice,[56] the syncretistic character of child sacrifice in ancient Israel would be quite clear.[57] But that is surely the case in any event. Child sacrifice is specifically identified with non-Israelites in 2 Kings 3:27, where the king of Moab offers his firstborn son as a sacrifice to secure the favor of the deity in a battle against the Israelites, as well as in 2 Kings 17:31, which speaks of the Avvites burning their children (or sons) in the fire "to Adrammelech and Anammelech, the gods of Sepharvaim."[58] Within Israel, the practice appears first in the time of the Divided Monarchy when "foreign influences were encroaching upon the cult" (2 Kings 16:3; cf. 21:6; 23:10).[59] The Deuteronomist explicitly identifies the practice of child sacrifice with the worship of the gods of the nations (Deut. 12:31). Jeremiah records child sacrifice to Baal (19:5; 32:35) in the late seventh to early sixth century. Psalm 106:37–38 alludes to the practice of child sacrifice specifically as a sacrifice to "the idols of Canaan," and Ezekiel's polemic against Jerusalem also points to child sacrifice in his time as a borrowing from the Canaanites. It was probably somewhere in the eighth to seventh centuries—but possibly earlier—that child sacrifice was incorporated into Yahwistic ritual, presumably by court and upper-class figures, from areas of Phoenician influence where the practice was widespread.[60] It seems to have continued or been revived in the postexilic period (Isa. 57:5).[61] Those who engaged in this practice probably did so as a part of their worship of Yahweh.[62] As far as one can tell, the purpose of such sacrifices was either dedicatory, as a foundation sacrifice for a city (1 Kings 16:34), or, more likely and more often, a sacrifice in time of calamity to gain the favor of the god(s) (e.g., 2 Kings 3:27).[63] As yet, the practice of child sacrifice is without archaeological evidence in Israel, though it has been argued that tophets,[64] cult places for the sacrifice of children and/or the incineration of corpses, have been found in Syria-Palestine.[65]

Ezekiel 8 has been seen as testifying to syncretistic developments during the late preexilic period within the royal, priestly, and upper-class
circles of Jerusalem as well as specifically again among the women.[66] Four
different "abominations" are recounted in the chapter, not all of which
are clearly understandable. The first is an "image of jealousy" (*sēmel
haqqin'â*, v. 3) at the gateway of the inner court of the temple, probably a
statue of some deity.[67] The second is a picture of seventy elders or leaders
engaged in an obscure ritual in a room covered with paintings of reptiles
and other beasts, those that were hybrid and unclean (Ezek. 8:7–13).[68] They
may have been Egyptian in origin, having to do with the worship of
Osiris,[69] but the iconography is reminiscent of scenes from Mesopotamia
and Asia Minor as well. The women weeping for Tammuz (Ezek. 8:14–15)
were participating in the cult of the Sumero-Akkadian vegetation deity,
Tammuz, whose descent into the underworld was an occasion for weeping, usually by women, as it meant the end of the time of fertility with the
end of spring.[70] The final "great abomination" described by Ezekiel is a
scene of twenty-five men (priests?) with their backs to the Lord in the temple and "prostrating themselves to the sun towards the east" (v. 16). In this
case, what appears to be a clear syncretistic appropriation of the cult of the
sun god may, however, be a case of heightened focus upon solar elements
in Yahwism. Recent studies have made us more aware of the presence of
solar symbolism in the biblical depiction of Yahweh.[71] Seals and ivories
from the ninth to eighth centuries show a dominance of solar symbols that
had not been the case earlier.[72] Ezekiel, however, clearly regards this solar
dimension as evidence of an idolatrous sun cult. Certainly, Josiah's removal
of "the horses that the kings of Judah had dedicated to the sun, at the
entrance to the house of the LORD" (2 Kings 23:11) was consistent with
Ezekiel's condemnation of a specific ritual focus on the sun. What may
have been a long-evolving association of solar elements with Yahweh came
to be regarded as heterodox or syncretistic by the prophetic and reformist
elements in seventh to sixth century Yahwism.

The divinization of the heavenly bodies in both Egyptian and Mesopotamian religions and the widespread appropriation of solar elements
generally in ancient Near Eastern religions would have facilitated an exaggerated focus on the sun by Yahwists in a temple that contained cosmic
symbolism from the beginning as well as a heightened resistance by the
prophets to practices that could be disconnected from Yahweh (turning the
back, v. 16) and associated with worship of the solar disc. Indeed, it is possible that the chapter is a kind of "Babylonian" interpretation of practices
that originated elsewhere or were a part of the heterodox Yahwism that

continued into the late preexilic period.[73] Some have argued that the "image of jealousy" was an Asherah statue,[74] and the weeping for Tammuz, which authentically represents a Babylonian ritual, may be an interpretation of other forms of weeping and lamentation that were regarded by Ezekiel as heterodox and therefore a form of rejection of Yahweh—whether or not that was the view of the weeping women.[75] How widespread any of the practices depicted in Ezekiel 8 were among the general populace is not known. They may have been prevalent primarily among the court and the upper classes.

In the sixth century, a colony of Jewish soldiers lived on the island of Elephantine at the southern border of Egypt near Syene (Aswan). Papyri documents in Aramaic from family and community archives along with many ostraca have been preserved to tell us something of the affairs of that community, including its religious life. The presence of a temple to YHW (=Yahweh) oriented toward Jerusalem (1 Kings 8:44–45), frequent references to that deity as "God Yahweh" (literally "Yahu"), "God of heaven," "Lord of Hosts," and the like, as well as an onomasticon of Jewish names that is overwhelmingly Yahwistic[76] while non-Jewish names bore divine elements such as Bethel, Eshem, Herem, and Anath—all attest to the Yahwistic character of the community.

At the same time, other data suggest that in fact other deities were also worshiped in this community. Money was collected not only for Yahu/Yahweh but also for the Aramaic deities Eshembethel and Anathbethel. Oaths were sworn "by Yahu" but also by Anathyahu, the Egyptian goddess Sati, and possibly by "Mesgida," the divinized cult place.[77] A person with a Yahwistic name (Malchiah) calls for help to the Aramaic god Herembethel. Worship of the Queen of Heaven seems to have been introduced into Egypt by Jews from Judah (Jeremiah 44) and was cultivated at a temple dedicated to her at Syene near Elephantine where the Arameans of that area were located. This may have been the goddess Anath, and the worship of the Queen of Heaven may have led to the assimilation of Anath to Yahu in the divine name Anathyahu.[78]

The fundamental issue under debate and not yet fully settled is whether in this very Yahwistic community—with its Yahweh temple, Yahweh names, and the references at Elephantine to Sabbath and Passover—the deities Eshembethel, Herembethel, Anathbethel, and Anathyahu were "hypostatic forms of Yahweh"[79] or actual deities worshiped or invoked on their own and not simply as aspects of Yahweh. With Anathyahu, as with the asherah in preexilic Israelite religion, the question remains as to whether we are encountering a hypostatic form of the deity or a separate goddess

perceived as a consort of Yahweh. The issue is whether Elephantine represented a heterodox Yahwism, which surely would have been unacceptable to the prophets and Deuteronomists but was nevertheless perceived
by the garrison as completely and exclusively Yahwistic, or a true syncretism in which the worship of specific Aramean deities was incorporated
into Yahwism. The dominance of Yahu at Elephantine makes it clear that
the Jews there understood themselves to be Yahwists, but the evidence for
the independent existence of such deities as Bethel and Anathbethel suggests that they were worshiped as deities and not simply as manifestations
of the presence of Yahweh.[80] The close proximity of the Jewish garrison at
Elephantine to the Aramean one at Syene, its distance and separation from
the main postexilic centers of Israelite religion, and the general intermixing
of Jewish, Aramean, Egyptian, Babylonian, Median, Persian, and other soldiers and their families within a relatively small area were circumstances
conducive to forms of syncretism within an isolated outpost of Israelite
religion.[81]

THE FORM AND CHARACTER OF THE CULT

If one takes the form and character of the cult as the criterion, then the
types of Israelite religion may be described somewhat differently, although
much of what has been identified via the criterion of orthodoxy still makes
up the ritual and ideology of the various types. The overlap means that it
is not necessary to repeat each feature that has already been discussed but
rather to show its place in another typology. The typology taken up here
is a fairly familiar one, particularly in the distinction between "official" and
"popular" religion. A somewhat more complex categorization, however, is
proposed to account for the literary, epigraphic, and artifactual data, one
that is coming more prominently into the study of Israelite religion.[82]

Family Religion[83]

Family religion and cult has to do with what went on in domestic households and in the larger circle of the clan. We are dealing with the "father's
house" or extended family (*bêt 'āb*) and the "clan" (*mišpāḥâ*),[84] recognizing
that in any family locality there may have been single households made up
of a single nuclear family—as, archaeologically, would seem to have been
the case for many houses—but also larger clusters of family units.[85] In addition to archaeological evidence, the primary biblical material comes from
the family stories of Genesis and those of Judges–Samuel with pieces of
data from elsewhere.[86] The picture painted here is necessarily more

schematic than the actuality, where one must recognize there would have been changes over hundreds of years and that practices would have varied to some degree over a long time span and in different localities.[87] Some changes would have been due to reform movements, such as that of the Deuteronomists, or the stresses of historical upheavals,[88] but not all the variation can be explained.

The Genesis narratives about the patriarchs reveal the cult of the *family god* as an important feature of family religion.[89] The personal god of the paterfamilias, the family god, was therefore also the god of the collective entity of the family or clan of whom the head of the family was leader.[90] That means that women who married into the family or servants within the family also worshiped the personal god of the father, who was sometimes called "the god of my father" or identified by reference to the name of the head of the family or an earlier head of the family, for example, "the God of Abraham" or "the bull of Jacob, "the God of Isaac" or "the Fear of Isaac."[91] So Eliezer, Abraham's servant prays, "Blessed be Yahweh, the God of my master Abraham" (Gen. 24:27). The family god, however, was not a nameless deity; nor was it willy-nilly any of the gods of Syria-Palestine. In the pre-Yahwistic period, the family god seems to have been the high god El. In the Yahwistic period of Israel's religion, from the time of the exodus onward (according to biblical tradition, which is probably correct)[92] the family god appears to have been Yahweh, though some see indications in the early period that Baal may have been the clan deity in some instances.[93] The family god was a personal and social god who provided protection and guidance for the family as well as the blessings of fertility and the continuity of life.

Within the family setting there may have been at least two kinds of *sacred areas* or *shrines*. One would have been within the domestic center or household. Holladay has noted that "about 45 percent of all houses in Level A at Tell Beit Mirsim exhibited signs of cultic activity"[93a] and that similar statistics are exhibited at Beer-sheba in the south and Hazor in the north during the time of the Divided Monarchy. The archaeological remains indicate that in any community a number of households had religious objects and a number did not and that the percentages varied from time to time, with a sharp increase toward the end of the Israelite and Judean states. While the religious objects suggest some sort of house cult, we can tell little about the actual character of sacred areas in the houses except to note some indications that offerings and other activities of worship took place on the roofs of houses.[94] We can identify the kinds of apparently religious artifacts found in domestic contexts. For example, at the Judean sites of Tell

Beit Mirsim and Beer-sheba, of those houses with religious objects about half had only one object, most often a pillar-based female figurine (and rarely more than one) but also horse and rider figurines (fig. 10), animal figurines or vessels, bird-shaped vessels, rattles, limestone altars, and fenestrated stands.[95] Where more than one object was found, there was nearly always a female figurine.[96] The limestone altars, which began to appear in domestic contexts toward the end of the eleventh century, and the fenestrated cultic stands were presumably used for incense offerings (fig. 12 and plate 7).[97] Libation vessels appeared in domestic contexts from the ninth century on. It is worth noting, therefore, that the sacrifices and offerings of family religion, insofar as they took place in more domestic settings, were primarily incense and libation offerings rather than burnt offerings of grain or meat.[98]

The other type of sacred area of family religion was the cultic center of the clan or extended family. Three kinds of evidence suggest that there were such centers established in the early period of Israel's history and possibly continuing down to the exile,[99] though affected by efforts at cult centralization: archaeological, toponymic, and biblical.[100] As an example of the former, one may cite the "Bull Site," an open cult area situated on a hill between Dothan and Tirzah in the tribal territory of Manasseh during the period of the judges. A bronze bull figurine, 17.5 cm long and 12.4 cm high, was found there together with a possible standing stone and another partial cult object (plate 2). There is no major tell near by, but the cult place is in the middle of a cluster of small sites dated to Iron Age I, small

Fig. 12. Limestone incense altar from Miqne-Ekron. (*After Gitin,* Eretz-Israel, *20, p. 53**).

Plate 7. Limestone incense altar from Megiddo, tenth to ninth century. (*Collection of the Israel Antiquities Authority*)

agricultural villages, probably Israelite. It has been suggested that this is a "high place" (*bāmâ*) erected by a farmer and used as the family shrine by the clan or *mišpāḥâ* that lived in the surrounding villages.[101] It cannot be determined if it is a purely family shrine, but presumably it was used and maintained by the people in the immediate area, who are likely to have been members of a single clan. The bull figurine is capable of being related to Yahweh, El, or Baal. It is not impossible that here (and in the possibly domestic religious context of the cult stand at Taanach) one finds antecedents within local and family religion of the bull iconography that is later associated with Yahweh in the north, particularly in the bulls Jeroboam set up at Dan and Bethel.[102]

The second type of evidence for family shrines or cult centers is toponymic and indirect. In the period of Israelite settlement in the hill country and among the number of new settlements that arose, there are several place names in the formation "Baal + clan name," for example, Baal-Shalishah (2 Kings 4:42; cf. 1 Chron. 7:37), Baal-Perazim (2 Sam. 5:20; cf. Ruth 4:18–22), Baal-Tamar (Judg. 20:33). These compound Baal names do not appear among the Canaanite sites on Egyptian and other topographical lists from the Canaanite era of the Late Bronze Age and before.[103] It has been suggested that these were "family cult places" for Israelite clans settling in these areas.[104] It is unclear whether the deity served at these presumed centers of family religion was Baal or Yahweh or a local deity of some sort. While it is quite possible that the deity was Canaanite Baal, this is the period in which the term "baal" was used quite freely in personal names, apparently as an epithet or alternative name for Yahweh, where other members of the same family bore Yahwistic names.[105] The same may have operated with the place names.[106]

There are several narratives in Judges and Samuel that tell about activities at family religious centers. The story of Gideon tells of his setting up a Yahwistic shrine, consisting of an altar for animal sacrifice, at the family settlement of Ophrah, but probably outside the town proper.[107] While the later Deuteronomistic narrative portrays "all Israel" as prostituting itself before the ephod Gideon set up at Ophrah (Judg. 8:27), it is likely that this was a cult center for the Abiezrite clan, to which Gideon belonged (Judg. 6:11, 24; cf. Josh. 17:2).[108] By juxtaposing the account of Gideon's building the altar at Ophrah against the command to tear down his father's altar to Baal, the narrative suggests the family character of the Ophrah shrine.[109] The concluding etiological notation about Gideon's building an altar there—"To this day it still stands at Ophrah, *which belongs to the Abiezrites*" (Judg. 6:24)—confirms its family character, as does the report that Gideon was buried "in the tomb of his father Joash at Ophrah of the Abiezrites" (Judg. 8:32).[110] The family character of the previously existing altar and asherah or sacred pole is also indicated by the report that they belonged to Gideon's father Joash (Judg. 6:25) and that Gideon was reluctant to tear them down for fear of his "family" (*bêt 'āb*) and the townspeople. The deity worshiped at the shrine built by Gideon was clearly Yahweh. The ephod he constructed of silver and gold, and for which the Deuteronomistic redactor condemns him, was probably a Yahwistic image or cult object.[111] While the deity for whom his father Joash built an altar is depicted in the story as Baal—thus the command to Gideon to tear it down—one cannot be certain that the deity worshiped there was in fact the Canaanite deity rather than Yahweh. That may have been the case, and the story may preserve a memory of an early clash between the worship of Yahweh brought by clans and tribes from the south and the preexisting worship of Baal in Canaan.[112] There are complications in the details of the story, however, that raise the alternative possibility that this was a Yahwistic family cult center but as heterodox (or more so) by later standards as Gideon's act of making the ephod at the explicitly Yahwistic shrine he built. Gideon's father bore the Yahwistic name Joash but is depicted as having set up a Baal altar. Gideon, who set up an altar to Yahweh and tore down the Baal altar of his father, had a Baal name, Jerubbaal (Judg. 6:32; 7:1; 8:35)![113] Joash's defense of his son against the townspeople who want to kill him becomes an anti-Baal statement that provides a Yahwistic etiology for Gideon's baalistic name, Jerubbaal—that is, "Let Baal contend against him" (Judg. 6:31–32). In this instance, we are probably dealing with a Deuteronomistic projection of Baal worship onto an early family shrine serving Yahweh but using the Baal name/epithet, a feature of early Israelite religion we have noted above. Hosea's later anti-Baal oracle—"no longer will you call me 'My Baal' "—is an indication, and rejection, of this earlier tendency to use the word "baal" in reference to Yahweh. What was done with ease by good Yahwists in the time of the league and the early monarchy was unacceptable in the ninth to eighth century conflict with the Phoenician god Baal, whose worship violated the exclusive Yahweh allegiance required of Israel.[114]

The account of Micah and his shrine (Judges 17–18) in the hill country of Ephraim has already been discussed as an example of early heterodox Yahwism. In this context, it needs only to be noted that the shrine was clearly a *family* cult center initiated by Micah's mother and set up in Micah's house with his son as the priest until he later hired a Levite.[115] The Levite was paid by Micah, called "my/his priest," and resided "in the house of Micah" (Judg. 17:10–13). The family shrine in this instance was quite complex. While it seems to have been confined to a *bêt 'āb* or extended family, it was a separate structure (*bêt 'ĕlōhîm,* "house of God") with cultic objects of various sorts and its own cultic official. The size of the *bêt 'āb* here is unknown but later in the story reference is made to the "men who were in the houses comprising the household of Micah" (Judg. 18:22), suggesting a sizeable multiple compound. The family compound may have been coterminous with the village itself.[116] If that was the case, then this episode, like the story of the family shrines at Ophrah in Judges 6–8,[117] would provide an illustration of the family cultic center serving also as the settlement sanctuary, and the family god interchangeable with the god of the settlement.[118]

While the accounts of Gideon's and Micah's family shrines do not tell us much about the activities that took place there, from other texts, particularly in Samuel, we learn of *sacrifices, meals,* and *festival celebrations* at such shrines. Brief reference is made to a visit by Saul to the *bāmâ* or shrine at his hometown of Gibeah in Benjamin, called both *Gib'at Ha'ĕlōhîm,* "Hill of God" (1 Sam. 10:5), and *Gib'at Šā'ûl,* "Hill of Saul."[119] While no activity is indicated, Saul is queried there by his *dôd,* about which van der Toorn writes, "The leadership of the family cult normally lay with the *dôd.* The *dôd* is no mere uncle, but the oldest living male of the extended family and as such its *paterfamilias* with both social and religious duties (cf. Lev 10:4; 25:49; Am 6:10)."[120] Before returning home on this occasion, however, Saul had visited at the family cult center of Samuel and his clan, a *bāmâ* in the territory of Zuph,[121] apparently outside Ramah, Samuel's home (1 Samuel 9).[122] This *bāmâ,* which seems to have been outside of and higher than the town,[123] was distinct from the major shrines of Bethel, Gilgal, Mizpah, and Shiloh, with all of which Samuel was associated as Yahweh's spokesman to the people. At the family cult center at Ramah, which was clearly a structure with one or more rooms in it (1 Sam. 9:22),[124] Samuel presided over a sacrifice, which he blessed, and a meal following the sacrifice, attended by about thirty people. While it has been suggested that this was a family sacrificial feast, like the one of which David speaks in 1 Samuel 20 (see below),[125] the character of the feast makes it difficult to say that with any certainty. With its invited guests, it is more like the sacrificial feasts carried out by Samuel (1 Sam. 16:1–13), Absalom (2 Sam. 15:11–12), and Adonijah (1 Kings 1:9, 18–19, 41, 49) as "anticipatory coronation banquets," in this case in anticipation of Saul's becoming king of Israel.[126] This may, therefore, have been more than a family shrine.

Clans did hold a yearly sacrificial feast (*zebaḥ*) that was attended by all of its members, even those not residing at home, for David used this occasion as an excuse for avoiding attendance at Saul's court on the occasion of the new moon festival (1 Sam. 20:6, 28–29). The family sacrificial feast was significant enough that David could claim the urgency of his being there.[127] His pretense that his elder brother had summoned him may point to a leading role on the part of that member of the family, or this may simply be an indication of the elder brother taking over the role of the father upon his death or because he is too old (1 Sam. 17:12). While no indication of the character of the sacrificial feast is given, it was probably not one of the main pilgrimage festivals celebrated by all Israel. It is unclear what was the relation of this occasion to the annual journey of Elkanah and his family to Shiloh to make a sacrifice (1 Samuel 1). They are both called *zebaḥ hayyāmîm*.[128] Whether or not these accounts reflect the same kind of cultic event, both reports, together possibly with the information in 1 Samuel 9, suggest that family religion in early Israel involved sacrificial feasts where the family made a sacrifice at a sanctuary, often the family cultic center, and then shared a meal from the sacrificial portions (1 Sam. 1:4–5; 9:23–24).

The sacrifice was carried out by the male head, but the other members of the family, wives and children, participated in the meal (Gen. 31:54). Even at a later time when Deuteronomic reform centralized worship and sacrifice in Jerusalem, the combination of sacrifice or offering by the males followed by celebratory meals in which the whole family took part, before the Lord and in a chamber or room adjacent to the sanctuary (*liškâ,* 1 Sam. 1:18 [LXX]; 9:22), was an important aspect of Israelite religion.[129] Such reports receive probable confirmation in the extensive evidence for food offerings and preparation of meals that has been uncovered archaeologically at various cultic sites.[130]

In this connection, it should be mentioned that the biblical texts identify the celebration of the feast of Passover as a family feast held within the *bêt 'āb* (Ex. 12:3, 21–24), as well as an all-Israel celebration (Deut. 16:1–8). When it functioned as a family feast and when it involved the gathering of all the people is a matter of debate. Josiah's reinstitution of the Passover suggests that it was an all-Israel occasion prior to the monarchy and fell into disuse as such during the rule of the kings and the focus on the fall festival (see below). At some point, however, possibly both early and late, Passover centered in the family. It may have had to do with celebration of God's bounty in the flock or with sacrifice to secure the welfare and fertility of the flock, but it came to be linked with the going out of Egypt. In any event, Passover joins with the texts discussed above to identify once more the place in family religion of sacrifice and the family meal. At a much later time, the feast of Purim was instituted and celebrated within the family, again as a time of feasting and celebration (Esth. 9:20–28, esp. 28).

Food preparation as a family religious activity in devotion to a deity is also evident in the report of offerings made and libations poured out to the Queen of Heaven by Judean refugees in Egypt in the sixth century (Jer. 44:15–30). The family character of this particular form of cultic service is shown by the description in Jer. 7:18: "The children gather wood, the fathers kindle fire, and the women knead dough, to make cakes for the queen of heaven." These offerings and libations are explicitly described as a former widespread practice, given up (presumably in Josiah's reform) but now—in new stress and crisis—to be taken up again. The role of the women or wives is particularly stressed in Jeremiah's account.[131]

The *šabbāt* should be mentioned in this connection. While we know little of its origin, it seems to have been a preexilic institution that gained importance in the exile and the postexilic period (see below on "Community Religion").[132] It was a day set aside as sacred to Yahweh and on which no work was to be carried out. The commandment calling for Sabbath observance was addressed to the individual Israelite and was obligatory for the whole family. Because it centered primarily around a period of rest and cessation from work, its locus in the family setting is obvious. At the same time, it was understood as an element of religious life that belonged to all Israel and commemorated, in the Deuteronomic version of the Sabbath commandment, the deliverance from Egypt. In the postexilic period, the Sabbath became more significant as a mark of identity for the Yahwistic community. The Sabbath, therefore, is one of the places where a religious practice was located in family life but belonged to the wider understanding and practice of Israelite religion.[133]

The same is to be said for *circumcision*, the removal of the male foreskin. While there are accounts of its practice as an all-Israelite event (Josh. 5:2–12), in most instances it seems to have been carried out within the family context by mother (Ex. 4:24–26) or father (Gen. 17:23–27; 21:4) or by another person, at least in the late postexilic period (1 Macc. 1:61). There is no indication of its being carried out in a sanctuary or by a priest. Its original function seems to have been as a rite of passage, either from puberty to young manhood or in preparation for marriage, and it was practiced by other ethnic groups in the ancient Near East.[134] Adult circumcision, therefore, would have been the original practice (cf. Genesis 34 and Josh. 5:1–12), with a later move toward circumcision of the infant (Lev. 12:3) as the ritual became increasingly regarded as a mark of identity, a sign of belonging to the community of Israel.[135] Once again, therefore, in the course of its history, a family practice came to be understood within the larger context of the faith of the Yahwistic community and one's identification with it, a move especially indicated by the connecting of circumcision with the Passover in the Priestly ideology of the exilic period and later (Ex. 12:48). Like the Sabbath, circumcision did not leave the family context but gained a socioreligious symbolic function that may have been foreign to its original character. While its original function indicates why it was associated with males, its development as a symbol of incorporation and belonging functioned along with other features of Israelite religion to center religious identity and practice upon the male members of the family. Furthermore, the rite of circumcision took on a symbolic function, as a covenant rite to be a reminder of ethical obligation. The circumcised heart would love and obey (Deut. 10:16; 30:6; Jer. 4:4; 9:25–26), the uncircumcised ear would not listen (Jer. 6:10).[136]

Among those elements of family religion that were not directly associated with cultic activities in the sanctuary, practices associated with birth and death stand out. As we have indicated, circumcision came to be one of the religious rites around the birth of a child. Naming was less a religious activity in the strict sense, but in Israelite literature it is often depicted as an act of thanksgiving or confession of faith, a fact reflected also in the propensity for theophoric names.[137] The association of fertility and the ability to bear children with Yahweh's will and blessing is seen particularly well in the story of the birth of Samuel. There the womb of the barren Hannah is understood to be closed by Yahweh, and she prays to the deity for a child, which is granted to her. His weaning is celebrated with a sacrifice at the sanctuary at Shiloh (1 Sam. 1:24–25; cf. Gen. 21:8). The conviction that childbearing was a blessing from the deity permeates the stories of family life in the Old Testament. That is why many regard the female figurines found in Israelite excavations as possible talismans "used in sympathetic magic to stimulate the reproductive processes"[138] or images of the mother goddess, whose service or devotion might bring the devotee the reward of fertility.[139] Any claim, however, about how these figurines were used remains quite speculative.

Like its beginning, the end of life also involved the family directly. Not all of the *practices associated with death* had direct religious associations or connotations, nor can we be sure that where we see religious death practices they were carried out generally and normally within the family. Two kinds of activities are attested either indirectly or in critical reaction. They are sacrifices for the dead and the veneration or worship of ancestors, both of which were quite common in the ancient Near East.[140] Because sacrifices for the dead were unacceptable in the Deuteronomic ideology (Deut. 26:14) and criticized in the psalms as pagan practices carried out by earlier generations (Ps. 106:28), one may assume that in some times and places they were offered, presumably by members of the family and at the family tomb. In later postexilic literature, we find further implicit criticism of food offerings placed on graves (Sir. 30:18). The recent work of van der Toorn has given stronger support for the possibility that the teraphim mentioned several times in the Bible are ancestor figurines or deified ancestors rather than household gods.[141] There are three narratives in which such teraphim are found in household or family contexts (Gen. 31:19–54; Judges 17–18; 1 Sam. 19:11–17). Van der Toorn associates these with the reference to the "god(s)" apparently located near the door of an Israelite home (Ex. 21:6) and suggests that family religion included a recognition and service of the spirits of the ancestors, presumably with offerings of various sorts. Located near the entrance of the house, such "gods" would also have served an apotropaic function, warding off evil of various sorts.[142] If this interpretation of Ex. 21:6 and of the teraphim is correct, then the veneration of the ancestors would have been more commonly and acceptably a part of family religion in the early period before the Deuteronomic effort at centralization and containment of religious ritual and deity worship.

The association of the teraphim with divination in a number of texts (1 Sam. 15:23; Ezek. 21:21; Zeph. 10:2; cf. 2 Kings 23:24) further suggests that such ancestor figurines may have been used in necromancy, that is, the consultation of the dead.[143] The only clear example of necromancy, however, is 1 Samuel 28, which does not seem particularly tied to the family. It may have been, however, that such consultation of the dead in order to divine the future or determine what the deity had in store and how the deity was directing the fate of the family or the individual member of the family was in fact an aspect of family religion and a part of regular and irregular inquiry of the deity. Inquiry of the deity via dreams, persons, oracular procedures, or the dead would have been a part of family experience, and the involvement of women in significant ways in such activities suggests an association with the family structure, the primary sphere in which women functioned generally. With regard to those matters that particularly concerned the family, as over against the nation as a whole—for example, birth and sickness—consultation of this sort at least would have taken place within the family or by family members in behalf of or on the part of other family members.

Three narratives explicitly inform us of such inquiry of the deity. When Rebekah's twin sons struggled within her womb, and she despaired of her life, "she went to inquire of the LORD," who gave her an oracle explaining the meaning of the struggle and what it presaged for her posterity (Gen. 25:22–23). Nothing is told about the medium of inquiry, but its family orientation and appropriateness is evident. So also, in the stories around the figure of Elisha, there is the account of the illness of the son of the Shunnamite woman, with whom Elisha was staying (2 Kings 4:18–37). The remark of the woman's husband when she says that she is hurrying to "the man of God" (v. 22) is revealing: "Why go to him today? It is neither new moon nor sabbath" (v. 23). Apparently it was customary for individuals in the family to visit and inquire of a seer, but it usually took place on a special day, the Sabbath, when the family rested, or at the time of the new moon, also a special feast day often associated with the Sabbath.[144] The story intimates that the woman went to ask the help of the seer in healing the child and such may have been the case. Another narrative, however, tells of a mother, this time at the behest of her husband, Jeroboam, going to a prophet to inquire "what shall happen to the child" (1 Kings 14:3, 5). Each of these stories is an instance of a typical family circumstance or crisis—the birth of a child and critical illness. In each case some sort of consultation is made to discern what will happen, and in one instance also to seek help. Such inquiry and consultation was not confined to the family and its circumstances. Nor was it necessarily restricted to the particular technique suggested in two of the stories. But they make it clear that family religion included such practices as consultation of the deity, and it is likely that all of the procedures that came to be rejected in orthodox and official Yahwism were available and used, though the family stories do not inform us in detail about that.

Closely related to the inquiry of the deity in time of family crisis was the resort to *prayer* under similar circumstances. Several works have identified the family sphere as the primary locus in which the prayers for help that are found in the Old Testament had their setting in life.[145] These prayers, commonly called laments of the individual, were prayed in the context of the family in times of sickness, crisis, and distress, and may have involved a ritual of some sort carried out by a member of the family or neighbor or possibly a person who was regarded as an expert in prayer and the practice of healing. Such prayers were rooted in the life of the individual and that person's relation to God and not in the official cultus of the main sanctuaries. They included an address to the deity and a dialogue in which the relationship was expressed in highly personal terms. The need was often sickness, a human distress experienced and dealt with primarily in the context of the family.[146]

Yet one cannot simply assign the individual laments to a purely family locus never connected to the broader worship of the community at the sanctuaries and under priests who ministered to and in behalf of the larger community.[147] Moreover, there are many instances of prayers embedded in narratives that are quite spontaneous and uttered in all sorts of circumstances, not necessarily related to the ongoing life of the family and its members. But those same narratives often are family stories, making clear that these prayers for help were very much at home, if not exclusively so, in the sphere of the family. The prayer for help was pervasive in Israelite religion. As it was prayed by the individual, it often centered in the family and so, as we have said, may have been accompanied by procedures that were carried out within the family structure.[148] That such prayer was sometimes joined with particular modes of deity inquiry often associated with magic is suggested by some of the narratives discussed above.[149]

When one considers that the protection, continuity, and well-being of the family were at the center of its concerns in all eras of Israel's life, it is not surprising that *blessing* should play a large part in family religion. While all blessing may not have had explicitly religious or theological formulation, the family stories are clear that the ultimate source of blessing was the deity, specifically the family god.[150] Often, but not always, the blessing was explicitly a prayer-wish for God's blessing.[151] The concerns of family life were the focus of the blessings. They took place at times of parting, both the taking leave of a journey[152] and the parting at the end of life.[153] In such a context, the blessing could have to do with the ongoing welfare of the one on whom the blessing was pronounced or for whom blessing was invoked,[154] or with the continuity and growth of the family represented in the ones who went off on a journey or were the bearers of the family name and heritage in the next generation(s),[155] or with God's protection during separation and times of absence.[156] The blessing of the father in old age or on the deathbed had much to do with insuring the continuity and growth of the family as well as its well-being and prosperity. It also was concerned with directing the future in terms of family relations, seeking to create a particular order or relationship, especially among brothers.[157] Not surprisingly, blessings were pronounced on those about to be married to secure for the couple a good future generally but especially children or posterity.[158] Blessing was most often spoken by family heads, but it was not an act reserved to them or simply to males. There were instances of brothers and mothers invoking blessing upon sons or daughters.[159] Generally it was pronounced upon males or sons as prospective family heads responsible for the family's welfare. When pronounced or invoked upon a woman, it had to do primarily with her fertility and the generational continuity that the family or clan mother provided for the family (Gen. 24:60; Ruth 4:11–12; 1 Sam. 2:20).

Blessing is one of the areas where the common distinctions between magic and religion are blurred. In most cases, the blessing had the character of a prayer and thus would be understood as a religious act. In some instances, the saying of the blessing, whether or not the deity was invoked as its author, seemed to carry an effective power that apparently could not be revoked, so that it seems to reflect a magical view of reality.[160] This seems particularly to have been the case with the blessing of the patriarch upon the next generation. In those contexts, the biblical tradition clearly gives the impression that the expression of the blessing was either a shaping of the future or an announcement of what its shape was going to be like.[161] Such potency and efficacy may not have been universally assumed for any blessing. But the distinction obvious to a modern reader of these texts may not have been of significance to the ancient Israelite.

One notices within some of the blessings that a curse was also pronounced, indicating that such cursing was possible within the family context. But it would be a mistake to set blessing and curse alongside each other as comparable features of family religion. Cursing was much less common in the family and usually occurred only in the context of the larger blessing (Gen. 27:29; 49:4, 6–7). In fact, within the legal traditions there were explicit prohibitions against curses pronounced against one's father or mother. That may well indicate that such curses happened, but they did not have religious validation. Their potency, however, may have had something to do with the prohibition against curses within the filial relationship, although the force of the commandment to honor parents was sufficient basis for the prohibition against cursing of parents.[162]

It is appropriate to conclude an examination of family religion by summarizing its *theology*.[163] The deity, whose particular identity was most often El or Yahweh but who could be identified as the god of the father/ancestor, especially in the earlier period of Israel's religion, was the Divine Kinsman.[164] Related to the individual members of the family as their creator, the one who formed them,[165] the Divine Kinsman was their guide and protector.[166] The relation between deity and family members was an enduring one, a relationship of trust that was not related to a particular act or event of history[167] but may have had its primary roots in an encounter with the deity by the family ancestor.[168] It was less vulnerable to the disobedience of the individual or the anger of God than was the relationship between Israel and Yahweh.[169] When trouble came, it more often was seen to reflect the deity's abandonment than the deity's anger and rejection.[170] Sin and forgiveness were not major themes of family religion. God was seen as one who turned to and helped the individual in trouble, protecting and being with the family and its members in times of distress.[171] The nearness of God was not a dangerous experience, as was the case with cultic nearness.[172] Instead, it was the deity's continuing presence with each person from birth to death,[173] letting the individual grow and prosper and helping when called upon. Children,[174] success,[175] prosperity,[176] and health[177] were the signal gifts or acts of the deity. There does not seem to have been sharp conflict with other deities in the family relationship with the family god, unless the story of Gideon's altar reflects such conflict, which is very uncertain.

Local and Regional Cults

The family's devotion to the family deity did not exclude worship and participation with others in the cult of the larger community, that is, within the context of a local or regional cult that encompassed a larger entity than a bêt 'āb or mišpāḥâ, presumably several clan or tribal units. Such local or regional cults are only recognizable indirectly for the most part. And it may be that what seems to belong to such religious expressions was perceived as either a part of family religion or a part of the cultic life of all Israel. Certainly within smaller communities, the line between family religious devotion and that of the larger community may have been fuzzy or vague because of the overlap between the larger family and the members of the village or town. We cannot be certain what social structure(s) supported such local or regional cults, although one must assume that either geographical proximity or clan relationships were at the heart of the matter. To the extent that such cults were devoted to different deities, one could assume that they provided locations for the gathering of persons from different areas who were devoted to particular deities.

In some cases, local cults may have been devoted to the worship of Baal or some other deity such as the Queen of Heaven. In fact, the reported temple of Baal at Samaria may be an example of a local cult devoted to that deity and imported from Phoenicia.[178] Some of the cultic centers identified in the stories of the ancestors may have continued as local cults of El under different epithets, but the identification of that deity with Yahweh would have occurred at an early time.[179] There is no reason not to suppose that most of them were centers for the worship of Yahweh.

The bāmôt or "high places," which may have been family shrines in some locations, also served as geographical or regional cult centers[180] comprised of altars for sacrifice and incense offerings and probably a room for eating the sacrificial meal.[181] The extent to which they were open-air shrines or buildings of some sort is a matter of debate.[182] They also would have included, in at least some instances if not regularly, stone pillars (*maṣṣēbôt*) and sacred poles (*'ăšērîm*).[183] During the time of the monarchy, some of the high places were structurally expanded[184] and priests were appointed by the king.[185] As the narrative of 1 Samuel suggests, such priestly figures may have been present at these high places at an earlier time.

We do not know where all the high places were, nor can we directly connect any particular excavated sacred place—or presumed sacred place—with a high place. There were other sanctuaries that did not bear that title, and there are excavated shrines in locations that may or may not have been associated with high places. Some of these may have been open-air shrines. Others had small temple structures, such as the one excavated at Arad (plate 6), or, as apparently was the case at Shiloh, a tent shrine.[186] A number of sacred structures have been excavated from the premonarchical and monarchical eras.[187] Others are attested in the biblical reports, including Bethel, Mizpah, Gilgal, Beer-sheba, Shechem, Mamre (or Hebron), and Dan.[188] Some of these, such as Dan and Bethel, were national shrines or chapels set up by kings, and as such were a part of the state religion of the kingdom of which they were a part, although both of these had an earlier history as family and possibly regional shrines. In the case of both Bethel and Dan, there is textual evidence that suggests their character as local cults of El (Bethel)[189] and "the god who is at Dan" (fig. 13).[190]

Among the clearest indicators from written sources of the presence of local cults of Yahweh in ancient Israel are the several references in the eighth-century Kuntillet 'Ajrud inscriptions to Yahweh of either Samaria or Teman. While it is not possible to identify any of the above cultic sites with certainty as local cults, the divine names "Yahweh of Samaria" and "Yahweh of Teman" are probably to be understood as "local forms or manifestations of the national god."[191] In both cases it is possible that we are dealing with a region. Teman always refers to the region of Mount Paran, west of Edom; Samaria could be either the region or the city of Samaria. Kuntillet 'Ajrud may have been under the control of the Northern Kingdom at the time of these inscriptions, which would account for a reference to "Yahweh of Samaria" in this southern locale. "Yahweh of Teman" was the deity of other visitors to the site, from the south, or was the local Yahweh of the region of which Kuntillet 'Ajrud was a part.[192] There are numerous analogies in Mesopotamia and Syria-Palestine to this form of divine name where the name of a national god is placed in genetival relation to a locale—X of Y.[193]

Such names identify a local manifestation of a deity whose domain was

Fig. 13. Greek inscription (second century) "to the god who is in Dan." (*After Biran,* Temples and High Places in Biblical Times, *p. 146, fig. 4 and pl. 20, no. 4)*

much broader. At these local or regional centers the national god was perceived to have a particular identity and character, not necessarily significantly different from other manifestations of the same deity. Yahweh of Samaria was Yahweh as worshiped in Samaria. But, as McCarter notes, the particular cultic expression of the deity at any place may have been influenced by various factors appropriate to the place. Thus, he suggests that the "cult of the Temanite Yahweh . . . may have preserved archaic liturgical forms and religious concepts, while that of the Samarian Yahweh . . . reflected the contemporary liturgy and theology of the national god [i.e., the state religion of the Northern Kingdom]." Where Israelites took over Canaanite shrines, "pre-Yahwistic practices and ideas are likely to have survived in adapted form."[194]

We cannot be sure which sanctuaries identified in the Bible or uncovered in excavations represented local cults of Yahweh. Nor can we say very much about what went on in these local cults other than what has been suggested above. Some probably contributed to the spread of practices deemed heterodox by the orthodox Yahwism of the prophets and Deuteronomy. Others would have had their own impact upon the larger religious expressions of the people, and in the premonarchical period would have served as sacred places for all Israel. That would have been the case with the sanctuary at Shiloh, which was a shrine visited by families in the region (1 Samuel 1) but also a central sanctuary for the people as a whole.

Wherever local cults of Yahweh existed, there was always the possibility that they would become somewhat autonomous and independent. We have no direct evidence of that happening, but there is some evidence to suggest that the Deuteronomic reform of Josiah in the late seventh century may have been aimed at curbing that tendency. The confessional claim of Deut. 6:4, "Hear, O Israel! Yahweh our God is one Yahweh," seems to have been an implicit polemic against the notion, whether specifically articulated or not, that there was more than one Yahweh, a view that the local cults could have served to nurture, even as they may have encouraged the idea that Yahweh's asherah was capable of being understood separately from the deity. In any event, the Josianic reform[195]—and that of Hezekiah before him—by closing down the local shrines and centralizing worship of Yahweh in Jerusalem, served to eliminate such local cults where they may have existed.[196]

Family religion and the religious activities of local and regional shrines are not easy to characterize because they were not institutionalized or codified in ways that give any systematic picture of their conceptualization. But that was not true of all types of religious practice and ideology in Israel. In turning to official national religion, we take up the religious expressions and ideas that belonged to the community as a whole, what we shall call "all Israel," and that were in various ways authorized, institutionalized, and inscribed in and by the institutions and traditions of Israel. Here, therefore, the community of "all Israel," which took changing shapes and political forms in the course of its history, provided the matrix for the religion, and the activities of political and religious leaders as well as the written legal, religious, and historical documents preserved in the Bible authorized and codified its forms and expressions. The four primary forms of official Israelite religion and the religion of the national entity correspond closely to the changing political forms of the nation and thus reveal the intimate connection between religious and political history. At the same time, these forms also contain significant dimensions of continuity that reflect the tenacity of religious practice over against the evolution of political structures.[197] The forms of official Israelite religion now to be discussed are (1) the cultus of the Israelite confederation, (2) the state religion of Judah (the South), (3) the state religion of Israel (the North), and (4) the religion of the Jewish community after exile.

The Cultus of the Israelite Confederation

It is not impossible that the local or regional cult centers were also the places where persons in the area gathered for the great festivals. But there is evidence that at an early time those festivals involved the larger people of Israel, that is, "all Israel,"[198] at a major shrine that served on those occasions as a sanctuary drawing together all the tribes who worshiped Yahweh. Several of the shrines are identified in biblical tradition with cultic activities involving the tribal confederation as a whole, particularly Shiloh, Gilgal, Mizpah, and the Shechem area. The worship of Yahweh was not confined to domestic and local expressions. The tribes of Israel were joined together not only around the need for security and protection but more importantly around their common allegiance to the covenant god of the league, Yahweh. The union of the tribes had its primary expression in the all-Israel cult of the tribal confederation, "the centralized, organized, communal exercises of celebration and instruction directed explicitly toward Yahweh, the God of united Israel, and subjectively or indirectly toward affirming and cementing the union of the people."[199] Such centralized expressions of Israelite religion, whose locus was not the family or geographically related communities but the larger transtribal community defined as the "people of Yahweh,"[200] continued beyond the time of the tribal league and into the monarchical period so that many features of the all-Israel cultus did not cease with the rise of kingship. From that time on, however, they became a part of the state religion, which needs to be recognized as a type of Israelite religion developing out of the cultus of the league but significantly affected by the institution of the monarchy (see below). In both contexts, there was a clear relationship between the cultus with its central focus on the all-Israel festivals and the solidarity of the confederation or the nation. That is, the cohesiveness and unity of the community rested on and was regularly rearticulated, reactualized, and thus solidified by theological and liturgical means rather than coercive ones.[201]

The chief occasions for worship or religious practices were the three annual pilgrimage festivals of Unleavened Bread (spring), Weeks (summer), and Booths or Ingathering (autumn).[202] The last two of these, and possibly also the spring festival,[203] were agricultural festivals in which the people celebrated the harvest and gave thanks to God for the produce of the land. The spring and autumn festivals, however, were not simply agricultural festivals. What drew all Israel together on those occasions was their character as celebrations of Yahweh's election and deliverance of Israel and as opportunities for renewing the covenant that bound them together as a people and more particularly as Yahweh's people.

The spring festival, held probably first at Gilgal but then later at the league sanctuary at Shiloh, was probably the major festival of the pre-monarchical confederation. The older traditions, such as Joshua 3–5 and Ex. 34:25 (and some of the later ones, such as the Priestly text in Exodus 12), connect this spring festival with the Passover. That is, the Passover is associated with the historical memory of the deliverance from Egypt and the entrance into the land and so was probably a part of the major spring pilgrimage festival to which the tribes of the league came at one of the major sanctuaries. The memory of this is suggested in those references to Hezekiah and Josiah instituting the Passover after it had fallen into disuse as an all-Israel tradition. Second Chronicles 30:5 tells of Hezekiah calling for all Israel and Judah to come keep the Passover, "for they had not kept it in great numbers as prescribed."[204] Second Kings is more specific about this: "The king commanded all the people, 'Keep the passover to the LORD your God as prescribed in this book of the covenant.' No such passover had been kept since the days of the judges who judged Israel, or during all the days of the kings of Israel or of the kings of Judah; but in the eighteenth year of King Josiah this passover was kept to the LORD in Jerusalem" (23:21–23).

In Cross's language, "this covenant-renewal festival becomes the cultic carrier of Israel's historical traditions."[205] That is, it is in the great spring festival that Israel in its earliest form as a confederation of tribes nurtured and kept alive the story of its foundation in the exodus from Egypt, the covenant at Sinai, and the conquest or settlement of the land:

> While it is true, obviously, that all elements of later twelve-tribe Israel did not engage in these epic events but came to share them as historical memories through the "actualizing" of them in the covenantal cultus, it also must be insisted that the pattern—Exodus from Egypt, Covenant at Sinai, Conquest of Canaan—is prior, cultically and historically, to the several elements of the pattern.[206]

Joshua 3–5 probably preserves the memory of the early cultus of the tribal confederation gathering at Gilgal to celebrate the Passover and possibly also the feast of Unleavened Bread, though the extent to which these were combined at this early period is unclear. Building upon the work of Hans-Joachim Kraus on these texts and the important role of the sanctuary of Gilgal in the early period of Israel's history, Cross proposes to reconstruct the spring festival from the Joshua materials as follows (and this can only be a rough approximation, for the materials are complex literarily and historically):

> (1) The people are required to sanctify themselves, as for holy war, or as in the approach to a sanctuary (Josh 3:5).
>
> (2) The Ark of the Covenant, palladium of battle, is borne in solemn procession, which is at the same time battle array, to the sanctuary of Gilgal.
>
> (3) The Jordan, playing the role of the Red Sea, parts for the passage of the Ark and the people of Israel. The repetition of the Exodus is the transparent symbolism in the processional (Josh 4:21–24). . . .
>
> (4) At the desert sanctuary of Gilgal, twelve stones were set up, memorial to the twelve tribes united in the covenant festival celebrated there: we must understand this festival to be the festival of the old spring New Year. It is explicitly called Passover, and the tradition of eating parched grain and unleavened bread, as well as the etiological notice of the suspension of manna, lends confirmation (Josh 5:10–12). The setting up of the twelve *maṣṣēbôt* of the *gilgal* is paralleled by Moses' setting up of the "twelve *maṣṣēbôt* for the twelve tribes of Israel" at Sinai (Exod 24:4).
>
> (5) We must note also the circumcision etiology (Josh 5:2–8), and finally
>
> (6) the appearance of the (angelic) general of the host of Yahweh (Josh 5:13–15: compare Ex. 3:2ff.; 14:19).[207]

The relation of the festival of Unleavened Bread to Passover is a difficult matter to figure out and there are various opinions. Joshua 3–5 draws the two together inferentially, and that may not be far wrong for the early period. That is, the spring festival of Passover celebrating the deliverance from Egypt may have included in its earlier all-Israel form the eating of unleavened bread. As the Passover disappeared as an all-Israel celebration and moved into the context of family religion, unleavened bread became the center of a major pilgrimage festival in the spring, thus detaching itself from Passover "as an independent custom preserved to commemorate the exodus from Egypt."[208] Thus, when Deuteronomy combines Passover and Unleavened Bread, now a full-fledged seven-day festival, it may have been "reverting to old custom."[209]

Alternatively, the festival of Unleavened Bread may have been, from the start, an agricultural festival that became a substitute for Passover as it fell into disuse. It marked the beginning of the barley harvest (late April or early May), and the eating of bread without leaven may have been to eat that which did not have anything from the harvest of the previous year in it.[210] Relatively early, at least in the oldest of the cultic calendars (Ex. 23:15;

34:18), this festival is connected with the history of salvation. The reason that Israel is to do this in the month of Abib is because "in the month of Abib you came out from Egypt." The association of both Passover and Unleavened Bread with the exodus and their setting in the spring would have led to the combination of Passover and Unleavened Bread in a single festival as is called for in Deuteronomy.

It is not easy to determine between these two options, whether (a) to assume an early joining of the two, which then fell apart into separate family (Passover) and all-Israel (Unleavened Bread) celebrations, only to be joined again in Deuteronomy; or (b) to assume separate and different kinds of all-Israel celebrations, both having to do with commemoration of God's provision (flock and crops), the exodus deliverance, and a spring setting that led to their subsequent joining in the Deuteronomic prescription even though one had been located within the family while the other was all-Israel.

The fall festival, apparently held at Shechem, at least for a period of time (as traditions in Joshua 8, 24, and Deuteronomy suggest), and which during the monarchy was the principal pilgrimage festival (at Jerusalem and at Bethel) was probably also a covenant renewal festival in which the historical events of Israel's deliverance were recalled and the stipulations embodied in the law read before the people, after which they swore allegiance and obedience. In other words, the spring festival, associated with Passover and Unleavened Bread and held probably at Gilgal and then at Shiloh, and the fall festival of Ingathering, which came to be identified as the festival of Booths, were "variant covenant festivals of old sanctuaries which at different periods or at different seasons played their role as sites of a pilgrim festival."[211]

This did not continue to be the case in the state religion of the monarchy, as we shall see. As Kraus remarks,

> In the early "period of the Judges" Israel had not yet broken with its semi-nomadic tradition [sic], and the encampment at the feast times in spring and autumn was still a reality. In the period of the kings this archaic pattern disintegrated, and with the rise of the Temple worship the Passover rite came to be observed in the villages and families. Only the feast of Unleavened Bread was celebrated at the central sanctuary.[212]

The fall festival, however, continued in its prominence and became the major festival of the state religion in the Southern Kingdom and in the Northern Kingdom.

The fall festival came to be accentuated in the tradition, being called "the feast of Yahweh" in Lev. 23:39 and simply "the feast" in Ezek. 45:25. The later designation of the fall festival as the feast of Booths or Tabernacles (*sukkôt*)[213] probably derives either from the practice of farmers to live in huts or temporary dwellings during the harvest or the fact that the celebration itself took place in huts. Leviticus 23:41–43 associates the living in huts or booths with the wilderness period, but this is presumably a historical connection provided by later tradition.

We see, therefore, that major festival celebrations in the spring and in the fall joined the natural and the historical, the annual agricultural celebrations and the regular remembrance and celebration of the one-time acts of Yahweh in delivering the people and constituting them as Yahweh's people bonded in covenant.

The third major festival fell between these two, that is, in the summertime. The festival of Weeks—called also in the older cultic calendars "the feast of harvest" (Ex. 23:16) and "first fruits" (Ex. 23:16; 34:22)[214]—was celebrated, according to Deut. 16:9, seven weeks from the time the sickle was first put to the grain of the barley harvest, which would bring one to the time of the wheat harvest.[215] This was a purely agricultural festival, celebrating the wheat harvest, the gathering in of "your produce from your threshing floors and your wine press" (Deut. 16:13), an occasion of much rejoicing. The festival of Weeks had no historical connection, although "later Jewish tradition regarded it as commemorating the giving of the law in the third month (cf. Ex. 19:1; 2 Chron. 15:10ff.)."[216] One notes that at the end of the law for the festival of Weeks in Deuteronomy there is a separate prescription: "Remember that you were a slave in Egypt, and diligently observe these statutes" (16:12). By its placing, the general injunction serves to make a historical connection that was not a part of the festival in its celebration by the all-Israel community.

We are not altogether sure what transpired at the festival of Weeks, but its center was an offering of the first fruits of the harvest. Leviticus 23 prescribes two loaves made with new flour and leaven, thus tying it back to the festival of Unleavened Bread from which the date of the festival of Weeks or First Fruits was set. The antecedents of all three of the festivals is uncertain. In the case of Weeks, however, there is little doubt that the Israelites inherited the custom of celebrating the harvest from their neighbors as they settled in the land and became increasingly agricultural in their economy. It may well be that the festival in form was taken over as is, with two major adjustments: the celebration of the harvest by first fruits brought "to Yahweh" and the fixing of it at what would have been one of the all-

Israel shrines. As the Priestly legislation indicates (Leviticus 23 and Numbers 28), the festival became increasingly a sacrificial one after the temple was built. But it was probably not a sacrificial rite in the time of the Israelite confederation. Even Deuteronomy does not associate sacrifice with either the summer or fall festival in any special way. It was the produce "from your threshing floors and your wine press" that the people were to bring.

Such regular festival occasions were not the only expression of the religion of the tribal league. The people also gathered together on ad hoc occasions for lamentation and fasting as they cried to Yahweh for help,[217] as, for example, in Judges 20–21 when all Israel went up against Benjamin because of the rape of the Levite's concubine by the men of Gibeah. The punishment was decided in an all-Israel assembly "before the LORD" at Mizpah, and a course of events included two occasions when "all the Israelites, the whole army (kol hā'ām)" went back to Bethel (20:26) or "the people (hā'ām) came to Bethel" (21:2). Another example is the occasion recorded in 1 Samuel 7 when Samuel gathered all the people to Mizpah so that he might pray to the Lord for them because they had been lamenting over the oppression of the Philistines. Occasions of this sort continued throughout the history of the people and are reflected not only in the narratives but in the community laments of the Psalter, Jeremiah, and Lamentations.[218] Thus, particular crises or significant moments in the affairs of the league might draw them together. Such significant moments are reflected in the accounts of Samuel's gathering of the people at Mizpah to select a king by lots and his gathering them at the ancient cultic center of Gilgal to "renew the kingship." Though these were not primarily religious or cultic affairs, at least in terms of their primary intention, they usually had religious dimensions to them. So on both of the occasions in Judges 20–21 when the people gathered at Bethel, they were there "before the LORD" (20:26) or "before God" (21:2), they wept and fasted, and they offered 'ōlôt and šĕlāmîm, burnt offerings and communion offerings or offerings of well-being. In one case, it is even reported that they built an altar. When Samuel gathered the people at Mizpah to pray for them, there was not only prayer, but fasting, confession of sin, and the pouring of libations. When the Philistines moved to attack, Samuel prayed and offered a burnt offering. The renewal of Saul's kingship at Gilgal, likewise, was accompanied by šĕlāmîm, "offerings of well-being before the LORD" (1 Sam. 11:15) and the report that Saul and all the Israelites "rejoiced greatly."[219]

All Israel also went into battle as a league sacral affair under the aegis of the deity.[220] The battles may not always have involved all the tribes, but the obligation of those summoned to "come to the help of the LORD" is clear from Judg. 5:23:

> Curse Meroz, says the angel of the LORD,
>   curse bitterly its inhabitants,
> because they did not come to the help of the LORD,
>   to the help of the LORD against the mighty.

Whether on particular occasions, as, for example, the choice of Saul as king, or on occasions of battle, inquiry of the deity via oracular procedures often accompanied such occasions. First Samuel 28:6 indicates that the primary means for this inquiry were dreams,[221] sacral lots known as Urim and Thummim,[222] and prophets.[223] Priestly involvement in divination or inquiry of Yahweh is attested early and late.[224] In the context of an all-Israel sacral assembly, such inquiry is reported, for example, on an occasion of military defeat caused by transgression of the requirements of holy war in Joshua 7 and in the gathering of the people at Mizpah "before Yahweh" so that a king might be chosen from among them (1 Sam. 10:17–24).

In all of this, one may identify some features or characteristics of this aspect of religious life in early Israel in distinction from the family religion discussed above or the possible local cults that seem to have been sporadically present in ancient Israel. The cultus of the league, itself a kinship structure,[225] provided a form of religion in Israel that transcended the family and its religion while incorporating both into the larger whole. The egalitarian and family character of the larger community was enacted in the shared sacrificial meal. To the extent that Passover was both a family meal and a remembrance of the deliverance from Egypt, it served to conjoin the sense of belonging to the micro- and the macrostructures of ancient Israel, the family and the league.[226] The cultic celebrations of the confederation took place at sites that may have served as family or local shrines. Symbols and titles associated with them functioned also as all-Israel symbols and divine designations. That was especially the case with the shrine at Shiloh, the ark that resided there primarily if not exclusively, and the title "Yahweh of Hosts."

Most significantly, the league cultus reinforced the unity of the tribes by the celebration of a common story, the creation of a common memory, and the traditioning of the next generation.[227] In the absence of coercive or economic means of binding the tribes or controlling individual and clan conduct, the festivals provided an ideological source of power that was seen as residing outside the tribal structure, that is, in the will of the deity, but actualized in its daily life and its political affairs. Internal affairs—between individuals and between clans and tribes—and external relations were controlled by the structure and divine will set forth in the covenantal framework, the foundation and ground of which was recalled and its claims renewed in the cult. That such control was not always effective is indicated by the intertribal conflicts recorded in Judges and in the move toward a monarchical political structure. In the gatherings of the assembly of Israel for fasting and lament, the larger community sought to effect the final outcome of their political predicaments by affecting the deity through the penitence and prayer of the people.

Theologically, the all-Israel cult saw its relationship to deity as historically created in an act of redemption from oppressive slavery. While families and clans that made up Israel had an ongoing relation to the family deity, Yahweh, their existence as a larger community was understood to have been effected in this historical moment. The character of the covenantal structure required a setting of limits on Israelite worship so that the possibility of turning to other gods was made a first order of business and strictly forbidden in the religion of the league. The polemic against other deities that was absent from family religion for the most part was a feature of the all-Israel cultus and probably from the beginning of the covenantal formulations. They set a moral structure for the larger community and incorporated sanctions that were not a major part of family religion in its relation to the family deity. The wrath of the deity and the sin of the people were assumed to be ingredients of political disasters. Even in the nonthreatening cult, the presence of the holy god, Yahweh, in the midst of the people was potentially dangerous to those who were present, looked on, or touched the divine throne, a concomitant of divine appearance that was not a feature of family religion.[228]

The State Religion of Judah

With the rise of the monarchy, another facet of Israelite religion, the religion of the state, came into being. It developed out of the all-Israel cultus of the tribal league and did not eliminate family religion and local cults except during reform movements under the power and authority of the king that sought to eliminate the influence of these other types. Such reforms were created by the very fact of state religion, an official religion under the aegis and influence of the monarch. It is in this context that one must differentiate to some degree between the state religion of the United Monarchy and its Judean successor and that of the Northern Kingdom, Israel.[229]

From the moment of David's transfer of the ark of the covenant into his tent sanctuary at Jerusalem (1 Samuel 6), the cult of all Israel began to undergo significant changes. The most notable features of the official cultus and religion of the monarchical era were the role of the king and the place of the temple. The shift toward a temple-based cultus under royal authority did not happen overnight, nor was the shape of official religion in this regard the same in the north and the south.

During most of the monarchical era, however, the kings' initiative and power with regard to the cults of both kingdoms is evident in several respects. For one thing, they established sanctuaries. It is likely that from the tenth century onward a number of sanctuaries were built or rebuilt by royal order or placed under royal control and administration for several reasons. We can only speculate what those reasons were. Some of them seem to have been strategically located near the borders of the kingdom to establish the boundaries of the kingdom under divine and royal authority.[230] Some may have been designed to keep religious practice under the direction and oversight of the royal administration. The most famous of these sanctuaries was the temple at Jerusalem, planned by David and built by Solomon, which became the central sanctuary and the center of state religion in Judah after the breakup of the United Kingdom in the reign of Rehoboam. The significance of these cultic building activities as an instrument of ideological social power is readily apparent.[231] David's movement of the ark to Jerusalem—consistently called "the city of David" in the tradition—was a first step in establishing that power, for the presence of the central symbol of Israel's God and of that God's presence would have been a powerful instrument in securing the support of those who were rooted in the old order of the tribal confederation and its covenantal allegiance to Yahweh. The election of Zion and the Zion theology began, in effect, when David moved the ark and made Jerusalem the religious center of the nation. A question remains at that point. As one scholar has posed it, "Was the archaic Ark tradition sufficient to meet the needs of a dynastic order in a world in which the building of a temple was a requisite component of the establishment of monarchic rule, in which the construction of a shrine simultaneously actualized and symbolized the divine sanction of human rule?"[232] The legitimacy of David's reign over the people, whether or not it depended upon it, would have been reinforced by the building of a temple as an abode for the deity who chose the king alongside the abode of the king himself.[233] The national sanctuary, now called a *hēkāl* or "temple,"[234] and more specifically dubbed "the temple of the kingdom" (*bêt mamlĕkâ*), became associated with the seat of government and the royal palace to the degree that in the eighth century in the Northern Kingdom,

the sanctuary erected by Jeroboam at Bethel can be called "the king's sanctuary" (*miqdāš melek*) by the chief priest of the national shrine.[235]

The examples of David and Solomon and Jeroboam include other
aspects of royal involvement and control of state religion. These figures initiated or reshaped the primary cultic events. Usually this was done in
marked dependence upon or continuity with existing all-Israel cultic practice. But David's transfer of the ark to Jerusalem also represented both
innovation and continuity, the former to establish his rule and his chosen
locale as the center of Israel's religious life and the latter to insure their
acceptability by the tribes.[236] The building of the temple, designed to
accomplish those same ends, was also both innovative and familiar—innovative in Israel's religious history but familiar to the people from the reli-
gio-political structures of their neighbors, structures from which they had
drawn the model of and desire for kingship.

Such cultic initiative continued in the history of the kings. As far as the
biblical tradition identifies this, it was primarily in the establishment of heterodox or syncretistic cults in the national shrines of both kingdoms and in
consequent reform movements. All of these moves seem to have been
related to social and political factors, from the marriage of kings to foreign
wives who established foreign cults[237] to the impact of Assyrian imperialism
and its accompanying religious practices.[238] To a significant degree, the
"paganizing" of Yahwism in the state religion was less a pervasive Israelite
phenomenon than it was a feature of the politics of the royal court. Its presence in the national shrine would have meant, of course, that its influence
went beyond that into the general populace. Epigraphic evidence, however, would lead one not to exaggerate the extent to which the worship of
Yahweh was significantly displaced or compromised among the people as
a whole.[239]

The king was also involved in appointing cultic officials. That is especially noticeable in David's appointment of Abiathar and Zadok as his
priests,[240] representing the two primary priestly families of the premonarchical period, the houses of Moses and Aaron. Here again, state religion
was created in continuity with the cultus of the tribal league, probably
reflecting conflict with the priestly families presiding at Shiloh and Hebron.[241]
But the activity of the kings in cultic appointments was not confined to this
one act or this one king. The Chronicler may be at least partly right in
ascribing to David the setting up of other cultic officials early in the time
of the monarchy. It has been argued, primarily on the basis of late material from Chronicles, that David and Solomon set Levites in various parts of
the kingdom with both cultic and political or administrative responsibilities.

The latter could have involved collecting taxes and managing royal estates.[242] Jehoshaphat appointed priests to new roles in his reform (1 Chronicles 19), and Josiah made the priesthood a focal point of his reform movement. Indeed, Josiah's reform of the cult is a major testimony to its control by the king.

One scholar, who has shown how "intimately interwoven religion and state were" in ancient Israel, has concluded, "The king, as head of state, was also the head of the national religion as his god's viceroy."[243] In light of that fact and the appointment of priests by kings to whom they were accountable, it is not surprising that the chief priest of Bethel, Amaziah, reported Amos's criticism as a conspiracy against the king and sought to ban the prophet from the kingdom. The state religion in both kingdoms was fully under the control of the king. As such it was an instrument of royal power and control in a way that was not true of other forms of Israel's religion.

The other primary feature of the religion of the state was the temple, together with the cultic activities that took place within it (fig. 14). These now were as inseparable from the ideology of kingship as they were from its initiative and control. Changes that took place were features of historical change in the context of the developing power and politics of kingship.[244] But change did happen. Rather than the mobile tent shrine, kingship brought with it a fixed sanctuary alongside or attached to the palace of the king. Whatever David's final decision with regard to the building of a temple or his degree of involvement in planning it,[245] he knew the connections between king and temple symbolized in the use of the term *hêkāl* for both temple and palace and represented in the traditional role of kings in the ancient Near East in temple building.

At this point, and on the way to further interpretation of the significance of the temple, it is necessary to look at the tradition of the tent shrine and the shift from tent shrine to permanent building sanctuary. What is the significance of the tent shrine and the problem with the shift away from it to *hêkāl*, temple?   .

We begin with recognizing the tradition, reflected in the tabernacle, of God's dwelling in a moveable shrine. Whatever was the earliest history of the traditions of the ark and of the tabernacle—and many would claim that these were separate shrines joined much later in the tradition—by David's time, there was a clear tradition that Yahweh had always dwelled in a tent. Other kinds of sanctuaries were around, presumably where the deity Yahweh was worshiped. But the abode of the ark as the central symbol of Yahweh's presence seems to have been a tent, at least according to the

Fig. 14. Drawing of a reconstruction of the Solomonic temple. (*After Wright,* Biblical Archaeology, *p. 138, fig. 92*)

tradition of 2 Samuel 7, the oracle of Yahweh to David. To what extent was that the case? There is some evidence to confirm that, apart from the tabernacle tradition. Although the Deuteronomistic material refers to a *hêkāl* at Shiloh, other sources refer to the shrine there as a tent or tabernacle, especially the poetic sources (e.g., Ps. 78:60). Psalm 132:7 refers to the shrine of the ark at Kiryat-Yearim as Yahweh's *miškĕnôt,* "encampment." The likelihood is that the primary dwelling of the ark was indeed a moveable tent.

David continued that tradition when he set up a tent shrine for the ark (1 Samuel 6). But wherein lay the resistance to the temple that is so firmly a part of the Nathan oracle, even though it is short-lived? If the tradition is correct, that resistance was strong enough for David to hold off building the temple and to leave the ark in a tent shrine. Cross suggests that an explanation of the conflict can be found in part in the mythic background of the two types of shrine. Baal's temple on Mount Ṣapon was founded to confirm his establishment of order, especially kingship among the gods. It served also to establish the rule of the earthly king. In other words, it was a manifestation of the typical Near Eastern royal ordering of cosmos and state. The temple thus served to tie the divine order and the human order, the eternal kingship of the deity and the eternal human kingship reflected in the dynasty. It was both the dwelling place of the deity and the dynastic shrine.[246]

The tent of El, which is reflected in some of the tabernacle terminology, reflects a different political structure. El was the divine patriarch, god of the father, of the league, of covenant. From Ugarit, we have now a reference to "El Berit," El of the covenant. El sat as judge in the assembly of the gods (*pḫr m'd*). In Israel the political counterpart was the tent of assembly (*'ōhel mō'ēd*), the shrine of the federated tribes bound together in a conditional covenant.

The "temple of Baal" and the "tent of El" thus symbolized alternate political ideologies. These alternate ideologies are reflected in the traditions
associated with the temple and the tent in ancient Israel. Psalm 132:5
speaks of the shrine David set up with "tent" language, that is, *miškānôt*,
which Cross plausibly translates as "tent-complex." This psalm also underscores the conditional character of the Davidic dynasty (v. 12). Over against
this, Psalm 89 exalts the king as the adopted son of the deity and declares
that, come what may, he and his line shall rule forever (vv. 20–38 [19–37]).

In fact, as Cross has pointed out, the temple in Jerusalem represented a
compromise and incorporated features of both the tent shrine of the confederation and the dynastic temple of Canaanite kingship.

> The portable Ark with its cherubim became the "center piece" usurp-
> ing the place of the divine image of the Canaanite temple. . . . The con-
> ditionality of temple and dynasty—*bêt* Yahweh and *bêt* David—per-
> sisted albeit intermittently until the end, thanks to the prophetic and
> traditional insistence that kingship was forfeit when the ancient
> covenant was violated and that the temple in which Israel trusted could
> be destroyed like Shiloh.[247]

David's tent shrine would have been the culmination of the development
of Israel's tradition of tent shrines, serving as a successor to the league tent
shrine at Shiloh. It may be reflected in some of the tabernacle description
in the Priestly tradition.

What David initiated in the move from league cultus to state religion,
Solomon carried out, building a temple on the pattern of the Canaanite
dynastic temple with Phoenician architects and builders.[248] Continuities with
the league cultus were indicated with the procession of the ark into the
temple (1 Kings 8). But with Solomon there were major changes in the cultus that shifted the focus away from the covenant renewal forms of the
league cultus and toward a celebration of the election of David and of Zion
by Yahweh as recipients of the deity's grace.[249] While the three pilgrimage
festivals apparently were still held at the central sanctuary, now in
Jerusalem,[250] Passover ceased to function as a pilgrim festival for the whole
community until Josiah restored it in the seventh century,[251] and the principal festival became the autumn one.[252] While we are not told of the details
of this festival under the monarchy, there are indications that its celebration
of the rule of Yahweh joined the demonstration of that rule in the historical events that founded Israel as a people with its manifestation in the rule
of the human king in Jerusalem, that is, in the foundation of the house of
David and of the house of Yahweh on Zion.[253] The festival would have pro-

vided the primary religious support for the primary political and religious developments of the monarchy.

The State Religion of Israel

The state religion of the Northern Kingdom after its breakaway from the South under Jeroboam I in 922 is a matter about which we have much less information.[254] The Judean royal ideology with its focus on the election of David and Zion, the covenant with David, and the character of the Judean king as the adopted son of the deity (e.g., Psalm 2) would not have been applicable to the Northern Kingdom of Israel. Indeed, it would have been necessary to counter that ideology. While we have little indication of how that was done, we are told that significant steps were taken in the direction of a countercultus to the state cultus in Jerusalem (1 Kings 12:25–33). The political character of Jeroboam's cultus is identified explicitly in the text:

> Now the kingdom may well revert to the house of David. If this people continues to go up to offer sacrifices in the house of the LORD at Jerusalem, the heart of this people will turn again to their master, King Rehoboam of Judah; they will kill me and return to King Rehoboam of Judah. (vv. 26b–27)

While the Northern Kingdom may in fact have been a more resolute repository of the traditions of the Israelite league as some would argue,[255] that does not seem to have been the intention of the founder of the northern cult. It was a political move to hold the loyalty of the people by providing a Yahwistic cultus in the North to replace the one in the South. The fact that Jerusalem had been the religious center of the state for only about seventy years and the temple had been built only about forty years before would have joined with the tenacity of the religious traditions in the North to enhance the possibility of Jeroboam succeeding. Whereas David and Solomon had set up a royal temple in the capital city Jerusalem, which was without previous Israelite tradition, Jeroboam created national shrines at two already existing sanctuaries at the northern and southern ends of his kingdom, in Dan and Bethel, both of which had long standing as Israelite sanctuaries.[256] Bethel had patriarchal associations as an El sanctuary.[257] Like Jerusalem, however, it came to serve a dual function as royal chapel and national temple (Amos 7:13).

In each one, Jeroboam placed a calf or bull (*'ēgel*) as a counter icon to the ark of the covenant in Jerusalem.[258] Within the polemic of Exodus 32, there is probably "a cult legend of the old sanctuary of Bethel claiming Aaronic authority for its bull iconography" and reflecting older traditions

of the worship of El.[259] The character or function of the bulls is a matter of
much debate. The analogy with the ark and the well-known function of
bulls and other animals as pedestals for divine images suggests that they
were so conceived here (fig. 7). But the use of bull language in divine epithets and the close association of deities with their animal identifications
would have opened up at a fairly early stage the possibility of the bulls
becoming objects of worship in a way to which the ark was not suscepti-
ble (plate 2).[260] There is no reason, however, for suspecting that these were
other than Yahwistic icons in origin.

Jeroboam's cultic activities necessarily included the setting up of a primary festival in opposition to the one in Jerusalem (1 Kings 12:32–33).
Indeed, the report of Jeroboam's alternative, "like the one that was in
Judah," is one of the clearest indicators of the primacy of the fall festival in
the Southern Kingdom. The reason for placing the festival one month later
than the one in Jerusalem[261] is unclear, though some have speculated that
it was so those who wished still to go to Jerusalem could do so.[262]

Jeroboam also appointed non-Levitical priests chosen from among the
people (1 Kings 12:31b). There is reason to believe that Jeroboam maintained significant continuities with older cultic tradition by confirming an
existing Mushite (or Mosaic) priesthood at Dan and an existing Aaronide
priesthood at Bethel.[263] The accountability of the priests at the national
sanctuaries to the king, indicated by Jeroboam's placing the priests of the
high places in Bethel, is confirmed by the words and deeds of Amaziah,
priest of Bethel in the eighth century.[264] Although there were two principal
sanctuaries in the state religion of Israel, Bethel seems to have been the primary one, as evidenced by the locating of the fall festival at that site (1
Kings 12:33). Jeroboam may have created other sanctuaries or more complex structures at the various shrines of the North called "high places" (1
Kings 12:31).[265]

Community Religion

The use of the term "community religion" to describe the type of religious
life and practice in the postexilic period is a convenience that is somewhat
appropriate but hardly definitive or specific enough to describe the type of
religion that developed and flourished in the sixth to fourth centuries. Like
other types of religion, this expression had clear continuities with other
types and was as much a historical stage as it was a particular type. But the
religious life of the province of Yehud after the return of Babylonian exiles
was different enough and significant enough to merit some effort at defining it on its own and in distinction from other types mentioned earlier.

The use by other scholars of the word "community" to characterize the postexilic Judeans has in mind the term *qāhāl,* "assembly," "congregation," or "community," a word that is used specifically to describe the totality of the returnees from Babylon (Ezra 2:64 = Neh. 7:66). This term, or some expanded form of it—"assembly of the exiles" (Ezra 10:8), "assembly of those returning from the captivity" (Neh. 8:17), "assembly of God" (Neh. 13:1)—served to designate the gathering of the people for political and cultic activities. Thus, Nehemiah called an assembly (*qāhāl;* Neh. 5:7, 13) to deal with the problem of the poorer members of the community having to pledge their fields and vineyards and their children as slaves as well as to borrow money to pay off loans to the upper class as well as to pay the king's tax. The community/assembly gathered for Ezra's reading of the Torah (Neh. 8:2) and for the marriage reform of Ezra rejecting the foreign women and children (Ezra 10:1, 12, 14). The congregation/community of the exiles (*qĕhal haggôlâ*) was the body from which others could be separated or excommunicated (Ezra 10:8), and there is specific reference to the Deuteronomic law calling for exclusion of foreigners from the "assembly (*qāhāl*) of God" (Neh. 13:1, citing Deut. 23:2–4[1–3], where there are four references to the "assembly of the LORD."[266]

The examples cited indicate that the "community" was a politico-religious entity that was convened to deal with special crises or issues that came up, a custom that was not common in the preexilic period.[267] As Blenkinsopp notes, "In all cases, we are dealing with a collectivity which defines itself over against others in the region, membership in which is regulated by incorporation in lists and genealogies, and which has its own procedures governing inclusion and exclusion."[268] The shape of the community was in ways closer to that of the premonarchical character of Israel rather than the monarchical state. The community was made up of the "houses of the fathers," a structure with roots in the premonarchical clan structures of the tribal confederation,[269] and consisted of lay and priestly bodies of leaders, both organized according to the "houses of the fathers" and operating under a governor.[270] Using Weinberg's model of a citizen/civic-temple community, Harold Washington has aptly summarized the character of the Judean community:

> The postexilic community was not, as often assumed, a purely religious association. Under the Persian-sponsored civic-temple community, land tenure, participation in the temple cult, and full citizenship were combined and brought under the umbrella of a genealogical system that defined membership in terms of family descent, within the "house of

the fathers," and accorded positions of political and economic leadership to the largest landholders.[271]

The books of Ezra and Nehemiah show the development of conflicts within the community or between elements of the community. Virtually every reconstruction of the history and religion of the postexilic community identifies groups and parties at odds with one another, though there is much disagreement about who those groups were and what the issues were that divided them.[272] What is particularly suggested by the literature is the conflict between the returnees from Babylon and those who remained behind, between "the people of Judah and Benjamin" and "the people of the land" (which included Israelites from the north), a conflict that seems to reach back to the early stages of the return and the time of Zerubbabel (Neh. 4:1–4).[273]

One of the more insightful efforts to explicate this conflict in terms of its earlier roots is that of Shemaryahu Talmon.[274] With others (e.g., Weinberg), he calls attention to the continuing agrarian character of the community and the fact that the returnees from Babylon did not simply all become urbanized in Jerusalem but settled largely in the villages. It was necessary, however, to place a number of the returnees in Jerusalem, and much of the leadership lived there (Neh. 11:1–2). The conflicts that developed, therefore, were not simply between urban and agrarian or between Jerusalem leaders and the people of the land. The critical impulse for defining the community and thus determining who was in and who was out came from the returnees from Babylon. As Talmon has noted, what happened in Judah, or the Persian province of Yehud, was largely shaped by the experience in Babylon.

> The enforced status of a confessional community had been regarded by the Babylonian exiles as a mere temporary adjustment to prevailing adverse circumstances. However, . . . once this new form of communal life had come into existence, it would not be discarded even when the conditions that brought it about were seemingly reversed or attenuated by the return to the land, which did not, however, put an end to the existence of an exilic community.[275]

A symbiosis of confessional community and nation evolved in the Persian period out of the experience of exile, so that "Jewish peoplehood would embrace communities that accentuate their national-religious heritage differently."[276] Thus was paved the way for the development of various parties and groups within the nation.

The "in-group/out group" ethos that had long characterized Israel's relations with its neighbors now took on different forms. Maintaining the character and identity of the community against external pressures, which had been so much a necessity during the exile, was carried over into the community so that issues of identity and practice, such as Sabbath, circumcision, sacrifice, and festivals, became internalized. "The need for a close circumspection of Jewish identity that had been especially pressing in the setting of a surrounding pagan-foreign majority in Babylonia-Persia was turned inward, so to speak. . . . Compliance with the specific-particular execution of these rites now became a criterion that set apart constituents of one Jewish 'inner group' from others."[277]

Thus, the confessional community increasingly marked itself off and set boundaries between itself and either the "people of the land" or foreign peoples. Specific acts of separation from acts of pollution and from foreign wives and their children marked the practice of community religion in this period, practices rooted in earlier laws but coming to prominence in this period. While persons could be added to the community that centered in the returnees and their practices and power (Ezra 6:21; Neh. 10:29), proselytism was not as prominent an activity as was the differentiation and separation from others and others' practices. The purity of "the holy seed," which centered in the returnees,[278] was protected by formal separation from foreigners, which may have included not only separation from the traditional surrounding nations (Neh. 9:1) but also separation from "non-Judean Israelites whose version of the biblical faith was at variance with the returnees' understanding of biblical monotheism."[279]

Separation, however, was not only separation from foreign elements and pollutions; it was also separation to Yahweh through the Torah.[280] The classic understanding of holiness was thus manifest in both positive and negative forms of separation, and the prophetic charisma as a mode of personal revelation fell by the wayside after a brief spurt in the early postexilic period in favor of "more rational and controllable forms of instruction" at the hands of a new class of leaders, the scribes or sages (see chapter 5), whose "authority rested on expert exposition of the hallowed traditions" rather than on more subjective and personal inspiration, which was not subject to checks and controls.[281]

The classic instance of this focus now on the Torah is the account of Ezra's reading of the law before the community (Nehemiah 8).[282] What comprised that law is much debated, with the usual conjecture that it was the Pentateuch or some form of it. But the occasion is important for its indication of the movement toward a Torah community that was focused upon obedience to the divine law as contained in the written Torah and led by leaders who were capable of interpreting and aiding in the understanding of the Torah. Henceforth the community religion of Israel/Judah would be scripture-oriented, and the study and interpretation of Torah would become a major function of the religious leadership. The synagogue became the center of such study, but it came in at a later time and seems to have served other communal functions as well.[283]

Samuel Balentine, along with others, has shown how this focus on the law was an important religious development that was at the same time consonant with the purposes of the Persian Empire in its provincial administration. That is, the codification of local law was an instrument of social control and political maintenance in the Persian provincial policy. Assuming that the "king's law," which Artaxerxes commissioned Ezra to administer in the province of Judah, was the Pentateuch or some form of it, Balentine suggests that it was the product of both internal and external factors:

> On the one hand, it represents an internal synthesis of traditional laws and customs that provided Yehud a sense of cultural and religious identity. On the other, it represents an essential aspect of imperial control, a standardized law that was approved and implemented with the support of the Persian authorities.[284]

A major religious, economic, and political center of the religious community of Judah was the temple, rebuilt by the returnees from exile, who, according to the book of Ezra, spurned the help of the Israelites and Judeans in the land when it was offered (Ezra 4:1–4). The temple and its sacrificial cultus became the center of religious life as had been the case in the state religion of the preexilic era. Built on the ruins of the Solomonic temple, the second temple symbolized significant continuity with its predecessor while manifesting some differences in its character and symbolism and in its modes of administration and support, the administration being at the hands of the priests under the leadership of the high priest (see chapter 5).[285] The lay members of the community, however, had a greater involvement in the temple, both in their voluntary economic support of the temple as well as in cultic participation, than in the preexilic period.[286] The function of the temple as an economic center of the community is evident by the various avenues of income and distribution, including income from the Persian government, taxes of various sorts, deliveries of wood, and voluntary contributions. As cultic offerings swelled to around a third of the total income, with the state taxes in addition, "the temple developed into the most important economic factor in the community of Judah."[287]

As with the placing of torah at the center of the community's religion, the temple cult also served the purposes of the Persians while providing a cultic center for that religion, for the construction and maintenance of regional temples was a feature of Persian imperial policy.[288] Because the temples were built and supported by funds from the Persian treasury, the Persian government effected a center of local stability but one in which it had a vested interest and thus some measure of influence or control. Balentine notes that this provided the Persian Empire a presence at the administrative center of the community's life. By the degree of financial support of the temples, the Persian king could exercise some control over the province. The connection to and support of the temple also kept the Persian presence as a part of the religious life, as the king decreed that prayers and sacrifices would be offered for the royal family (Ezra 6:10). Further, the temple supported and enhanced the empire's aims for political and social hierarchy in the region in a way that would help maintain Persian control and social and political stability.[289] Balentine describes this relationship thus:

> Through the High Priest appointed by the Persians, temple personnel with conscious loyalty to the Empire, and a strata [sic] of educated, urban elite with vested interests in a local, nonmonarchic system of governance, the Persians developed a coalition of power within the temple that was loyal to the Persian agenda.[290]

As the sacrificial cult developed in the temple, a particular element came more to the fore: the concern for atonement of sin, represented especially by the celebration of the Day of Atonement (see chapter 3), which may have anteceded the postexilic period but is probably to be associated particularly with the community religion of that period. The experience of divine judgment associated with the destruction of Jerusalem and the exile led to a heightened emphasis on the sin of the people and the need for reconciliation, an emphasis reflected in the system of sacrifice and also in the personal piety of the individual.[291]

If the community religion of the sixth to fourth centuries grew out of the exile and was formed in the light of and around the realities of the Persian Empire, while not being wholly shaped by either context, that religion also included different ways of dealing with the end of kingship. There were elements that hoped to reinstate it in the figure of Zerubbabel (see Haggai, for example), but this failed in the face of the realities of the dominance of Persia over the province of Judah. Isaiah 55:3–5 seems to suggest a democratization of the messianic idea or the Davidic promise so that the covenantal promises to David were to be for the whole nation.[292] There were other elements that reduced the role of the king to that of a prince (*nāśî*) ruling alongside a Zadokite priest, a civic ruler on the model of the earlier clan chieftain rather than the royal ruler of the monarchical period (e.g., Ezek. 43:18–44:3; 45:1–8; Zechariah 4).[293] It has even been argued that in the law of the temple in Ezekiel 40–48 this term refers to the Judean governor under Persian rule.[294]

The developments reflected in Ezekiel, especially chapters 40–48, and in Zechariah represent the main trend within the community religion of the postexilic period. As Paul Joyce describes this trend with specific regard to Ezekiel, "The 'messianic' figure is at best on the fringes of what for Ezekiel is the real focus of future expectation, namely the restored sanctuary."[295] As the temple and its cult under the administration of the priestly group but with lay involvement became the center of the religion of the community, the royal figure and the prophetic hopes associated with it were muted or transformed in favor of an emphasis on temple and cult. With regard to the Chronicler, Peter Ackroyd states, "It is not a Davidic monarchy which the Chronicler hopes to see restored; it is the expression in the life of the community, particularly in its being gathered around the temple and its worship, of what David had established."[296]

One of the conflicts that developed in the postexilic community would seem at first glance to be less a religious matter than some of the others. But its implications for the religion and theology of the community were far reaching, since it insured the continuation and development of prophetic and legal dimensions of Yahwism having to do with wealth and property, and justice for the weaker and poorer members of the community.[297] The conflict was between the poorer members of the community and the upper class over the economic bondage that developed out of the debts of the poorer members and the system of credit that called for loss of property or bondedness to pay off debt and even the selling into slavery of children to cover debts. The primary and telling witness of this conflict is Nehemiah 5, where a report is given of a large outcry on the part of the poorer members of the community over their having to pledge the labor of their children to get credit to pay for food and the (Persian) king's tax, as well as having to pledge or mortgage their fields, vineyards, and houses to get grain during a period of famine. Their fundamental situation is well described in the final words of the protesters: "We are powerless, and our fields and vineyards now belong to others" (Neh. 5:5). Nehemiah's laying the responsibility for these acts upon the "nobles and the officials" identifies the social and structural conflict here. The fact that this upper class or aristocracy seems to have responded to Nehemiah's indictment and call for redress indicates that there were at least some elements in the community who were sensitive to the long-standing legislation and guidelines in the community that called for amelioration of debts and who resisted high-handed encroachment on the property of those who were in economic deprivation (Neh. 5:12–13; cf. 10:32 [31]). That the occasion described in Nehemiah 5 was not an isolated instance is suggested by the number of references in postexilic literature to oppressive economic measures against the poor, widows, orphans, and aliens (e.g., Isa. 58:6–7f.; Mal. 3:5; Job 7:2–3; and probably a number of Psalms that cry out against economic injustice).[298] Albertz has suggested that there were opposing elements in the upper class or aristocracy, some of whom went along with the Persian system of financial support without concern for the situation of their poorer compatriots, and others of whom were sensitive to their needs and worked to ameliorate them. By a close reading of the text (indeed, a reading between the lines in some cases), Albertz suggests that one can see in the accounts of the redresses in Nehemiah (including the actions of Nehemiah in 5:14–19 but also in the creation of didactic psalms and proverbs about the wicked and the righteous) efforts on the part of this latter element of the upper class to demonstrate solidarity with the poor and effect a change of attitude on the part of others.[299] Within the poor or lower class, Albertz argues, an eschatologizing of prophecy developed that saw no possibility in the present reality but anticipated God's intervention in history in behalf of the poor and to do away with the unjust structures that even Torah piety could not overcome (e.g., Isaiah 56; 29:17–24).[300]

It is within such a development toward a more eschatological prophecy on the part of deprived elements within the community, though possibly on its fringes, that some would place the development of apocalyptic.[301] Such an understanding has been called into question in more recent studies as it has been observed that apocalyptic and millenarian movements do not necessarily occur only among deprived groups but may have their locus among power-holding elements, such as priests and scribes.[302] In other words, apocalyptic movements that expect an imminent and radical divine intervention to undo the structures of present reality in vindication of those who are righteous (pious or innocent) and who view that reality, both present and future, in sharply dualistic terms of good and evil can occur in a variety of social locations, and can involve both groups of the deprived and groups of the powerful. In light of the debate about the social location of apocalyptic and the sharply different views about the difficulty of dating apocalyptic literature, it cannot be determined at this point to what extent apocalyptic thinking belonged in any central way to the religion of the postexilic community. That it grew out of that community and may have been related to social and religious developments, including various conflicts, is likely, but caution in being too specific about its role in postexilic community religion is in order.

INTERACTION OF FAMILY RELIGION
AND OFFICIAL NATIONAL RELIGION

The presentation of Israelite religion in terms of types vis-à-vis different social and political contexts shows some of the diversity and complexity of that religion. It runs the risk, however, of giving an overly segmented picture of what was connected and interactive in many ways. While some indications of that have been noted along the way, a more nearly complete picture requires identification of some other ways in which family religion—and to some extent the religious features of local or regional sanctuaries—interacted with official national religion and its continuation in postexilic community religion. Three areas of such interaction illustrate the connectedness in the midst of the diversity, or the overlapping of features across different social groupings and the religious practices and ideas that were characteristic of them.

The first of these is the penetration of kinship categories into all parts of Israel's life, including its religion. At an early stage, the "nation" was itself a family or a congeries of kinship units. Its larger character as a league or confederation of tribes was couched in kinship terms, so that kinship-in-law became the means by which individual units were conjoined in a politico-religious whole.[303] Cross has summarized the kinship character of the league as follows:

> The league was also a kinship organization, a covenant of families and tribes organized by the creation or identification of a common ancestor and related by segmented genealogies. Such genealogies are in substantial part constructs, based as much on "kinship-in-law" as real kinship, and the genealogies tend to be fluid, shifting to reflect social and historical changes and developments. The league in ideal form was conceived as twelve tribes, related at once by covenant and kinship.[304]

He notes further that the "name" of the league, *'ām Yahweh,* "people of Yahweh," is a kinship term "perhaps better translated the 'kindred' of Yahweh," but also "in some contexts must be translated the 'militia of Yahweh,'" and in other contexts the *'ām Yahweh* is a community of worshippers, a cultic association."[305] These tribal and kinship relations never fully dissipated, therefore, even under the state.[306]

Furthermore, the family deity was the national deity. Yahweh's relation to the nation was the same as to the family: personal, or better, that of kinsman. The god of the family was the high god El/Yahweh, at one and the same time the "creator of the heavens and the earth" and also the one who delivered the enemies of the family ancestor into his hand (Gen. 14:18–19). The head of the family addresses the family god as "Judge of all the earth" (Gen. 18:25). The deity who blessed and guided the destiny of the family did so for "all the families of the earth" (Gen. 12:3).

One of the primary codifications of official and orthodox Yahwism was the book of Deuteronomy. It was set as a Mosaic address to the assembly of Israel and was intended to define the life of the people politically, religiously, and socially. Within its bounds, however, familial categories and family-oriented perspectives were appropriated even as the family was set within the context of the experience and religion of all Israel. The category of "brother" became in Deuteronomy the primary way of speaking of other members of the larger community and not just those in the immediate family.[307] The family relationship became a moral category. Family laws are a prominent part of the Deuteronomic code.[308] An intergenerational perspective is present throughout the book, and requirements for instruction of the young, *within the family circle*, about the fundamental claims of the official national religion are given. The home was seen as the locus of teaching and of shaping the next generation for participation in the official all-Israel cultus and for living by the covenant between Yahweh and the people. Some laws that are at the heart of the Deuteronomic social ethic but may be regarded as idealistic or unrealistic in their present all-Israel framework probably arose out of the kinship situation, for example, the remission of debts in Deut. 15:1–11.[309]

One other feature of Israelite religion that is associated with both family religion and official public cult is prayer. It has been discussed here primarily in relation to family religion, particularly in regard to the prayers for help of the individual, which often have their need and may have their setting in life in the family or clan group. But there were clearly ways or moments in which individual prayer was associated with the public cult of official religion and with its theology. Psalm 22, in some ways a classic individual lament that incorporates family imagery directly into its language by addressing the deity as one who has watched over the petitioner from birth, also specifically alludes to the cries of the "ancestors" (*'ābôt*) who trusted in God and were delivered (Ps. 22:5–6[4–5]). It is possible that such a

reference could be to the family ancestors alone, but the immediately preceding allusion to the "praises of Israel" (v. 4[3]) suggests that here the petitioner draws upon the experience of the ancestors of Israel and not just
those of the immediate family as grounds for encouragement. So also in
Psalms 42–43, the petitioner remembers going with crowds in procession
(fig. 15) to "the house of God" with shouts and songs of thanksgiving,
"keeping festival" (ḥôgēg; Ps. 42:5[4]), and desires again to be brought to
"your holy hill and to your dwelling," in order to sacrifice at "the altar of
God" (43:3–4). The one who cries out here does so in marked connection
with the theology and ritual of official all-Israel religion. There are other references to the temple[310] or to aspects of the ideology of official national religion[311] in the individual prayers for help marking their assimilation to the
official cult and theology. Some individual prayers may have been adapted
for use by the congregation in the all-Israel cult.[312] Psalm 22 and a number
of others point to a ritual of thanksgiving after prayer has been heard and
answered that takes place in the sanctuary with offerings, sacrifice, and
praise. While such thanksgiving offerings and meals may have occurred in
local sanctuaries or even domestic shrines in some instances, there are also
indications that the paying of these vows by the petitioner was in the midst
of "the congregation" (qāhāl, Ps. 22:22; ʿēdā, 111:1), "the great congregation" (Ps. 22:26[25]; 35:18; 40:10–11[9–10]; "the assemblies" (maqhēlîm, Ps.
26:12); "in the presence of all his people" (Ps. 116:14, 18).[313] The story of
Hannah's thanksgiving offering and sacrifice together with her song of
thanksgiving is the clearest report of such occasions. As we have noted, this
may not have been on the occasion of an all-Israel festival and no reference to a gathering of others is indicated, though the sanctuary involved
was one of the all-Israel centers. The references above from the Psalms,
however, place such occasions very much in a public context. We must
assume, therefore, that the ritual of thanksgiving belonged very much to a

Fig. 15. Drawing of worshipers with
arms outstretched in either imploring
prayer or adoring praise. From Kuntillet 'Ajrud. (*After Beck,* Tel Aviv *9*
[1982], fig. 3)

cultic event that often or at different times was on the occasion of an all-Israel gathering, while at other moments it could have taken place in a more localized setting with the focus on the family, as was the case with Hannah's thanksgiving vow. To the extent that the king may have been the one speaking in the voice of some of these individual prayers, they would have belonged quite directly to the state religion during the time of the monarchy.[314]

CHAPTER 3

Sacrifice and Offering in Ancient Israel

There seems to have been no period in ancient Israel's history when sacrifice was not an important part of religious practice—from the oldest accounts of family and tribal sacrifice to the systematic organization of the sacrificial ritual reflected in the Priestly material of the Pentateuch that belongs to the later stages of that history, the time of exile and afterwards. The legislative parts of Leviticus and Numbers focus major attention on the sacrificial cultus. Deuteronomy 12 opens the Deuteronomic code with a program for the centralization of worship, but this means primarily slaughter and sacrifice. First Kings 9 not only sets prayer and sacrifice at the center of the dedication of the temple by Solomon but tells of regular sacrifices and offerings by Solomon in the temple. Not only was sacrifice carried out by Samuel, Saul, and David (the latter on the occasion of setting up the ark in Jerusalem to establish it as the religious and political center of his kingdom [2 Sam. 6:17], but Jeroboam's chief reason for creating a counterreligious center to Jerusalem when the Northern Kingdom split off was so that the people would not continue to go to Jerusalem to offer sacrifices (1 Kings 12:27). There is no level of the literature that is our primary source for Israel's religion that does not identify sacrifice as a major aspect of that religion. Even when sacrifice increasingly came to be spiritualized (e.g., Ps. 50:12–14, 23; 51:18–19[16–17]) and "scripturalized," that is, the subject of literary and exegetical activity vis-à-vis texts on sacrifice, rather than the focus of liturgical and ritual activity,[1] it maintained a significant place in Israel's religious conceptuality if not its actual practice. Its centrality is self-evident even from the most cursory reading of the texts that inform us about Israelite religion and is confirmed by comparative data as well as archaeology's identification of altars of various sorts and sacrificial remains.

While the previous chapter noted the place of sacrifice at various points in the different types of Israelite religion, here we shall examine the practice and ideology or conceptuality of sacrifice in more detail.[2] Some distinction between "sacrifice" and "offering" needs to be recognized. "Offering" is a broad term that can refer to any sacred gift or donation brought to the altar or cult place to be given over to deity and the deity's cultic personnel.[3] "Sacrifice" generally refers to those gifts that are totally or partially burned in the ritual of offering. The use of the expression "sacrifice and offering" (*zebah* and *minhâ*) as a way of talking about the whole conglomeration is found in several places (e.g., 1 Sam. 2:29; 3:14). While, therefore, sacrifice is the focus of attention in this discussion, other types of gifts or offerings, such as first fruits and tithes, which are not technically sacrifice, come into view also.

TYPES OF SACRIFICE

The categorization of the different sacrifices by way of the different names is possible but more complex than may appear at first glance. That has already been suggested by the discussion of the way that the term *minhâ* functioned. One should recognize further that the different terms for sacrifice reflect different concerns. In general, three principal orientations are reflected in the terminology, and a particular term may operate within more than one category depending upon how the sacrifice is applied:[4]

1. Terms indicating either the manner of performing the rite, for example, *zebah*, "slain offering," or *'ôlâ*, "ascending offering," or the material to be used in the sacrifice, for example, *qĕṭōret*, "incense offering."
2. Terms indicating the place of a sacrifice within the order or process of cultic operation or the calendar of cultic activity, for example, *pesah*, "sacrifice of the Passover (*pesah*) festival," or *tāmîd*, "daily offering."
3. Terms indicating the purpose or motivation of a sacrifice, for example, *neder*, "votive offering," or *tôdâ*, "thank offering.

Because there are so many different sacrifices and terms for sacrifices, it would not be profitable to list and characterize each one.[5] Rather, we shall identify some of the main kinds of offerings that are prominent in both the Priestly codes of sacrifice and in the practice of sacrifice as that is attested in other literature.[6]

Burnt Offering (*'ôlâ*)

The word *'ôlâ*, customarily translated "burnt offering," comes from the root *'ālâ*, meaning "to go up" or "to ascend." The derivation may well be associated with the smoke that comes from the offering and "goes up" to the deity, for this particular type of sacrifice was burned entirely on the altar, over against others that were burned partially or not at all, with some portions being consumed by priests or other participants. The prescription for the "burnt offering," which was not a part of Mesopotamian sacrificial practice but does seem to have been a type of sacrifice practiced generally in Syria-Palestine and Anatolia, is found in Leviticus 1–7, especially chapter 1.[7] This represents a rather late conception of a sacrificial practice that was much older and may have been handled in different ways at different times. The procedure could involve different animals, from bull to bird, apparently depending upon the economic status of the person sacrificing. While there are differences in the process depending upon the animal, the essential requirement was for an unblemished male animal if it was from the herd or flock (fig. 16). The presenter placed his hand over the animal to identify it as his offering for his need or benefit.[8] Having been slaughtered by presenter or priest, the animal's blood was splashed or poured out against the altar and the animal burnt so that its smoke or odor might rise up pleasantly to the deity.

The tradition depicts the *ʿōlâ* being offered throughout the history of Israel's religion, and there is no reason to doubt its antiquity.[9] It does not always seem to have required the presence of a priest (e.g., Genesis 22), but there may have been occasions when the reported burnt offerings of a king or other leader, in fact, involved the participation of a priest. The Levitical procedure is a conceptual presentation that does not necessarily inform us about actual procedure in every instance.

It has been proposed that the primary function of the burnt offering was to attract the deity's attention "with the objective of evoking an initial response from the deity prior to bringing the primary concerns of his worshippers to his attention."[10] This is suggested by several accounts of the presentation of burnt offerings, for example, Balaam setting up several burnt offerings whose sole purpose is so that "perhaps the LORD will come to me" (Num. 23:1–6) and the burnt offerings offered by Elijah and the priests of Baal on Mount Carmel to get a response from the deity (1 Kings 18).[11] Levine summarizes the function of the *ʿōlâ* as follows:

> [O]ne normally invited the deity to a common, shared sacrificial meal (like the one described in I Samuel, chapter 9) after he had been invoked by means of an *ʿōlâ*. There are instances, albeit infrequent in biblical literature, where the *šelāmîm,* or the *zebaḥ* generally, constituted the sufficient rite. The fact that in so many cases a sequence of composite rites is projected, and not a single sacrifice, indicates just

Fig. 16. Worshiper carrying a sacrificial kid, from Mari in Mesopotamia, mid-third millennium. (*After* ANEP, *no. 850*)

what we are saying, i.e. that the 'ôlâ was normally utilized for the purpose of invoking the deity preparatory to joining with him in a fellowship of sacrifice, which was the context for petition and thanksgiving, and for the expression of other religious attitudes of this character.

On this basis, it is eminently clear why the šelāmîm sacrifice, understood as a gift of greeting, a present to the deity, would follow the 'ôlâ and not precede it. Until the deity indicated his readiness to "come" to his worshipper, it would have been less appropriate to offer such a gift to him.[12]

Such an interpretation of the essential function of the burnt offering makes very good sense of both narrative accounts and the order of sacrifices to which Levine has drawn attention.

At the same time, it must be recognized that there are indications in Priestly legislation (e.g., Lev. 1:4; 9:7; 14:20) and narrative texts (e.g., Job 1:5; 42:8; and possibly 2 Sam. 24:25; cf. Ezek. 45:15, 17) that the burnt offering was seen as having an expiatory or atoning function also, especially at earlier stages before the institution of the ḥaṭṭā't offering (see below on the purification offering).[13] One does not have to assume that the same intent was present in every instance of a particular sacrifice. Indeed, the burnt offering is also associated with joyous occasions, such as the fulfillment of a vow or a freewill offering (Lev. 22:17–19; Num. 15:3). The pervasiveness and frequency of this sacrifice cautions us against being confident we can always comprehend its function or motivation.

Grain or Cereal Offering (*minḥâ*)

We have already noted that the term *minḥâ* functioned to speak about offerings or gifts generally but that it also had a specialized use with reference to the grain or cereal offering. That specialized use is particularly noticeable in the Priestly sacrificial legislation where the ordering of the sacrifices sets the procedure for the grain offering immediately after that of the *'ôlâ*, (Leviticus 2). The grain offering could come in several forms in the Priestly taxonomy, probably reflecting actual and varied practice over a long period of time. It might be presented as coarse grain in the ear, as fine flour, or formed into cakes. In the process, it was mixed with oil, frankincense, and salt (Lev. 2:1–2, 13, 15). It could be cooked in an oven, on a griddle, or in a pan. While at earlier stages the grain offering was burned on the altar in its entirety, in the priestly administration part of it was burned and part consumed by the priests (Lev. 2:8–9).[14] There are indications that at some period, possibly during the time of the monarchy as well as after the exile, the grain offering was sacrificed daily in the evening and by itself.[15]

The close association of the *'ôlâ*, and the *minḥâ* is evident, especially in the later Priestly tradition of sacrifice, for example, in the cultic calendar of Numbers 28–29 and the summary of the cultic calendar in Lev. 23:37. One notes further that the sequence of burnt offering (*'ôlâ*), grain offering (*minḥâ*), and sacrifice of well-being (*zebaḥ šelāmîm*) that is found in the Priestly legislation of Leviticus 1–7 is attested elsewhere (Josh. 22:23, 29; 1 Kings 8:64 [2x] = 2 Chron. 7:7; Jer. 33:18; and Amos 5:22), suggesting that this order of sacrifice, whether conceptually or procedurally (see below), had some fixity in the understanding of the relation of the sacrifices to each other. That might be seen as simply a part of the later Priestly concern for systematizing the whole understanding of sacrifice. But the appearance of this sequence in Amos suggests its antiquity. Indeed, one might well see in the Amos castigation of *'ôlâ*, *minḥâ*, and *šelem* a kind of ABC of the sacrificial cultus, that is, a citing of the traditional first three sacrifices as a way of condemning the whole order. That would suggest that the ordering of these three and the ordering generally of the sacrifices was clearly present in preexilic practice and was not a late development. Milgrom has suggested that the

> procedure for the *minḥâ* (Lev 2) was probably inserted between the procedures for the *'ôlâ* (ch. 1) and the *šelāmîm* (ch. 3; 3:1 is a subsection of 1:2; cf. 1:3), because the *minḥâ* became the regular accompaniment to the *'ôlâ* (e.g., Lev 14:20; Num 28–29), and especially because

it was the *'ôlâ* of the indigent, serving the same wide-ranging functions, including expiation.[16]

If so, the insertion belongs to a fairly long tradition.[17]

The fact that the grain offering can be joined with both the *'ôlâ* and the *šelem* offering (see below), and the fact that there are a number of indications of the offering of grain as a discrete sacrifice tends to confirm the view, which goes back at least as far as the Rabbis and Philo and is present in Mesopotamian sacrifical tradition also, that the cereal offering, as Milgrom suggests in the quotation above, was a concession to the poorer members of the community who could bring a cereal offering in place of an *'ôlâ* or *šelem* offering.[18] In an Assyrian conjuration we read: "(Then) the *baru*-priest brings you (an offering of) cedar (perfume), the widow (only) magda-(and *kukkusu*)-flour, the poor woman (some) oil, the rich from his wealth brings you a lamb."[19] In another context, the point is made even more succinctly: "The widow makes her offering to you (pl.) with cheap flour, the rich man with a lamb."[20] Within the Priestly tradition itself, there is explicit provision for the poor that includes the move to grain offering instead of animal or bird (Lev. 5:11).[21]

The fact that grain was so accessible to all classes, particularly in a heavily agricultural society, makes it quite understandable that a gift of grain could serve a variety of purposes. That is why the *minḥâ* functions to refer to gifts in general as well as to a specific type of sacrifice or offering. Gary Anderson has given a plausible accounting for the varied use of this term in the Bible and Northwest Semitic texts generally. Rather than assuming, as has been traditionally the case, that there was a historical shift from the broader use to a narrow specialized usage reflecting a growing specialization and fixity of sacrificial practice and away from the freer and more spontaneous earlier practice, Anderson indicates how different social contexts led to varied meanings and understandings:

> We would suggest that both the usage of *minḥâ* as tax or tribute payment and as cereal offering could co-exist at one time in Israelite culture. For the common Israelite, the term *minḥâ* would have referred to a gift, most often a gift given to the Temple cult. Because Israelite society was primarily grain oriented, the *minḥâ* payment given to the Temple was usually grain. This basic datum was further "rationalized" by the priestly specialists in the Temple. For them there was a need to organize and categorize the variety of offering types which were received. A typical Judean farmer need not be specific regarding these matters; he simply contributed a tenth of whatever it was he produced. But the priests—who had to deal with a variety of agricultural and

pastoral gifts and revenues—needed a more elaborate taxonomy to order their experience. No doubt a large impetus for this ordering came from Temple lists and tariffs. In order to deal meaningfully with the income of the Temple, a precise lexicon of cultic contributions had to be in place. This would explain the need to specialize further a term like *minḥâ* from "a gift" (which was most often grain) to "a cereal offering." . . . Once the new lexical meaning was established it could be used elsewhere in Israelite society. . . . [The Priestly classification] does not reflect a crudely materialistic view of the cult; rather it reflects the attempt of each and every cultic center to provide order and meaning to the wide variety of gifts and offerings which it receives.[22]

The fundamental meaning of the word *minḥâ* is, of course, our best clue to its function. That is, it was understood as a gift to the deity, presumably to seek the benevolence and help of the deity, whether in a particular situation or as a regular part of one's life. So David says to Saul: "If it is the LORD who has stirred you up against me, may he accept an offering (*minḥâ*)" (1 Sam. 26:19). If the cakes that were baked for the Queen of Heaven in Jeremiah are examples of the *minḥâ*, as is likely, then there too one sees explicitly the offering as a gift to secure the beneficent activity of the deity: "But from the time we stopped making offerings to the queen of heaven and pouring out libations to her, we have lacked everything and have perished by the sword and by famine" (Jer. 44:18).

Offering of Well-Being (*zebaḥ* and *šělāmîm*)

One of the primary and most ubiquitous forms of sacrifice in ancient Israel, this particular sacrificial type is often joined with or replaced by the word *zebaḥ*, signifying a slain sacrifice. Thus, we have *zebaḥ*, *zebaḥ šělāmîm*, or simply *šělāmîm*, all apparently referring to the same kind of sacrifice, though *zebaḥ*, while often associated with the *šelem* sacrifice— particularly in the Priestly ordering of the sacrificial cult—means a slaughtered offering whose meat was eaten by the worshiper.[23] When *zebaḥ* is joined with *ʿôlâ*, the combination may refer to offerings and sacrifices in general or identify two of the primary forms of sacrifice. *Zebaḥ* is thus the larger category, of which *šělāmîm* is a specific and important example. When the word *zebaḥ* is used, the *šelem* offering is often what is in mind.

The translation of the term *šelem* is much debated. The different proposals are tied either to etymological possibilities around the root *šlm*, "be whole, sound" and its noun cognate *šālôm*, "peace, well-being," or analyses of its function, for example, "communion offering," because of the presumption that the *šelem* was to effect communion between deity and presenter. The translation "offering of well-being" is a guess but consistent with etymology and the context in which the sacrifice functioned.

The two most conspicuous features of the *šelem* offering are its consumption by human beings and its use on celebratory occasions. While the burnt offering was consumed entirely on the altar and thus given over to the deity for consumption and the grain offering largely given over to the priests, the *(zebaḥ) šelem,* or offering of well-being, was offered to the deity but provided meat for the offerer and others participating (Deut. 27:7; Jer. 7:21), including the priest(s) (Lev. 7:28–36). The fat or suet of the slain offering was burned on the altar (Leviticus 3; 1 Kings 8:64) and the rest consumed. What is most important, however, is the association of this offering with celebratory occasions, both those reflected in the festivals and in the more personal occasions of celebration (Num. 10:10). In the Levitical ordering of the *šēlāmîm* sacrifices, the *šelem* or *zebaḥ šelem* is specifically associated with three kinds of celebrative and often personal sacrifices: the thanksgiving offering given in gratitude for God's deliverance (Lev. 7:12–15), the votive offering made in payment of a vow to the deity to secure the deity's aid (Lev. 7:13; Prov. 7:14), and the freewill offering, "the spontaneous by-product of one's happiness whatever its cause" (Lev. 7:13).[24] The *šelem* offering could, therefore, be either public or private, a part of the great festival or royal occasions or a part of a particular individual's worship of the deity in thanksgiving or fulfilling a vow. It belonged, therefore, both to official religion and to family religion. The latter, with its special moments, which would have included marriage, restoration to health, birth, and the like, would have provided many moments appropriate for freewill and thanksgiving offerings as well as votive offerings (1 Sam. 1:21).[25]

Purification Offering (*ḥaṭṭāʾt*)

In the Levitical ordering of the sacrifices, two expiatory offerings follow the burnt offering, the grain offering, and the offering of well-being, a grouping we have noted has relatively ancient standing as indicated in Amos and other texts. The two expiatory offerings are the *ḥaṭṭāʾt* (Lev. 4:1–5:13; Num. 15:22–31) and the *ʾāšām* (Lev. 5:14–6:7). They came to prominence apparently later in the history of the sacrificial cult in ancient Israel, taking over expiatory functions that may have belonged primarily to the *ʿōlâ* sacrifice earlier.

The particular intention and force of the *ḥaṭṭāʾt* has been a matter of much debate, reflected in the two primary ways of translating this word: sin offering and purification offering. Was the primary focus of the offering a matter of purification, whether with regard to sin or other forms of impurity, or was the *ḥaṭṭā't* primarily aimed at expiation for sin, which thus brought about purification? These are closely connected in the texts, but it is difficult to gain a completely harmonious view from all the data.

Recent studies by Milgrom of the various regulations and practices involving the *ḥaṭṭā't* have suggested that this sacrifice was not essentially a sacrifice for sin committed but a sacrifice to purify, an understanding that is indicated by its grammatical form and that of the verb from which it comes, that is, *ḥiṭṭē'*, "to purify."[26] Individuals who sought to effect purification by the *ḥaṭṭā't* included the person who sinned unintentionally (Leviticus 4), the mother after childbirth (Leviticus 12), the person with a genital discharge (Leviticus 15), and the Nazirite who had completed a vow of consecration (Numbers 6). The last three of these examples make it clear that the purification effected by the *ḥaṭṭā't* was not necessarily the purification of sin. It was rather the purification of altar and sanctuary, accomplished by putting blood on the altar or other parts of the sanctuary (e.g., Lev. 4:5–7; 16:14–19), that was effected by this offering. The purification, therefore, was in order to overcome cultic impurity, whether from the effects of sin or from other kinds of impurity manifest in individuals and things. The great concern was for the maintenance of the purity of the sanctuary as the place of the deity's abode or manifestation.

This understanding of the *ḥaṭṭā't* is surely correct fundamentally. There remains, however, the question of what is meant by the forgiveness that is effected by the *ḥaṭṭā't*. That is, the ritual, which served to purify the sanctuary and its elements of contamination brought about by the impurity or sin of the individual or the community, also accomplished something for that individual or community. For the inadvertent sinner, whether priest, ruler, one of the people, or the entire community (Leviticus 4), the text indicates that the priest should make expiation (*kippēr*) for him or them (vv. 20, 31), or should make expiation "on his behalf for the sin that he has committed" (vv. 26, 35), and "he shall be forgiven." For the person impure for other than reasons of sin, the same formula of expiation or purgation was used with the result that she or he would be clean (Lev. 12:6–8; 14:19–20). In both cases, the final outcome was a purifying of the individual also. The fact that the text indicates that the purification of the inadvertent sinner was forgiveness does suggest that there was some way in which the *ḥaṭṭā't* made expiation for the sin itself, that is, brought about the necessary purification, which in this instance was forgiveness.[27] Thus, the ritual of the *ḥaṭṭā't* offering, which surely centered around purification, accomplished that for the sanctuary and the impure or sinful individual. Baruch Levine has described this latter outcome as follows:

> Once certain acts are performed, purity resulted, just as in other instances forgiveness resulted. That is to say: As a result of the performance of certain rites, God grants expiation or atonement. In such instances, expiation, forgiveness, etc. are not the direct *physical effects* of the rites performed. Such acts are prerequisite, but not causational. It is God who grants the desired result![28]

The Day of Atonement. The Priestly texts of the Old Testament record in some detail a separate expiatory ritual called the Day of Atonement (Leviticus 16; 23:26–32; Num. 29:7–11). While the ritual of the Day of Atonement involved more than sacrifice, it placed the *ḥaṭṭā't* offering at its center and served a purifying and expiating function that makes it appropriate to consider it in relation to that dimension of the sacrificial system. The Day of Atonement was, in effect, an occasion of purification and expiation.

The fact that this ritual is not mentioned in any clearly preexilic texts or referred to in major postexilic texts that tell of other cultic matters, such as Ezekiel, Ezra, and Nehemiah, has led most scholars to assume that the Day of Atonement ritual was instituted in the postexilic period.[29] This assumption has been contested in recent years, particularly by Milgrom, who argues that the ritual was instituted as an annual event on the tenth and final day of the fall festival already in preexilic times.[30] While one would expect more explicit indication of this than is present, the argument from silence that is the primary basis for the judgment about a postexilic origin is not a strong one.

There are internal and external indications that the procedures that came to be known as the Day of Atonement may not have been regularized at the beginning, serving instead as a kind of emergency purification ritual.[31] Somewhere along the line the ritual became fixed as a particular day, that is, the tenth day of the seventh month, Tishri, in the fall. The set ritual indicates the character of the occasion as both purifying the sanctuary and its accoutrements of defilement from the sins of the people and purifying or expiating the sins of the people. Such purification or purgation could happen at any time through the *ḥaṭṭā't* offering. The institution of a day of purification and atonement created a special ritual to cleanse the sanctuary "of impurity from *deliberate* [italics mine] sins and from any other lingering impurity not yet rectified."[32] There were two dimensions to the ritual centering around two goats, one "for the LORD" and the other "for Azazel" (Lev. 16:8–10; cf. v. 26). The goat on which the lot fell "for the LORD" was slaughtered as a *ḥaṭṭā't* offering and its blood sprinkled in the sanctuary to purge it of impurities.[33] As for the other goat, the priest would lay hands on it and confess the "iniquities," that is, the deliberate sins and transgressions of the people. Having been confessed, they were now transferred to the goat who was sent away into the wilderness "for Azazel" (Lev. 16:10, 20–22). Verse 16 (cf. vv. 21–22) identifies the dual purpose of the ritual, the removal of impurities and the removal of sins: "Thus he shall make atonement for the sanctuary, because of the uncleannesses of the people of Israel, and because of their transgressions, all their sins."[34]

The Azazel of this text and its ritual have been the subject of much discussion. Azazel may be "the name of a demon who has been eviscerated of his erstwhile demonic powers by the Priestly legislation."[35] But the Azazel of this text has no personality, carries on no demonic actions, and the goat is not a sacrifice to a demon. The term should probably be interpreted with reference to analogous rites, which suggest that it be understood as a term for elimination.[36]

It is customary to see in this chapter and in the final form of this ritual the joining of two quite different rituals—one a ceremony of ritual and expiation involving sacrifice and the sprinkling of blood, the other an act of transferring the sins of the people to a goat who was sent into the wilderness for "Azazel," thus taking away the sins.[37] There are indeed two dimensions to the ritual, but they are not necessarily to be seen as separately evolving procedures only lately and artificially joined. Purification and elimination rites were common in the ancient Near East, though not necessarily joined as they are in this instance.[38] But there is an analogy elsewhere in the Priestly ritual for the sacrifice of an animal and the sending away of another one. In the purification of a person with "leprous" or scale disease of some sort, two birds were used (Lev. 14:2b–8, 49–53; cf. Zech. 5:5–11), one of which was sacrificed while the other was set free. The living bird was dipped in the blood of the slaughtered bird, and the diseased person was sprinkled with the blood, much as the sanctuary was sprinkled with the blood of the slain goat in the Day of Atonement ritual. The live bird was then sent away, carrying the impurity of the diseased person with him. The analogy suggests that the two-goat ritual of purification and scapegoating may have been an early form of the atonement ritual, not necessarily originally attached to sanctuary cleansing or fixed days but a means of purification and removal of both sins and impurities.[39]

Whenever this atonement ritual was instituted, it joined with the purification and expiatory sacrifices to further effect both the removal of pollution from the holy things and the holy people. In so doing, the iniquities of the people along with the inadvertent sins were removed, from one perspective, or cleansed and purified, from another. The significance of such purification and expiation needs further discussion. Its achievement through the sacrificial system and related rituals, as one means of accomplishment, is evident in the ḥaṭṭā't offering and the larger context of the Day of Atonement.

Reparation Offering ('āšām)

As with the ḥaṭṭā't offering, there is a difference of opinion over how this sacrifice should be designated. While the Hebrew is commonly translated "guilt offering" because of the association of the root 'āšam with becoming guilty and incurring guilt, more recently it has been recognized that the 'āšām offering is primarily to make reparation for an offense of which one is guilty. Thus, this offering, like the ḥaṭṭā't, is expiatory in some sense or is intended to deal with particular kinds of sins and their effects or with violation of the sacred and the dangers that evokes.[40] Leviticus 5:14–26 (6:7) together with Lev. 19:20–22 and Num. 6:10–12 give us the major instances in which the 'āšām offering is indicated. There one sees that it regularly involves bringing something to the Lord and making restitution and payment of a fine. That is, the whole procedure is a kind of compensation or reparation, a point further indicated by the fact that the 'āšām or reparation offering is seen as having an equivalent in silver or money (Lev. 5:15, 18; 5:25[6:6]; cf. 2 Kings 12:17).[41]

The earliest instance of an 'āšām offering is one that was sent by the Philistines with the ark when they sought to allay the anger of the Lord after the battle of Ebenezer and the capture of the ark.[42] The golden mice and tumors that were sent with the ark were an 'āšām or compensation to the Lord of Israel for what they had done to Israel. This was not an altar sacrifice but a monetary or valuable gift offered to Yahweh of Israel because of the taking of the ark.[43] The violation of sacral space and things is one of the reasons indicated in Leviticus for bringing a reparation offering (Lev. 5:14–16). Milgrom has seen such violation or "misappropriation" of sacral things as the primary sphere of concern in the 'āšām offering, while Levine suggests that it is inadvertent misappropriation generally, whether of sacral things (Lev. 5:14–16; Num. 6:8–12) or property of others (Lev. 5:20–26[6:1–7]; 19:20–22), that is dealt with by the reparation offering.[44] Both perspectives account for a significant amount of the information provided in the biblical texts and analogues from the ancient Near East. It is difficult to provide a single conception of the 'āšām that neatly accounts for all the material. The matters that are fairly clear are (a) the connection of the sacrifice to reparation for wrongdoing, including fines and restitution of what was misappropriated as well as the reparation offering itself; and (b) the convertibility of the sacrifice and its manifestation in both objects of value or money and sacrificial animals.

The distinctions between the *ḥaṭṭā't* or purification offering and the *'āšām* or reparation offering are sometimes rather blurry, but both offerings directly address and deal with the fact and consequences of sin, seeking to overcome its effects by purification and reparation. In the process the forgiveness of God is received by the sinner. The question of the antiquity of these two sacrifices in Israelite religion remains much debated. They appear primarily in what are generally regarded as postexilic texts, though Milgrom and others would date the sacrificial texts much earlier. While it is safe to conclude that these sacrifices were significantly a part of the ritual of the second temple, we cannot preclude the possibility that they were operative at an earlier time.

Other Offerings

There were various other offerings in the sacrificial ritual of ancient Israel. For example, in the regulations for the worship at the central sanctuary, Deuteronomy twice sets forth a series of offerings that members of the community are to bring to the sanctuary: "You shall go there, bringing there your burnt offerings and your sacrifices, your tithes and your donations, your votive gifts, your freewill offerings, and the firstlings of your herds and flocks" (12:6; cf. v. 17). So also Lev. 7:12–18 and 22:18–30 bring together the thanksgiving offering, the freewill offering, and the votive offering. These different references in Leviticus and Deuteronomy suggest two main categories of offerings that may overlap with the ones already discussed but are sufficiently characterized and distinguished that one should take account of them in order to see how thoroughly the practice of offering and sacrifice were a part of the individual and communal life of the people.

The common denominator in the different offerings described in the references above is that they were brought to the sanctuary as demonstrations of thanksgiving. Some of these, such as the tithe and the presentation of first fruits, were regularized and expected of the community as a whole. Others, such as the votive, freewill, and thanksgiving offerings, were individual offerings that, while regularized in the Priestly sacrificial legislation, were related to, evoked by, or responsive to particular experiences of individuals in the community.

The *tithe* seems to have functioned as a kind of regular tax, primarily of agricultural products—grain, wine, and oil (Num. 18:27; Deut. 14:22–23)—

but also, according to some texts or at some point, flocks and herds. When it originated is unclear, but by the time of the eighth-century prophets, it was a regular practice, at least in the Northern Kingdom (Amos 4:4). It was a common feature of the cultures of Syria-Palestine, present at Ugarit in the second millennium and within the Phoenician-influenced Punic culture of Carthage many years later. At Ugarit, the tithe, collected from the villages where the agricultural products were harvested, was a secular tax due to the king or one of his servants.[45] While described in the biblical texts as an act of religious devotion to the deity, its character as a royal tax in Syro-Palestinian culture generally is well indicated by 1 Sam. 8:10–17: "These will be the ways of the king who will reign over you. . . . He will take one-tenth of your grain and of your vineyards and give it to his officers and his courtiers" (vv. 11, 15).

As a sacral phenomenon in ancient Israel, the tithe seems to have served three functions, though to what extent these overlapped with each other or were operative at different times is difficult to tell. The Deuteronomic law interprets the tithe as a celebratory gift to God, implicitly serving as an expression of thanksgiving that was to be enjoyed and shared by the members of the family as an act of devotion, at the central sanctuary if possible (Deut. 14:22–26). The tithe also functioned as a support for the priests and the priestly service, but more specifically for the Levites, since the priests who were not Levites received portions of sacrifices, first fruits, and the like.[46] This provision of the tithe to support the Levites is first identified in Deuteronomy (14:27–28; 26:12), but the tradition is fairly consistent in iden-tifying the tithe as a tax or gift for the Levites (e.g., Num. 18:21–32; Neh. 10:37–38; 13:10–12). Deuteronomy gives a clear rationale for this as it places the Levites with other categories of persons who did not have reg-ular means of support off the land and so had to be provided for. Every third year the tithe was to be stored up and made available to the Levites, resident aliens, orphans, and widows throughout the land (Deut. 14:28). The tithe thus served as a celebratory thanksgiving gift and as a kind of welfare system.[47]

The first fruits of the harvest and the firstborn of flocks and herds were offered to the Lord of Israel as both thanksgiving for the blessing of the Lord as reflected in the harvest (Deut. 26:1–11) and for the support of the priesthood (Num. 18:12–13; Deut. 18:4). The offering of first fruits seems to have been associated especially with the celebration of the harvest at the pilgrimage festival of Weeks (Ex. 23:16; 34:22; Num. 28:26). While Deuteronomy does not explicitly associate the first fruits offering with one of the pilgrimage festivals, it does describe the ritual by which individuals came to the sanctuary and offered their first produce of the harvest to the priest while declaring in a kind of credal statement what the Lord had done to deliver and provide for the community. The act was an individual or family presentation, but it was set firmly in the context of the experience of the community as a whole. The presentation of the firstborn may have served originally the same purposes as the first fruits of the harvest, that is, a dedication to the deity of the first of the flocks and herds as an acknowledgment of the rule and provision of the deity (Deut. 15:19). In the tradition, it came to be associated particularly with the Passover and the festival of Unleavened Bread (Exodus 13). This may have had to do with indications that firstborn sons were also dedicated to the Lord (Ex. 13:1–2; 22:29; 34:19–22; Num. 18:15) and redeemed (Ex. 13:15; 34:19; Num. 3:12–13; 18:15). The dedication of firstborn males is so clearly a part of the cultic tradition of Israelite religion that it raises the question of whether or not sacrifice of firstborn sons was a practice at one time. There is, however, no indication that such was the case except possibly in exceptional or aberrant situations (see chapter 2). The redemption of the firstborn was a way of recognizing the right of the deity over the family and the community, but the actual dedication involved either a life of service (Num. 3:11–13; 1 Sam. 1:11, 28) or a monetary or animal substitution (Ex. 34:20; Num. 18:16ff.).

It is not clear at what point the first fruits offering became specifically a means of support of the priests, but by the postexilic period that was the case and probably earlier. The provisions for sacrifice also make it clear that either all or portions of other sacrifices were to be given over to the priests as provision (Num. 18:8–24; 1 Sam. 2:12–17).

Individual offerings of various sorts could be brought to the sanctuary apart from the prescribed sacrifices and offerings discussed above. Thus, we are told of freewill offerings and votive gifts that were voluntary offerings presented to the deity, the latter either accompanying a vow or offered after the accomplishment of something sought by means of a vow (e.g., 1 Sam. 1:11, 21–28).

The Psalms attest to the practice of the *tôdâ*, the vow of thanksgiving made by a petitioner to the Lord and fulfilled when the prayer had been heard and answered. That is, the lament psalms, which are prayers for help, often included vows to give thanks to God and offer sacrifices in response to God's answering the prayer (Pss. 66:13–15; 116:12–19). So the individual brought a *tôdâ* or thanksgiving offering to the sanctuary when deliverance, that is, a response to prayer, had been experienced in some fashion. While this offering or sacrifice was an individual expression, it seems to have taken place in the context of a larger congregation, indeed, of the worshiping community as a whole (Pss. 22:23–26[22–25]; 40:10–11[9–10]; 66:16; 116:14). And even as the individual Israelite made a kind of declaration of faith as a verbal expression of thanksgiving when bringing the offering of first fruits (Deut. 26:3–10), so also the thankful petitioner made a public declaration of what the deity had done and how he or she had been helped and delivered. Such a declaration was intended to elicit praise and acknowledgment from those who heard it, whether that was a small group like the family or a larger gathering of worshipers (Pss. 22:24[23]; 30:5[4]; 40:4b[3b]).[48]

THE PURPOSES OF SACRIFICE AND OFFERING

The study of Israelite sacrifice has been dominated by the effort to develop a theory of sacrifice that would explain the rituals of sacrifice in some coherent way and identify a fundamental rationale or intention behind the complex ritual. More recently, there has been widespread and appropriate recognition that many things went on and were accounted for or taken up, consciously or unconsciously, in the presentations of sacrifice and offering. Furthermore, because sacrifices and offerings were usually part of a larger ritual, one cannot fully comprehend or account for them without taking account of the larger context where matters of purification and holiness, the transcendent and the human, the sacred and the profane, were operative in many and complicated ways (see chapter 4).[49]

Support and Welfare

From the preceding discussion, it is evident that the system of sacrifices and offerings served social purposes. These included a formal means of providing for two groups of people in the community: first, the clergy who were occupied with religious matters (e.g., Lev. 7:28–36; Num. 18:8–24; Deut. 14:27–29; 18:1–8; 1 Sam. 2:12–17; 2 Chron. 31:2–19; Neh. 10:37–39; 12:44; 13:5, 10), and second, within the Deuteronomic system of tithes, persons within the community who did not have clear access to the allotment of the land and its economic productivity—resident aliens, orphans, and widows (Deut. 14:28–29; 26:12–15).

At this point, Israelite religion provided for important social functions that have been a part of many traditional communities who have used a system of offerings to release clergy from other occupations and to provide charity for the economically deprived. Israelite religion happens to have systematized this in specific ways that did not leave matters purely voluntary. The community was required to provide this economic support for these two groups and given a system to insure that it happened. The uncertainty of the provision was only in the uncertainty of the harvest, an insecurity that was shared by all members of the community.

Order and Movement

The sacrificial legislation of the Pentateuch has been the object of considerable anthropological analysis. That analysis has tended to see the system of sacrifice as largely a reflection of the concern for order, its breakdown and its restoration. This involves the maintenance of boundaries between orderly categories, usually binary in form—for example, clean and unclean, holy and profane, natural and social, sick and whole, inside and outside, life and death—though sometimes more complex, as reflected, for example, in the Priestly school's assignment of the fauna of the earth to three ("fish of the sea," "birds of the air," and "cattle," "all the wild animals of the earth," "every creeping thing that creeps upon the earth"—Gen. 1:26). Sacrifice and the rituals of which it was a part had to do with maintaining these orders, restoring them when they became disordered, and moving or transferring things and people from one category or status to another category or status.[50] When the holy was profaned—as, for example, when the sanctuary was polluted or risked pollution by the impurity of the people— sacrifice was part of the ritual for either the restoration of holiness and purity (so the Day of Atonement ritual as either emergency or regular ritual) or for maintaining it regularly, as in the practice of daily sacrifices, whenever that was instituted. When the sick person was restored to health and moved from sick to whole, from unclean to clean, then sacrifice might be a part of the ritual of cleansing and expiation of impurity and sin, as in the case of scale-diseased persons (Leviticus 14). While normal bodily discharges created uncleanness that could be reversed to cleanness, more serious and irregular discharges required not only a ritual of washing but also the *'ôlâ* (burnt offering) and the *ḥaṭṭā't* (purification offering) sacrifice to overcome the pollution (Lev. 15:13–15, 29–30). When a person moved from the sphere of the profane to the holy, as, for example, in the consecration of a priest, sacrifice was a part of the ritual (Leviticus 8–9). Indeed, the very act of sacrifice was a transfer of something from the profane to the holy, from human possession to the divine.[51]

Such an analysis makes considerable sense of the system of sacrifice as one encounters it in the Priestly legislation reflected in such works as Leviticus, Numbers, and Ezekiel, legislation that points to a developed system in the postexilic period that probably has antecedents in an earlier time. Whether such implicit notions of order and disorder were operative in the practice of sacrifice at all times is difficult to say. At all times, there were symbolic understandings at work. At all times, sacrifice may have involved a movement from the profane sphere to the holy, from the human to the divine. Further, there are indications that the sacrificial system, even as it is reflected in the didactic ordering of Leviticus 1–6, was known in some fashion as early as the eighth century, as the prophet Amos seems to attest to it (Amos 5:21–22). It is less certain that the ordered society with the coherent set of symbols presumed in these analyses was always operative or functional in all spheres of Israelite religious life.[52] The sacrificial offering of the family that is attested more than once in the books of Samuel (e.g., 1 Sam. 1:4–5, 21, 24; 2:19; 20:6) may be accounted for only tangentially by the customary symbols of holiness and purity that are so dominant in the priestly system of sacrifice. Here family solidarity and identification with and acknowledgment of the god of the family may be much more dominant impulses (see chapter 2).

One should note further that within the system of sacrifice as we can discern it, there are various forms of order that do not necessarily have to do with the system of symbols generally set forth in the anthropological analyses, but do reflect what anthropological interpretation has helped us see about the concern for movement across boundaries and the different spheres. Recent study of the Priestly legislation has uncovered different orderings that seem to have served different purposes, though there is debate about what those different purposes are.[53] In Lev. 1:1–5:26 (6:7), the sacrifices are divided into two categories, those of "pleasing odor to the LORD" (burnt offering, cereal offering, and offering of well-being) and those having to do with purification and expiation (purification offering and reparation offering). It has been suggested that this ordering of sacrifice is primarily didactic.[54] That is further indicated by the fact that the ordering of the first part of this system is the oldest ordering preserved in the biblical texts (Amos 5:21–22) and so seems to have been a quite traditional way of listing and referring to the whole system.[55] A second order of the sacrifices is found in Lev. 6:1(8)–7:38. There the focus is on "administrative details, especially the allocation of various parts of the sacrificial victim to those entitled to eat them."[56] Yet a third order, however, is discerned in the texts that seems to have been the procedural order actually followed when more than one sacrifice was to be made on any occasion. According to the procedural order, the purification (or sin) offering was made first and then the burnt offering and other offerings.

One finds in the procedural order a fundamental clue to the religious significance of the sacrificial system. The initial act was the sacrifice that removed the impurity that might have polluted the sanctuary and the altar (the place where the deity dwelled and met the people), pollution arising from the effects of sin or other forms of impurity. The burnt offering followed this, having also an expiatory function in part but serving to evoke the deity and prepare for the full communal participation of the worshipers.[57] Once these initial and crucial sacrifices were made, further burnt offerings and offerings of well-being could be presented. With regard to this stage, A. F. Rainey summarizes as follows:

> The former include both the voluntary gifts of individuals and the calendral offerings (symbolizing the constant devotion of the people as a whole). The peace offerings represented the communal experience in which the Lord, the priest and the worshipper (along with his family and the indigent in his community, Dt 12, 17–19) all had a share. The ritual approach was therefore: expiation [or purification], consecration, fellowship.[58]

The ordering of the sacrifices when the ritual was complex thus involved various movements and transfers. The meaning and purpose of sacrifice, however, is not fully comprehended simply by binary categories and notions of order and movement across categories. Though these were clearly present, other social and religious purposes and effects were at work in the various dimensions of sacrificial activity.[59]

Flesh and Blood

In the didactic or conceptual rendition of the offering of well-being in Leviticus 3, the following concluding comment is made:

> All fat is the LORD's. It shall be a perpetual statute throughout your generations, in all your settlements: you must not eat any fat or any blood.
> (Lev. 3:16b–17; cf. 7:22–26)

This brief statement is a clue to the fact that the sacrificial ritual of ancient Israel had much to do with flesh and blood. Or to put it succinctly, sacrifice was a means of permitting the consumption of flesh or meat, and the handling of the blood was a crucial part of the procedure that enabled its consumption. The material that demonstrates this dimension of sacrifice belongs to the Holiness Code and so represents a Priestly perspective that is echoed by other and somewhat different Priestly voices in the Noah story, where permission to eat flesh is given but not the eating of "flesh with its life, that is, its blood" (Gen. 9:4).[60] The particular association of this concern for not eating any blood with the offering of well-being is due to the fact that this offering was explicitly eaten by the people. The prohibition against eating the blood is reflected a number of times in the biblical documents (Lev. 17:10–17; 19:26; Deut. 12:16, 23–24; 15:23; 1 Sam. 14:31–35). The offering of well-being, which involved the presentation of the choice fat parts to be burned on the altar, turned the slaughter of animals for food consumption into a sacral act. One cannot be altogether sure of the underlying rationale for this, but analogies from the ancient world as far apart as early Sumerian mythology and Greek mythology suggest that the killing of animals was seen as incurring a kind of guilt that had to be dealt with in some fashion.[61] Sacrifice turned the act of slaughter into a sacral ritual, involving dedication to the deity that would serve to assuage the feelings of guilt from killing the animal.

The special treatment of the blood, beginning with the prohibition of eating bloody meat but incorporating the specific requirements of dashing or sprinkling blood against the altar (as one finds it in priestly sacrificial ritual), or pouring it out on the ground (as one finds it in Deuteronomic regulation of profane slaughter away from the central sanctuary), was also a part of the way by which the consumption of flesh was rationalized. Its life was in the blood, and that part was not to be consumed. Priestly development of that notion suggests that the blood was assigned by the deity for the purpose of expiating the sin of killing or murder that took place in the slaughter of the animal:

> The Levitical enactment postulates that "the life of the flesh is in the blood, and I have assigned it to you for making expiation for your lives upon the altar; it is the blood, as life, that effects expiation" (Lev 17:11). . . . [T]he expiation involved here is nothing less than ransom for a capital offense. Under the Levitical dispensation, animal slaughter *except at the authorized altar* is murder. The animal too has life (older versions: "a soul"), its vengeance is to be feared, its blood must be "covered" or expiated by bringing it to the altar.[62]

This analysis of one of the functions of sacrifice thus uncovers an important social and economic dimension of the practice. That is, it serves to sanctify an important part of the economy and the food production system. Hallo speaks of meat consumption as "a privilege routinely accorded to priesthood, aristocracy, and royalty and sporadically, notably on holidays and holy days, to the masses of the population."[63] One may assume that in Israel's economy, meat was an important food source, not only for the priests, whose access to it was explicitly insured by the sacrificial system, but for the populace also. Because the use of sacrifice for the feeding of the deity was not the dominant notion that it was in Mesopotamia and because sacrificial meat was shared by priest and sacrificer(s), one does not have to assume that this consumption was largely a privilege of rank, though it clearly was one of economic status, as those sacrificial regulations that provide for grain offerings by the poor make clear (see above).[64] That sacrifice was, in a significant way, related to the need to justify meat consumption and make sure that the act did not in some fashion bring guilt upon those who slaughtered and killed is indicated further by the concern in the Deuteronomic reform of the seventh century—as reflected in the book of Deuteronomy—for making sure that people could slaughter and eat meat even though the altar was now centralized and it was not easy to bring a sacrifice from the slaughtered animal to the sanctuary. Deuteronomy 12:15–27 provides for a nonsacrificial slaughter away from the altar and ties it explicitly to the desire to eat meat. While there is an implicit indication that sacrificial slaughter at the altar is preferable, permission is given for slaughter of domestic animals for consumption in the towns:

> If the place where the LORD your God will choose to put his name is too far from you, and you slaughter as I have commanded you any of your herd or flock that the LORD has given you, then you may eat within your towns whenever you desire. (Deut. 12:21)

But the permission makes sure that the blood is to be poured out, either on the altar in the case of the burnt offering, or on the ground in the case of other sacrifices and slaughter; it is not to be eaten (Deut. 12:23–24, 27). As the vital power of life, the blood was able to cleanse from sins or impurities and so was sprinkled and dashed on the altar or other parts of the sanctuary, or it was used to purify the impurities of sick persons, new priests, and the like. If not used in some form of purification or expiation, it was poured out.

Food and Gift

The sacrificial notions just described have primarily to do with social and religious purposes and effects for the participant(s), the offerer(s) of the sacrifice, or the consumers of the meat that is slaughtered but not sacrificed. But sacrifice also had important functions vis-à-vis the deity. As often noted, the primary explicit purpose of sacrifice in ancient Mesopotamia was the care and feeding of the gods. Hallo, for example, has claimed that the one clearly common thread running through both Sumerian and Akkadian myths about the relationship between human beings and gods is that the former were created to relieve the gods of the need to provide their own food: "The sacrificial cult was literally taken as a means of feeding the gods and specifically, beginning with the end of the third millennium, their cult statues."[65] He notes, as others have, that Israelite sacrificial practice, which involved consumption of sacrifice by both priests and laity, moved in another direction.[66] But remnants of this notion of sacrifice as food for the deity persisted in ancient Israelite religion, even if in fairly muted form. The whole notion of the burnt sacrifice producing an odor pleasing to the deity involved a highly anthropomorphic conception of Yahweh smelling and responding positively to the sacrifice as human beings respond to the pleasing odor of cooked food. For example, in Gen. 8:21, when Noah sacrifices burnt offerings to Yahweh, the text says that Yahweh "smelled the pleasing odor" (cf. Lev. 26:31). One of the main ways of identifying a larger category of sacrifices is those with "an odor pleasing to the LORD" (e.g., Lev. 1:9, 13; 2:2, 9; 3:5, 16; Num. 28:13, 24). Further, several times, the sacrificial regulations of the Priestly code and the Holiness Code speak of sacrifice as "food" (Lev. 3:11) or "the food of their God" (Lev. 21:6; cf. 21:17, 21, 22; Num. 28:2). The notion of sacrifice as food is muted and perhaps even vestigial at this point, but the language betrays a notion that in some way, the act of sacrifice provided sustenance for the good of the deity.[67] Such an understanding carried with it an implicit concern to appease the deity.[68] That is certainly suggested in the deity's response to the pleasing (or soothing) odor of the sacrifice in Gen. 8:21, for there it has a placating effect leading to Yahweh's decision never again to curse the earth. The same sense of propitiation may be inferred from Lev. 26:31, as well as 1 Sam. 26:19, where David says to Saul: "If it is the LORD who has stirred you up against me, may he accept [lit. "smell"] an offering."[69]

Explicit resistance to the notion of sacrifice as food for the deity was also a part of the conceptuality of sacrifice in ancient Israel. Even though the Priestly code and the Holiness Code use the language of "odor pleasing to the LORD" and speak of Yahweh "smelling" the odor of sacrifice, Ezekiel and later literature tend to avoid using these terms except, in Ezekiel's case, with regard to idolatrous worship (Ezek. 6:13; 16:19; 20:28).[70] Psalm 50 contains an explicit polemic, in the form of divine speech, against the notion of sacrifice as food for the deity:

> If I were hungry, I would not tell you,
>   for the world and all that is in it is mine.
> Do I eat the flesh of bulls,
>   or drink the blood of goats?

Offer to God a sacrifice of thanksgiving,
and pay your vows to the Most High.
(Ps. 50:12–14)

If, however, the notion of sacrifice as food for the deity was not prominent in ancient Israel, the function of sacrifice as food for human beings in
order to effect or generate solidarity and community is evident in the centrality of table fellowship as part of the ritual of sacrifice.[71] That is, of course,
connected to the way in which sacrifice enabled meat consumption, but it
went beyond that. The gathering of family, clan, or community around a
meal was frequently an aspect of the sacrificial process—often its final outcome—as is well indicated in the Deuteronomic legislation for slaughter/
sacrifice and for the festivals:[72]

> Most Israelite sacrifices resulted in a meal shared by the worshippers.
> The company of diners would consist of family (Deut 12:18; 1 Sam
> 1:3–5) and a circle of invited guests (Exod 34:15; 1 Sam 9:12–13;
> 16:3–5). As such, sacrifice may be understood as table fellowship with
> Yahweh for whom a portion of the meal was set aside by burning. . . .
> Those sharing the sacrificial meal would have seen it as a way of
> strengthening family and group associations, but also as a way of mak-
> ing personal contact with Yahweh. Commensality builds a relational
> bridge over which benefits can cross from the realm of divine power
> into the communicants' lives. Exodus 24:9–11 and Judg 6:19–24;
> 13:15–23 are narrative reflections of the ritual concept of table fellow-
> ship with Yahweh. Nevertheless, the Hebrew Bible is always careful to
> note that human worshippers dine *before* Yahweh, not actually *with*
> Yahweh (Exod 18:12).[73]

The Exodus narratives referred to above demonstrate the joining of sacrifice with the building and cementing of relationships. The literary and
transmissional history of Ex. 24:1–11 is complex and the object of much disagreement. But the present form of the text attests to the place of sacrifice
and meal in the uniting of the community in relation to the deity it was
committed to serve. That is, the literary record of the beginning of the Yah-
weh-Israel covenantal relationship places at its foundation the ritual of sacrifice and a meal of tribal representatives in the presence of the deity. "A
meal is a social contract that is binding for both parts. This contract is rec-
iprocal, both parts contribute something."[74] In this context, it is sacrifice and
meal that bring the contractual, or better, covenantal relationship about. So
also, the binding of the relationship of Jethro the priest of Midian with
Moses, Aaron, and the elders of Israel, an account that is probably a reflec-

tion of the origins of Israelite worship of Yahweh (see chapter 1), is set in the context of a sacrificial meal (Ex. 18:12; cf. Ex. 2:20).

As we have noted previously, the sacrificial meal was a major feature of the thanksgiving offering and ritual as the community (whether large or small is difficult to say) joined with the one whose prayers had been answered or whose vow was being fulfilled in an act of thanksgiving that may have included dimensions of communal reconciliation and restoration.[75]

It is the *tôdâ,* or thanksgiving sacrifice, along with the *nĕdārîm,* or votive offering, that particularly point to the character of sacrifice in ancient Israel as *gift* to the deity. Increasingly, students of Israelite sacrifice in its larger context have seen here the primary purpose or fundamental principle underlying the complex and varied ritual of sacrifice.[76] A number of features or aspects of the practice of sacrifice and offering indicate Israel's understanding of the presentation of sacrifice as a gift to the deity. The payment of a vow suggests a gift to the deity in return for the deity's help. The very character of the vow assumes that the deity desires the gift and responds in the light of the vow, as well as suggesting that without the offer of the sacrificial gift the deity might not respond. The vow indicates that as gift, the vow and sacrifice had an instrumental character, in some manner effecting, from the perspective of the offerer, divine assistance and returning a gift to the Lord in both thanksgiving and obligation.

So also, first fruit and tithe offerings have the character of gift brought in return for what the Lord has given. Not infrequently, there is specific reference to what the Lord has "given" when a sacrifice or offering has been brought (e.g., Lev. 23:38; Deut. 16:17; 26:10–11). Here again, thanksgiving and obligation join as motivating forces for the offering, and the gift further symbolizes the recognition of the one who is Lord of the land and provider of life. The gift is thus symbolic as well as instrumental, indicating an acknowledgment of the divine gift and the source of the blessing received (Deut. 26:1–10).

Some of the technical terminology of sacrifice also indicates its gift nature. Thus, the word "gift" (*mattānâ*), while not a frequently used noun, occurs with reference to offerings as a whole[77] as well as to a particular category of offerings (Lev. 23:38). Two terms that most frequently have to do with sacrifice—"bring near" (*hiqrîb*) and "(grain) offering" (*minḥā*)—have secular uses in the sense of bringing tribute in Judg. 3:17–18 and Ps. 72:10. The latter term, *minḥā,* occurs elsewhere with the meaning "tribute."[78] The noun *qorbān,* "offering," derived from the same root as the verb "draw near," is a priestly term used to refer to typical sacrificial offerings but also to anything that is presented as a gift at the sanctuary, including draft animals and wagons (Num. 7:3), silver (Num. 7:13), and gold and jewelry (Num. 31:50—in this case war booty), all of which are to be understood as gifts for Yahweh.[79] Thus, it has been suggested that these terms originated in the realm of diplomacy and the practice of acknowledging human sovereignty and were brought into the sacrificial language by the priests precisely to identify that activity as a tribute or presentation to the divine ruler that served the same purpose—acknowledgment of Yahweh's rule and authority over the people.[80]

As we have said, no single theory of sacrifice or definition of its purpose adequately explains all its intended effects in ancient Israelite religion.[81] But the function of sacrifice as gift, that is, as "offering" is clear. There was indeed, in many if not most instances, a sense of quid pro quo as the worshiper gave because of having been given, either help or forgiveness and expiation. The gift was understood as appropriate to the divine act of help or blessing. At the same time, the gift, like tribute to a king, expressed a sense of loyalty and devotion to the deity who ruled over Israel.

The prophetic critique of sacrifice, which is regularly put in the mouth of the deity, did not mean that the various views of sacrifice described above were under question or the very practice itself suspect. The prophets' objection to sacrifice as it was practiced was its tendency to substitute for all other aspects of the covenantal obligation of the Israelite. They reacted to the substitution of sacrifice for obedience to the covenantal stipulations, to the divine directives for Israel's life in community. In their sharp criticism, they asserted a divine rejection of sacrifice, but this was because it came to be assumed by some that sacrifice by itself sufficiently covered the obligations of the individual to the deity. The rejection of sacrifice by the prophets in behalf of the deity was not a rejection of the notions of sacrifice described above but of an assumption that the gift to the deity, appropriate as both gratitude and acknowledgment, was a substitute for obedience to the requirements of torah for the moral life and the practice of justice and compassion in the larger community.[82]

CHAPTER 4

Holiness and Purity

Both secular and religious life in ancient Israel were permeated with a concern for holiness and a proper guarding of what was sacred. While the various expressions of this reflect notions of taboo and dimensions of power and so belong to a common category of experience in other religions, the many ways in which holiness was achieved and protected came to be understood as directly related to Israel's God. The holiness of Yahweh was to be reflected in various ways in the society. A large body of legal material developed over the centuries to encourage and provide for achieving and guarding holiness, and extensive prophetic oracles attest to the seriousness of the concern for holiness and the frequent violation of the sacrality of the community.

The most extensive collection of rules and regulations to determine, achieve, or protect holiness and purity is found particularly in the Priestly legislation of Exodus through Numbers and in the related body of rules known as the Holiness Code (Leviticus 17–26). But these are not the only places where the concern for and identification of the holy is to be found. Not only does Deuteronomy have a strong notion of the people of Israel as holy, but narrative reports and prophetic oracles all testify to a perduring concern for the sacral in ancient Israel's religion. While an elaborate cultic apparatus and procedure developed in the course of Israel's history to clarify and guard the realm of the sacred, the sense of the sacred and the experience of taboo were features of the religion of Israel at all stages.

Holiness or sacredness, expressed primarily in the various forms of the root qdš, was joined with the related category of purity (tāmē'). In each case there was an opposite category. For holiness, the opposite was profane or common, and for purity, it was impurity. These categories, however, existed in somewhat complex relation to each other. The holy and the clean were related categories, and so the holy needed also to be pure or clean. Thus, when the Israelites were instructed to "consecrate themselves" at the holy mountain Sinai in order to meet there the holy God, they were told also to wash their garments (Ex. 19:10). Holiness and purity, however, were not the same. Purity, for example, was not an attribute or category applied to the deity, unlike holiness, which was a primary attribute from which Israel, or facets of its life, derived its holiness. Purity could be a feature of something that was holy as well as of something that was common, but nothing that was impure could ever be holy. In some sense, impurity was the true converse of holiness. An act of purifying oneself, as, for example, a woman purifying herself after her menstrual period, could be described as a consecration or sanctification, that is, with a verbal form of the common root for holiness, *qdš* (2 Sam. 11:4). While one must not too easily equate purity and holiness, these dimensions of Israel's social and religious life have enough contiguity that it is appropriate, if not indeed necessary, to give some attention to them together.

HOLINESS AND POWER

The experience of the holy manifested itself in features that partook of taboo. The dedication of spoils, for example, meant that they were not to be touched or taken, and doing so brought danger. The story of Achan's taking of the dedicated things in Joshua 7 is a good illustration of this. But the story also makes it very clear that the sacrality of the dedicated things was not because of anything inherent within them, any *mana* or potency with which they were laden. The sacrality and the danger lay in that they were set apart to the deity, Yahweh. Indeed, the word "holy" and its derivatives from the root *qdš* mean "separated, withdrawn, set apart." But this seems regularly to have meant separated to Yahweh (Ex. 19:6; 20:8–9; 31:15; Lev. 20:26; Deut. 7:6; 14:2, 21). Not every reference to something as being holy can be seen in immediate relation to Yahweh, but the expression "holy to Yahweh" is sufficiently common and the elaborated notions of holiness in the law codes so thoroughly tied to the command of the deity and the relation to the deity that one can read an animistic notion of holiness into Israel's religion only with great difficulty. Even when Uzzah was killed for having touched the ark of the covenant to steady it, the destruction is described as being due to the wrath of God, who struck him down (2 Sam. 6:7).

That the ark was also the dwelling place of Yahweh contributes to an understanding of this event as a divine act (albeit a puzzling one) that happened because of Uzzah's apparent violation of the line between the holy and the common rather than because of an inherent danger in the ark itself, as if one were to touch an electric current.[1] It is precisely the absence of a mechanistic or animistic kind of sacrality in this event that makes it so problematic. The danger came explicitly from the divine decision. So also Achan's punishment for taking the dedicated things from the destruction of Jericho was the outcome of a complex procedure and a divine decision rather than being from actual contact with the taboo items (Joshua 7).

There was clearly potency in the holiness of anything, and the community may have responded to the awareness of something being holy or consecrated by treating it as innately potent. In 1 Samuel 4–6, a relatively early account of the involvement of the ark of the covenant in a military engagement, the presence of the ark is understood to be potent. As the palladium for the deity, it brought the power of the God into the camp (1 Sam. 4:7–8). While in its first entrance the ark seems to lack any power, before the story is over, its potency, or more precisely the power of the God who dwells there, is thoroughly demonstrated.

The association of the ark, power, and the holiness of the deity is transparent in 1 Sam. 6:19–20. While the Hebrew text ascribes the death of some of the men of Beth-shemesh to their looking into the ark, the Greek text, which is generally preferred by commentators and several of the contemporary translations (e.g., NRSV and NAB), tells of the death of seventy of the descendants of Jeconiah because they did not rejoice at the return of the ark. In both texts, the people then say, "Who is able to stand before the LORD, this holy God?" The slaughter of the seventy men by Yahweh did not occur because of the inherent taboo character of the ark that destroys the one who looks inside it. Rather, it happened because the descendants of Jeconiah did not rejoice with the Beth-shemesh folk at the return of the victorious warrior enthroned on the ark.[2] At the same time, what happened— and one may assume that includes the presence of the ark as well as the destruction of the Jeconiah group—is summed up by the exclamation about who can stand before this *holy* God. The combination of moveable object, power, and holiness did, therefore, place Israel's experience with the ark in the category of fetish and taboo. The ark was "replete with power" and an object through which the holiness of the deity was manifest. This is what taboo is all about.[3] But the source of that power and holiness was not the object itself or some totem inscribed on it, but the God who was enthroned on it. That is true of the Hebrew text of 1 Sam. 6:19 as well as of the Greek, even though the former ascribes the divine response to something the people do to the ark, that is, look in it.

The story of the ark thus marks a significant way in which the holiness of objects in ancient Israel may have shared the customary taboo character of many religious things. At the same time, it underscores the fundamental fact about holiness as a feature of Israelite religion—that is, its derivation from the holiness of the deity, a point made programmatic for the life of the people in the Holiness Code, as they are commanded to be holy as the Lord is holy (see below).

The power associated with what was holy is suggested also by the notion that ritual impurity was associated with things that represented the forces of life and death, such as carcasses and corpses (Lev. 11:24–40; Numbers 19), skin or scale diseases (Leviticus 13–14), and genital discharges (Leviticus 12, 15).

> The common denominator of these impurities is that they symbolize the forces of death: carcasses/corpses obviously so; the emission of blood or semen means the loss of life; and the wasting of flesh characteristic of scale disease is explicitly compared to a corpse (Num 12:12). . . . [T]he conclusion is manifestly clear: if *ṭāmē'* "impure" stands for the forces of death, then *qādôš* "holy" stands for the forces of life.[4]

Whether or not all dimensions of the impurity-holiness opposition reflected this particular power, it would seem to be the case that the power for life and the power of death were dimensions of the various ways in which holiness was guarded and impurity was avoided. Milgrom has made a cogent case that the prohibitions against the shedding of blood (Gen. 9:3–6; Lev. 17:1–9) and the ingesting of blood (Gen. 9:4; Lev. 17:10–16; 19:26; cf. 3:17; 7:26–27; Deut. 12:16, 23–25; 15:23), reflected a deep sense of the inviolability of life. While animals might be killed to provide food, their life was sacred and the blood of sacrificial animals was to be poured out on the altar (Ex. 24:6; Lev. 17:6; cf. 1:5, 15; 3:2, 8, 13) and/or the ground (Deut. 12:16, 23; 15:23) and so returned to the Creator. Its pouring out on the altar could also atone for or ransom the life of the sacrificial donor(s) (Lev. 17:11). With its vital power, blood could also serve purifying, sanctifying, and protective functions in such cases as a person recovering from skin disease (Leviticus 14) and the consecration of the altar (Lev. 4:5–7) or of priests (Lev. 8:23–24).[5] That such an understanding of the significance of the blood and regulations for handling it and not consuming it when slaughtering animals may have had a long history in ancient Israel is suggested by the story of the famished Israelites taking the captured Philistine herds and flocks and slaughtering them in a manner that did not drain the blood and so resulted in their ingesting the blood. This act was condemned by Saul, who made provision for the proper slaughter of the animals so that the blood was drained out of the animal onto the ground and not ingested (1 Sam. 14:31–34).[6]

THE PERVASIVENESS OF THE HOLY

There is no clearer indication of the degree to which holiness permeated Israel's religion and indeed its life than looking at the many dimensions of societal existence where the sacred came into play in explicit and often critical fashion. Thus, holiness could be ascribed to many different kinds of things, but it also was a way of life. It had to do with morality and it had to do with ritual. Holiness was an aspect, a characteristic of a thing or person that could come and go. But it also could be perduring. Thus, a shrine, a "holy" place where the deity was worshiped remained in a permanent state of holiness, but the people might sanctify or hallow themselves for a particular occasion, as they did at Sinai. From other perspectives, the people were enduringly holy or were summoned to manifest a permanent holiness, a separation from other groups, as evidenced in their devotion to the holy god, Yahweh, and as demonstrated in the totality of their ongoing existence. Holiness as a feature of something could be either positive or negative, that is, encounter with holiness could enhance life or destroy it. Space and time, daily life and extraordinary events, divine and human, animate and inanimate—no sphere of life or realm of being was shut off from the sacred.

The range of things or categories that could be regarded or designated holy was thus very wide, comprising objects, places, people, and acts or deeds. Some of the particular things that were called or became holy are fairly obvious, such as priests or vessels used in ritual procedures. But the land was holy, and war could be holy. A journey could be sacred or common (1 Samuel 21). Comprehending the depth of the experience of the holy as a fundamental dimension of Israelite religion involves a broad look at that range of categories of the holy.

The Holiness of Yahweh as the Ground of the Sacred

The starting point or the foundation of all dimensions of the sacred in ancient Israel was the holiness of the deity (see chapter 1). This is obviously indicated in the Holiness Code (Leviticus 17–26), which prescribes a way of holiness for the people that is rooted in the holiness of the deity:

> Speak to all the congregation of the people of Israel and say to them: You shall be holy, for I the LORD your God am holy.
>
> (Lev. 19:2)

The prophets carried on such an understanding also as they identified Yahweh as the "Holy One" or "holy God"[7] or referred to the "holy name" of Yahweh.[8]

In the Priestly tradition—the origins of which are much debated and located from Solomonic times down to the late postexilic era but probably reflect developments from the late preexilic era into the postexilic period—holiness as derivative from the deity is further indicated in various textual allusions to Yahweh's "sanctifying" something, for example, the Sabbath (Ex. 20:10–11) or the seventh day (Gen. 2:3), the priesthood (Lev. 21:8,[9] 15, 23; 22:9), the firstborn (Num. 3:13; 8:17), and the people (Lev. 22:16, 32). The deity is depicted as showing himself to be holy or manifesting holiness in various ways, for example, in righteous acts (Isa. 5:16) or before the eyes of the nations.[10]

But the holiness of Yahweh is something that also seems to be vulnerable to human acts. There are instances in which persons are said to have failed to maintain the holiness of the deity by their actions,[11] as well as injunctions to act in a manner that does not profane the name of the deity but upholds Yahweh's holiness (Lev. 22:32). Human actions can be nonreflective of the holiness of the deity and so profane or make profane the deity and the deity's name. In Ezekiel, such profanation of the deity seems to be specifically at the point of not attending to the holy things, that is, to the distinction between the holy and the profane or common, between what is *qōdeš* and what is *ḥōl*, or to the distinction between the clean and the unclean, between what is pure (*ṭāhôr*) and what is impure (*ṭāmē'*), as well as to maintaining the sanctity of the Sabbath (Ezek. 22:26). In other words, priestly profanation of the deity, priestly failure to manifest the deity's holiness, took place as the religious leaders did not uphold the system that identified holiness in the community. In what seems to be one of the postexilic definitions of priestly duties, those duties are identified as responsibility for teaching the people the distinctions between holy and profane or common, and between unclean and clean as well as for keeping the Sabbath holy (Ezek. 44:23–24).[12] The distinctions so identified by Ezekiel are understood in the Holiness Code to be precisely reflections of the deity's holiness in the midst of the community. The laws regarding maintaining the distinction between clean and unclean animals conclude with the repeated Holiness Code formulation to "be holy, for I am holy" (Lev. 11:47; 20:25–26).

Such profanation of the deity or the name of the deity did not seem to indicate any diminishment of the holiness that was intrinsically a part of Yahweh's character (and that of many other gods as well).[13] Activity so labeled was rather a failure to be holy or act in a manner that uncovered and signaled the holiness of the deity. The notion of profanation of the deity assumes therefore the binding relationship between deity and the people and a connection between divine holiness and human holiness, a connection such as is suggested in the Holiness Code's identification of Israel's holiness as grounded in and reflecting Yahweh's holiness.

Holiness in the Spheres of Space, Personality, and Time

Rooted conceptually in the holiness of Yahweh and Israel's experience with the holy God and the numinous power of that holiness (see Ex. 19:9b–25; 20:18–21; Isa. 6:1–5),[14] the realm of the sacred was broad and comprehensive, in this respect, not unlike the experience of the holy in various other religions.[15] Thus, holiness could accrue to places, things, and persons.

Holy places. The first of these is well exemplified in the sanctuaries and shrines that were understood to be sacred precisely because the deity was present there in some form or at some time (cf. Gen. 28:10–22; Ex. 3:5). Thus, the tabernacle was called "the holy place" (Ex. 26:33–34) and the innermost sanctuary where the ark rested was the "holy of holies" or "most holy place" (Ex. 26:33–34; 1 Chron. 6:34(49). But specifically religious sites were not the only holy places. According to both the Deuteronomic Code and the Priestly circle (Deut. 23:9–14; Num. 5:1–4), the war camp was holy. In both instances, the holiness was explicitly understood to derive from the presence of the deity with the people in the camp. Ritual purity in the midst of military engagements is also suggested by the encounter of David with Ahimelech in 1 Samuel 21, when David indicates that his soldiers regularly stay pure—away from women—and thus holy, while on active duty.

Holy things. The ark itself was a good example of a holy thing or instrument (see above on holiness and power). But many other sorts of things could be holy, from the rest of the sanctuary furniture, such as the altar (Ex. 29:37) and the menorah (Ex. 30:26–29), to the offerings brought to the sanctuary (e.g., Lev. 27:9–10; see the discussion of gradations of holiness below), to clothing (Ex. 39:1), property or real estate (Lev. 27:14–25), seed (Lev. 27:30), fruit (Lev. 27:30), money (Lev. 27:23), and such products as incense and oil (Ex. 30:25).[16]

There is a particular and somewhat unusual accrual of holiness to the mixture of certain things, such as planting two different kinds of seeds together or wearing a garment out of mixed threads (Deut. 22:9–11; Lev. 19:19). Mary Douglas has suggested that such laws belong to a system of orderliness in life that is guarded by dietary laws and other such regulations. In this instance, the violation of the orders and distinctions in thread and seed require the forfeiture or sanctification of the material rather than allowing it to be a part of everyday life and thus creating in that life a kind of undercutting of the categories that insure the smooth and unchaotic movement of life.[17] Such mixtures, however, could function in the holy sphere because they carried that symbolic value. Thus, the priest's garments, being holy, could be made of a mixture of wool and linen, because that mix was understood to be holy, thus not available in the common spheres of life but available to the realm of the sacred.[18] Other mixtures were so dangerous to the normative order of creation that they were prohibited altogether, for example, the sexual union of different kinds of animals or of animal and human, because such mixings were "bound up with the power and danger of sexuality."[19]

Holy persons. The most obvious and perhaps important instance of personal holiness is that of the priests. In the Priestly tradition, their holiness was seen as secured by an elaborate ritual of sanctification (Exodus 29; Leviticus 8–9). The priests (Aaron and his sons) were brought forward from the congregation, that is, separated out, clothed in priestly garments (another mark of distinction and separation), washed with water to purify them, and anointed with oil, a process that is described as sanctifying or consecrating (*qiddēš;* cf. Num. 21:12).[20] Various offerings were then made by the presiding figure—in the Priestly tradition seen as Moses—and further sprinkling of oil and also blood was carried out. The first part of this ritual of consecration thus began the process of sanctification by a complex of acts that separated the priests from the rest of the congregation or community, before whom the ritual was carried out.

At that point, the priests were to remain seven days within the tent of meeting, "keeping the LORD's charge so that you do not die" (Lev. 8:35). Milgrom has pointed out the liminal state of this period, a time when the priest or priests were moving steadily in a temporal way away from the congregation and increasingly into a condition or sphere of holiness but also a time of danger:

> They are consecrated as priests only at the end of the week, and during this liminal period they are highly vulnerable, not to demonic assault—the world of demons has been expunged from Priestly notions—but to human sin and impurity. . . . Each day's rites will remove them farther from their former profane state and advance them to the ranks of the sacred, until they emerge as full-fledged priests.[21]

As Milgrom has noted, various features of this seven-day period are comparable to other rites of passage involving a liminal state, including the seclusion of the priest candidates, their silence, their sexual continence (cf. 1 Sam. 21:4–5), and their prohibition from acts that, if carried out, involved breaking a taboo and so endangerment (see below on holiness and taboo).[22]

This transitional stage came to an end when the priests, now having passed through the liminal stage, were deemed fully consecrated and reintegrated into the full community, symbolized by their carrying out the ritual of sacrifice and the blessing of the people (Leviticus 9). The climax and confirmation of the full consecration of the priests, as well as of the tabernacle (Lev. 8:10–11), was the appearance of the deity to the congregation, a sign that the sacrality of the community and the sanctification of the sanctuary and priests was secure.[23]

The Levites, who had responsibilities for guarding and taking care of tabernacle materials and for carrying them (Num. 3:14–39; 4:1–33), went through a ritual process somewhat comparable to that of the priests (Num. 8:5–22). But it was more of a purification ritual than a consecration. The Levites were not characterized as holy, but they were separated from the rest of the Israelites and cleansed or purified in order to make them ready for the work of the sanctuary. This period of service was limited to the period of time between age twenty-five and age fifty (Num. 8:23–26). The clearest suggestion that there may have been some implicit sense of the holiness of the Levites rests in their being separated out and ritually purified for the performance of their duties and in the fact that they were regarded as substitutes for the firstborn of all the Israelites, whom the Lord had consecrated "for my own" (Num. 3:11–13; 8:17–18). So while there is no explicit indication of the Levites being characterized as holy in the Priestly circle, they were a part of the process of separating out individuals and purifying them for the service of the holy God in the sanctuary. And in the Chronicler's witness to the rituals of sacrality, the Levites were indeed designated as holy (2 Chron. 23:6; 35:3).

The Nazirite was another category of holy person (Num. 6:1, 8), one attested through the range of Israel's history. The term itself meant "consecrated" or "separated out" and probably meant "separated to God."[24] One became a Nazirite by means of a vow, temporary (Num. 6:13) or lifelong (so Samson and Samuel). The vow was to a discipline that effected a kind of sanctification. The laws and stories having to do with Nazirites focus upon the particular abstentions that were standard to the vow—no drink, no cutting of hair, no contact with the dead.[25] It is important to recognize that, unlike the priests and Levites, Nazirite was a category of holy persons that could include women (Num. 6:1), although that inclusion of women was carried out within the patriarchal structures that dominated Israelite family and religious life. Numbers 30 reveals the detailed ways in which a woman's vow was under the control—the approval or disapproval—of father or husband. That is, a man's vow had to be fulfilled, but a woman's vow could be annulled by either her father or her husband. The vow of consecration and its reflection of holiness, while seeming a binding matter of relationship to the holy God—and actually so in the case of males—was subject to human control by way of the familial structure that ordered the subordination of women to their fathers and husbands.

With regard to members of the community generally, the concern was for their purity and the preservation of the holiness of the sanctuary and everything and everyone connected to it. Thus, the rules and regulations for lay people had more to do with pollution and the effecting of holiness than with consecration and sanctification to a status of holy.

The requirements for the maintenance of holiness on the part of those who were consecrated were various. Aside from the general distancing from pollution that would defile the person and anything that he touched, there were specific regulations to guard the purity and holiness of the consecrated individual. These included staying clear of corpses (Lev. 21:1, 10–11; Num. 6:6–8), not drinking wine or beer (Lev. 10:9; Num. 6:3; Ezek. 44:21), not marrying prostitutes or defiled women (Lev. 21:7–9, 14),[26] exercising care in cutting the hair (Lev. 19:27; 21:5; Num. 6:5; Deut. 14:1), and avoiding unclean food (Ex. 22:30[31]; Ezek. 44:31).[27]

As has been indicated above, there was within the traditions of Israelite religion a definite notion of the people as a whole being holy. The consecration of the firstborn to the Lord was a specific and representative example of that larger claim that is attested in the Sinai tradition of Exodus (Ex. 19:6), the Book of the Covenant (Ex. 22:30[31]), the Holiness Code (Lev. 19:2), and Deuteronomy (Deut. 7:6; 14:2, 21; 26:18–19). The requirements for such holiness would have included the kinds of specific prohibitions and disciplines indicated in the preceding paragraph, but went far beyond that. The modern designation "Holiness Code" for Leviticus 17–26 attests to the degree to which it placed all of the rules and regulations of Israel's life, social and familial as well as ritual, as means by which the holiness of the people was demonstrated and maintained. In like manner, the Book of the Covenant and the Deuteronomic Code identified the means of effecting and preserving sacrality for the people—their separation out from other communities and their identification with Yahweh—with the whole of the various statutes and ordinances that they set forth (cf. Num. 15:37–41). It is at this point that the conceptions and manifestations of holiness in the legal literature of ancient Israel joined hands with prophetic notions of holiness.

Thus, the prophet Isaiah viewed the antithesis between the holy God and the unholy people as manifest in all the different ways that their personal and social sins polluted their life (see below).

Holy times. Time as well as space partook of sacrality in Israelite religion. One of the responsibilities of the priests identified above was to keep the Sabbath holy to Yahweh. While the regular and significant observation of the Sabbath may have come later in Israel's history, its character as a day set apart, consecrated, "holy to the LORD," is indicated in the prescription for the day in the Decalogue (Ex. 20:8; Deut. 5:12) and other legal formulations (Ex. 31:12–17; 34:21; 35:2), as well as in the lists of priestly responsibilities (Ezek. 22:26b; 44:24) and prophetic injunctions (Neh. 9:14; 13:17–18; Isa. 15:13; Jer. 17:22, 24, 27; Ezek. 20:20–21, 24).[28] As the Sabbath became increasingly a mark of identity for the Jewish people, the holiness of the Sabbath coincided with the holiness of the people as a way of marking them off distinctively from other nations. Thus, time was set apart— even as space was set apart—to be God's time, time when the common things did not go on. The hallowing of the Sabbath was in treating it as utterly different from other days. That did not happen in cultic or ritual processes, as was true of the sacrality of other things but particularly in the absence of work. The sacrality of the Sabbath came to be so sharply protected that in the Priestly tradition, the violation of the Sabbath, like the violation of other commandments, was punishable by death (Ex. 31:14–15; 35:2; Num. 15:32–36). Two social functions thus joined in its hallowing: the effecting of a significant identifying mark that would help keep the community together and avoid syncretistic meldings, and the provision of rest for persons caught in the bondage of unceasing labor and toil (Deut. 5:14b; cf. Ex. 23:12). The former function is underscored by the Priestly claim that keeping the Sabbath was a mark of Yahweh's sanctification of the people. The second function had its larger extension in the provision for a sabbatical year of release (Deuteronomy 15) and for a jubilee year of restoration (Leviticus 25).[29]

While the Sabbath seems uniformly to have been regarded as sacred time, that is not as clear with the festivals. Certainly acts of sacrifice at the sanctuary brought the participants into the realm of the holy, but it is particularly in the Priestly tradition, though not alone there,[30] that the pilgrimage festivals were viewed as "holy convocations." Such terminology applied to certain days of the festivals, thus indicating that here also there was some gradation of holiness. In the Holiness Code, the sacredness of the holy convocations was linked to that of the Sabbath by the prohibition of work on both types of occasions (Lev. 23:3, 8, 21, 25, 28, 31).

Jenson has suggested that the deeming of a particular moment or day in the festival as a "holy convocation" (*miqrā' qōdeš*) was linked to "an increased activity around the sanctuary on such an occasion":

> Most of the additional sacrifices were burnt offerings, the sacrifice par-
> ticularly associated with God and thus an appropriate offering for a
> holy day. Even when the occasion was not a pilgrimage feast, there
> were a significant number of public sacrifices. Since no work was
> allowed, many could come from the immediate surroundings to take
> part in the celebrations. The *ḥaṭṭā't* sacrifice probably guaranteed that
> a degree of purity appropriate for the holiness of the day was attained
> at the sanctuary. It is likely that special care was taken to attain a high
> degree of purity on these occasions, both by priests and non-priests.[31]

The Complex Interaction
of the Spheres of Holiness

It would be a mistake to read the above discussion as a catalog of unre-lated items that were regarded as sacred. Holiness was so much a feature of the nature of the deity Israel worshiped and of Israel's worship in gen-eral that it can be misleading to treat each item or sphere of holiness sep-arately. Not only is that a distortion because the holiness of the deity formed the ground of the sacred in other spheres, but rarely did something belong to or enter the sphere of the holy apart from its relation to other things that were holy. The relation of holy things to the deity is well illus-trated by the sanctuaries. Both temple and tabernacle were holy spaces because of the presence of the deity. Thus, all else associated with them came into the sphere of holiness, whether it was the ark, which rested in the shrine and was also the dwelling place of the deity—in at least some conceptions of the ark—or the monies that came into the treasuries of the temple. While these had a distinct social and economic function having to do with the upkeep of the sanctuary and the sanctuary personnel, a func-tion presumably reinforced by their sacred status, their very presence in the sanctuary would have vested in them a degree of holiness, even though that is rarely stipulated. Occasionally the extant texts are explicit about the consecration of the economic resources of the temple. So Solomon is recorded by both Kings and Chronicles as having put in the temple all the "holy things" of David, or the things that David had consecrated: "silver, gold, and all the vessels in the treasuries of the house of God" (2 Chron. 5:1; cf. 1 Kings 7:51). And other kings are reported as having brought the holy things of their ancestors or their own into the house of the Lord—sil-ver, gold, and utensils (1 Kings 15:14 // 2 Chron. 15:18; 2 Kings 12:18).

Such separation of the royal wealth and sometimes the booty of royal conquests was an act of piety that reinforced the religious standing of the king and provided revenues "set apart," and thus available when tribute was demanded by foreign powers (1 Kings 15:18–19; 2 Kings 12:19[18]).

So also everything having to do with the priesthood was understood as sacred, because the priest entered the sacred space at sacred times to handle things that had been consecrated and set apart to the Holy One. Jenson has suggested that the holiness of the high priestly garments is expressed by the way their materials and weave were aligned with the materials of the tabernacle and that what he calls the "Holiness Spectrum" "correlates the personal with the spatial dimension."[32]

Thus, holiness in one area required holiness for whatever impinged upon that area, and the holiness of one thing worked to protect and safeguard the holiness of another. It is precisely this complex interrelationship and the ripple effect of encounter with the holy that effected such a complicated system of sacred spheres. The priestly community had primary responsibility for effecting and safeguarding that system and so enjoyed status, power, and financial support to do so. That such effecting and safeguarding had a self-serving dimension does not diminish the degree to which the Israelite community really found in this interaction of spheres the effecting of a realm that seemed to enhance the openness of the community to the divine and, certainly in the Priestly tradition, the preservation of the community in the face of the danger of the encounter with the holy God.

Yet not everything belonged to a network of holiness. The holiness of the Nazirite was the result of an act of dedication to the holy God that did not depend upon proximity to the sanctuary or to holy things, though entry into the period of consecration or departure from it, if the Nazirite vow was temporary, brought the Nazirite before the Lord, that is, into the holiness of the sanctuary (e.g., Num. 6:13–20), and fundamental rules of ritual cleanliness and purity were central to the period of the vow.

So also the Sabbath was not correlated to cultic or ritual activities. Its rootage in family life seems to have separated it out from the usual connections to the spheres of holiness even though it was by definition a piece of sacred time, "holy to the LORD."

Finally, one needs to note that one of the major documents preserved from Israel's religious history, the Holiness Code of Leviticus 17–26 with its view of the people in all their daily interactions with one another as exemplifying or embodying holiness, did not therefore see holiness as confined to certain spheres, specifically the cultic. In some ways, the network of holy acts, persons, places, and times became more complete and complex as holiness was the ground and rationale for all that was done or happened. To the extent that the community was to be holy because the Lord was holy (Lev. 19:2), no area of life and no time or space was relegated to the common or the profane, at least implicitly. Such an understanding seems to lie behind the prophetic emphasis on holiness as a requirement of the people that should be reflected as much in social life as in cultic ritual.

GRADATIONS OF HOLINESS

One might expect from what is said above that the clear indication of distinctions between what was holy and what was not, what was clean and what was impure, meant that these were simply two different realities, two spheres that could be distinguished from each other. What would have been required was understanding what characterized one sphere and what characterized the other, acknowledging that there could be movement from one to the other. That is, some thing, person, or place was holy or it was not.

But the matter is not that simple. There were also gradations of holiness, so that one thing or person or place could be more holy than another. There was, from some perspectives, a clear hierarchy of holiness that began with Yahweh of Israel and moved down. Such gradations seem to have become more common in the development of a more systematic approach to sanctity and purity as we know it in the Priestly legislation.[33]

One of the clearest and broadest manifestations of some gradation in holiness is found in the tripartite division of humanity in the Priestly system into levels of holiness that corresponded to three covenants with God: humanity (Gen. 9:1–11), Israel (Gen. 17:2; Lev. 26:42), and the priesthood (Num. 25:10–12; Jer. 33:17–22).[34] This division also represented increasing (or decreasing, depending upon where one starts) degrees or requirements of holiness. So Israel was held under a stricter requirement than all other peoples if they were to be a holy nation. Thus, the food laws that distinguished between acceptable and unacceptable animals for consumption reflected a perceived distinction between Israel and the nations (Lev. 20:23–26) or served to effect and guard such a distinction. And Deuteronomy grounded the holiness of the people in their rejection of the religious practices of the "nations that are before you" (Deut. 7:1–6) as well as in the rejection of certain practices associated with the surrounding nations, such as laceration and veneration of the dead (Deut. 14:1–2), even though it is clear that such practices went on and had some acceptability within orthodox Yahwism or were at least borderline between orthodox and heterodox Yahwism (see chapter 2). The shaping of Deuteronomy 14, with its reference to the holiness of the people at the beginning and end of the chapter and its focus upon the dietary laws, suggests that, as is indicated in the Holiness Code, those laws became a mark of distinction between Israel and the nations, probably by the late preexilic period. The point is made explicit in the instruction to abstain from eating animals that died on their own—as over against being slaughtered—while permission is granted to sell such meat to resident aliens and foreigners (Deut. 14:21).

The priests, however, had even more stringent and specific requirements than the people, at least in certain respects, because they moved in and out of the spatial sphere of holiness and dealt with holy things. They were responsible for maintaining and protecting the holiness of that sphere and the things that came into it. The differentiation between the holiness of the priests and that of the people, as well as distinctions within the ranks of the priesthood, are the focus of the story of the rebellion of Korah in Numbers 16–17 and in Priestly legislation that follows it. These chapters are complex in their composition and redaction.[35] They seem to reflect an internecine conflict between priestly groups in ancient Israel. But as such, they testify to significant differentiations. The rebellion against Moses and Aaron is said to be because they set themselves above others when in fact "all the congregation are holy." Graded and hierarchical holiness is specifically acknowledged but only to be attacked. The formulation indicates an explicit awareness of the difference between the priests and the rest of the congregation in terms of sacrality. The story may reflect some actual conflict in the community about the accessibility of ordinary Israelites to the sacral sphere. But the primary issue was probably one of priestly grades or of the claims of rival priestly houses (see chapter 5). That is, what develops at the primary level of the narrative as a distinction or grade between the priestly elements is identified and then fixed in law in the chapters that follow. The fact that such gradation of the Levitical priests did not always exist in ancient Israel is a reflection of the tendency to move toward an increasingly hierarchical and graded spectrum of holiness, one that served to support and reinforce the power of the Jerusalem priesthood, more specifically the Zadokite priests.[36] At the same time, one is given a glimpse of the way that spheres of holiness were affected by internal societal conflicts and the struggle for power among varying and even warring groups in the religious establishment. Indeed, this particular gradation of holiness served to identify and sustain one group ahead of and over the other, although the narrative and legislative accounts give an etiology that roots it in definitions of sacrality and relative degrees of participation in the sancta (Num. 16:1–11).

It has been suggested that lying behind all levels of the story in Numbers 16–17 is a further hierarchical dimension to the sacrality of persons, and that is the distinction between the high priest or chief priest and all the other priests.[37] There were various ways in which that distinction was made in ancient Israel, some of which have to do specifically with the sanctification of the high priest and his participation in the sphere of holy space, the sanctuary. For one thing, there was at some point a more detailed and elaborate ritual of consecration.[38] Whenever there was a new high priest, the ordination into the sphere of holiness took place (e.g., Ex. 29:29; Lev. 16:32; Num. 35:25), while for other priests the initial ordination of the Aaronide priests was sufficient in perpetuity (Ex. 40:15). The higher status and holiness of the high priest was further indicated by the more elaborate set of garments of the high priest, which included mixed cloth (see above) and were called holy (Lev. 16:4),[39] the access of the high priest to the most holy place of the sanctuary (Lev. 16:3–4, 11–19), and the greater restrictions on the high priest with regard to marriage, mourning, and purity (Lev. 21:1–15; Ezek. 44:22).[40]

Distinctions between the priests and the Levites is another place where gradations in holiness may be inferred. While the history of the relationship between Levites and other priests is a complicated subject, the Levites would have played a significant role at an early time, if information in Judges–Samuel is any indication. Some of the administrative functions to which they were assigned, while generally understood as reflecting a late cultic development, may have been a part of their assignment as early as the United Monarchy.[41] But in the course of Israel's religious history, and at least to some extent out of the rivalry of priestly groups and the effort to maintain power on the part of the Jerusalem priests and their descendants, the Levites came to occupy a subordinate, albeit important, cultic role, at least in the Priestly schema. Some indication of this form of priestly gradation is indicated in the following summary:

> [T]he Levites were to guard the sanctuary, while the priests protected the holy items inside. The Levites were not allowed access to the holy things on pain of death (Num 4.15). They were directed to serve Aaron, and were under the authority of him and his sons. They did not serve Yahweh directly in the sanctuary as did the priests; rather they guarded the sanctuary from defilement on the outside and performed the hard labour (עבודה) of its dismantling and erection. Only the priests could safely pack and cover the holy items (Num 4.5–20), and subsequently the coverings provided the necessary barrier between the holiness of the Tabernacle and the Levites.[42]

Within the later traditions, there is some difference in the matter of whether or not the Levites were actually regarded as "holy." They are never characterized as holy in the Priestly tradition, and their initiation is understood as an act of purification (Num. 8:6–7, 21) rather than sanctification, as in the case of the priests (Lev. 8:10, 30). But their taking the place of the firstborn (Num. 8:16–18) suggests a kind of consecration, in that the firstborn were so regarded (see above). The Chronicler explicitly characterizes the Levites as "holy" (2 Chron. 23:6; 35:3), but the gradation seems to be recognized in the assignment of Aaron and his sons "to consecrate the most holy things" (1 Chron. 23:13).

Within the spatial sphere, distinctions and grades of holiness could be maintained, according to the Priestly tradition. This is reflected, for example, with regard to the sanctuary, more specifically, the tabernacle, where zones and grades of holiness were maintained as indicated in table 4.1.[43]

GRADED HOLINESS

Boundaries	inner curtain		outer curtain		entrance
Grade	I	II			III
Zone	Holy of Holies	Holy Place			Court

The significance of the zones may be indicated by the fact that the inner sanctuary was distinguished from the holy space where the sacrifices were brought by designating it as "*the* holy place" or "the holy of holies." There was also a gradation of material in that the costliness of the material seems to have grown in proportion to the closeness of the material to the deity or the place of the deity's presence. So also greater proximity increased the lethal potential in the holiness of objects associated with the deity (see below).

That such gradations may sometimes reflect an agenda other than guarding the sacred has already been suggested. Pressing that point further, David Wright has noted that "the social hierarchies of a particular society determine its gradation of ritual space and the access that groups may have to its different parts."[44] He compares Ezekiel's program for the postexilic temple and its cultus with those of the Priestly tradition. In the former, the priests (Zadokites), who are judged as having been faithful when the people went astray, are given access to the inner court (Ezek. 44:15–27). But the Levites are kept from such access and assigned custodial roles because they joined the people in going astray (vv. 10–14). Foreigners and the uncircumcised are prohibited from the sanctuary altogether (vv. 6–9). The people remain in the outer court (v. 19). The prince or political ruler does not enter the inner court but is allowed to enter the vestibule of the east gate from the outside (44:3; 46:2). Wright, following Smith, observes appropriately:

> The book's gradation is not descriptive but prescriptive; yet not just prescriptive, but revisionist. It is a polemical reformulation of social and religious relationships. The Zadokite priests are exalted while the Levites are demoted and castigated. Civic leaders—kings—are criticized for their breach of purity rules and are restricted in the future from access much beyond laypersons and Levites. . . . By changing access to the temple, the prophet is changing the constitution and organization of society.[45]

While the Priestly tradition is not as polemical, there are similar distinctions, and the more implicit social distinctions and categories are still enhanced:

> The access laws in P and elsewhere do not just protect the sanctuary from encroachment and sacrilege, they sustain the borders between categories of persons in society. To carry it further, encroachment prohibitions do not just protect potential encroachers and the community from God's wrath, they protect the group from the confusion of social boundaries and thereby from social dissolution.[46]

SANCTIFICATION AND DESANCTIFICATION

There were various ways in which something or someone or some place could be consecrated and thus made holy. The fairly elaborate process by which priests were sanctified or consecrated to the service of Yahweh has been described above. But there were other ways in which something could be brought into the sphere of holiness. This might happen formally and appropriately by such means as anointing with oil (Ex. 30:22–38; Lev. 8:10–12; 21:10), the slaughter and sacrifice of an animal (Lev. 8:14–17), or by simply offering it and setting it aside, as in the case of certain sacrifices

(Ex. 28:38; Lev. 22:2–3) or of the individual himself or herself, as in the case of the Nazirite. In this last case, however, certain ritual processes seem to have been connected with entering the holy state, for example, shaving the head (Numbers 6). Or sanctification might happen more informally, less ritually, and sometimes inadvertently, for example, by coming into contact with something or some area that was holy (Ex. 29:37; 30:29; Lev. 6:11, 20[18, 27]). In Ezekiel's program, the priests were not to take their vestments or the offerings into the outer court and "so communicate holiness to the people" (Ezek. 42:12; 44:19; 46:20).

A particular kind of consecration took place in the dedicating of something as *ḥērem,* that is, placing something under a ban or devoting it to the ban. In this process of consecration, valuables, animals, and people could be separated off and dedicated to the Lord so that others no longer had access to them. Such consecration was particularly associated with war and its booty. It is not clear how often the spoils of war were so consecrated, but there were clearly instances of its happening, and even the Deuteronomic ideological leveling through of the practice of *ḥērem* in the recounting of the early wars of conquest is a testimony to an understanding of sanctification as an act of dedication that probably originated in a vow to set apart the spoils of war—or something else valuable—exclusively to Yahweh's use or domain in return for Yahweh's beneficence and assistance (Num. 21:1–4). Whatever was so dedicated was either to be destroyed (e.g., Lev. 27:28–29; Num. 21:4; Josh. 6:17–18, 21) or given over to the holy sector, that is, to the priests and the sanctuary (Num. 18:14; Josh. 6:19, 24).

Something that had been consecrated could be removed from the holy sphere and thus desanctified by redeeming it (e.g., Leviticus 27). This could be by payment, as is indicated for several types of redemption in Leviticus 27, or by substitution of another item. The redemption of the firstborn Israelite is of particular interest, for in the Priestly system redemption was accomplished by the dedication of the Levites but also by the payment of a sum for those firstborn above the number of Levites (Num. 3:44–51; 18:15–16). The Nazirite moved back into the profane sphere by presentation of sacrifices and shaving "the consecrated head" (Num. 6:13–20). The transition back into the common sphere was marked by the drinking of wine (Num. 6:20).

CLEAN AND UNCLEAN: PURITY

While holiness and purity are distinctive categories and notions, they also interlock sufficiently in Israelite religion so that neither concept and its experiential regulation can be understood without attention to the other. As Wright has observed, "Impurity receives its dynamic definition in relation to the sacred; impurity is a threat to the holy and contacts between these two spheres bring grave punishments and effects."[47]

Much of the priestly structure of legislation is aimed toward the protection of holiness, which means its protection from impurity and the dangers to the sphere of the sacred that the encounter with impurity involves. Thus, while holiness had its *opposite* in the common or the profane (*ḥōl*), it encountered its *opposition* in the presence of impurity (*ṭāmē'*).

That does not mean that no distinction between pure and impure or between clean and unclean operated apart from the sacral sphere. But any impurity became a problem when it came in contact with the sancta—the sanctuary, personnel, and things belonging to the realm of the holy. That is why an impure people or an impure land could not be joined with a holy God.

Recent study of the laws having to do with cleanliness or purity has suggested that there were two broad categories of these: impurities that were tolerated, regulated, and not dangerous, and impurities that were prohibited and dangerous because they either represented wrongdoing of some sort or they polluted the sancta.[48] Regulation of these impurities was established also, involving ways of moving from an unclean state to a clean state, of overcoming the threat of impurity to the sacral sphere, and of cutting out or eliminating the threat, that is, eliminating the one who had brought about the pollution.

The tolerated category had its own gradation and could be divided into minor impurities or defilements and major ones.[49] Minor impurities, exemplified, for example, in a variety of pollutions that came from some kind of contact with a polluting agent (such as an animal carcass [Lev. 11:24, 27]) or a person with a major pollution (such as a person with a bodily discharge), were not contagious, and the restoration to a pure state customarily took a day. Further gradation is indicated for these minor or tolerated impurities by the fact that some required a more extended purifying process of bathing or washing. Thus, the *touching* of an animal carcass only required the passage of time until evening, when the individual returned to a state of purity (Lev. 11:24, 27, 39). It is not altogether clear whether one may infer bathing as a part of the process. That may be inferred because it was clearly expected in many of the other minor pollutions, such as those having to do with bodily discharges (Ezekiel 15).[50] *Carrying* an animal carcass or *eating* some of it, however, required not only the passage of time until evening but also washing the clothes of anyone who carried or ate the animal (Lev. 11:25, 28, 40), and in Lev. 17:15, there is the explicit requirement of bathing as well as washing the clothes for the one who eats a carcass.

The major pollutions, however, were contagious, so that contact with a person who was impure from a bodily discharge could pollute the one who made contact. These pollutions, which included such things as contact with a human corpse, skin disease, and bodily emissions from the genitalia, took longer to return to a state of purity, normally seven days. The purification process tended to happen by way of sacrifice rather than washing, especially the *ḥaṭṭā't* sacrifice, the purpose of which was the purification of the sanctuary and the other sancta against the danger of pollution by contagion.[51]

It was at this point that the major defilements became not only contagious but dangerous. In itself, their contagion generally was not dangerous to the one who "contracted" the impurity. It required isolation for a period of time and removal from contact with the holy, but such impurities, while significant enough to require an extended time for the return to purity, did not pose any threat of harm to the one who was so polluted. If, however, such pollution spread to the realm of the sancta, then the impure one was in real danger (Lev. 7:20–21; 22:3–9) because the sphere of the holy, which was Yahweh's domain, was in danger. Thus, the Priestly description of the regulations for Israelites encamped in the wilderness required expulsion from the camp of persons with the skin disease *ṣāra'at,* or having a bodily discharge from the genitals, or having been in contact with a corpse because "they must not defile their camp, where I dwell (*šōkēn*) among them" (Num. 5:3). The conjoining of the impure and the holy was explosive and dangerous to the one responsible and to the whole community, which might suffer the effects of such violation of the sacral sphere.

The prohibited impurities were dangerous by definition, threatening the welfare of the impure person and by extension the whole community because they threatened the holiness of the community in its parts, that is, the sancta, and as a holy people.[52] Such pollution, when it occurred, whether intentionally or unintentionally, because it was a violation of a prohibition, effected guilt on the polluted one and polluted the sanctuary. But there is a difference in the further effects of the pollution, depending upon whether or not it was inadvertent. Wright has laid out these differences succinctly as follows:

> The general features of unintentional prohibited impurities are, then, the pollution of the sanctuary (outer altar or shrine) and the consequent requirement of sacrifices (always a *ḥaṭṭā't*) except in the case of some sins that have been repented of (which require an *'āšām*). Since a sin

has been committed, there is the potential for divine punishment (*kārēt*). But inadvertency—which implies a repentant spirit—defers such a penalty, and allows reparation. When inadvertent sins involve bodily pollution arising from tolerated impurities, corresponding purification and restriction requirements are to be followed. With intentional prohibited impurities pollution increases and the evil-doer's life is forfeit. Not just the outer altar or the shrine is polluted, but the heart of the sanctuary as well, the most sacred room. Purification comes through the sacrifices of the Day of Atonement.[53]

The seriousness of this concern for purity and the danger of polluting the holy is well demonstrated by the penalty that was to be enacted against those who polluted by violating the prohibitions and engaging in wrongdoing, disobeying the commands of Yahweh. Two technical expressions indicate the extreme character of the penalty: "he shall bear his punishment" (*nāśā' 'et 'awōnô*) and "he [she, they] shall be cut off" (*nikrat*). Both of these imply divine punishment.[54] The former is a more general indication that the one who has violated the prohibitions protecting the purity and the sanctity of the community and the sanctuary is subject to punishment. The term *kārēt*, however, indicates not only that the punishment is from God but that the individual shall be cut off from "his people" (Lev. 7:20, 21, etc.) or "Israel" (Num. 19:13) or "the assembly" (Num. 19:20). Specifically what such "cutting off" meant has been a subject of debate. It has been suggested that it once referred to expulsion from the community, from one's kin, but a more likely interpretation is that it had to do with cutting off one's life or one's line. That is, *kārēt* may have involved either premature death by the intervention of God or the loss of one's progeny, cutting off the lineage. A further possibility is that the one guilty of violating the sacred was understood to be cut off from his or her ancestors in the afterlife. The fact that in two cases, the worship of Molech (Lev. 20:2–3) and the violation of the Sabbath (Ex. 31:14), there seems to be a requirement for both judicial execution and *kārēt* suggests that the latter was not simply capital punishment.[55]

While *kārēt* was to be applied in quite a number of different offenses, the great majority of them clearly had to do directly or indirectly with matters of purity and the protection of the sacred.[56] Thus, violations of the rules that kept the sacred times in order could invoke the *kārēt* penalty: eating leavened bread during the festival of Unleavened Bread (Ex. 12:15–19), working on the Sabbath (Ex. 31:14), and working and not fasting on the Day of Atonement (Lev. 23:29–30). Failure to be cleansed after contact with a corpse resulted in *kārēt* (Num. 19:13, 20). The holiness of the sanctuary was protected by making the eating of the fat of a sacrificial animal or blood a sin punishable by *kārēt* (Lev. 7:25–27). The use of the anointing oil for ordinary purposes or the sacred incense for personal perfume was also punishable by *kārēt* (Ex. 30:22–38). And while there is not always specific reference to *kārēt* in the extant texts, there were other pollutions that stood under the pain of death, for example, the failure of the priests to wash their hands when they entered the tent of meeting to minister (Ex. 30:20–21).

It would be a mistake to assume that specifically cultic matters or things related to the cult and to sanctuary ritual were the only or even primary modes of dangerous pollution.[57] The sins of the people generally could pollute the community, the temple, and the land (Ps. 106:39; Ezek. 14:11; 20:43). Thus, idolatry (Jer. 7:30), adultery (Num. 5:11–31), improper sexual acts (Leviticus 18), rape (Gen. 34:5, 13, 27), and necromancy (Lev. 19:31) were understood to pollute the community and the land (Jer. 3:1–9). The prophets described Israel or the land as defiled because of the sins of the people—religious and social—but particularly because of idolatry, sexual sins, and profaning the Sabbath (Jer. 2:7; Ezek. 14:11; 20:43; 36:17; Hos. 5:3; 6:10; Micah 2:10; Hag. 2:13–14). Images of pollution became ways of speaking of the condition of the people: the impure woman (Jer. 2:23; Ezek. 36:17; Lam. 1:9; possibly 4:14) and the person with skin disease (Lam. 4:15; cf. Lev. 13:45). The paradigm of purity and pollution was so significant to Israel's religion that its whole history on the land could be understood in terms of that paradigm—from the wilderness days (Ezekiel 20), to the taking of the land by virtue of the Lord casting out the inhabitants because their practices defiled it (Ezekiel 18), to the pollution of the land by the sins of the people leading to their loss of the land. Tikva Frymer-Kensky concludes, "In the face of such pollution, the temple and its cult could not be enough to save Israel, and thus necessitated the land being destroyed and the people sent into exile. The Exile is thus seen as a necessary result of the pollution of Israel."[58]

A particular feature of the purity spectrum in Israel's religion was the system of dietary laws and the distinction between clean and unclean animals, the subject of much discussion in the contemporary analysis of the holiness rules operative in Israel's religion, particularly rising out of the groundbreaking work of Mary Douglas.[59]

These dietary regulations are found primarily in Leviticus 11 and Deuteronomy 14, though there are scattered examples elsewhere.[60] They prohibited the eating of certain quadrupeds (camel, hare, rock badger, and pig), water animals that do not have fins and scales, certain birds (e.g., eagle, vulture, osprey) and winged insects.[61] In addition, these regulations identified an animal that dies of itself as unclean and forbade the eating of such a carcass (so Deut. 14:21; cf. below) or required washing and the passing of a day to rectify the impurity acquired in the act of eating (Lev. 11:40). Finally, Deut. 14:21b joins with Ex. 23:19 in the much-discussed but still enigmatic prohibition of boiling a kid in its mother's milk.

While it is possible to suggest reasons not identified in the texts for the resistance to eating some or all of the animals identified in the catalogs of dietary laws, some of which may have involved a quite specific social purpose (see below), the rationale that is given in virtually all of the texts is specifically the maintenance of the people's holiness. The limits on food that could be eaten was a manifestation of Israel's separation to the Lord. As Milgrom has put it, "The diet laws which limit Israel's edible flesh to only a few of the animals permitted to other peoples constitutes an experiential mnemonic, confronted daily at the dining table, that Israel must separate itself from the nations."[62] Following this line of thought, Wright has made a cogent case for regarding the dietary laws as having a place in the system of sanctification in Israelite religion. But it was more symbolic. Existing in some form prior to and independent of the full formulation of Priestly legislation—an earlier history perhaps reflected in Ex. 22:30; Deut. 14:3–14; and Lev. 11:2b–23 as an early stage of Priestly formulation—the prohibitions against eating certain animals served to give symbolic character to the diet of the Israelites, which underscored and expressed their holiness, that is, their separateness and singularity among the nations.

The determination of which animals were clean and edible and which were not is probably best understood as a combination of preexisting custom with regard to some animals, possibly the pig, for example, and the application of developed criteria in the case of others.[63] There may have been various reasons for aversion to some animals. Wright suggests as possibilities hygiene, simple dislike or aversion (as, for example, modern aversion to brains and entrails), economic detriment (some animals competing for the same food as humans, for example, the pig), or nationalism (not eating something because a neighboring people eat it). He adds:

> Though, in my view, the criteria had a foundation in traditional aversions, they reoriented these traditional taboos and consequently included new animals among those considered abominations. The change from the traditional approach of designating particular animals as impure, to using criteria served to abstract and unify the perceptions about abominable animals. This abstraction, unification, or systematization of determination of such animals was accompanied by a new

unified rationale for avoiding such animals (as Milgrom says): so that
Israel might be a holy people.[64]

The conclusion of the Deuteronomic catalog of forbidden animals is
worth noting in this regard. It forbids the eating of anything that dies of
itself but allows the Israelites to give it to a resident alien or to sell it to a
foreigner (Deut. 14:21). There was nothing wrong with the meat, no inherent aversion to it or some hygienic reason for not eating it. The reason the
Israelite did not eat it is expressly stated in Deuteronomy at the conclusion
of the verse: "For you are a people holy to the LORD your God." The final
verses of Leviticus 11, probably a late stage of the text, also conclude that
catalog by an extended grounding of the dietary laws in the holiness of the
Lord and the consequent necessity for Israel to be holy (Lev. 11:43–45).
Furthermore, the somewhat earlier piece of dietary legislation in the Book
of the Covenant prohibiting the eating of any meat that had been "mangled
by beasts in the field" is grounded in the prior claim, "You shall be a people holy to me, therefore . . ." (Ex. 22:30[31]).

VARIATIONS IN THE IDEOLOGY OF HOLINESS

While the above discussion has indicated the depth of concern over holiness and purity and some of the conceptual and practical complexity as the
community attended to that concern, it is appropriate to identify a little
more clearly some of the differences in the understanding of holiness that
may be identified in the literary remains of Israel's religion. Some of these
differences reflect changing developments in that religion, but they also
apparently existed in some tension with each other over long periods of
time. There will be no effort here, therefore, to place these differences in
some precise chronological order. That involves achieving a level of certainty about dating the strata of the Pentateuch that is very difficult to do
in the light of our present state of knowledge.

Priestly Writings

The concern for the maintenance of holiness and purity was a first order of
business for those circles that came to dominance in the exilic and postexilic periods and worked to shape the community of Israel into a theocratic
and sacral community. At the same time, it must be recognized that many
of the fundamental notions expressed in the Priestly writings, both in
regard to specifics and general conceptions, had antecedents. A starting
point for articulating some of the particularities and differences in Israel's

understanding of the realm of the sacred may be found in looking at the Holiness Code, itself a document out of priestly circles, in relation to other Priestly literature.[65]

The most obvious difference was the close tie between holiness and the sanctuary in the Priestly conceptuality generally, whereas the Holiness Code understood holiness as a characteristic of the land as a whole. Holiness in the Priestly order of things was found in the sanctuary and the sancta associated with it. That is, various persons and things were holy in relation to the sanctuary and the cultic rituals of purification that took place in the sanctuary or under the direction of the holy persons, the priests. The common or profane was the customary state for people and things generally until some particular step was taken that brought a person or a thing into the realm and category of the holy, a state that was often temporary. Within the ideology of the Holiness Code, however, the land and the people existed in a state of holiness and were always under obligation to demonstrate that holiness, to achieve or maintain it by the whole realm of human conduct, moral and social as well as ritual. Holiness, therefore, did not involve simply being set apart for participation or use in the cultic sphere, though that clearly happened also in the Holiness Code conceptuality. But sacrality was understood to permeate the people and the land and had to do with the totality of life. Thus, the Priestly source restricted holiness of persons to the priests and the Nazirites, while the Holiness Code, though recognizing and protecting the holiness of the priests in its regulations, expanded the holiness of persons to include the whole community, even as it expanded the sphere of holiness from the sanctuary to the land.

The expansion of the realm of the holy in the Holiness Code to include the people and the land in distinction from the Priestly restriction of that realm to the sanctuary and the priesthood carried even further. Whereas holiness in the Priestly conceptuality was essentially tied to the cultic realm, in the Holiness Code the sphere of holiness included the moral as well as the cultic. Thus, members of the community aspired to a holiness like that of Yahweh in all aspects of their life. Matters having to do with sexual morality, prohibition of idols, proper treatment of parents, and social justice, joined with proper sacrificial procedure, avoidance of unclean things and animals, and participation in the appointed festivals to characterize the holiness of the people.[66]

The difference between the Priestly conception of holiness and that of the Holiness Code has been described as a distinction between static and dynamic, respectively.[67] The same distinction could be described in terms of ascription of holiness and achievement of holiness.[68] In the Priestly understanding, holiness belonged to the sanctuary and the priests. For the Holiness Code, holiness was that which the community constantly worked at by its conduct in all spheres of life: "Sanctification is an ongoing process for priests (21:8, 15, 23; 22:9, 16) as well as for all Israelites (21:8; 22:32)."[69]

With regard to pollution, matters were similar. Milgrom has summarized the differences as follows:

> P [Priestly source] holds that the sanctuary is polluted by Israel's moral and ritual violations (42) committed anywhere in the camp (but not outside) and that this pollution can and must be effaced by the violator's purification offering and, if committed deliberately, by the high priest's sacrifice and confession (16:3–22). H [Holiness Code], however, concentrates on the polluting force of Israel's violation of the covenant (26:15), for example, incest (18; 20:11–24), idolatry (20:1–6), or depriving the land of its sabbatical rest (26:34–35). Pollution for H is nonritualistic, as shown by the metaphoric use of *ṭāmē'* (e.g., 18:21, 24; 19:31) and by the fact that the polluted land cannot be expiated by ritual, and hence, the expulsion of its inhabitants is inevitable (18:24–29; 20:2).[70]

It is difficult to locate these differing understandings of holiness with certainty in social and historical settings. Views on the order and dating of both the Priestly source and the Holiness Code vary considerably. Certainly, the Priestly orientation seems to reflect a community that was dominated by a priestly leadership exercising significant control over the community as it sought to live and act before a holy God. There may have been various points in Israel's life when that was the case, from the late preexilic period to the late postexilic time. Clearly, the Priestly structure of holiness was a form of the official state religion, whether before or after the exile. Walter Houston has aptly sketched the hypothetical circumstances in which the Priestly and Holiness Codes could have come to dominance:

> But there will be no surprise that men in such a social position, officials and leaders in the most conservative of all social institutions, at a time when the traditional social structure was coming under tremendous pressure, or, still more, at a time when it had to be constructed anew out of the ruins of occupation and deportation should seek to mark out an area within society where role and action could still be governed by position and by traditional expectation, so old symbols could still retain their meaning, and pollution could be understood as something objective. . . . Others at the same historical turning point, their own roles governed far more by personal achievement and moral choice, saw salvation in attempting a very different kind of social planning.[71]

One can recognize in the Holiness Code's expansion of the sacral to the realm of the moral and the social a consistency with prophetic assertions about holiness. As Israel Knohl has pointed out, this is particularly the case with regard to the prophecy of Isaiah, where the holiness of God is the ground for an understanding of Israel's holiness demonstrated or manifest in its justice and righteousness, its treatment of widow, orphan, and poor (e.g., Isa. 1:4; 5:16, 23–24), though a number of prophets assert the holiness of Israel's deity as central to the character of the deity.[72] Knohl sees a distinction between the Isaianic understanding of how holiness is to be demonstrated and that of the Holiness Code at the point of Isaiah's rejection of the sacrificial apparatus and the Sabbath and festivals. While that is indeed the case, this may have been a matter of weight and emphasis. The Holiness Code, with its prescriptive and ideological character, set forth the joining of the cultic and the moral. Isaiah preached in a context where only one of these spheres was perceived to be a matter of holiness—whether ideologically or only in practice—and his preaching was a corrective away from the emphasis reflected in the Priestly literature and toward the Holiness Code's insistence on the moral sphere as the locus of holy living.

Deuteronomy

It has become customary to think of Deuteronomy as representing a "secularizing" tendency when compared with other legal and ritual texts in the Pentateuch. An early expression of this notion is to be found in Gerhard von Rad's argument that the ark was "demythologized" in Deuteronomy, moving from being treated as a sacral object because it was the dwelling place of Yahweh to being simply a box that contained the tablets of the Decalogue. Moshe Weinfeld has argued extensively that a process of demythologization and secularization was carried through in the book of Deuteronomy.[73] To the extent that sacrality is understood to be centered in the sanctuary and the ritual of sacrifice, one could argue such a case.

But there are significant problems with this "secular" reading of Deuteronomy. Even for von Rad's interpretation of the ark of the covenant, it will not work. While one seems to be far away from the picture of the powerful holiness of the ark that is described in 1 Samuel 4:1–7:1 and 2 Samuel 6, with its narrative of the destruction of individuals who look into or touch the ark of God (see above), that is not as much the case as it seems. In Deuteronomy, the ark is the receptacle for the tablets of the law, but Deuteronomy also so identifies the law with the promulgator of it, that is, with Yahweh, that the law is virtually a surrogate for Yahweh. The presence of the ark and the inscribed law within it is in some sense the presence of Yahweh with the people. The ark was still understood to be the place of the presence of Yahweh and so still sacral even if that point is not made explicit.[74]

More recently, Norbert Lohfink has argued for a more nuanced accounting of the Deuteronomic data, one that suggests Deuteronomy envisioned a different kind of sacrality than the sacrifice-oriented understanding of the Priestly circles.[75] Rather than perceiving holiness as centered primarily in a sanctuary and cultic personnel responsible for a sacrificial ritual that maintained the sacredness of the community, Deuteronomy centered holiness— in this respect not unlike the Holiness Code—in the land and its people. The critical texts are found in Deut. 7:6; 14:2, 21; and 26:19. In all three, the declaration is made that Israel is a "holy people to the LORD your God." The repetition of this claim makes it difficult to argue for a "secular" mentality in the Deuteronomic ideology. The point is made at three quite different and significant places. The first is the demand for the ban or destruction of the "seven nations" because of the danger that they will turn the Israelites away from the exclusive worship of Yahweh (Deut. 7:1–6). Thus, the holiness of Israel was the ground to guard against apostasy. The second instance prefaces and concludes regulations that come more into the cultic sphere: laceration and tonsure for the dead and the dietary regulations of Deuteronomy. Here holiness is specifically set in relation to categories of cleanliness and pollution, as it is in the Priestly tradition, but obedience to these regulations is because of the existing sacral character of the community. The bracketing of these regulations by explicit reference to the holiness of the community does serve to weight them significantly on the scales of what manifested holiness in Israel. Finally, in Deut. 26:19, holiness is directly tied to the whole covenantal relationship, both its ground and its outcome.

What is clear from these texts is that the holy-profane distinction was not between priest/sanctuary and people but between Israel and the nations. That is obviously the case in Deut. 7:6. But also in Deut. 26:18–19, the line that is parallel to the clause "for you to be a people holy to the LORD your God" is "for him to set you high above all nations." Furthermore, in both texts, as well as in 14:2, Israel is called Yahweh's "treasured possession." In 7:6 and 14:2, the further point is made that "the LORD your God has chosen you *out of all the peoples on the earth* to be his people, his treasured possession." The specific holiness regulations that follow in chapter 14 relative to clean and unclean animals were regulatory for *all* the people. There is no particular reference to priests and a special sphere of holiness that they inhabited. Purity and holiness were features of Israel's existence that distinguished it from all other peoples, not a line of demarcation within Israel.[76] As noted earlier, one of the specific signs of this identification of all Israel as the sphere of the holy, those who were "before the Lord" and separated out from all the rest of the nations, is the fact that in the Deuteronomic dietary laws, framed by the declarations of Israel's holiness (14:2, 21), food that might not be eaten by Israelites could be given to a *gēr*, a resident alien, or sold to a *nokrî*, a foreigner. This allowance is immediately followed by the reminder: "For you are a people holy to the LORD your God" (14:21).

At this point, there is a congruence within various traditions. Both Deuteronomy and the Holiness Code laid weight upon the people as a whole as the holy or sacral sphere.[77] The line between common and holy was that between Israel and all else. Being set apart was fundamentally the act of Yahweh to set apart a people to himself. The Holiness Code recognized within Israel the line between priest and layperson, but the fundamental distinction was between Israel and other peoples.[78] This perspective is found within the Book of the Covenant also (Ex. 22:30[31]), specifically in regard to dietary restriction.[79]

It is difficult to tell when this understanding of the sphere of the holy as the congregation or assembly of Israel came to dominate Israelite religion. Some of these texts may well be dependent upon others.[80] But it is fundamental to understanding Israel's religion that, while there is an interpretive tendency to identify Israel's understanding of holiness with the Priestly tradition's formulations and ritual, there was a dominant strain within that religion that placed the focus upon the people as a whole and understood holiness to be broadly applicable both in the sense of who was holy and also in the sense of what was required to manifest that holiness. This understanding continued to influence the life of Israel in the later postexilic period as the community under Ezra and Nehemiah saw the boundary line between holy and profane, pure and impure, as, once again, the distinction between the community of Israel, the returned exiles, and the peoples of the lands, that is, the nations. The conflict between the community of returned exiles and the peoples around them was an appropriate setting for the application of this understanding of holiness, but it would be a mistake to assume that the issue of Israel's relation to other peoples only came to the fore at that time. Indeed, the books of Ezra and Nehemiah indicate that the heavy focus on the difference between Israel and the peoples and the subsequent actions designed to keep that distinction a sharp one by complete separation of the community from the surrounding peoples— such as sending away the foreign wives—was specifically due to the reading of the ancient law (Neh. 13:1–3, 23–27), with Deuteronomy being explicitly quoted (Deut. 23:3–6; 7:3). That is, the separation from other nations was understood as a return to a longstanding religious tradition and its correlative practices.

These various traditions cohere, therefore, in presenting one self-acknowledged rationale for the various laws that guard purity and holiness. They were there to mark the distinction between Israel and the other peoples. Other functions might be present and other distinctions operative, but this is the one that is made explicit and wide ranging in the religious traditions of Israel. Such weight upon the entire community as holy stood in some tension with the specific Priestly focus on sanctuary and priests. But these other ideologies did not preclude more specific recognition of holy things, places, persons, and acts within the broader framework of an understanding of the people as holy. That broader framework allowed for a more comprehensive understanding of the holy without negating very concrete encounters with the holy and the development of guidelines within cultic, personal and familial, and social spheres of life for the achievement and manifestation of holiness and purity. The tension between holiness ascribed and holiness achieved and between ritual and moral definitions of holiness was a perduring one that continued to be present in those religious traditions and practices that developed in different ways from the religion of ancient Israel.[81]

CHAPTER 5

Leadership and Participation in Israelite Religion

RELIGIOUS LEADERSHIP IN ANCIENT ISRAEL

In any religious system, significant power and control are vested in the religious leadership. The leaders serve in no small way to define the religious practice of the community, whether in conformity to other dimensions of the system or in distortion of them. They provide varied forms of mediation between deity and people. They may be bearers of the continuities of religious practice in some instances—for example, priests—or they may be disruptive elements, breaking with the customary conventions, ideologies, and practices, as, for example, in some Israelite prophecy. An examination of their roles in ancient Israel is a necessary part of describing the religion of that community, especially with regard to its social functions.

THE PRIEST

Throughout Israel's history, the priest and the priestly community exercised a fundamental role in maintaining the order of life in the community and stood at the center of religious practice, whether carried out in a family setting or at local or state levels. Thus, one of the narratives of premonarchical Israel recounting priestly activity deals with the activities of a priest exclusively in relation to a house shrine and in direct relationship to the household rather than to any wider religious community (Judges 17–18). The priest is described as "his priest," referring to the head of the household. On the other hand, Samuel is depicted as carrying out priestly responsibilities, specifically sacrifice, at what seems to be a local shrine at Ramathaim (1 Sam. 9:11–14). The presence of priests presiding over the national shrine and over the religious activities of the state is evident at a number of places in the history of Israel's religion.[1]

At all levels, priestly responsibility for ritual purity and proper order served to keep the community from the threats of impurity and disorder (see chapter 4). The anointing of the priest, and particularly the high priest, served to "sanctify" him "by removing him from the realm of the profane and empowering him to operate in the realm of the sacred, namely to handle the sancta."[2] The priestly instruction and setting forth the norms for community life, individually and corporately, insured that the community would not fall apart by failure to keep the stipulations of the covenantal agreement between Yahweh and Israel and thus damage relations between people and deity and among members of the community. By the authority invested in them, the divine word could be spoken and the divine service properly carried out. Priestly authority and function were, by definition, set to maintain the order of the larger community and, where pertinent, smaller segments of that community.[3] The mediation of the relation between people and deity lay heavily in their hands so that the priesthood bore a major responsibility for maintenance of that relationship—and thus of the social order—by the way in which they carried out their duties.

Various narratives attest to the role that priests played or could play in maintaining the social order through their role as guardians of the temple and the cultic affairs of the community (plate 8). Thus Amaziah, chief priest at the national shrine at Bethel during the eighth century, sought to remove Amos from prophesying in the Northern Kingdom because of the social and political unrest it could provoke—and possibly was in fact doing, though we have no record of that (Amos 7:10–17). His couching of Amos's prophecy as a conspiracy against the king and the national sanctuary, called by the priest "house of the kingdom" and not "house of Yahweh," was a reflection of his role in maintaining political and social order.

In a text from a later time, a prophet in exile, Shemaiah, addresses a priest in Jerusalem, Zephaniah, calling for him to rebuke Jeremiah for prophesying a long exile. The grounds for the prophet's address to the priest is that the Lord has appointed Zephaniah priest, "so that there may be officers in the house of the LORD *to control any madman who plays the prophet, to put him in the stocks and the collar*" (Jer. 29:26). The claim is that the priestly office has responsibility for oversight of those matters where the religious and the political collide. The line of authority is suggested by the sequence *Yahweh* (appointer of the) *priest* (who can regulate, even imprison the) *prophet*. Potential and real conflict arose out of the conflicting claims of the priest (under legitimate divine aegis) to oversee and overrule the prophet, who may have stood outside the structures of priestly authority but bore legitimate credentials of his own as the bearer of the word of the Lord.

Breakdown in the relationship between deity and people and thus in the

Plate 8. Partially marred inscription on an ivory pomegranate, apparently reading "For the house of the Lord, holy [to] the priests." (*Collection of the Israel Antiquities Authority*)

order and life of the community inevitably found the priesthood culpable in some fashion (1 Sam. 2:12–36; 3:4–17; Amos 7:10–17; Jer. 1:18; 2:8, 24; 4:9; 5:31; etc.). The significant amount of criticism against the priests that is found in the biblical literature is a direct reflection of a history in which breakdown was a major dimension. The equally significant amount of priestly literature, that is, of rules and regulations that had to do with the functions of the priests, is an indication of how critical their responsibilities were in the religious life of ancient Israel. The line between responsibility for the religious life and responsibility for the sociopolitical life of the community, a line so very fuzzy in the work of the prophets, was also considerably blurred for the priests, particularly in light of the fact that the sociopolitical order and stability were understood to be intimately tied to the community's relationship with the deity.

Priestly Responsibilities

In what is probably a fairly archaic text, the blessing of Moses in Deuteronomy 33, the blessing given to the tribe of Levi in effect sets forth a job description for the priests in ancient Israel (Deut. 33:8–11). Three kinds of responsibilities are assigned to the priestly community in this blessing: divination, instruction, and sacrifice. These did not exhaust their duties, but they were at the heart of them.[4] In other ways, they mediated the relationship between deity and people, for example, in the invoking of the blessing of Yahweh on the people (Num. 6:22–27 (see plate 9); cf. Deut. 21:5; 1 Chron. 23:12)[5] or in the giving of an oracle of salvation in response to the lament or prayer of an individual or the people, but these activities are in various ways offshoots or dimensions of the three duties mentioned in Deut. 33:8–10 that lay at the heart of the priestly leadership of the community.

Divination. As indicated in Deuteronomy 33:8, priestly divination took place essentially through the form of designated lots or the "casting" of the Urim and Thummim, devices on analogy with dice that seemed to function in binary fashion, that is, giving a yes or no answer to a critical question or issue, though it is possible that more complex responses were given by the different forms of lot.[6] Priestly texts depict these divinatory devices as part of the priestly paraphernalia (Ex. 28:30; Lev. 8:8), along with the ephod, worn by the priest, whose character is quite obscure but whose function seems to have included divinatory activity (e.g., 1 Sam. 30:8; cf. Judg. 18:5, 14).[7] Priestly leadership in divinatory activity is suggested by several texts.[8] When David seeks the answer to questions having to do with the outcome of an expected conflict with Saul at Keilah, it is the priest Abiathar who brings the ephod forward (1 Sam. 23:6–12). There is no indication of how

Plate 9. Silver plaque from Ketef Hinnom with quotation of the priestly benediction from Num. 6:24–26 (seventh century). (*Collection of the Israel Antiquities Authority*)

the priest dealt with the ephod, but its divinatory function in this text is clear. The involvement of a priest in divination via the Urim and Thummim is best indicated by 1 Sam. 14:23–46.[9] This episode, having to do with Jonathan's violation of his father Saul's sacred oath and the consequences of that act, has been discussed in some detail by Huffmon.[10] As he notes, the priest uses divination to uncover the violation of an oath for the king and to identify the culprit, that is, Jonathan. The question to be answered is a binary one, and the response Saul seeks—"give Urim" for one answer and "give Thummim" for the other answer—suggests something of the way the Urim and Thummim would have functioned to answer the question.

It is important to recognize several features of this particular incident. One is that it arises out of the need to make a decision and to discern what will happen as a basis for making the decision. In fact, the priest's call for consultation is in order to manipulate the process so that the king will discover—in this case by the failure of the process since no answer is given— what the rest of the group knows, to wit, that Jonathan has violated the oath. The second stage of the divination process leads to the discovery of the violation. Huffmon notes in conclusion:

> In this procedure the outcome of the divination had to be Jonathan, as perhaps everyone but Saul knew. It is publicly seen as a discovery or uncovering of the truth by resort to divinely directed divination, but actually the outcome was controlled by the priest, responding to public opinion.[11]

In both this instance and the account of the procedure to determine who violated the ban at Jericho (Joshua 7)—presumably by casting lots—a strain in the societal situation is handled and necessary courses of action are sanctioned by depersonalizing and objectifying the decision, even if the community, and the individuals involved, were already aware of the necessary or appropriate outcome. The divination thus "constitutes a technique for establishing an effective consensus upon a rather particular project."[12]

Later tradition assigned a continuing consultative activity via the Urim to the priest Eleazar, who stood beside the political leader, Joshua, and inquired of the Lord via the Urim *in the sanctuary* (Num. 27:21), a spatial restriction of priestly divinatory activity that is not surprising in the tradition but seems not to have been so restrictive at an earlier time (but cf. Judg. 20:27–28) The choice of a scapegoat in the Day of Atonement ritual, which probably comes from a later time than may be presupposed by the texts above, shows the priest casting lots to determine the divine decision to designate which goat shall be for the Lord and which for Azazel (Lev. 16:8).

In summary, priestly divination may be said to have involved the determination of an answer to a question that involved either discovery, decision, or the discernment of the future on the basis of which decision could be made. The process seems to have been by way of technical manipulation, involving "a pre-arranged code, using written lots or designating Urim and Thummim for binary questions."[13] Divination thus served to give proper answers without there seeming to be a bias or individual control. In Parks's summary formulation:

[D]ivinatory procedure has the effect of stamping with a mark of special legitimacy a particular decision or a particular kind of response to crisis. Paradoxically, divination appears to have a derandomizing function; establishing consensus, it renders action more predictable and regular.[14]

The involvement of the priest was critical precisely at the point of giving divine reassurance and divine legitimation to the actions taken. It insured the maintenance of the safety and order of the community by "the integration of anomalous, dangerous ventures into the traditional religious schema."[15]

The inquiry of the priest via lots or Urim and Thummim points to a broader phenomenon of inquiry already identified above, the oracle of salvation that came in response to a prayer to the deity. While there is not a lot of direct evidence connecting the priest to such words, some texts clearly suggest that (e.g., 1 Sam. 1:17; 2 Chron. 20:13–17; Joel 2:17–22[16]). The response of the priest Eli to the prayer of Hannah in 1 Sam. 1:17 suggests a priestly function of mediating the divine response to a prayer for help. Eli's words to her—Go in peace and the God of Israel will grant your request (1 Sam. 1:17)—are not simply a pat on the back to a person in distress. This is a formal response assuring the one praying that God will respond to the prayer in some form of help. There are a number of such oracles, most of which center around the divine assurance, "Do not fear," and the grounds on which that assurance can be based. Most of them do not identify the mediator of the divine word, but it is likely that such words were communicated by a priest, though it is possible that a prophet or some member of the community delivered them to the petitioner in a formal process of lament and response.[17]

Teaching. A further responsibility of the priests according to the blessing of Levi in Deut. 33:10 was the teaching of *tôrâ,* that is, of the ordinances and the law. This may well have grown out of more divinatory practices,[18] inquiry of the priest bringing a decision via lots or Urim and Thummim as described above but also instruction about ritual or cultic matters, what was permissible and what was not—matters of purity and holiness, for example. Some see such instruction as a later dimension of the priestly office,[19] but the prophets make it clear that it was a well-known and fully assumed responsibility of the priests during the whole prophetic period and so probably much earlier. Micah, Jeremiah, Ezekiel, and Malachi all characterize the priests specifically as the source of *tôrâ* or instruction and in some cases distinguish this function from the prophet's responsibility for word or vision and the elders for wise counsel:

> They shall keep seeking a vision from the prophet;
> instruction shall perish from the priest,
> and counsel from the elders.
> (Ezek. 7:26; cf. Jer. 18:18; Micah 3:11; Mal. 2:7a)[20]

Two texts from the early postexilic period provide examples of what such instruction by the priest may have been like and show its similarity to oracular inquiry. In Zech. 7:1–8, the people of Bethel send representatives to the priests at the temple (and to the prophets) to ask a question about cultic practice: "Should I mourn and practice abstinence in the fifth month, as I have done for so many years?" (v. 3). The answer comes in this instance as a divine word through the prophet Zechariah to both priests and people. The substance of the inquiry is about proper cultic behavior. The means for determining that is through an oracle from the priests. Similarly, Haggai portrays the inquiry of the priests for decision and direction on cultic practice:

> Ask the priests for a ruling [tôrâ]: If one carries consecrated meat in the fold of one's garment, and with the fold touches bread, or stew, or wine, or oil, or any kind of food, does it become holy? The priests answered, "No." Then Haggai said, "If one who is unclean by contact with a dead body touches any of these, does it become unclean?" The priests answered, "Yes, it becomes unclean." (Hag. 2:11–13)

In both instances, the instruction of the priests is about ritual practice. A number of times in priestly ritual instruction in Leviticus, one encounters the introductory word: "This is the tôrâ, the ritual/instruction for the burnt offering . . ." (Lev. 6:2[8], 7[14], 18[25]; 7:1, 7, 11; cf. 11:46; 12:7; 13:59; 14:54–57). The various "instructions" given in these instances have to do with types of sacrifice, distinctions between clean and unclean animals, a woman's uncleanness, and skin diseases. One may assume, in light of the various commonalities between the prophetic and legal texts, that such instruction was regularly a responsibility of the priests and a means for ordering and preserving the cultic apparatus, insuring conformity of the members of the community to the rules and regulations of the cultus and avoiding impurity and pollution, improper sacrifice or Sabbath observance, and in general the violation of ritual taboos that might endanger the community.[21] This is confirmed by both Ezekiel (44:23; cf. 22:26) and the Priestly legislation (Lev. 10:10), which identify teaching the people the distinction between holy and common, clean and unclean, as a fundamental responsibility of the priests (cf. Deut. 24:8).[22]

One must not assume, however, that priestly instruction was confined to purely cultic matters, although the weight of specific evidence focuses on such matters. Hosea's critique of the priests for lack of knowledge and for forgetting the *tôrâ* of God (4:6; cf. Jer. 2:8), when placed alongside the specific indictment of the people for violation of the commandments in that same chapter, suggests that the priests were responsible for proper instruction in all dimensions of the law. Deuteronomy assigns to the priests responsibility for the preserving of the Deuteronomic law and a regular reading of it every seven years (Deut. 31:9–13, 24–26). To whatever extent such a process was carried out, it implicitly placed upon the Levitical priests a responsibility for the teaching of the whole of the law. If the entrance liturgies of Psalms 15 and 24 were to represent priestly questions to those who entered the sanctuary, as many presume, that would further identify the priestly instruction with moral as well as cultic behavior, or, to use the language of a later Jewish teacher, with "the weightier matters of the law" (Matt. 23:23) as well as with the important ritual practices of right sacrifice, cultic purity, and holiness.

While it is not presented in the texts as a major function of the priestly office, Deuteronomy attests to a role that may be related to the teaching responsibility: the consultation of the Levitical priests, as well as the judge, who are at the central sanctuary, when a judicial decision is too difficult to resolve otherwise (Deut. 17:8–13). The involvement of the priests seems to be tied to their function and competence as teachers of the law (see v. 11). The Deuteronomic provision is similar to the reform of Jehoshaphat in the ninth century, establishing a superior or central court in Jerusalem for disputed cases and comprised of priests and elders under a dual leadership of chief priest and governor of the house of Judah. It may be that such a priestly responsibility came into being at this time. Ezekiel 44:24 attests to a judicial responsibility for the priests in the postexilic period.

Sacrifice. The third of the priestly functions mentioned in Deuteronomy 33 is sacrifice. There is no specific reference to the priestly Levite in Judges 17–18 sacrificing, but the condemnation of Eli, priest at Shiloh, is because of the corruption of the priestly sacrificial responsibility on the part of his sons (1 Sam. 2:12–17) and testifies at an early stage to regulations and procedures for bringing sacrifices to the priest at the sanctuary and for the priest's carrying out a sacrificial ritual that included the priest's eating of some portion of the sacrifice. The Levitical legislation indicates various particular procedures that came to be the responsibility of the priest when sacrifices were made, including presenting the sacrifice on the altar and burning it and dealing with the blood of an animal sacrifice (Leviticus 1–7). The priest's involvement in the sacrifical procedures seems to have been closely associated with the altar as the place of most direct contact with the divine. There are even texts that speak about the priests' involvement in the sanctuary as simply "going up to the altar" (2 Kings 23:9; cf. 1 Sam. 2:28).

The sacrificial system was also a major source of income and support for the priesthood (see chapter 3). While a priest might be paid a wage (e.g., Judg. 17:10), it was clearly understood that there was a "priest's due" from the sacrifices that were offered (e.g., Lev. 2:1–10; 6:14–18; Deut. 18:3), a priestly portion that was carefully protected by financial penalties if eaten even unintentionally (Lev. 22:10–16).[23] Some have argued plausibly that the expression used to speak of ordaining the priests, that is, "to fill the hands," may refer to the priestly portion of sacrifices, though that is not the only possible meaning of this somewhat enigmatic expression.

As Rodney Hutton has noted, there is a direct link between the social maintenance of the priest by a payment system rooted in the sacrificial system and the role of the priest in providing social maintenance by risking danger in

> "bearing the sin" of the offender and thereby purging the sancta of the contaminating effects of the offender's sin. . . . [A]ccording to priestly ideology the priest did exercise a crucial social function, fraught with danger from contact with the combined powers of the uncontrollably numinous and of deadly contamination. He was the equivalent of the modern nuclear reactor supervisor who must channel the tremendous energy of the reactor while at the same time facing potential death in preventing radioactive contamination, core meltdown, and nuclear catastrophe, and who must supervise the decontamination of the environment in the case of disaster, which in cultic terms was an everyday occurrence.[24]

Developments in the History of Priesthood

In the course of the history of the priesthood in ancient Israel, there were developments that affected the roles and responsibilities of the priests. The most notable one was the demotion of the Levites from full participation in priestly functions to a secondary position with subordinate duties that did not include officiating at the altar. This is most pronounced in Ezekiel's vision of the temple in chapters 40–48 (Ezek. 44:10–16), as well as in Chronicles (e.g., 1 Chron. 23:2–6) and the Priestly legislation of the Pentateuch (e.g., Num. 3:5–10; 8:19, 22). The book of Deuteronomy does not seem to know a distinction between priest and Levite or a relegation of the Levites to a secondary position in the ritual and worship activity of the community, but that is a little deceptive when the evidence is examined more closely (see below).

The literature gives different kinds of rationales for the distinction that came to operate in the postexilic period and may have been present earlier. On the one hand, it is grounded in the Levitical disobedience indicated at two points. One is found in Ezekiel's claim that the Levites went far from the Lord and were idolatrous like the rest of Israel (Ezek. 44:10, 12); the other is reflected in the rebellion of Korah and other Levites and their subsequent punishment (Numbers 16), which is seen in the end as a reminder "that no outsider who is not of the descendants of Aaron, shall approach to offer incense before the LORD, so as not to become like Korah and his company" (Num. 17:5[16:40]).[25] On the other hand, the subordinate role of the Levites is understood to be part of David's organization of the temple worship and its maintenance (1 Chron. 23:2–6).

While it is very difficult to uncover the history of the priesthood and account for the development described above, some observations may be made toward a sense of the whole. The careful order and classification of priests that is now found in the priestly oriented literature represents a somewhat later development and would not have been the way things were at the beginning if one can take a clue from the story of Micah's appointment of a family or household priest in Judges 17–18. Here priesthood is linked with a family shrine rather than with the later official national cult. Levitical descent is not required but seems to be a clear plus in that Micah believes himself to be in better stead with Yahweh for having now a Levite as priest and not just a member of the family. The fact that this Levite had lived in Bethlehem and thus was associated with Judah raises the question of whether the term "Levite" was originally a job title rather than a tribal name.[26] On the basis of this story and other evidence, Lawrence Stager has suggested that the priesthood in early Israel performed an important socioeconomic function as it "helped 'absorb' a surplus of young males, especially for those who were not firstborns and, as the frontier was closing, stood little chance of inheriting much of the patrimony or of pioneering new land."[27] Samuel would have been another such "youth" who became a priest. Many families from all over Israel would have dedicated their sons to the Levitical order, and, as Deuteronomy indicates (10:8–9; 18:1–8), they would have been landless and dependent upon patrons among the tribes or individual or corporate support for their livelihood, as was the case with the young Levite attached to the house of Micah. So while some were indeed born to the priesthood, others were recruited across clan and tribal boundaries.[28]

The development of an official state religion brought about a centralized priesthood associated with the court. The presence of two main priests in the court of David, Zadok and Abiathar, points to priestly rivalries that may have developed at an earlier stage. Both the Judean cultus with its two priests and the Northern Kingdom cultus with its two state shrines established by Jeroboam have been seen to reflect rivalries and conflicts between Aaronide (Zadok) and Mosaic (Abiathar) priestly lines, conflicts that are signaled in various Pentateuchal stories.[29] Others would see these conflicts as indicating a rivalry involving an early Mosaic priesthood that served tribal interests and continued on into the monarchy under whom another and official state priesthood (Zadok—Aaronide) was established alongside the Mosaic or Levitical priesthood (Abiathar) and eventually came to dominate, forcing the Levitical priests into a subordinate role.[30]

The evidence from Deuteronomy and the Deuteronomistic History may point to a more complex development during the later monarchy than appears to be the case on the surface, as Steven Tuell has noted in a careful study of references to the Levites in Deuteronomy and Samuel–Kings.[31] On the basis of a number of texts he reaches the following conclusion:

> Already in the First Temple period, evidence of a very complex subsystem within the one category "Levitical priest" can be found. At the head of the priestly class is הכהן, *the* priest.[32] Other subgroupings are headed by the elders of the priests.[33] Then, there are the guardians of the threshold,[34] and the second order of the priests:[35] groups twice mentioned together, and in company with the chief priest. Finally, there are "the Levites," bearing the Ark in procession in Jerusalem,[36] and "the Levitical priests" outside of the city, serving a vital function in the land: arbitrating disputes,[37] pronouncing blessings,[38] taking part in occasional rituals, and diagnosing leprosy.[39]

Tuell's analysis suggests that something more was going on than simply priestly rivalry, although that came to play a significant part.[40] But the priestly responsibilities developed in more complex ways and produced various groups within the general category even before the dominance of the Zadokite priesthood and the clear relegation of the Levites to a subordinate role in the postexilic period. This is reflected not only in Deuteronomy and the Deuteronomistic History but also in the Priestly system's assignment of guard duty (Num. 1:50–53) and the "work" or "service" of assembling and disassembling the tabernacle and moving it (Num. 1:50–51; 3:5–9) to the Levites as well as in the law of the temple in Ezekiel 40–48.[41]

In any event, by the postexilic period the special place and roles of the Levites was firmly established. They were in charge of the work in the temple, tending to its furnishings, the sacred vessels, and the like. They were gatekeepers and they were musicians responsible for the musical praise of the Lord (1 Chron. 23:1–6; cf. 2 Chron. 5:12–14; 7:6). The Levites were in charge of the temple treasuries and storerooms (1 Chron. 26:20; 2 Chron. 8:15) as well as responsible for collection and distribution of offerings (2 Chron. 31:11–16) and the collection of the temple tax (2 Chron. 24:4–7; 34:9). In addition, they continued as scribes and teachers as well as administrators and judges (1 Chron. 26:29; 34:13).[42]

THE PROPHET

At the point of the Levitical responsibility for leadership in music, one encounters an example of a priestly-Levitical function that overlaps with prophecy. In 1 Chronicles 25, the musicians "prophesy" with their musical instruments, a not uncommon connection between music and prophecy (e.g., 1 Sam. 10:5; 2 Kings 3:15).[43] The customary sharp distinction between priest and prophet as religious roles covers or distorts ways in which these two leadership roles overlapped or shared functions. Such overlap is not too surprising when one considers, for example, that two of the major prophetic figures of ancient Israel, Jeremiah and Ezekiel, came from priestly lineage (Jer. 1:1) and, in the case of the latter, probably had that designation (Ezek. 1:3).

The most obvious way in which priest and prophet functioned similarly in Israelite religion is the fact that oracle inquiry could be sought from either priest or prophet. The priest may have had particular devices by means of which a divine word or decision could be received, for example, Urim and Thummim or the ephod, but the prophet seems early on to have been a source of divine direction or an oracle. There is some indication that this was the earliest primary role of the prophet. That is, a prophet was a seer to whom people came and paid money or brought presents to get a divine word of some sort (1 Samuel 9). In the eighth century, Micah testifies to prophetic divination, which he condemned primarily because it was a monetary operation (Micah 3:11; cf. 3:6–7).[44] The word "peace" (šālôm), which certain prophets are condemned for uttering, seems in Micah's context to have been a response to oracle inquiry. Jeremiah condemned prophets for saying "Peace" when there was no peace (and thus uttering a "false" prophecy), but in Micah the condemnation is because "peace" was a positive response to the divinatory inquiry and one that came when suitable compensation was provided, whereas a negative word ("war")[45] was given when there was not satisfactory remuneration to the prophet.

Shared religious functions between prophet and priest are evident also in the way in which apparently priestly speech forms were used also by prophets, for example, the *oracle of salvation*, which appears in the prophetic literature associated with, among others, both Jeremiah and the prophet of the exile whose oracles are preserved in Isaiah 40–66 (e.g., Jer. 30:10–11; 42:11–12; Isa. 41:8–13, 14–16; cf. 1 Kings 22:5–6, 12), and the *priestly torah* (e.g., Isa. 1:10–17; 33:14–16; Micah 6:6–8).[46] One needs to be careful about assuming that such forms are "taken over" from priestly genres. They may have simply been shared modes of speech and oracular activity. The oracle of salvation was a common mode of speech among prophets or prophet-like figures in Mesopotamia in the Old Babylonian period at Mari and in the later Neo-Assyrian period as well as in the first millennium Aramean milieu (e.g., the Zakkur inscription ca. 800 B.C.). The fact that the basic prophetic speech form in the ancient Near East, including Israel, seems to have been some type of oracle of salvation announcing deliverance against or from an enemy[47] has been one of the grounds for suggesting an even closer connection between prophet and priest, that is, the possibility that the prophets of ancient Israel, or at least some of them, were directly connected with the cult and under priestly supervision.[48]

There are numerous places in the literature where priest and prophet are paired in a way that suggests a close association of the two (e.g., Jer. 4:9; 5:31; 6:13; 13:13; 14:18). The prophetic bands or guilds, the *nĕbî'îm* or the *bĕnê hannĕbî'îm* (on which see below), may have been particularly associated with cult centers and under the supervision of priests. They were found at major cultic centers, such as Bethel (1 Kings 2:3) and Gilgal (2 Kings 4:38). And priestly control of prophetic bands as well as possibly of individual prophets is intimated in the eighth century in the effort of Amaziah, chief priest of Bethel, to control the activities of the prophet Amos in the Northern Kingdom (Amos 7:10–17) as well as in seventh-century Judah, where the prophet Jeremiah seems to be subject to, or presumed subject to, priestly control. On one occasion he was beaten and put in the stocks by a priest because of his prophesying (Jer. 20:1–2). Even more indicative of formal oversight of prophetic activity by priests is the written reprimand of the priest Zephaniah by Shemaiah because he did not rebuke Jeremiah, "who plays the prophet" inasmuch as Zephaniah had been appointed priest "so that there may be officers in the house of the LORD for any madman who plays the prophet" (Jer. 29:26–27).

Furthermore, some of the individual prophets, whose stories are told in the historical books or whose writings are preserved in the prophetic books, engaged in cultic activity or had clear connections to the temple, the latter suggesting a possible significant involvement in cultic matters. Thus, Samuel, who is seen at one point standing at the head of a band of ecstatic prophets (1 Sam. 19:20) and engaging frequently in prophetic activities, also led in the ritual of sacrifice (1 Sam. 9:13, 23) and indeed is first encountered in the biblical record as "ministering to the LORD in the presence of the priest Eli" (1 Sam. 2:11; 3:1). Elijah also both headed a band of prophets and officiated at a sacrifice (1 Kings 18).

Prophets received visions (Isaiah 6) and gave oracles (for example, Jeremiah and Hananiah in Jeremiah 28) in the main temple of the state. Hananiah's oracle was a typical oracle of salvation, but both were uttered in the temple before priests and prophet. Elsewhere prophet and priest are spoken of in the biblical tradition as functioning together in some capacity in the temple, though there is no detail to determine the character of that relationship other than its locus in the state shrine (Jer. 23:11; Lam. 2:20).[49] In one instance, the sons of a "man of God" (see below for this term) are reported to have had a chamber in the temple (Jer. 35:4). It has been argued that some of the prophets whose writings are preserved in the Bible were cult prophets, as evidenced by hymnic or liturgical elements, absence of criticism of the cult, and oracles of salvation against the enemy. The most likely candidates are Joel, Nahum, and especially Habakkuk, but the evidence is more suggestive than definitive.[50] The involvement of prophets in cultic activity within a sanctuary may well have changed and modulated over the course of Israel's pre- and postexilic history. That is certainly suggested by the way in which "prophecy" seems to have become a part of second temple worship in the form of the Levitical musicians referred to above (1 Chron. 25:1–8; 2 Chron. 20:14; 29:25; 35:15).[51]

Both of these types of religious leadership shared the fundamental task of mediating the covenantal relationship between the God of Israel and the people. The dominant way of viewing the prophet in contemporary discussion, especially that influenced by anthropological and sociological analogies, is as intermediary or mediator, that is, as "links between the human and supernatural worlds."[52] This may have happened most often in the communication of messages from the divine world to the human, whether solicited or unsolicited, but it may have involved healing acts as well, also mediating divine action (1 Kings 17:17–24; 2 Kings 4:18–37; 20:1–11 // Isa. 38:1–8).

The common ground between priest and prophet, however, does not diminish the significant differences in their role characters and functions. Several biblical texts differentiate the role of priest and prophet as major religious figures in ancient Israel (Jer. 18:18; Ezek. 7:26; cf. Micah 3:11).

Torah, or instruction, was the responsibility of the priest according to this traditional differentiation, counsel the task of the sage or wise person, and the prophet was the one who brought vision, word, or oracle. The prophet, therefore, was one whose *primary function was to receive messages from the deity*, possibly in ecstatic trance or through dreams or visions (see below). The vision was a means of prophetic reception and not a part of priestly mediation of the torah.

There were some other significant differences between priest and prophet. In the classic analysis of Max Weber, it has been noted that the priest might assume the role by lineage or be appointed, while the prophet tended to be a figure whose authority was by divine calling and often involved spirit possession, suggesting a more charismatic kind of authority. The extended contemporary investigation of prophecy has rightly challenged some of Weber's conclusions, particularly the distinction between charismatic and institutional, indicating how often it can be seen that prophets may have had strong institutional bases and were under some external control by human authorities and not simply subject to possession by divine power (see above). Wilson's study of central and peripheral prophecy has suggested a more complex and nuanced view of the relation of prophecy to official establishments and institutional order. But there remained a core of difference in most cases between the calling of the prophet, which was constantly under attack, and the generally accepted appointment or inherited position of priests that is consistent with Weber's observation.

A further differentiation at the social level between priesthood and prophecy was the fact that women could and did become prophets even though they did not become priests, at least as far as the evidence indicates. Elsewhere in the ancient Near East, women were found among the oracular speakers or intermediaries who most closely paralleled the prophets of Israelite history, at Mari and Emar, for example.[53] Several examples of women prophets in Israel are attested in the biblical record, enough to suggest that the actuality was probably even more extensive.[54] The most obvious example is the prophetess Huldah, whose oracle concerning Josiah is reported in 2 Kings 22:14–20. This account, in which several officials, including the priest Hilkiah, went to inquire of the prophetess and then reported the prophetic oracle back to the king, is reminiscent of the frequent report of oracles to kings or queens at Mari by third parties who received the oracle from the prophet and then passed it on, though in those cases the oracle was usually unsolicited. The prophet Isaiah was married to a prophetess (Isa. 8:3), and Ezek. 13:17–23 reports a judgment against certain women who "prophesy out of their own imagination." Furthermore, named women are identified as prophets from the earliest period (Miriam and Deborah)[55] to the latest (Noadiah).[56] Insofar as any detail is given in the reports of these prophetesses, their activities correspond to the activities of male prophets. As Bowen has indicated, the somewhat peculiar references to bands and veils in regard to the female prophets of Ezekiel 13 may suggest a more specialized prophetic activity associated with pregnancy and childbirth.[57] This would be in accord with indications of healing activities on the part of other Israelite prophets, for example, Elijah, Elisha, and Isaiah.

The Character of Israelite Prophecy

Terminology. While not a decisive indicator of role and function for professional figures, religious or otherwise, several terms give some clues to the character of prophecy in ancient Israel. The most common term is the Hebrew word most often translated as "prophet," *nābî'*, a noun from the Semitic root *nābā'*, "to call, proclaim, name."[58] The word has been understood as both an active participle, meaning "proclaimer," or, more likely, a passive participle, "one who is called." Either definition fits the role. While the active participle is a less likely meaning, it would point to one of the main activities of Israelite prophets, the announcing or proclaiming of the divine word, whether solicited or not. The prophets were clearly often, if not always, persons who acted under some sense of divine call or compulsion, as is indicated in a number of the written records of Judean prophets (Isaiah 6; Jeremiah 1; Ezekiel 1; cf. Amos 7:14–15), and the call seems to have played a part in the authorization and authentication of prophecy (see below).

More recently, Daniel Fleming, on the basis of new texts from the northern Mesopotamian cities of Mari and Emar that have provided us with the first formal cognates to the Hebrew noun *nābî'* in a West Semitic setting, has argued that the meaning of the word is "the one who invokes the gods," and points to several places in the biblical record where the prophetic activity was precisely calling on the name of God, particularly the famous contest between Elijah and the prophets of Baal on Mount Carmel (1 Kings 18), where each party in the contest sought to invoke its god for a display of power. The contest was won when one of the prophets failed to invoke the deity or evoke his power.[59]

Two of the terms that designated prophets reflect their function as seers or diviners of the future: *rō'eh* and *ḥōzeh*. Both of these are active participle forms of words for "seeing." The former seems to have functioned earlier in the history of Israelite prophecy, gradually being displaced by the terms *ḥōzeh* and *nābî'*. This transition of terminology is reflected in 1 Sam. 9:9, where inquiry of the deity is identified as an activity involving a prophet (*nābî'*), who was formerly called a "seer" (*rō'eh*). But the identification of a prophet as a "seer" did not disappear, and the term *rō'eh* continued to function alongside *ḥōzeh* and *nābî'* to refer to prophetic figures (Isa. 29:10; 30:10).

Yet a third term appears a number of times as a way of designating a prophet. It is the expression *'îš hā'ĕlōhîm*, "man of God," that is, one who is seen as authorized by God and acting as God's representative. This term is used for, among others, Elijah (1 Kings 17:18) and Elisha (e.g., 2 Kings 4:10, 16, 21, 25). In some instances, the word "holy" (*qādôš*) is used to refer to the "man of God."

First Samuel 9:5–10 gives a glimpse of all three of these terms in use, apparently at an early stage in the history of prophecy. It is the account of Saul's search for his lost donkeys. In the search, he and the boy with him consult a "man of God" who divines the future for a fee. The term "man of God" is the primary designation in the story for the figure Samuel, but he is also called a "seer" and it is in this context that a narrative insertion reports on the shift from "seer" to "prophet" to designate the person to be consulted when one wished to "inquire of God." The factuality of the story is, of course, impossible to determine, but it is likely to preserve with some accuracy the way these terms were used at an early stage. The terms may represent some role differentiation in the early period, but the nuances of difference became lost and there was probably considerable fluidity in the applicability of the terms. The passage suggests a distinction, but it does so in terms of historical development in nomenclature rather than in terms of roles.[60] While one may be tempted to draw sharp lines suggesting different types of prophecy or differences between early and later prophecy, the continuity of character and activity is more evident than any major distinctions, whether in terminology, manifestation of possession, function, or relation to official religion.

Prophetic Groups. As already indicated, prophets functioned in ancient Israel both in groups and singly. That is, there are a number of attestations to bands or groups of prophets, sometimes called *nĕbî'îm*, "prophets," and sometimes called *bĕnê hannĕbî'îm*, often translated as "sons of the prophets," but actually simply meaning "belonging to the prophetic group." These may have been connected with cult centers (see above) and were sometimes found in association with named prophets whose activities are reported apart from their connection with the prophetic bands, for example, Samuel, Elijah, and Elisha.[61] The "prophets" often functioned in a central role, giving oracles to political leaders, as in the story recorded in 1 Kings 22. But they did not always function in relation to the establishment and may have lived and worked more on the margins of society or in relation to particular shrines or locales, that is, in relation to local religious activities rather than in connection with official or state forms of religious activity. The account of Amos's encounter with the priest of Bethel suggests that the chief priest may have had some control over the "prophets," but the evidence there is quite indirect. Jeremiah's frequent references to "the prophets" who speak a false word or give oracles of salvation may have reference to groups of prophets who functioned primarily in relation to the political establishment. But that seems less the case with the prophetic bands associated with Elijah and Elisha. In any event, as best one can determine, the prophetic bands, like individual seers and prophets, were expected to mediate between the deity and the community or the individual, giving a divine word about the future, especially announcing the outcome of wars or divine deliverance in the face of some threat or danger.

That not all prophets were associated with prophetic groups is well indicated by 1 Kings 22, where the prophetic group is depicted under the leadership of a named prophet, Zedekiah, but the prophet Micaiah is portrayed as a completely separate figure, clearly outside the establishment though well known to it. So it was that Israelite society included throughout the monarchical period a number of prophets who functioned primarily or often as individuals, sometimes intimately connected with the political and religious establishment, as, for example, in the case of the prophets Nathan and Gad in David's court or the prophet Isaiah, who had direct connections with the kings over a long period of time and was consulted by the king or took the initiative in bringing divine words to the king. Even those individual prophets who were not centrally located vis-à-vis the state and official religion in the earlier period, that is, in the tenth and ninth centuries, sometimes directed divine words to kings while also being consulted by individuals in the communities. Classic examples of this combination, at least in the Northern Kingdom, are found in the legends associated with Elijah and Elisha (1 Kings 17–2 Kings 10).

Relation to the Social Order. The relation of the prophetic groups and the individual prophets to the society and particularly to religious and political dimensions was quite complex. Our understanding of that relationship has been illumined by Wilson's analysis of the function of prophets as either *central* to the political and religious establishment—helping to provide maintenance of the social order and its stability, promoting social welfare— or *peripheral* to the main social order and working often to effect change and to destabilize the existing structures. Such prophetic activities, however, cannot be understood simplistically. As Wilson points out, peripheral intermediaries or prophets might seek to arrest social change by reaffirming traditional values, working conservatively in behalf of the old gods and in the face of rapid social change. More often, they sought innovative changes in the society. Peripheral prophets even served a stabilizing function by allowing minority groups to express and vent their frustration, thus relieving their discontent. Furthermore, central and peripheral prophets could exist in the same society at the same time, as is probably reflected in the stories of prophetic conflict in ancient Israel (see below), and prophets could move in and out of these "positions," going, for example, from a more peripheral status to a more central role, as seems to be the case in the depiction of the prophet Elisha in the Deuteronomistic History.[62]

Samuel seems to have been a member of the central cultic establishment who gave political and religious leadership and functioned at times as a prophet. His opposition to the institution of kingship can be understood as an effort to preserve and promote traditions associated with Shiloh and other cult centers. But the Saul constituency would not have seen his position as maintaining the social order. Elijah is fairly consistently presented as "a peripheral prophet who used prophecy in an attempt to reform Israel's central cult, which had been infiltrated by the worship of Baal."[63] Amos in the eighth century seems to have been a central prophet in Judah and a peripheral prophet in Israel.[64] A classic case of the encounter of central and peripheral prophets is the account of prophetic conflict in 1 Kings 22, where the four hundred prophets under the leadership of Zedekiah are clearly related to the political establishment and serve to provide oracles of salvation, supporting divine words for the political leadership, in this case with regard to military endeavors. Over against this group and clearly distinguished from them was Micaiah, whose oracle arises out of a vision of the heavenly council in deliberation and its effect is a thoroughly destabilizing one, to wit, the death of the political leader.

In all of these examples, it is clear that Israelite prophecy is to be seen in significant relation to social structures and groups. Validation of the prophet's role is, at least in part, provided by the society or elements within the society. The authority of the prophetic word or oracle was a critical factor in the response of the leadership or of the people. That authority was manifest in several ways, particularly through accounts of prophetic power such as miracles and predictions. Even the Deuteronomic law assumed the predictive power of the prophet as a test of prophetic authority. The denunciation of some prophets by the deity through the agency of other prophets (for example, Ezekiel 12) was because of their lying visions, prophesying out of their imaginations. They claimed a power and an inter- mediary power that they did not have, at least according to the opposing prophetic voice and in some instances according to the test of prophetic prediction by the ensuing events.

The prophetic call narratives also dealt with the issue of prophetic authority and prophetic validation or authentication before the society. It has been suggested that the narratives themselves functioned only secon- darily this way, with reference to the later collection of prophetic oracles rather than the actual career of the prophet whose call is reported.[65] That is, the call narratives served to ground the authority of the prophetic book that grew out of the work of a particular prophet.[66] The acceptance of the prophet by the people or the particular group with whom a prophet was associated was dependent more upon the prophet's activity or behavior. At the same time, there are some indications that the prophetic claim to be called served within the prophet's own experience to answer challenges to his or her claim to be the intermediary of the divine word. At least that seems to be the case with regard to Amos, who refers to his call in response to the effort of the priest Amaziah to bring him into line and prohibit his prophetic activity in the Northern Kingdom (Amos 7:10–17). In this conflict between priest and prophet, the attestation of a divine call or commission distinguishes the prophet's authority from the priest's oversight.

Relation to the Divine World. The stories of prophetic conflict, for exam- ple, the encounter between Micaiah and Zedekiah and the four hundred prophets (1 Kings 22), the encounter between Amos and the priest Amaziah, and the encounter between Jeremiah and the other prophets active in Judah (represented especially by the prophet Hananiah [Jeremiah 28]), may all be understood in relation to the social and political context of Israel and Judah, reflecting either conflicts between central and peripheral prophets or particular historical and social circumstances at the time of the conflict.[67] Such analysis, however, is incomplete on its own. Israelite prophecy—and perhaps ancient Near Eastern prophecy generally—cannot be understood simply in terms of its social, religious, or political world. It has to be under- stood from a frame of reference outside the realia of social existence though never separated from them. Prophetic authority and prophetic activ- ity were derivative of an experience that can only be understood as reflect- ing or claiming a transcendent ground. This is attested particularly in two ways. One was the call experience already referred to, involving the prophet's encounter with the deity through a theophanic experience in which the prophet was called or commissioned (perhaps more than once) and given a specific task even in the face of objection or resistance on the part of the prophet. There is little indication of Amos's validation by any social group, for example, though such may have been the case within his Judean context. The ground of his resistance to the representative of official state religion is solely his conviction of operating under a divine commission.[68]

The other indication of self and societal transcendence was the prophet's vision of the heavenly assembly and his or her role as a herald or messenger of the decree of the divine council with regard to events on earth. Prophetic oracles and prophetic narratives attest to a starting point for prophetic speech and activity in a transcendent world identified by the image of the council of the Lord, the heavenly assembly (e.g., 1 Kings 22:19–23; Isaiah 6; Jer. 23:16–22; Amos 3:7). Both formally and conceptually the prophetic oracle was a message, not simply from the deity but from the divine world, where the decrees of the council of Yahweh were set forth and transmitted as a divine proclamation or message by the prophetic herald: "Thus says Yahweh." This conceptuality is so much a feature of Israelite prophecy that it must be taken into account as much as defining a particular position for prophecy vis-à-vis society. The word of the prophet to the society in which the prophet lived and functioned was rooted firmly in a relationship to the divine effecting a mediation of the divine word to the contemporary community of the prophet. The sociopolitical and religious character of prophecy was not simply due to the particular concerns of the prophet or the prophet's group in addressing the human world. It came out of a sociopolitical transcendent world that was understood to be the source of governance for what happened in the royal court and the law court, in battle and exile, in the streets and the sanctuaries. Heaven spoke through the prophet; earth listened in anticipation. The social world of the prophet was to be found in heaven as much as on earth. This is the meaning of the intermediary role.

Where conflict arose between prophets and prophetic groups, the issue was regularly understood as one of truthful message, authentic encounter with the divine, and access to the divine will and the divine word. While the accusation of false prophecy may have been in relation to whether or not the word of the prophet would come to pass, it was also a claim about whether or not the prophet had access to the transcendent world of the deity, whether or not the prophet was sent by the deity (Jer. 23:21–22, 32). That was the primary ground for prophetic intermediation. Thus, the groups of prophets were regularly identified not simply in relation to a particular prophet but also as prophets of a particular deity—Yahweh (e.g., 1 Kings

18:4, 13) or Baal (1 Kings 18:19, 22, 25, 40; 2 Kings 10:19; cf. Jer. 2:8; 23:13) or Asherah (1 Kings 18:19)—and prophesied in the name of the deity (Jer. 2:8; 23:13, 25), as indicated by the form of the prophetic oracle introduction: "Thus says . . ."[69] This identification with a deity and orientation toward the divine world was as much a factor in prophetic conflict as the relative social positions of the prophets.[70] It was possible for prophets to operate and function primarily in relation to the sociopolitical matrix of which they were a part rather than in relation to an experience of the divine world, but that could become the grounds for rejecting the prophecy as false. At the same time, it is clear from the record that prophets did announce contrary decrees from the same deity.[71]

Modes of Revelation

The question of how a prophet received a message from the deity is difficult to answer. Often the text will say something like, "The word of the LORD came to . . ." (e.g., Jer. 2:1; Ezek. 17:1; 36:16; Zech. 6:5; 8:1, 18). This may have been by way of an audition or a vision. The latter is clearly indicated in a number of prophetic texts that represent visionary experiences (e.g., 2 Sam. 7:17; 1 Kings 22:17, 19–23; 2 Kings 6:16–17; Isa. 1:1; 6:1–13; Jer. 14:14; Ezek. 1:1; 7:13; Amos 7–9; Obad. 1; Nahum 1:1; Hab. 2:2; Zechariah 1–6; 13:4)—whether or not in some sort of trance or ecstatic state, as seems to have been the case with Ezekiel—and is further suggested by the prophetic superscriptions referring to what the prophet "saw" (Isa. 2:2; 13:1; Amos 1:1; Micah 1:1; Hab. 1:1). There is enough interchange of word and vision, of "saw" and "heard" in prophetic book superscriptions (Isa. 2:2; Amos 1:1; Micah 1:1) that it is difficult to distinguish in any significant way between auditory and visual reception of the divine message. First Kings 22:19–23 is a classic instance of a prophet—in this case a peripheral prophet, not a part of the main group of prophets consulted by the political establishment—recounting a vision of the heavenly assembly that served to provide a message to communicate to the king.[72]

The textual evidence from Israel and elsewhere leaves the relationship between vision (ḥāzôn) and dream (ḥălôm) as prophetic revelatory vehicles very ambiguous. There is no doubt that dreams were a mode of divine revelation in the ancient Near East, and there are texts that associate prophecy and "dreaming." But those that do, specifically Deut. 13:2–6(1–5) and 1 Sam. 28:6, set dreams alongside prophecy and, in one case, Urim and Thummim as *different* modes of divine revelation. The texts suggest differentiation between prophecy and dreaming even more than similarity. In any event, the textual data from Israel and other locales where prophetic activity was apparent do not show any fundamental difference in the character of prophetic vision and reported dreams when both things are actually described.[73]

Some analysts of prophetic activity in the ancient Near East have called attention to the fundamental distinction between divination and prophecy precisely at the point of the means of revelation rather than the content. In Mesopotamian culture, for example, one can recognize two primary modes of revelation, both of which were also present in Israelite culture.[74] One form of mediation and revelatory discernment was divination and particularly extispicy (examination of the entrails of animals for divination purposes), an activity carried out by professionals who dealt with critical matters of the kingdom, such as the security of the city, conduct of war and military enterprises, and gaining information from the gods by "careful analysis of material and physical evidence and omens by applying traditional and highly refined codes of interpretation."[75] In the Israelite context, this would have been by such devices as Urim and Thummim or by lots. The other form of discerning the divine word or will was through "intuitive divination" or prophecy, where the word of God was ascertained through some sort of psychic experience of revelation, that is, communication or information received from the deity through immaterial means.[76] The communication was requested or sought (e.g., 1 Kings 22; Jer. 37:17; 38:14–16; Ezek. 14:1–5; 20:1–3), or it could come spontaneously, either with oracles of salvation or with words of judgment (e.g., 2 Sam. 7:4; 12:1; 1 Kings 20:13, 28; Jer. 26:1–6).

There are instances in which the prophetic word came in an experience of trance or ecstasy, and some forms of the verb "to prophesy" seem to refer to more ecstatic activities in which the prophet or prophets were posssessed by some power.[77] Not only is that evident in the stories of early prophecy in Israel, as, for example, in the accounts of Saul's frenzy (1 Sam. 10:5–13; 19:20–24), but the depictions of Elijah (2 Kings 3:14–19) and Ezekiel, who experiences the "hand of Yahweh" or the "spirit of Yahweh" upon him (Ezek. 2:2; 3:12, 22) and is transported from one place to another by the spirit (Ezek. 3:14), suggest that ecstatic or trance experiences were fairly common if not always the rule. Music seems to have played a role on occasion in stimulating the ecstatic experience (1 Sam. 10:5; 2 Kings 3:15), but there are also instances of self-laceration to accomplish the same end (1 Kings 18:28; Zech. 13:6). Efforts to distinguish between "acceptable" and "unacceptable" prophecy in ancient Israel, between legitimate and illegitimate or between true and false prophecy on the basis of the presence or absence of ecstatic experience will not work. Ecstasy was probably frequently but not always present, a part of the experience of those who were regarded as "true" prophets and those who were "false," experienced by both central and peripheral prophecy.[78]

Note should be taken of the different ways in which prophetic communication to others took place. Along with the proclamation of a message in verbal form with the messenger formula "Thus says . . . ," the prophet could and did communicate the divine word by means of symbolic acts, some of which were momentary, single acts (Jeremiah 19; 25:15–29; 28:10–11), some of which were prolonged endeavors (Isa. 8:1–4; 20:1–6; Jer. 16:1–4; Ezekiel 4; 24:15–27). Interpretation of the symbolic action may or may not have been a part of the communication.

Prophetic Activity

The particular activities of prophets in ancient Israel have already been indicated in the discussion above but need to be summarized here. The primary function of the prophet was the giving of oracles from the deity, oracles that had to do with military activities, illness and the threat of death, cultic faithfulness, and the responsibilities of king and people, of leaders and populace, to serve the deity in accordance with the deity's wishes. Cross has suggested that the prophetic agenda can be understood as falling into three primary tasks.[79] As messenger from the divine assembly with the decree of the assembly and the deity, the prophet was responsible for:

1. Representing the divine king to the human king (e.g., 1 Sam. 10:1ff.; cf. 1 Kings 11:29–39; Jer. 23:1–6)
2. Proclaiming God's justice and the requirements of covenant (e.g., 1 Sam. 15:26–29; 1 Kings 21; Micah 3:9–12)
3. Announcing and interpreting the deity's interventions (1 Samuel 7; 1 Kings 22; Amos 5:18–20)

As with Near Eastern prophecy generally, much of the prophet's activity was in relation to the political leadership. That is consistently the case from Samuel and the prophets associated with David's court through Elijah and Elisha down to Jeremiah and the end of kingship in Israel. But from the start, prophets gave oracles to individuals who consulted them whatever their status, and, increasingly in Israel's history, they directed oracles to the wider community or to segments within the community.[80]

Even as some of the oracle inquiry of the prophet was directed toward determining the prospects for recovery of health for someone ill or near death (e.g., 1 Kings 14:1–18; 2 Kings 1:2–4; 8:7–10; cf. 2 Kings 20:1), so it seems that prophets sometimes were involved in the healing of persons.[81] Several narratives show prophets engaged in healing activities, specifically Elisha's healing of the Syrian commander Naaman (2 Kings 5:1–19) and Isaiah's healing of Hezekiah (2 Kings 20:7 // Isa. 38:21). But there are also reports of prophetic resuscitation of the dead (1 Kings 17:17–24; 2 Kings 4:18–37; 13:21). While the Elijah-Elisha stories are replete with legendary materials, they may be assumed to reflect understandings of prophetic activity with some authenticity. As Hutton has pointed out, the close association of healing with prophecy is suggested by 1 Kings 17:24 where the widow responds to Elijah's healing of her son by the words, "By this ('attâ zeh) I know that you are a man of God."[82]

The fact that prayer accompanied the prophet's healing activity in some instances is a pointer to another intermediary activity on the part of prophets: intercession in behalf of others, especially intercession to seek the removal of the divine judgment upon the people. The association of prophecy with intercession is made even in a text that does not deal directly with prophecy. In the Genesis narratives, Abimelech is promised that Abraham will pray for him "because he is a prophet" (Gen. 20:7). But the association of prophecy with intercession to avert divine wrath or judgment, which is reflected also in the Mosaic intercessory prayers of the Pentateuch, was much more extensive than that nonprophetic text would suggest. There are several recorded instances of intercession on the part of such prophets as Elijah in behalf of a dying or dead child (1 Kings 17:20–21), Isaiah in behalf of the sick King Hezekiah (2 Kings 19:4), and Amos (Amos 7:2, 5) and Ezekiel (Ezek. 9:8; 11:13) in behalf of the people to save them from judgment. Even more indicative are the various texts that suggest that intercession was peculiarly a prophetic activity. Thus, Yahweh tells Jeremiah on several occasions not to intercede in behalf of the people (Jer. 7:16; 11:14; 14:11–12) and even swears that the intercession of Moses or Samuel, both prophetic figures whose prayers for the people are a part of the biblical tradition, would not be sufficient to avert the divine wrath announced against the people of Judah (Jer. 15:1). Perhaps the clearest pointers to the responsibility of the prophets for intercession in behalf of the people are two texts from Ezekiel in which the deity indicates a specific expectation that a prophet would intercede for the people in order to bring about divine relenting: "And I sought for anyone among them who would repair the wall and stand in the breach before me on behalf of the land, so that I would not destroy it; but I found no one" (Ezek. 22:30). That the ones in the breach are assumed to be prophets is indicated by Ezek.

13:4–5: "Your prophets have been like jackals among ruins, O Israel. You have not gone up into the breaches, or repaired a wall for the house of Israel."[83]

Religious Dimensions of the Prophets' Messages

While prophets were not always directly connected to the religious activities and practices of ancient Israel in a formal sense, it is clear from the above that their function within the society, whether on the center or the periphery, whether in behalf of social order and maintenance or disrupting that in behalf of either return to old values or the instigation of change, was a highly religious one. As intermediaries their role was to communicate the word and will of the deity and in some instances to mediate with the deity in behalf of the people, though primarily through prayer rather than through the procedures of sacrifice and the cult. In various ways they were influenced by and influential upon the religious practices of the cult.

One of the clearest manifestations of the influence of the cult upon the prophets was the fact that their oracles were often shaped by the form and content of worship. Calls to worship were transformed into prophetic oracles of judgment (e.g., Amos 4:4–5) and priestly instruction or torah became a vehicle for calls to proper covenantal behavior (Isa. 1:10–17; Ezek. 33:14–16; Micah 6:6–8). The hymnic praise of the sanctuary greatly influenced the prophet whose message is preserved in Isaiah 40–55.

More significantly, the critique of worship practices was a frequent theme of the prophet's oracles. This was directed toward worship that violated the covenantal obligation to worship Yahweh alone, as in the prophetic oracles announcing judgment against the people for the worship of Baal, the Queen of Heaven, Tammuz, or any other deity than the official and national god of Israel (e.g., 1 Kings 18; Jeremiah 2, 44; Ezekiel 8; 14:6–8; Hosea 2). The prophetic critique of the worship practices of the cult was also directed toward the incongruity between cultic activities and the treatment of others, between the worship of Yahweh and the treatment of the Israelite neighbor. Thus, Isaiah, Amos, and Jeremiah, along with other prophets, denounced various customary worship practices and announced doom on the sanctuaries where worship took place if the obligations to the deity were not carried out, specifically the just and compassionate treatment of other members of society.

But the protest against formal religious practices was not a rejection of the cult per se, though some of the prophets' messages have been so interpreted. It is clear from what has been said above that a number of prophets had direct associations with the religious establishment and spoke their oracles in the sanctuary before the people. The loci of prophetic proclamation were many and varied. Not all of them were formally religious centers. But the temple was a major center of prophetic preaching, the proclamation about the temple dependent upon the practices of the people at any particular time. Both divine support of the central shrine (Isaiah) and threats to its continued existence (Jeremiah) were dimensions of the prophetic word. Further, in a later period, prophets, such as Haggai and Zechariah, were leaders in the move to reinstate the official cult in the postexilic period, though prophecy came to play a lesser role in the centuries after the return from exile, at least as far as the record indicates.

THE KING

While prophets and priests clearly played significant and varied roles in the religion of ancient Israel, it is much less clear what functions the king may have had in the Israelite cultus. Obviously, the question arises only for the official state religion of the United Monarchy and the Northern and Southern Kingdoms (see chapter 2), though the figure of the king influenced the later religious developments through the form of the messianic hope. Insofar as one can tell from the literary remains of Israel's history and comparative materials, the king seems to have played a part in the religious life of Israel in two broad ways.

Cultic Legitimation of the Social Order

As in other societies of the time, the Israelite king—and that includes kings of both Northern and Southern Kingdoms—provided a legitimation of the monarchy's social control and dominance through the royal temple cult.[84] In the state religion, the king served as the chosen ruler of the national god of Israel, Yahweh—symbolized and actualized in the king's anointing (e.g., Ps. 2:2)—and thus exercised a representative function in behalf of the deity over people and land.[85] The king's rule on earth was a reflection of the divine rule of the whole cosmos. The cosmic implications of the king's rule are vividly expressed in Psalm 72, where the fertility of the land and the existence of people in peace and well-being is dependent upon the king in Jerusalem. As the "son" and heir of the deity, the king claimed right over the land and its productivity to exercise in behalf of Yahweh (see Psalms 2, 72). Such oversight could be benevolent or malign, but it inevitably meant the king's drawing to himself the resources of the people in support of Yahweh's cultic establishment, for example, a lavishly appointed temple, as well as of the other rightful prerogatives of the king as Yahweh's

anointed, such as a court and palace with staff and courtiers to maintain.
As Keith Whitelam puts it:

> It is this portrayal of the king's fundamental position as the central sym-
> bolic figure in a well defined social and political order that allows royal
> ideology and ritual to address the twin problems of the justification for
> monarchy against opposition to its development as well as addressing
> the problem of any threats from urban factions who might try to usurp
> the king's position and claim the throne for themselves. . . . The signifi-
> cance of this royal world-view is that it provides religious sanction for
> the obedience of the state population to its king on the basis of the
> appeal to the rule of law.[86]

There were significant nuances of difference between the way in which
the royal theology legitimated monarchical rule in the Southern Kingdom
and the way it did in the North. The covenant theology of the tribal league
carried over into the royal ideology and helped to provide the legitimation
of the monarchy.[87] This is especially reflected in the careers of Saul and
David, where obedience to covenantal stipulations on the part of the king
was an issue of fateful significance. The Northern Kingdom seems to have
carried forward this covenantal ideology to some degree so that the monarchy did not have the stability it did in the South, though it is not altogether
clear whether the instability in the North reflected older ideological forces
at work or was motivated by "dissatisfation with the performance of the
existing king or by personal ambition."[88] The very prompt response of the
northern tribes to Rehoboam's perpetuation of Solomon's more despotic
royal practices by completely withdrawing from the kingdom is indicative
of a resistance to the ideology of kingship developing in the South, or at
least to some of the practices of royal power implicitly undergirded by that
ideology. There the earlier covenantal forms were transformed into the
royal ideology of divine sonship by adoption and unconditional rule by
eternal decree. Such an ideology, which had as its central foundations the
choice of David and Zion, the king and the temple place, served to give
powerful support to the structures and prerogatives of monarchy by link-
ing them to the cult, what Cross has called the "*bet Yahweh–bet David*
typology":

> In its mythic dimension, the Temple of Zion and the kingship of the
> Davidic house are fixed in the "orders of creation," and thereby given
> eternal stability. Covenantal forms in their conditionality gave way to
> eternal forms in the royal cult. This applied both to the covenant of the
> league (the so-called Sinaitic covenant) and the covenant of David,

which despite the continuance of the term *bĕrît* was transformed into
an eternal decree in the new context of the Temple cult.[89]

The character of the national shrine at Bethel in the Northern Kingdom
as both "a/the temple of the kingdom" while also being regarded as "the
king's sanctuary" (Amos 7:13) is a sharp indicator of the overlap between
state cult and royal position, even in the Northern Kingdom. The aim of
Amaziah, the chief priest of the Bethel shrine, to force Amos to leave the
country because of the political unrest his prophecies have stirred up or
might do is a further indicator of the sociopolitical legitimation provided by
the royal cultic establishment. The temple at Bethel was both royal and
national shrine and thus the king could, through a representative cultic
figure, exercise political and social control.

The frequent building of sanctuaries on the part of the kings and their
role in dedicating and setting up the cultic apparatus in these temples was
a visible way of identifying the king with the divinely sanctioned order.
Thus, David and Solomon were both involved in planning and building the
temple at Jerusalem, but there were temples built by Jeroboam in the North
at Bethel and Dan, and there may have been a royal sanctuary at Samaria[90]
or at Shechem,[91] though the arguments for such are speculative in both
instances. To the extent that the king may have been involved in organizing the cultic establishment, as the Chronicler reports David did extensively
and as 1 Kings 12 also reports for Jeroboam in the North, he served further
to exercise authority over the religious establishment and thus implicitly to
provide a grounding for the monarchy's control of Israelite life.[92] The
leadership of the king in establishing the official state cult is especially
noticeable in the case of Jeroboam, who drew upon ancient traditions in
creating new cult images (bulls) to replace the ark, which was in the temple in Judah, setting them up in old sanctuaries in Dan and Bethel,
installing new priests dependent upon him, and introducing a new major
fall festival to rival the festival in Jerusalem (see chapter 2).[93]

The ideology and character of kingship in ancient Israel was not sharply
dissimilar from its manifestation in other ancient Near Eastern societies.[94]
There existed in Israel, however, two significant checks on the dominance
of the royal ideology: (a) the involvement of the people in the choice of
kingship and of kings, and (b) the prophetic critique of kingship and of the
worship practices of Israel in the temple in Jerusalem as well as in other
shrines.[95] Whereas in Mesopotamia, kingship was understood to have "come
down from heaven" as a gift of the gods, and individual kings were called
and chosen by the gods, there existed in ancient Israel an old tradition

whereby kingship was itself the choice of the people—indeed, with divine resistance to its introduction—and the people were seen to participate in some way in the choice of ruler as well as the national god. While the involvement of the people in the election of the king is most prominent in the relatively late law of kingship in Deuteronomy 17 and is absent from such sources of royal theology as the royal psalms, the will of the people played a role in the ascent of persons to the throne from the early stages in the history of kingship.[96]

In the Northern Kingdom especially, prophetic critique seems to have been effective at times in restraining, if not undoing, monarchical social control, as in the case of Jehu's rebellion (2 Kings 9–10). As others have noted, it was the prophets who seem to have been the primary bearers of the more conditional understanding of kingship in the North.[97] In Judah that was less the case, although Jeremiah was apparently perceived as a serious threat to the social and political order, if the royal reaction to his prophecies as attested in the book of Jeremiah has any basis in reality.

If the king led in the establishment of the official state religion, centered in the central sanctuary—Jerusalem in the Southern Kingdom and Bethel in the Northern Kingdom—but present also in other royal sanctuaries (such as the one at Arad in the South and Dan in the North—see above and chapter 2),[98] and the temple cultus helped to undergird the royal theology and the claim of the king, especially in the South, it is to be expected that the king would also take the initiative in matters of reform of the state cultus. A number of these are reported, not all of which are historically certain:

> Asa (1 Kings 15:9–24 // 2 Chronicles 14–16[14:2–16:14])
> Jehoshaphat (1 Kings 22:41–51 // 2 Chron. 17:1–21)
> Athaliah (2 Kings 11 // 2 Chron. 22:10–23:21)
> Joash (2 Kings 12:1–17[11:21–12:16] // 2 Chron. 24:1–14)
> Amaziah (2 Chron. 25:14–16)

Such enterprises are regularly couched in the literature as moves to bring the worship practices into conformity with the official theology as represented in both the Sinaitic and Jerusalem traditions. But they also functioned to maintain royal control of the religious institutions and establishment and thus served a sociopolitical purpose as much as or more than they did a religious one. Hezekiah's cultic reform in the eighth century in Judah involved actions intended to bring worship practices into line with the Yahwistic tradition, particularly the exclusive worship of Yahweh and the distaste for divine images, or to effect such exclusivism and rejection of divine images beyond previous practice. While the historicity of Hezekiah's reform has been debated, it is likely that it involved at least the destruction of the bronze serpent, Nehushtan, and the dismantling of altars throughout the kingdom.[99] But there was a sociopolitical rationale for this reforming activity as well, as indicated in the following summary of Hezekiah's reform:

> This action can be seen as part of Hezekiah's plan to unify the kingdom of Judah, to centralize the cultic apparatus (with its fiscal infrastructure) in the Jerusalem Temple, and to attract northerners to Jerusalem's cause.[100]

One might well argue the same for Josiah's reform a century later, which seems to have had many of the same goals, although his ambitions for political unity seem to have been much larger, incorporating the Northern Kingdom into the kingdom of Judah.[101] As Albertz has described this far-reaching effort to centralize the cult and purify it of elements foreign to the official state cult, or to eliminate features that had been previously acceptable in the state cult, "it was at the same time a broad national, social and religious renewal movement which sought to use the historical opportunity offered by the withdrawal of Assyria to reconstitute the Israelite state fully."[102]

It is difficult to discern how accurate the reports of the Deuteronomistic Historian and the Chronicler are with regard to the reforms of such kings as Asa, Jehoshaphat, Joash, and Ahaz.[103] The latter two kings, however, demonstrate some of the ways that political and religious dimensions of the national life were joined together. In the case of Joash, the reform, as reported in Kings, centered around repair of the temple (2 Kings 12:1–16). It shows the king as responsible for upkeep of the cultic apparatus and having final authority in determining how temple revenues would be handled. The passage suggests that there was a temple tax, assessed upon citizens for upkeep of the temple and dispensed by the priests. Joash's reform had its impetus in the tendency of the priests to hold onto the money and not use it for repairs. So Joash instituted what Lowery calls a "user fee,"[104] which was dispensed by a joint administration of bureaucratic and priestly elements (2 Kings 12:10). The interaction of priestly and royal elements in tending to and supporting the cultic establishment is evident in the story, but the dominance of the king is also a marked feature of the account, one that is consistent with the role the king played in the establishment of the central cultus.

Ahaz's reform centered in his building of a second altar on a Syrian model. This apparently had to do with his accommodation to the Assyrians and the problem of how to assimilate the Assyrian gods to the stringent and intolerant Yahwistic state cultus. Ahaz managed this by a compromise that centered in his providing a new altar for the worship of Yahweh and moving the old altar to the side where the king could perform the rituals expected of an Assyrian vassal. Lowery concludes, "The brilliant double altar solution secured Ahaz's reputation as a loyal Yahweh worshiper and simultaneously showed him to be a loyal vassal to Assyria."[105]

The King's Participation in the Cult

The other major religious role of the king was as a leader in cultic activity. While the biblical data do not give us a lot of information about this, what is there tends to confirm what one would expect from the practices of kingship elsewhere. In Ugarit, for example, the king was involved in ritual activities that included ablutions, prayer, and especially sacrifice.[106] In Israel, also, the king on various occasions officiated at major cultic occasions, particularly in prayer and blessing and the offering of sacrifices. Both David and Solomon are depicted as leading the assembly of the people in standing at the altar and making sacrifices as well as blessing the people (2 Sam. 6:13, 17–18; 1 Kings 3:3; 8:5), both activities that were customarily in the hands of the priests. Elsewhere, kings are mentioned as presenting offerings and sacrifices in ways that suggest they officiated at the presentation (e.g., 2 Sam. 24:25; 1 Kings 12:32; 2 Kings 16:4). In Psalm 110, a royal psalm, the king is called "a priest forever" (Ps. 110:4). It cannot be inferred from these texts, however, that administering the sacrificial system was regularly a part of the royal responsibilities. In most of the cases mentioned above, the sacrifice went on in the context of the building of a new altar or a new sanctuary and thus was a one-time service of dedication and consecration. In one case—Ahaz's building a new altar like the one in Damascus—the text indicates that the king came to the altar and offered sacrifices, obviously to dedicate it, and then told a priest to offer the regular sacrifices at the great altar (each day understood), while the old bronze altar would be the king's personal entre to the deity or, as suggested above, the place where the king sacrificed to the Assyrian gods.[107] The one suggestion of regular priestly duties associated with the royal house is a single note in one of the lists of persons in David's administration (2 Sam. 8:18) to the effect that "David's sons were priests."[108]

The account of David's bringing the ark to Jerusalem in 2 Samuel 6 has often been read as evidence of a regular ritual procession of the ark into the temple. That narrative, however, is more likely to reflect a particular and standard ritual, "the introduction of a national god to a new royal city," something that was quite common in the ancient Near East.[109] In this case, of course, the ark was the "cult image" of the national god. The Assyrian inscriptions that tell of such an event describe a pattern not unlike what one encounters in 2 Samuel 6: "ceremonial invitation of the national god into a royal city, the presentation of sacrifices and 'feasts and banquets of choice dishes' for all the people of the land."[110] David's procession of the ark into the royal city of Jerusalem followed by sacrifices and offerings and then a feast for the people was just such an introduction of the deity into the new city. Even David's dancing, while clothed with a linen ephod, was a part of the ritual act. It is to be noted that in all of the Assyrian reports alluded to above, "special emphasis is placed on the role in the proceedings played by the king, whose pious service to the deity in question is thus stressed."[111] On the basis of the comparisons with the Assyrian texts, McCarter notes appropriately with regard to David, "He appears unambiguously as the patron and founder of the cult of Yahweh in Jerusalem."[112]

The King and the Central Festival[113]

The character of the central festival in the time of the monarchy has been one of the most debated topics in Israelite religion during the past century. Three hypotheses have dominated the discussion. H.-J. Kraus proposed that the feast of Tabernacles was the primary festival during the monarchy and centered in a celebration of Yahweh's choice of David as king and Zion as the divine abode.[114] The basic textual grounds for this hypothesis are 2 Samuel 6 and 7, 1 Kings 8, and Psalm 132, all of which have to do with ritual celebration of the promise to David and the establishment of Jerusalem as the place of the divine dwelling. A counterproposal came from Artur Weiser, arguing that the center of the cultus was a covenant festival, celebrated at the new year in the autumn to renew the encounter between God and people as well as the covenant bond established at Sinai. The center of the festival, Weiser saw, was the theophany of Yahweh, but the occasion was liturgically complex and included such elements as the proclamation of the divine name, the rehearsal of the history of salvation, the putting away of foreign gods, and the renewal of the covenant. Many of the psalms are to be seen as having their setting in life in this festival.[115]

While both of these reconstructions of the central festival have had some adherents, neither has claimed a large following. Nor has either one received as much vigorous debate as the third and earlier reconstruction of the central festival, which was Sigmund Mowinckel's argument for an enthronement festival of Yahweh as the central and large cultic event, again occurring at the new year feast of Tabernacles. According to Mowinckel's reconstruction, the festival centered in the declaration "Yahweh has

become king," a declaration occurring in several psalms that have come to
be designated "enthronement psalms" (Pss. 47, 93, 96, 97, 99), but it
includes celebration of the deity's creative activity, victory over all other
gods, the judgment of gods and nations, the election of Israel, and the
covenant made at Sinai. In addition to the enthronement psalms, Mowinckel saw many other psalms in connection with various aspects of the
festival.[116]

While it is not likely that one can find in one of these proposals a consensus about its appropriateness to the data available, which in this case
are largely textual, several observations can be made from the discussion
and the evidence about the central festival and its relation to kingship.

1. The few allusions to the fall festival suggest that it indeed had the
prominence during the time of the monarchy that has been ascribed to it
in these proposals. One may assume that a number of psalms and other
hymns were related to it and played some part in the celebration of the festival.

2. There is a clear stress upon the rule or kingship of Yahweh as a central and climactic element not only in enthronement psalms proper but
elsewhere in psalms and poetry. As noted in chapter 1, the kingship of
Yahweh is a notion that belongs to earlier rather than later elements of
Israel's religious thought and practice, as evidenced by its prominence in
early Israelite poetry (Ex. 15:18; Num. 23:21; Pss. 68:25; 24:9; and possibly
Deut. 33:5).

3. The expression *yahweh mālak* probably means "Yahweh has become
king (and thus reigns)." Such a translation neither denies the eternal character of Yahweh's reign nor implies anything about a dying and rising god.
The expression is more a proclamation of Yahweh's enthronement and rule
than an actual royal investiture.

4. In several poems (Exodus 15, Deuteronomy 33, Psalm 68), a pattern
may be discerned that includes Yahweh's coming to deliver and create a
people and his victory, which leads to the celebration of kingship and the
establishment of his sanctuary. In this pattern, Near Eastern mythic elements and Israel's historical experience came together.

5. The emphasis on Yahweh's election of David and Zion that is at the
heart of Kraus's proposal is appropriate, but in his reconstruction it is
viewed too narrowly and in isolation from or over against other notes that
are sounded in harmony with these themes. The choice of Jerusalem would
inevitably and early on have had larger connotations than simply establishing this city as the place of the temple. It also was the place where Yahweh dwelled, was enthroned, and ruled. The ark went up in victory as well

as to establish and choose a sanctuary. Mythic and cosmic overtones were there from the earliest times in the so-called ark narrative, and in Psalms 47, 68, and 132.

6. Along these lines, Cross has suggested a possibly fruitful direction in underscoring the joining of the motif of exodus and conquest with the motif of creation and kingship in the royal cult around the central festival. Yahweh entered in victory, having delivered his people, but this was also the ascent of the king to the throne. The institution of kingship and the temple brought the latter (which has many mythological overtones) more to the fore, and these were united with the interest in the choice of David and Zion.[117] The actual ritual activities of the king or the specific place of the king in the drama of the festival are not evident from the texts themselves.

THE SAGE-SCRIBE

The prophecy of Jeremiah alludes to three categories of leadership alongside each other: priest, prophet, and the wise (18:18). This last category represents, in some respects, more of an intellectual leadership than a religious one.[118] That is, the wise men and women were not directly associated with the cult; their sphere of operation was more the family, the school, the bureaucracies of the state, and the like. But their wisdom and instruction had to do with moral matters as well as court counsel and table manners, and to the degree to which wisdom was associated with "the fear of the LORD" (e.g., Prov. 1:7; 9:10; Job 28:28) the wise were seen as instruments for the instruction in true Yahwism as it had to do with the wholeness of everyday life. (It is not always clear when one is talking about a profession that is schooled and trained and when one is dealing with a more nebulous group of those who have gained their wisdom in experience more than in formal training.)

The book of Jeremiah also indicates that in speaking about a group called "the wise," it has in mind scribes who wrote and copied important texts and interpreted or taught them as well (8:8–9). Here one encounters a different term and a different role, describing persons who must have received some schooling and training in literary skills and perhaps in traditions of law and history. Scribes appear on the lists of royal officials (e.g., 2 Sam. 8:16–18; 20:23–26; 1 Kings 4:1–6; 18:18, 37; 2 Chron. 24:11–12). Their specific duties are not well spelled out, though it has been suggested on the basis of analogies that they drew up official edicts and that in the time of Hezekiah were involved in important diplomatic missions (2 Kings

18; Isaiah 36).[119] One may assume that they functioned as secretaries of some sort (à la Baruch with Jeremiah) in the general administration of the state.

The association of scribe and wise suggests that while some distinction must be maintained between the roles of "wise" (ḥākām) and "scribe" (sēper), there was significant overlap. Almost by definition, the scribe belonged to the learned and wise element of society and was so characterized.[120] The particular point at which that impinged on the religious life and practice of ancient Israel was in the way that, running from Jeremiah in the seventh to sixth centuries through Ezra to Ben Sira in the second century, the scribes were persons associated with wisdom and with the keeping of the law, that is, with its preservation and transmission. Thus, in Jeremiah, the condemnation of the scribes is that they claim to be wise and to have the law with them, but they betray their wisdom and the law that has been entrusted to their keeping (Jer. 8:8–9).[121] Ezra is called both priest (Ezra 7:11; Neh. 8:2) and scribe (Ezra 7:6, 11; 8:1) and sometimes both in the same context. What this dual role means for the actual profession of Ezra is unclear, but in both respects he is specifically identified with the law (Ezra 7:6, 10–12; Neh. 8:1–2). In Ben Sira's famous account of the duties of the scribe (38:34–39:11), he begins with the duty of devoting oneself to "the study of the law of the Most High" (38:34) and goes on to describe the many ways the sage/scribe seeks out wisdom and understanding.[122]

It is not surprising that the wise teacher and scribe should be associated with the law, for it was necessary both to preserve and hand it down and to teach it. The scribe was not alone in this enterprise. As we have noted, the priest also had responsibility for teaching the Torah.[123] But "the pivotal position of scribes as tradents of traditions also put them in a primary position with respect to their meanings."[124] This also meant that they could and did respond to the text, giving interpretive glosses or making scribal comments and corrections, a feature of the text that is evident in the present form of the Hebrew text of the Bible but even more visible in the Qumran texts, where it is possible to see the work of scribes correcting earlier texts.[125] By Jeremiah's time, such scribal activity with regard to the biblical text, specifically the Torah, is evident. In the postexilic community, that role became even more prominent as the mode of revelation was increasingly centered in scripture and its interpretation. The more charismatic modes of revelation associated with prophecy fell back in favor of the more objective—but not fully constricted—interpretation of scripture as the way by which the community discerned the will of God.[126] As that happened, especially in the postexilic community religion and onward, the scribes came

more to the fore among the leadership of the community, a fact symbolized and actualized in the leadership role of Ezra and its focus on the law,
both read and interpreted. As Fishbane has noted, this function was fully
consistent with and supportive of "the Persian policy of reviving and restoring local legal traditions" (see chapter 2).[127] It also meant that the Torah,
rather than becoming a dead letter, became the basis of teaching and interpretation. Out of such activity developed the rich store of interpretation that
began in the biblical text itself and continued on in the life of the communities that studied it and lived by it.[128]

CULTIC PARTICIPATION IN ANCIENT ISRAEL

The cultic assembly in ancient Israel was a gathering of the people for the
worship of Yahweh. Its constituency would seem to be self-evident, but the
biblical materials indicate that there were various ways in which participation in the formal worship of the deity was defined and delimited, both
with regard to the most formal occasions of the official state cult and with
regard to less formal or more ad hoc cultic moments. Two issues are
implicit and explicit in various ways in the literary forms of narrative, legislation, and psalm and prophetic speech: (a) who was permitted to take
part in the forms of worship and who was excluded; and (b) what were
the requirements for participation in worship? While these matters have
been touched on in the discussion of the role of women in family religion
(chapter 2) and the cult of the asherah (chapter 1) as well as in the discussion of purity, a more focused examination will be offered here with
particular attention to the formal elements of the cultus of Yahwism.

Exclusion of Foreigners

At several points in the legislative material and in the narrative accounts of
Israel's worship practices, restrictions against the involvement of non-
Israelites in the cultic assembly of Israel are articulated, sufficient to suggest
that the line between Israelite and non-Israelite, which affected other
aspects of social practice, also was determinative for participation in formal
religious activity.

In Deut. 23:3–7, a series of regulations prohibit some ethnic groups
(Ammonites and Moabites) from being admitted to the "assembly of the
LORD," while others (Edomites and Egyptians) may be admitted at least by
the third generation. Reasons are given for these distinctions, but they may
be rationalizations, and it is very difficult to say when such regulations may
have been operative in ancient Israel. What is important in this instance is

that the "assembly of the LORD" can refer to a gathering for religious purposes, but it is by no means restricted to that. It seems to have in mind the
adult males (see Deut. 23:1) meeting together in formal session for religious, military, or political purposes.[129] In some ways, participation in the
assembly was tantamount to citizenship.[130] The regulations cannot be read
as aimed primarily at exclusion of foreigners from cultic activity, though
that may have happened.[131]

From a later, postexilic context, there are indications of restriction of foreigners from temple worship. Ezekiel 44:5–9 purports to set guidelines for
who may be admitted and who is excluded from the temple, specifically
prohibiting "foreigners" from the sanctuary and from any duties in the sanctuary. Exodus 12:43 prohibits any "foreigner" from eating the Passover
meal. The account of Nehemiah's angry removal of the Ammonite Tobiah
out of his occupation of a room in the "house of God" may reflect this
development, though this act is presented as a response to a hearing of
Deut. 23:4–9 and thus an interpretation of that text as excluding foreigners,
at least an Ammonite, from the temple (cf. Lam 1:10). So also the prophetic
declaration that foreigners may enter "my house" to sacrifice and pray (Isa.
56:3–8; cf. 1 Kings 8:41–43) may represent a reaction to the postexilic
restriction of foreigners from cultic participation, a move that developed
out of a broader reading of the Deuteronomic regulation (cf. Lev. 22:25)[132]:

> The same broad construction of the law was evident during the period
> of the Return to Zion in the fifth century B.C.E. At that time, many Jew-
> ish men were found to have married foreign women, including
> Ammonites and Moabites but also others such as Ashdodites (from
> Philistia). Based on their interpretation of Deuteronomy 23:4–9 in com-
> bination with 7:1–4 and other verses in the Torah, Ezra, Nehemiah, and
> the leaders of the community insisted on the dissolution of all mar-
> riages.[133]

The reason for the dissolution of the marriages to foreign women (Ezra
9–10; Neh. 13:1–3, 23–29) may have been that there was no other way to
comply with the law since there was apparently no formal process for conversion at that time.[134] The exclusion continued, for in later second temple
times, foreigners or Gentiles were barred from the inner courts of the temple in Jerusalem, but by this time there were procedures for conversion. In
the tension reflected between the Ezekiel restriction and the Deutero-
Isaianic inclusive vision of the Temple, the Deuteronomic-Ezekiel impulse
won out.[135]

The situation is different with regard to the resident alien (*gēr*) or stranger who resided in Israel on a relatively permanent basis.[136] Milgrom has summarized the situation for the resident alien as follows:

> Though the *ger* enjoyed equal protection with the Israelite under the law, he was not of the same legal status; he neither enjoyed the same privileges nor was bound by the same obligations. Whereas the civil law held the citizen and the *ger* to be of equal status (e.g., Lev 24:22; Num 35:15), the religious law made distinctions according to the following underlying principle: The *ger* is bound by the prohibitive commandments but not by the performative ones. For example, the *ger* is under no requirement to observe the festivals. The paschal sacrifice is explicitly declared a voluntary observance for the *ger*. Whereas an Israelite abstains from the sacrifice on pain of *karet*, the *ger* may observe it provided he is circumcised (Exod 12:47–48; Num 9:13–14). In fact, the injunction to dwell in *sukkot* is explicitly directed to the "Israelite citizen" (Lev 23:42), which, by implication, excludes the *ger*. Similarly, the *ger* may participate in the voluntary sacrifical cult if he follows its prescriptions (Num 15:14–16; Lev 22:17ff.)[137]

What this seems to mean is that the resident alien, for the most part, was not excluded from participation in the ritual practices of Israel's cultic life, specifically the festivals and the sacrificial cult. The critical thing, however, was that the alien was prohibited from activities that might create impurity in the land and endanger its holiness or reflect the worship of gods other than Yahweh of Israel.[138] The resident alien was not required but was permitted to participate in those actions that involved the active worship of Yahweh. By the third century, the situation had changed as the possibility of formal conversion made it possible for a non-Israelite to become a member of the Israelite religious community, and so exclusion of non-Israelites became the pattern.[139]

Participation of Women

The significant role of women in the family religion of ancient Israel and in the more heterodox aspects of Israelite religion, at least by the standards implicit and explicit in the main strands of the prophetic, Deuteronomistic, and priestly movements, has been observed in chapters 1 and 2. But there is the further issue of the place that women may have had in the cultic activities of Israelite worship more generally, a question that has been much discussed and debated.[140]

As Phyllis Bird has observed, the basic sexual division of labor and the distinction between the domestic sphere as the realm of women's labor and the public sphere, including the major social institutions, as primarily a male domain, means that women rarely occupied major leadership roles in the official cultus.[141] What can be said then about women's participation in a cultus that was so regularly defined in terms of male leadership and male participation (e.g., Ex. 19:15; 23:17; 34:23; Deut. 16:16; 23:1; cf. Judg. 20:2)? Bird's summary generalizations, arising out of a sophisticated analysis of the data, come as close as one can probably get to an accurate answer:[142]

1. While leadership of the cultus appears at all times to have been under male control, women were not excluded absolutely from cultic service or sacred space. There seems to have been an increasing level of restriction, correlating with increasing centralization, specialization, and power.

2. Males occupied the positions of greatest authority, sanctity, and honor, and performed tasks requiring technical skills and training. This is reflected particularly in the restriction of the priestly role to males (see above).

3. Women's service in the cult seems to have been confined largely to maintenance and support roles, probably such things as weaving and sewing of vestments, hangings, and other materials for cultic use (see Ex. 35:25–26); the preparation of cultic meals or food used in the ritual; and the cleaning of cultic vessels, furniture, and quarters.[143]

4. Women had a more public involvement in official cultic activities as singers and dancers. While in the later period of the monarchy and the second temple period the musicians in the cultus seem to have been males (see above), at an earlier time two women (Miriam and Deborah) are depicted as leading in the singing of praise, both of whom are called "prophet" (Ex. 15:20–21 and Judg. 4:4; 5:1),[144] and Ps. 68:25 indicates that women formed a recognized group among the temple musicians in the procession into the sanctuary:

> Your solemn processions are seen, O God,
>   the processions of my God, my King, into the sanctuary—
> the singers in front, the musicians last,
>   between them girls playing tambourines.
>   (Ps. 68:25–26[24–25])[145]

Young women dancing seems to have been an expected part of the yearly festival at Shiloh (see 1 Sam. 1:3), though the particular function or significance of this is not indicated by the text (Judg. 21:19, 21)

5. The social context for the involvement of women in some of these formal roles may have been their association with priestly houses, hence their living near sanctuaries and thus having access to the sacred space, or as women without families who placed themselves in the service of the

sanctuary and under the guardianship of the authorities in the cultus. Such possible social settings are quite plausible but can only be speculative without more data to support them.

6. Although not all such religious acts were formally connected with the main cultus, women also prayed (e.g., 1 Sam. 1:10–16),[146] sought oracles (1 Kings 14:2–5; 2 Kings 4:22–23), made vows (Num. 30:3–15; 1 Sam. 1:11, 24–28), pronounced blessings (Ruth 2:20; 4:14), and participated in the festivals, whether at local shrines or at the central sanctuary (e.g., Deuteronomy 16). Presumably in this last case, they contributed to the preparation of the meals for the festival celebrations. Women are specifically identified as a component of the assembly gathered for major occasions of covenant renewal, reading the Torah, and the like (e.g., Deut. 29:10; 31:12). In the time of Nehemiah and Ezra, women and wives were regularly a part of the assembly at the reading of the Torah (Neh. 8:2), the service of penitence (Ezra 10:1), the renewal of covenantal obligations (Neh. 10:29–30[28–29]), and the celebration of joy (Neh. 12:43). The participation of the women seems to have been confined to their presence, but nothing further is indicated for the male participants, except possibly in Neh. 12:43, where the sacrificial activity may be confined to the males. At some stage in Israel's religion, women could take the vow of a Nazirite, a provision specifically indicated in the Priestly legislation (Num. 6:2).

The one major issue of debate in the current discussion is the nature of women's involvement in the sacrifical cult of ancient Israel. Both Bird and Winter have argued that their involvement was minimal, animal slaughter and sacrifice as an act of worship being confined to males.[147] A distinction is drawn by Bird between the woman's *presentation* of a sacrificial animal to a priest at the end of her days of purification after the birth of a child and the priest's actual *offering* of the animal (Lev. 12:6–7). Nor does she regard the sharing of a sacrificial meal as an act of sacrifice.[148]

This reading of the place of women has been recently contested on several occasions by Georg Braulik, specifically in relation to the Deuteronomic legislation.[149] Braulik has made theoretical, linguistic, and historical observations that are pertinent. The theoretical one has to do with the character of sacrifice. It is not to be seen as confined to a single act, for example, the actual slaughter of an animal, but includes the whole of the ritual that it encompasses. Braulik notes that the meal is central to the meaning structure of the sacrifice, and that this is a fully participatory event, comprising several ritual activities, not just sacrifice. The event described in 1 Samuel 1 is called a "sacrifice" but obviously involves more than simply the slaughter. Clearly a meal is indicated. Every indication is that women were fully involved in such sacrificial meals. Both in the earlier period as reflected in 1 Samuel 1 and 2 and in Deuteronomy, this was a family event and the wife was fully involved. In the case of Elkanah and Hannah, while the text at one point describes Elkanah as sacrificing (1 Sam. 1:4), elsewhere it speaks of the two of them going up together to the sacrifice (2:20), even noting the fact when Hannah does not go up (1:22), and in one instance identifies *both* of them as sacrificing or slaughtering (1:25). In the Masoretic Text, Hannah is the dominant acting figure in the report of the bringing of Samuel and the bulls to the sanctuary in payment of the vow (1 Sam. 1:23–2:1).[150]

The Deuteronomic legislation includes the women generally and addresses the wife as well as the husband in the "you" of the various statutes and ordinances. Noting that the wife is not listed in the various regulations that identify who was to participate in the pilgrimage festivals in the central sanctuary (e.g. Deut. 12:7, 12, 18; 14:26; 15:20; 16:11, 14), Braulik concludes,

> This can mean one of two things: either the free woman and house-
> wife was included in the "you" or the family mother had to stay at
> home alone, take care of the house and do all the work, while the
> whole family, including the slaves, went off on a pilgrimage, enjoyed
> the sacrificial meal and rejoiced in Jerusalem. The second alternative is
> highly improbable. Such an interpretation would run contrary not only
> to the older pilgrimage tradition (1 Samuel 1), but also to the equal
> esteem for men and women shown elsewhere in Deuteronomy. . . .
> Evidently, the "you" (*'attâ, 'attem*) of the list addresses women as well
> as men.[151]

If one can make that assumption, then the following kinds of acts were part of the ritual in the legislation that includes the lists of participants:

> offering a burnt offering (12:14)
>
> presenting burnt offerings on the altar, flesh and blood, and
>   pouring out the blood of the other offerings on the altar
>   (12:27)
>
> setting aside the tenth of the harvest (14:22)
>
> consecrating the firstborn of the herd and flock to Yahweh
>   (15:19)
>
> giving a freewill offering (16:10)
>
> keeping the festival for Yahweh your God (16:15)
>
> bringing the first fruits to Yahweh and the confession spoken
>   before and after the presentation (26:5, 10, 13)[152]

When one turns to the Priestly legislation, the situation is not radically different. In addition to sacrifices that women brought in relation to purification after childbirth (Leviticus 12) or after menstrual periods or other bodily discharges (Lev. 15:19–33), it is clear that women were included in the provisions for other forms of sacrifice. Following clues from earlier rabbinic exegesis, Mayer Gruber has noted that "one of the characteristic features of the cultic legislation of P is the use of the neutral, nonsexist expression *nepeš* and *'ādām,* both meaning 'person,' in referring to cultic acts which can or should be performed by either men or women or to cultic offenses committed by either men or women."[153] Among those texts where these words are used and imply either male or female agents are Lev. 2:1; 4:2, 27; 5:1–4, 15, 17; 7:20; 20:6; and Num. 15:27, 30–31. This means that women along with men would be participants in offerings of grain as well as the procedures for purification offerings after unintentional sins. But one may infer that in fact many other sacrificial acts were open to women in the Priestly legislation, as the rabbis suggested long ago with reference to Lev. 1:5.[154]

There remain two other rather enigmatic references to women with possible cultic significance that should not be overlooked. One is the reference to "the mirrors of the women who served (*ṣĕbā'ôt*) at the entrance to the tent of meeting" (Ex. 38:8). This allusion to "serving/ministering women" is given little interpretive context.[155] The use of the term *ṣābā',* which elsewhere not only refers to military service but to the cultic service of the Levites (Num. 4:3, 23, 30, 35, 39, 43; 8:24) when referring to an activity at the entrance to the "tent of meeting," surely refers to a specific role for certain women in the cultus.[156] The difficulty is defining what that is. Marie-Therese Wacker has noted that there are "maximalist" and "minimalist" interpretations of the meaning and function of these women. Some have seen the mirrors as suggesting identification with a goddess, either Egyptian[157] or Hittite and North Syrian, and one connected with the weather god.[158] This might suggest these women were in the service of Yahweh and his consort. On the other hand, the mirrors might be understood simply as a further indication of the largesse of the community in giving of its fine things for the building of the tabernacle. In either interpretation, there is a clear indication that women functioned in some official way in relation to the main cultus.

The second category of women in what might be an official cultic function is the *qĕdēšâ,* a term that seems to mean simply "holy woman" or "consecrated woman" and has a male parallel, *qādēš,* but is often translated as "cultic/sacred prostitute."[159] While much of modern scholarship has assumed that this reference was to women who engaged in sexual activities as a part of cultic rites, that is less and less certain in the light of more recent data and studies.[160] The association of the term with prostitution arises primarily out of the fact that in all three instances where the term *qĕdēšâ* appears, the Hebrew word for "harlot" (*zônâ*) occurs in a way that looks as if it is a synonym (Gen. 38:21–22; Deut. 23:18–19[17–18]; Hos. 4:14). Furthermore, Herodotus tells of a Babylonian custom whereby every woman in the land, sometime in her lifetime, had to sit in the temple of Aphrodite and have intercourse with a stranger. This claim was then picked up in other literature.[161]

Cognate terms are now known from Mesopotamia (e.g., *qadištu*) and Syria (Ugaritic *qdšm* and *qdšt*). In both cases, the terms clearly indicate cultic functionaries, but in neither case does one find indication of sexual activity as a cultic function. All the instances of the two Hebrew terms, *qĕdēšâ* and *qādēš*, occur in contexts where they are identified as foreign and unacceptable practices or they are present but condemned. The association of the feminine term with the word for "harlot" may reflect some degree of sexual activity, but it may also be a way of referring to its connection with worship practices that were regarded as idolatrous and apostate, the condemnation of which is often put in sexual terms, as, for example, in Jeremiah. Until further knowledge is gained, one must be content with seeing in the *qĕdēšâ* a female official or class in the formal cults of the Fertile Crescent, who may have also had an Israelite counterpart, but one that early on came to be condemned as reflecting foreign cults.[162] Analogy with Mesopotamian parallels would suggest that the role may have involved such activities as wet-nursing and midwifery; analogy with the Ugaritic parallels might suggest a kind of Levitical service in the sanctuary.[163]

Torah Obedience

Finally, a word must be said about the fact that participation in Israelite worship was dependent upon obedience to the Torah and that within the laws there were various restrictions upon participation that depended upon purity and holiness and required various ritual acts of sacrifice and purification before appearing before the Lord in worship for fear that the presence of the impure and the unholy might profane the sanctuary. This concern for pollution of the holy has been dealt with in chapter 4 in some detail and so does not need repeating here except to note its significance for the question of who may worship in the sanctuary. In addition, there were further restrictions on participation in the cultic assembly, such as genital impairment or birth by illicit union (presumably incest—Deut.

23:1–2), or other forms of physical deformity, mutilation, or defect, such as blindness, lameness, broken limbs, itching disease, and the like (Lev. 21:16–23; 2 Sam. 5:8).[164]

Along with these requirements for purity and holiness there were the requirements for moral uprightness in relation to the neighbor and before God. Such prerequisites to cultic participation are well identified by the prophets, who denounce the people for their going to the sanctuaries to worship in the face of violation of covenant obedience in their dealings in the marketplace and the court (Amos, for example). A more formal indication of the necessity for moral uprightness is suggested by the entrance liturgies in the Psalms. These question and answer psalms, notably Psalms 15 and 24, seem to have had their setting in life in the entry of pilgrims into the temple, where the priest and the entrants antiphonally would ask the question about what requirements were necessary for entering the sanctuary and the answer would come back defining the requirements. Thus, one finds in Ps. 15:1–2:

> O LORD, who may abide in your tent?
> Who may dwell on your holy hill?

and then the response:

> Those who walk blamelessly, and do what is right,
> and speak the truth from their heart.

A similar question and answer form in Psalm 24 suggests it served a similar function. Furthermore, there are prophetic texts that seem to have had a similar setting in life, such as Isa. 33:14–16 and Micah 6:6–8. All of these texts identify restrictions on cultic participation having to do with adherence to the requirements of the covenant for neighbor justice and fairness. So there were kinds of moral and human acts that also could determine participation, along with those qualities of person that might temporarily or by happenstance prohibit one from entering the sanctuary and thus profaning the holy place of the deity.

Epilogue

There is no clear point at which one can say that the religion of ancient Israel came to an end. On the contrary, the community that worshiped Yahweh of Israel in the cultus of the second temple and studied the Torah to discern the way of the Lord continued without interruption but in varying directions. In the Hellenistic era, various segments of the Jewish community gave emphasis to different dimensions of the religious tradition. Yet there was no cessation of the religious devotion that characterized the religion of Israel in the Iron Age before and after the destruction of Jerusalem and the exile and return of many Judeans. The decision not to present the religion of Israel in this volume in a primarily historical mode has at least some justification in the very fuzzy lines that mark the beginning and end of Israelite religion.

In this study, the parameters of that religion have been defined largely by the literature of the Old Testament or Hebrew Scriptures and the religious movements and developments reflected in them and out of which those sacred writings grew. The canonizing of this religious literature insured some continuity in the religion underlying it. So it was that the worship of Yahweh/Adonai/the Lord remained powerful and compelling on into the centuries that followed. While other religions of early Israel's time and place disappeared from the scene, Yahwism took new forms in continuity and discontinuity with what has been described in these pages. Prophets moved off center stage as scribes moved on. The anointed of the Lord, the king, became a part of the hope for the future, for some not yet realized and for others revealed in Jesus, a Jewish carpenter from Galilee. Sacrifice became spiritualized in different ways in Judaism and Christianity, but it did not remain in the forms it had taken in the course of ancient Israel's religious history.

Three streams flowed out of Israel's religion, all of them lively to this day and each comprising a remarkable array of diverse forms. Judaism kept the same canon of scripture and placed the emphasis of religious life on obedience to God's Word as revealed in the Torah. Christianity kept the canon and added to it, placing emphasis not on torah, about which it has remained ambivalent to this day, but on the "end" of the law in the form of the incarnate Christ, who is for Christians the Word of God made flesh. Islam took up another canon as the Word of God, seeing in the Koran the confirmation of earlier revelations and thus their replacement, and setting forth a new and rigorous combination of law and doctrine. In each stream, the monotheistic thrust so central to the religion of ancient Israel perdured, securely at the center of Judaism and Islam and in Christianity leading to the central doctrine of the Trinity as a way of accounting for the revelation of God in Jesus Christ without abandoning what Jewish and Gentile Christians had come to know about the oneness of that God. In each stream, the character of God and God's way with the community of faith echoed the depiction of the gracious and compassionate Lord of Israel, slow to anger and plenteous in mercy but by no means acquitting the guilty. In each stream, prophetic voices rose up from time to time, and different claims were made in their behalf.

Yet the tensions and conflicts discernable in the ancient religion of Israel became ever heightened as these different religious movements went their own way while claiming to be the true inheritors of the faith of Israel. Religious kinship has not made Jews and Christians and Muslims at home with each other. It may have exacerbated the conflicts that the combination of proximity and difference was bound to inspire. The treatment of the other remains at the center of the moral and ethical values of these three religious descendants of Yahwism, but the test that is often failed is the treatment of the other whose religious kinship seems not nearly as evident as the strangeness.

In such fashion the religion of ancient Israel lives on, transformed, persistent, resilient, asking in its new forms about the faithfulness of those who walk the way of the Lord and pray to the Creator God. That faithfulness depends in no small measure on the contemporary community hearing rightly what its mothers and fathers in the faith said and did and believed. Better understanding of this past may offer some clues for the present and guide us into the future. It may also tell us a little more about why we are the way we are, inform us about the good and the bad of our religious history, and offer some clues for how to walk together in mutual respect and understanding.

Abbreviations

AB	Anchor Bible
AnBib	Analecta biblica
ANEP	J. B. Pritchard (ed.), *The Ancient Near East in Pictures Relating to the Old Testament* (Princeton University Press, 1954)
ANET	J. B. Pritchard (ed.), *Ancient Near Eastern Texts*
AnOr	Analecta orientalia
AOAT	Alter Orient und Altes Testament
BA	*Biblical Archaeologist*
BAR	*Biblical Archaeology Reader*
BARev	*Biblical Archaeology Review*
BASOR	*Bulletin of the American Schools of Oriental Research*
BBB	Bonner biblische Beiträge
BHT	Beiträge zur historischen Theologie
Bib	*Biblica*
BibInt	Biblical Interpretation Series
BibOr	Biblica et orientalia
BN	*Biblische Notizen*
BWANT	Beiträge zur Wissenschaft vom Alten und Neuen Testament
BZAW	Beihefte zur *ZAW*
CAD	*The Assyrian Dictionary of the Oriental Institute of the University of Chicago*
CBQ	*Catholic Biblical Quarterly*
ConBOT	Coniectanea biblica, Old Testament
CRBS	*Currents in Research: Biblical Studies*
ErIsr	*Eretz-Israel*
FRLANT	Forschungen zur Religion und Literatur des Alten und Neuen Testaments
HAR	*Hebrew Annual Review*
HBT	*Horizons in Biblical Theology*
HSM	Harvard Scientific Monographs
HSS	Harvard Semitic Studies

HTR	*Harvard Theological Review*
HUCA	*Hebrew Union College Annual*
IBC	Interpretation: A Bible Commentary for Teaching and Preaching
IEJ	*Israel Exploration Journal*
Int	*Interpretation*
JAOS	*Journal of the American Oriental Society*
JBL	*Journal of Biblical Literature*
JCS	*Journal of Cuneiform Studies*
JNES	*Journal of Near Eastern Studies*
JNSL	*Journal of Northwest Semitic Languages*
JSOT	*Journal for the Study of the Old Testament*
JSOTSup	Journal for the Study of the Old Testament, Supplement Series
JSS	*Journal of Semitic Studies*
NCB	New Century Bible
OBO	Orbis biblicus et orientalis
OBT	Overtures to Biblical Theology
OTL	Old Testament Library
PEQ	*Palestine Exploration Quarterly*
RB	*Revue biblique*
RelSRev	*Religious Studies Review*
RSR	*Recherches de science religieuse*
SBLDS	Society of Biblical Literature, Dissertation Series
SBLMS	Society of Biblical Literature, Monograph Series
SBLSBS	Society of Biblical Literature, Sources for Biblical Study
SEÅ	*Svensk exegetisk årsbok*
Sem	*Semitica*
SJLA	Studies in Judaism in Late Antiquity
StudOr	Studia orientalia
TBei	*Theologische Beiträge*
TBü	Theologische Bücherei
TDOT	G. J. Botterweck and H. Ringgren (eds.), *Theological Dictionary of the Old Testament*
UF	*Ugarit-Forschungen*
VT	*Vetus Testamentum*
VTSup	Vetus Testamentum, Supplements
WBC	Word Biblical Commentary
WMANT	Wissenschaftliche Monographien zum Alten und Neuen Testament
ZAW	*Zeitschrift für die alttestamentliche Wissenschaft*
ZDPV	*Zeitschrift des deutschen Palästina-Vereins*

Notes

Introduction

1. On this point, see Albertz, "Biblische oder nicht-biblische Religionsgeschichte Israels?" 27–29.

2. See Miller, "Deuteronomy and Psalms."

3. The most recent English-language treatment of Israel's religion also takes a more topical approach to the subject. See Niditch, *Ancient Israelite Religion*.

4. See Miller, "Israelite Religion"; Zimmerli, "History of Israelite Religion"; Albertz, *History of Israelite Religion*, 1:1–21 (and the bibliography listed there); Arnold, "Religion in Ancient Israel"; Toorn, "Currents in the Study of Israelite Religion."

For discussion of some of the broader methodological issues and particularly the question of the relation of the history of Israel's religion to Old Testament theology, see *Jahrbuch für Biblische Theologie* 10 (1995), entitled "Religionsgeschichte Israels oder Theologie des Alten Testaments?"

Chapter 1. God and the Gods

1. See excursus 1 for evidence on this point.

2. In an essay that argues for a much more polytheistic and syncretistic Yahwism than this author believes to have been the case, Manfred Weippert writes, "In one respect, however, is this polyphonous, often quite dissonant choir united: that Yahweh is Israel's God and Israel the people of Yahweh. . . . Yahweh is the national god of Israel." See "Synkretismus und Monotheismus," 145 (translation mine). For the considerable recent discussion of the issue of monotheism and polytheism in ancient Israel, see Keel, ed., *Monotheismus im Alten Israel und seiner Umwelt*; Lang, *Monotheism and the Prophetic Minority*; M. Smith, *Early History of God*; Ackerman, *Under Every Green Tree*; Shanks and Meinhardt, eds., *Aspects of Monotheism*; Gnuse, *No Other Gods*; and especially various essays in W. Dietrich and Klopfenstein, eds., *Ein Gott allein?* A helpful and extended review of recent scholarship on the development of monotheism in Israel is provided by Gnuse in chapter 2 of his monograph.

3. See Deut. 33:2; Judg. 5:4–5; Ps. 68:7–8; Hab. 3:3 (cf. v. 7). McCarter has suggested that the plaster inscription from Kuntillet 'Ajrud in the Negeb recounting a theophany of El/Baal should be included in the list of appearances of Yahweh from the southern region (see excursus 1). Other inscriptions from Kuntillet 'Ajrud refer

to "Yahweh of Teman" as well as to "Yahweh of Samaria." These names suggest that there were local cults of Yahweh in the monarchical period, that is, local manifestations of the deity at cult centers where the national god was perceived to have a particular identity and character, not, presumably, significantly different from other manifestations of the same deity. Yahweh of Teman is Yahweh as worshiped in Teman. On the evidence for local cults of Yahweh, see chapter 2 of this volume and McCarter, "Aspects of the Religion of the Israelite Monarchy." Unlike McCarter, however, this author would regard the Shema of Deut. 6:4, "Hear, O Israel, Yahweh our God is one Yahweh," as probably a polemic against local cults and the tendency toward splitting off or hyper-differentiation of particular characteristics or manifestations of Yahweh. To the extent that Yahweh was himself in origin a local manifestation or split off of the high god of Canaan, El, into a separate and distinct cultus, as is suggested below, the concern was warranted. The resistance to the "asherah," in the Deuteronomic circles particularly, probably arose out of the same fear of a separate cultus being formed around the sacred cult object or "asherah" of the deity Yahweh (see below).

4. Cf. Cross, "Reuben, First-Born of Jacob."

5. For a helpful summary statement of this evidence and the geographical location of these names, see Mettinger, *In Search of God*, 24–28.

6. The text of Ex. 18:27 suggests that Sinai, while it is probably to be found in the general region of Edom and Midian, was understood to be some distance from the actual locale of the Midianite priest, Jethro.

7. On the southern and Midianite origins of Yahwism, see Weinfeld, "Tribal League of Sinai."

8. See Mettinger, *In Search of God*, 15–17.

9. For a brief summary of the Greek transcriptional evidence and further bibliography, see Mettinger, *In Search of God*, 28.

10. Cross, *Canaanite Myth and Hebrew Epic*, 66. For the most detailed spelling out of the linguistic, historical, and philological evidence for the formation and meaning of the divine name, cf. pp. 60–75. A more recent review of the matter and later bibliography may be found in David N. Freedman and Michael O'Connor, "*yahweh*," *TDOT* 2:500–521.

11. See, e.g., Num. 10:36; Deut. 33:2–3; and Ps. 68:18. On these texts, see Miller, "Two Critical Notes on Psalm 68 and Deuteronomy 33"; and Cross, *Canaanite Myth and Hebrew Epic*, 100–102. Cf. Josh. 5:13–15; 10:12–14; Judg. 5:20; and Hab. 3:3, 5, 10–11. The sense of the word *ṣĕbā'ôt* as the object of a verbal divine name may have become lost at a fairly early stage and the name simply understood as "Yahweh of Hosts," that is, as Yahweh the creator and commander of the hosts of heaven and earth. The assumption that the divine name could not take a construct according to the rules of Hebrew grammar needs to be reassessed in light of the presence of such divine titles as *yhwh šmrn*, "Yahweh of Samaria," and *yhwh (h)tmn*, "Yahweh of Teman," in the inscriptions from Kuntillet 'Ajrud. Yahweh Sebaot is at least analogous to these other names if it represents the particular manifestation of El that split off into a separate and distinct cultus, even though the Kuntillet 'Ajrud names would not represent such a radical step. For discussion of this linguistic issue, see Emerton, "New Light on Israelite Religion." While Emerton is inclined to see "Yahweh of Samaria" as a reference to the local manifestation of

Yahweh in Samaria, he does not think that "Yahweh of Teman" refers to a local manifestation. It refers to the God who comes from the southern region.

12. Procreative imagery, both male and female, is used to speak of Yahweh's creation of Israel in Deut. 32:18.

13. The epithet "creator/maker of (heaven and) earth" appears frequently as an epithet of Yahweh in what may be early tradition (Gen. 14:19) and late (e.g., Pss. 124:8; 134:3; and Second Isaiah). It is also known from an eighth-century inscription found at Jerusalem (?), although the text is broken and the divine name in front of "creator of earth" is missing. For discussion, see Miller, "El, Creator of Earth."

14. Cross, *Canaanite Myth and Hebrew Epic*, 71.

15. An analogue for such a division is provided in the Old Akkadian period in Mesopotamian religion where *annunītum,* which was an epithet of Inanna and with Inanna forms a compound, split off and became an independent deity after the Old Akkadian period, gaining her own epithets. See Roberts, *Earliest Semitic Pantheon,* 147.

16. "Many of the traits and functions of 'El appear as traits and functions of Yahweh in the earliest traditions of Israel: Yahweh's role as judge in the court of 'El (Ps 82; Ps 89:6–8) and in the general picture of Yahweh at the head of the Divine council; Yahweh's kingship (Exod 15:18; Deut 33:15; Num 24:21); Yahweh's wisdom, age, and compassion (*yahwê 'ēl raḥūm wĕḥannūn*) and above all, Yahweh as creator and father (Gen 49:25; Deut 32:6)." (Cross, *Canaanite Myth and Hebrew Epic*, 72). For inscriptional evidence in support of the identification of Yahweh and El in preexilic Israel, see Miller, "El, The Creator of Earth."

17. Indirect evidence has been proposed to argue for the worship of Yahweh in Syria and in Edom. On the former, see Dalley, "Yahweh in Hamath in the 8th Century BC"; on the latter, see Rose, "Yahweh in Israel—Qaus in Edom?" While the arguments proposed in each case are intriguing and not to be dismissed, the data are too slight and the speculation too strong to make a case for either one. Further evidence may, however, as in all matters, lead to a revision of this conclusion.

18. Cf. Albertz, *History of Israelite Religion,* 1:61–66. Albertz explores the possible social roots of the sole worship of Israel in the "relatively simple social structure" of the exodus group without "far-reaching social differentiation, division of work, or institutional division of society," which seems to be connected to the flourishing of polytheistic systems.

19. Following the earlier suggestion of Albright, David N. Freedman has claimed to see in Genesis 49 reference to father, mother, and son gods as a kind of triad in pre-Yahwistic patriarchal religion. The data, however, are too incomplete or depend too much on emendation and interpretation of difficult texts to place much weight on this suggestion.

20. Examples include Chemosh of the Moabites, Qaus of the Edomites, and El (or Milkom, which may have been a name of El) of the Ammonites. See Lemaire, "Déesses et dieux." On the last of these, for which we have virtually no data apart from proper names, see Tigay, "Israelite Religion," 171; and Lemaire, "Déesses et dieux," 142–43.

21. Cross, "The Epic Traditions of Early Israel," 37. Cf. Cross, *Canaanite Myth and Hebrew Epic,* 271.

22. Cf. Ex. 6:7a and Jer. 31:33 as well as other formulations, such as Ex. 15:17a;

19:4–6; Deut. 7:6; 32:9. Cf. M. Weippert, "Synkretismus und Monotheismus," 145, although he sees the covenant expression of this relation as relatively late. On this formula, see Rendtorff, *Covenant Formula*.

23. Deuteronomy provides the clearest documentary evidence for the influence of suzerainty treaty forms on the shape of Israelite covenant. The influence of this model, however, may reach back into the earlier pact of the league that bound the tribes together. For the relation of treaty to covenant, see Mendenhall, *Law and Covenant in the Old Testament*; Baltzer, *Covenant Formulary*; Hillers, *Covenant*; idem, *Treaty Curses and the Old Testament Prophets*; McCarthy, *Treaty and Covenant*; idem, *Old Testament Covenant*; and Weinfeld, *Deuteronomy and the Deuteronomic School*. For the claim that the covenant relationship does not arise in Israelite religion until the eighth century or later, see Perlitt, *Bundestheologie im Alten Testament*; Nicholson, *God and His People*.

24. On the three fundamental types of power or dimensions of social structure— economic, ideological, and coercive—see Runciman, *Treatise on Social Theory*, 2:12–20. Cf. Mann, *Social Sources of Power*, vol. 1, chapter 1. On the combination of coercion and consent, see Berlinerblau, "Preliminary Remarks for the Sociological Study of Israelite 'Official Religion,'" in 159–60.

25. Examples of this include Solomon and Rehoboam's corvée and Ahab's manipulation of the procedures of justice to get at Naboth's vegetable garden. Needless to say, those close to the court would have also benefited from this expansion of a centralized economic power.

26. Cross, "Kinship and Covenant in Ancient Israel."

27. Cross has suggested that the intimate relationship with the family god was expressed in the earliest period of Israel's history in the image of the Divine Kinsman, who fulfills the mutual obligations and receives the privileges of kinship. "He leads in battle, redeems from slavery, loves his family, shares the land of his heritage (*naḥǎlāh*), provides and protects. He blesses those who bless his kindred, curses those who curse his kindred [Gen 12:3]. The family of the deity rallies to his call to holy war, 'the wars of Yahweh,' keeps his cultus, obeys his patriarchal commands, maintains familial loyalty (ḥesed), loves him with all their soul, calls on his name" ("Kinship and Covenant in Ancient Israel," 7).

28. Genesis 49:25–26 offers an especially clear statement of the deity as dispenser of the blessings of fertility in nature. Freedman has suggested that the deity or deities represented in this text are pre-Yahwistic, but at an early stage the text would have been understood as referring to Yahweh ("Who Is Like Thee among the Gods?" 321–27).

29. The solar associations of Yahweh have been noted especially by Stähli, *Solare Elemente im Jahweglauben*; Taylor, *Yahweh and the Sun*; and Keel and Christoph Uehlinger, *Gods, Goddesses, and Images of God in Ancient Israel*, 248–62. They conclude as follows:

> The correlation of the iconographic symbols for the sun and the heavens with epigraphic documentation that gives evidence for a contemporary context, in which Yahwism was dominant, leads one inevitably to formulate a hypothesis that the movement in which the Phoenician Baal took on celestial and solar attributes and became Baalshamem is

to be seen as part of a larger shift in religion concerning the entire Levant, a shift that affected Israel as well. Like the Phoenician Baal, the Israelite Yahweh took on the characteristics of a celestial/solar "Most High God" during the Iron Age IIB as well. Some biblical texts also show Yahweh in the role of Baalshamem. In Ps 104:1–4, Yahweh has characteristics strongly associated with the sun and is surrounded by winged servants. (261)

Cf. M. Smith, "Near Eastern Background of Solar Language."

Keel and Uehlinger have also identified a movement toward astralization of the heavenly powers in the later preexilic period that may have involved increasing lunar associations with Yahweh (298–316).

30. There are many other metaphors present in Israel's conception of its God, some from nature (e.g., rock and eagle), some from kinship (e.g., father and mother). All of these participate in the complex profile of this deity. Here we are identifying those that seem to dominate and control the shape of the deity in Israel's history. Among those works that treat the images and metaphors of Israel's notion of deity are Mettinger, *In Search of God*; and Korpel, *Rift in the Clouds*.

31. For an elaboration of the shaping of Israel's early historical memory in the categories of myth, see Cross, *Canaanite Myth and Hebrew Epic*.

32. See, for example, the way in which the experience of slavery in Egypt and the liberation by Yahweh are motivating elements in the laws of the Book of the Covenant and Deuteronomy (e.g., Ex. 20:2; 22:20–23[21–24]; 23:9; Deut. 5:6, 15; 15:15; 24:17–18).

33. Cf. Hanson, *People Called*.

34. On the covenantal character of Judg. 5:31, see Moran, "Ancient Near Eastern Background."

35. Both the prose (Judges 4) and poetic (Judges 5) accounts of the battle with Sisera describe it in highly synergistic fashion.

36. See, for example, vv. 2, 7–8, 11, 13–18, 23, and the extensive report of Jael's killing of Sisera. The interpretation of vv. 13–18 vis-à-vis the question of whether it is a reprimand of nonparticipating tribes or a recounting of those who did participate is a matter of debate. Verse 23 makes it clear that there was nonparticipation along with willing involvement of people and leaders (vv. 2, 9, 13). For a presentation of the minority view that vv. 13–18 recount participation rather than nonparticipation, see Miller, *Divine Warrior*, 96–97; Cross, "Epic Traditions of Early Israel," 37 n. 67; and idem, *From Epic to Canon*, 54–55 n. 7.

37. See von Rad, *Holy War in Ancient Israel*, 41–42. Note that the Moabites are called the "people of Chemosh" in an archaic poem in Num. 21:27–30, where the context also indicates the designation has in mind the Moabite militia defeated by Sihon and the Amorites. While we have little information about the Moabite national deity Chemosh, whose name, unlike Yahweh's, is known from the Ugaritic pantheon, this text and the Mesha stele suggest significant similarities with the contemporary Israelite deity in character and in relation to his subject people, the Moabites. The report of Mesha king of Moab's sacrifice of his firstborn in battle (2 Kings 3:27) may suggest a significant departure in religious practice. But there is no reference to Chemosh in the Kings account, and such practices are attested by royal

figures in ancient Israel also even if always condemned as a corruption of Yahwism learned from the other nations (2 Kings 16:3). On Num. 21:27–30, see Hanson, "Song of Heshbon and David's *Nîr.*"

38. The role of the ark as the battle palladium of the divine warrior Yahweh is indicated in the archaic poem of Num. 10:35–36 as well as in Ps. 24:7–10, where the ark, though not mentioned, is to be assumed as the throne on which the triumphant Yahweh enters the city gates and the doors of the temple. Cf. the reference to "you and the ark of your might" in Ps. 132:8. On the song of the ark in Num. 10:35–36, see Miller, *Divine Warrior*, 145–47.

39. On this narrative, see Miller and Roberts, *Hand of the Lord*, and the bibliography cited there. The authors are inclined to date this narrative close to the occasion of which it speaks, while others assume it belongs to a much later period. At whatever time it originated, it attests to the power of this image in Israel's understanding of its God.

The military practices and the divine conceptions associated with them in this story as well as in other texts discussed here are reflective of widespread ancient Near Eastern modes of understanding the role(s) of deity or deities in the practice of war. See, e.g., Miller, *Divine Warrior;* M. Weippert, "'Heiliger Krieg' in Israel und Assyrien"; and Kang, *Divine War in the Old Testament.*

40. For elaboration of the way in which prophetic functions are linked in significant ways to the notions of Yahweh as warrior, judge, and king, see Miller, "Sovereignty of God." On the particular association of the prophets with the warrior activity of Yahweh, cf. Miller, "Divine Council and the Prophetic Call to War."

41. On the Day of Yahweh, see von Rad, "Origin of the Concept of the Day of the Lord"; and Everson, "Days of Yahweh." Cf. Hanson, *Dawn of Apocalyptic.*

42. See Miller, "Faith and Ideology in the Old Testament."

43. See Schmid, *Gerechtigkeit als Weltordnung.*

44. For studies of Israelite religion that see the kingship of Yahweh as a central feature, see de Moor, *Rise of Yahwism;* and especially Mettinger, *In Search of God,* 92–122.

45. See e.g., Num. 23:21; Pss. 29:10; 68:24; and possibly Deut. 33:4–5. The imagery of deity as king was widespread in the ancient Near East long before Yahweh appeared on the scene and was a feature of the characterization of both El and Baal. See, e.g., Schmidt, *Königtum Gottes in Ugarit und Israel;* Mettinger, *In Search of God,* 93; and Korpel, *Rift in the Clouds,* 281–86.

46. Note that in Exodus 15 the exalted status of Yahweh above all the gods is acclaimed as being demonstrated in the defeat of the Egyptian army at the sea. Cf. Pss. 95:3 and 89:6–15 (5–14).

47. Miller, "Sovereignty of God," 130.

48. The joining of these two is spelled out in detail in Mettinger, *In Search of God,* 92–122.

49. See Kraus, *Worship in Israel;* Cross, *Canaanite Myth and Hebrew Epic,* 99–105 (and the bibliography cited by Cross in n. 44); and Miller, *Divine Warrior.*

50. See the comment of Cross, *Canaanite Myth and Hebrew Epic,* 111:

> Late Prophetic and proto-apocalyptic eschatology was born of this wedding of kingship and Conquest themes in the cultus. The Day of

> Yahweh is the day of victory in holy warfare; it is also the Day of Yahweh's festival, when the ritual Conquest was reenacted in the procession of the Ark, the procession of the King of glory to the Temple, when "God went up with the festival blast, Yahweh with the sound of the horn . . . for Yahweh is king of the whole earth" [Ps. 47:6, 8].
>
> In apocalyptic, the battle of the sons of light and darkness—the Second Conquest—becomes a central feature of the "last days."

The claims for a possible mock or sham cultic battle at the center of the New Year's festival (à la Mowinckel), which have always been questionable and without evidence in the biblical material, have been called into even more serious question by the argument of Karel van der Toorn that such a cultic activity was no part of the Akitu festival in Mesopotamia. See van der Toorn, "Babylonian New Year Festival."

51. Norman K. Gottwald has also noted the sociopolitical importance of the three images of Yahweh discussed above, as the following paragraph reveals:

> In Israel *as a cult community*, Yahweh is the sole jealous *patron deity* working against divisiveness and waywardness in the ranks of his worshippers. In Israel *as a popular army*, Yahweh is *commander-in-chief*, "a man of war," arousing the faint-hearted and solidifying common military efforts. In Israel *as a customary and quasi-legal community*, Yahweh is *arbitrator and judge* pressing toward standardized practices in securing the integrity of the egalitarian community. In Israel *as a polity or realm of self-rule*, Yahweh is the ultimate and sole *sovereign*, the surrogate king, who guarantees the diffusion and decentralization of power within the several sovereign groups of the community. All of the symbols of Yahweh in his various guises refer with positive reinforcement to socioeconomic desiderata in the community and to the assurance that power will be used in ways that preserve the system externally and internally. (*Tribes of Yahweh*, 615)

The significant difference between Gottwald and the analysis of the dominant images of Yahweh in these pages is that those images are seen here to be both positively reinforcing and negatively critical. They are capable of disrupting the structure that they have helped to reinforce and that maintains them as important features of its theology-ideology. One problem with Gottwald's structural-functionalist and historical-cultural-materialist approach, which in this writer's opinion is often illuminating and productive, is that it does not seem to allow for or take adequate account of the anti-ideological dimension, the capacity of the ideology to subvert its proponents. That is, these images had critical as well as constructive functions. They had destabilizing as well as reinforcing potential.

52. While using a somewhat different rubric, that is, "selfish human motivations," J. J. M. Roberts has characterized ways in which the kingship of Yahweh undergirded social, economic, and political aspects of Israel's league structure and life:

> Israel's covenantal recognition of Yahweh as king and its acceptance of the covenantal law in the tribal assembly probably reflected a rejection

of Pharaonic rule and of Canaanite kingship, both of which had been experienced by different elements in the assembly as oppressive. Assuming that this is correct, however, the creation of this rival theological ideology for self-government was not without its selfish human motivations. By uniting under a divine overlord, the tribes gained a supratribal strength that aided them in their struggle to wrest living space from the established city-states in Canaan. Moreover, by vesting that unifying power in a divine king rather than in a human king they preserved the maximum freedom for the pursuit of their own tribal interests as well as scoring a propaganda victory against their opponents in the struggle for Canaan. The burden of taxation that was needed to support Israel's divine king was far less than that required to support the human kings of the Canaanite city-states. Thus, for large elements of the population of Canaan capitulation to the Israelites offered the advantage of lower taxes as well as relief from the economic disruption that hostile Israelite tribes could cause to the cities that opposed this confederacy. As N. K. Gottwald has correctly noted, the Israelite confederacy in no way represented the renouncement of the human exercise of coercive power; it simply redistributed the power in a less centralized fashion than the contemporary monarchies. While Yahweh was the acknowledged suzerain, the actual governmental power lay in the hands of the tribal leaders and the religious authorities. Moreover, while that power was diffuse and apparently ill-defined, it was clearly enough recognized that any shift in its distribution could provoke intertribal warfare. ("In Defense of the Monarchy," 384–85)

It is worth noting that social theorist W. C. Runciman has argued that "our traditional vocabulary of motives" (such as Roberts uses with his reference to the "selfish human motivations" within the early league structures) "furnishes a perfectly adequate provisional grounding for hypotheses about the causes of the modification or preservation of one rather than another set of institutions and the evolution of the society in question from one to another mode or subtype of the distribution of power." See *Treatise on Social Theory*, 2:32–33. Roberts argues that there is a "human and self-serving element" in the earlier structure and in the monarchical one that developed out of it.

53. For a full-scale development of the claim that early Yahwism arose in a resistance to the urban and imperial-feudal structures of Late Bronze Age Canaan and was a function and expression of the particular "socio-economic and communal-cultural existence" of early Israel, see Gottwald, *Tribes of Yahweh*, 692.

That historico-territorial factors entered into the conception of Yahweh is suggested by the account of Ahab's wars with the Arameans in the Northern Kingdom in the ninth century (1 Kings 20). Gottwald has summarized the territorial horizon of Canaan in the Late Bronze Age that was the geographical background for the formation of the Israelite league:

Maximal Canaanite ruling-class domination over the populace was exercised in cities of the plains and valleys, whereas cities in the highlands, although apparently organized by elites, were less effective in extending control over their hinterlands. The correlated differentials in Egyptian and Canaanite elite control according to regions were functions of a complex set of variables affecting accessibility and profitability to overlords. Specifically historico-territorial factors were at work. The city-states in the productive plains and valleys were close together, with the result that rural populations were easily dominated by urban elites.

The city-states in the highlands were farther apart. Population was much sparser in the hills than in the plains and valleys because of the difficulty of cultivating a thicketed and forested region with bronze tools and with an undependable water supply. Trade was inhibited by the rough terrain and the region's relative remoteness from the main coastal and valley communication arteries. It was always possible for groups resisting domination by the highland city-state elites to withdraw into relatively inaccessible areas and to escape direct control. It was just such hilly regions that served as base areas for the Amarna 'apiru and for the later Israelites. (395–96)

In the conflict with Aram, the Israelites were specifically seen by the Arameans as worshiping a god of the hills or highlands (*hārîm*) who exercised domination in that region (1 Kings 20:23, 28). The only way for the Arameans to defeat the Israelites was to draw them out into the valleys where the power of the Israelite god(s) did not work. That territorial restriction, however, is specifically rejected by the Yahweh representative in the story, and the deity's power over other geographical areas is asserted and demonstrated in the defeat of the Aramean army at Aphek.

The text thus associates Yahweh and Israelite strength with the areas where historically the Canaanites had not been as firmly in control, while at the same time implicitly contrasting the Aramean assumption that Yahweh was a local or regional deity with the Israelite, or prophetic, insistence that the sovereignty and power of Yahweh was more universal in scope, or at least not geographically restricted in a narrow sense.

54. The enthronement of the divine king on a moveable ark, the deity's abode in a tent shrine, and the likelihood that there was no fixed central sanctuary for an extended period of time are consistent also with the lack of a central government reinforced in a central and national cult, as in the monarchical period. See 2 Sam. 7:5–7 and Cross, *Canaanite Myth and Hebrew Epic*, 231, who speaks of "the typology of the Tent of 'El and the royal temple of Ba'al (in Canaanite mythology) and their foundation in patriarchal and monarchical social structures." He regards the tent shrine of early Israel, recrudescent in the Priestly theology, as reflecting the Tent of El typology.

55. Psalms 2 and 132 make this especially clear. See Roberts, "Zion in the Theology of the Davidic-Solomonic Empire," 99. He notes a similar approach in Assyria and Babylon.

56. See Brueggemann, "Social Significance of Solomon," 124.

57. Ibid. It is apparent, however, that the construction proposed here differs from

that of Brueggemann in not claiming "a radically changed definition of Yahweh, from a transformative agent to a guarantor." The conceptuality remained fundamentally the same, if expressed in different ways by different elements within the community and at different times. Further, Yahweh's role vis-à-vis social and political structures was not necessarily at one time stabilizing and at another transformative. At any one time or within any single sociopolitical structure, Yahweh was able to and did function in both ways. Cf. Roberts, "In Defense of the Monarchy," 386–87.

58. Cross, *Canaanite Myth and Hebrew Epic*, 224. Numerous examples from the United Monarchy as well as from the history of both kingdoms are cited by Cross on pp. 224–29.

59. See Amos 3:13–15; 5:4–5; 7:10–17; 8:1–3; Jeremiah 7 and 26; Ezekiel 9–11; and Micah 3:9–12.

60. In this regard, see Weinfeld, "Zion and Jerusalem as Religious and Political Capital"; and Roberts, "In Defense of the Monarchy," 386–87.

61. Gottwald, following Morton Smith, Bertil Albrektson, and others, has called attention to some of the basic common elements within the ancient Near Eastern notions of the high god that were present in the characterization of Yahweh as well as the particular mutation that took place in the cult of Yahweh. In the "common Near Eastern symbolic structure of religion" that premonarchic Israel shared, he sees the following six trait categories:

The high god is
        individuated and elevated
        active in the world
        conceived by natural and human analogies
        powerful, just, and merciful
        in bond with a people or a region
        interpreted by human representatives

Gottwald sees the following early Israelite mutations in this paradigm:

The sole high god
        usurps the entire sacred domain
        alone is active in the world
        is conceived by egalitarian sociopolitical analogies
        is coherently manifest in power, justice, and mercy
        is in bond with an egalitarian people
        is interpreted by egalitarian functionaries

Such an analysis of common traits and particular mutations has much to commend it in characterizing the God of Israel in relation to the divine milieu and the common theology of the ancient Near East. The analysis does not depend utterly upon Gottwald's general sociological approach for its claims to accuracy. However, the place where the largest questions can be raised is in a matter that is crucial to his construction—the use of the term "egalitarian." The egalitarian impulse cannot be denied in this writer's opinion, but that it is as sharply present in the premonarchical period as Gottwald claims is less clear. Yet where Gottwald's analysis represents a claim that Yahweh was a god who was not tied to class or group and who was understood to be particularly attentive to the cries of the weak and the powerless and required a largely just society measured by the way the weakest elements were treated, that would seem to be generally on target for the history of Israel's religion.

62. In taking note of the various myths that describe the conflicts of El to establish his headship in the family of the gods as well as other theogonies of the ancient Near East, Cross has made the interesting and provocative association of the patriarchal character of the deity with the patriarchal structures of society:

> The myths of 'El present static or eternal structures which constitute nature and the uneasy order of a patriarchal society. They do not seek to explain the historical course in the rising or falling popularity of a god's cult. In the cosmic family of the gods the patriarch always stands between the old (or) dead god and his lusty and ambitious son. It is this structure the myth describes, a "primordial" structure. The older theogonic pairs, at least at first, must inevitably be incestuous. Moreover, patriarchal society creates settings in which the temptation to incest on the one side and revolt against the father on the other side constantly threaten family peace. In the court history of David these forces are dramatically revealed. The rape of Absalom's sister Tamar by Amnon, another son of David, began a conflict which included fratricide and ultimately the revolt of Absalom against David. The transfer of power was signalized by Absalom's violation of his father's harem, and the episode ended only in a test of arms in which Absalom fell. The succession to David's throne by Solomon whom David appointed king in his last days also was marked by fratricidal conflict and harem intrigue. This is the pattern of life of men and gods who live in the extended families of patriarchal society. (*Canaanite Myth and Hebrew Epic*, 42)

In addition to the myths of El, Cross has in mind the theogony of the Babylonian Creation epic and the patricide and incest in the Harab myth. On the latter, see Jacobsen, *Harab Myth*; and Miller, "Eridu, Dunnu, and Babel."

63. Cf. Scharbert, "Formgeschichte und Exegese von Ex. 34, 6f"; Dentan, "Literary Affinities of Exodus XXXIV 6f."; Schmidt, *"De Deo,"* 86ff.; Fishbane, "Torah and Tradition," 280–81; idem, "Revelation and Tradition," 352–53; idem, *Biblical Interpretation in Ancient Israel*, 335–50; Dozeman, "Inner-Biblical Interpretation of Yahweh's Gracious and Compassionate Character"; and Spieckermann, "Barmherzig und gnädig ist der Herr."

64. See the extended study of Spieckermann, "Barmherzig und gnädig ist der Herr," which seeks to establish the formula, "the Lord is merciful and gracious, slow to anger and abounding in steadfast love," as being as central to Old Testament religion as other brief predications, such as "your God from the land of Egypt" (Hos. 12:10) or "I am who I am" (Ex. 3:14). Spieckermann sees the weight of usage of this formula in the exilic and postexilic period but argues that it has a long prehistory reaching back to Yahweh's incorporation of the attributes of El as reflected in the

five uses of the formula, *'l rḥwm wḥnwn*, "God/El gracious and merciful." On the question of the antiquity of the formula, cf. Miller, "Psalms and Inscriptions," 330 n. 42.

65. The italicized words are the core of the formulation and apparently the most oft-quoted part, but the whole passage is picked up again and again in biblical texts as well as being alluded to in the inscription from Khirbet Beit Lei (see below).

66. On the presence of such epithets in relation to El in Ugaritic and Amorite religion, see de Moor, *Rise of Yahwism*, 228; Cross, *Canaanite Myth and Hebrew Epic*, 72; and Spieckermann, "Barmherzig und gnädig ist der Herr," 3.

67. See Num. 14:18–19; 2 Chron. 30:9; Neh. 9:17, 31–32; Pss. 86:15; 103:8; 111:4; 145:8; Jer. 32:18; Joel 2:13; Jonah 4:2.

68. See e.g., Ex. 20:5–6 // Deut. 5:9–10; Ex. 22:26 (27); Deut. 4:31; 7:9–10; Neh. 1:5; Pss. 51:3(1); 78:38; 86:5; (cf. 112:4); 116:5; Isa. 48:9; 54:7–8; 63:7; Jer. 15:15; 30:11b // 46:28b; Dan. 9:4; Micah 7:18–20; Nahum 1:2–3. There are differences of opinion among scholars as to which references are explicit citations of the formula and which allude to or build upon it.

69. The inscription is given with some variant readings in Davies, *Ancient Hebrew Inscriptions*, no. 15.007. This author's own reading of the inscription as a result of extensive study of it in Jerusalem in 1980 is:

pqd yh 'l ḥnn nqh yh yhwh

This may be vocalized and translated as follows:

pĕqōd yah 'ēl ḥannûn
naqqeh yah yahweh

Be mindful, Yah gracious God
Absolve, Yah Yahweh

The repeated "Yah" is a shortened form of the divine name. All of the words in the inscription appear in the extended form of the cultic formula of Ex. 34:6–7. For a discussion of the reading and arguments in favor of understanding *yh* as the divine name, see Miller, "Psalms and Inscriptions," 328–30.

70. See Liebreich, "Songs of Ascents and the Priestly Blessing"; idem, "Psalms 34 and 145 in the Light of Their Key Words"; and Fishbane, "Form and Reformulation of the Biblical Priestly Blessing"; and idem, *Biblical Interpretation in Ancient Israel*, 329–34.

71. The inscription can be found in Davies, *Ancient Hebrew Inscriptions*, nos. 4.301 and 4.302. For the reading and interpretation of these silver amulets, see, among others, Barkay, *Ketef Hinnom*, 29–31; cf. 35; Rösel, "Zur Formulierung des aaronitischen Segens"; Riesner, "Der Priestersegen aus dem Hinnom-Tal"; Korpel, "Poetic Structure of the Priestly Blessing"; and Yardeni, "Remarks on the Priestly Blessing."

72. On this term as it is used in the Old Testament, see Sakenfeld, *Meaning of Hesed in the Hebrew Bible*.

73. See 2 Kings 19:22; Pss. 71:22; 78:41; 89:18(19); Isa. 1:4; 5:19, 24; 10:20; 12:6; 17:7; 29:19, 23; 30:11, 12, 15; 31:1; 37:23; 41:14, 16, 20; 43:3, 14; 45:11; 47:4; 48:17; 49:7; 54:5; 55:5; 60:9; Jer. 50:29; 51:5; cf. Hos. 11:9, 12; Hab. 1:12; 3:13.

74. See Isa. 5:16; Jer. 31:23.

75. This accounts for the frequent references to Yahweh's "holy habitation" (Pss. 46:4; 68:5; Isa. 63:15; Jer. 25:30).

76. See, for example, the Isaianic tradition rooting its moral demands in the notion of Yahweh as the Holy One of Israel, who as such "shows himself holy by righteousness" (Isa. 5:16) and uncovers and cannot tolerate the unrighteousness of the people; the claim of the Deuteronomist and others that Israel was a people holy to the Lord (e.g., Deut. 7:6; 14:2, 21; 26:19; 28:9; Jer. 2:3; Isa. 63:18); and Hosea's perception of the divine struggle over compassion for Ephraim as a resolution in behalf of compassion because Yahweh is the Holy One (Hos. 11:9; cf. v. 12).

77. On the antiquity of the formula and its Near Eastern parallels, see de Moor, *Rise of Yahwism*, 227–29.

78. See Ex. 20:5 // Deut. 5:9; Ex. 34:14.

79. See, e.g., Ex. 20:5; 34:14; Deut. 4:24; 5:9; 6:15; 32:16, 19, 21; Josh. 24:19; Ps. 78:58.

80. See, e.g., Isa. 26:11; 37:32; 59:17.

81. Especially in the Decalogue (Ex. 20:4–5; Deut. 5:9).

82. The aniconic issue has been the subject of considerable scholarly discussion in recent years. While not exhaustive of that discussion, the following works represent the various issues and points of view that have arisen: Schroer, *In Israel gab es Bilder*; Mettinger, "Veto on Images and the Aniconic God"; idem, "Aniconism— A West Semitic Context for the Israelite Phenomenon?"; idem, *No Graven Image?*; Schmidt, "Aniconic Tradition"; van der Toorn, ed., *Image and the Book*; Dick, *Born in Heaven, Made on Earth*; Berlejung, *Theologie der Bilder*; idem, "Macht der Bilder"; Lewis, "Divine Images and Aniconism in Ancient Israel"; and van der Toorn, "Currents in the Study of Israelite Religion."

83. This prohibition is present in virtually all the legal collections of the Pentateuch, the Decalogue (Ex. 20:4; Deut. 5:8), the Book of the Covenant (Ex. 20:23), the Holiness Code (Lev. 19:4), the covenant curses (Deut. 27:15), and the so-called "Ritual" Decalogue (Ex. 34:17). By the time of the Priestly legislation, it is to be fully assumed.

84. De Moor, *Rise of Yahwism*, 52–54, has pointed to indications in hymnic literature about Amun-Re of the deity's imagelessness, or at least that Amun-Re's image is hidden. There may be some parallel to what took place in Israelite religion, but it does not seem to have been as pervasive and full-blown as there.

85. For a sensitive treatment of the graven image as an aspect of religion in Mesopotamia, see Jacobsen, "Graven Image."

86. See, e.g., Niehr, "In Search of Yahweh's Cult Statue," 95.

87. So also Albertz, *History of Israelite Religion*, 1:64.

88. None of the legal formulations of the prohibition of divine images are necessarily earlier than the eighth century in their present form. That, of course, does not tell us very much about how archaic the prohibition was in Israelite religion. See Dohmen, *Bildverbot*; and Mettinger, "Israelite Aniconism," 175–77.

89. The presence of female figurines is another issue to be looked at below. If it could be determined in any definitive way that the tenth-century cultic stand found at Taanach (plates 3 and 4) includes an imageless representation of Yahweh between two cherubim, as several scholars have proposed, then we would have an

early testimony to the aniconic principle. We would also have the unusual situation of a cult object with an imageless Yahweh alongside an imaged Asherah. But the interpretation of the stand is by no means certain, and one register that is assigned to Yahweh does in fact contain solar and equine or bovine imagery. On this cultic object, see excursus 2.

90. For summaries of this evidence, see Dever, "Material Remains and the Cult in Ancient Israel," 573–74; Hendel, "The Social Origins of the Aniconic," 367; and idem, "Aniconism and Anthropomorphism in Ancient Israel," 212–18. Dever writes: "It may be significant that no representations of a *male* deity in terra cotta, metal, or stone have ever been found in clear Iron Age contexts, except possibly for an El statuette in bronze from 12th century Hazor and a depiction of an El-like stick figure on a miniature chalk altar from 10th century Gezer, and neither is necessarily Israelite" (figs. 5 and 6). Hendel is more inclined to see the Hazor image as coming from an Israelite cultic site but does not believe that any of the male images that are potential candidates for Yahweh figures are in fact that. The general picture is agreed upon by both scholars. Male images of deity, that is, Yahweh images, are rare to nonexistent in excavated Iron Age Israelite sites. For further discussion of the archaeological and iconographic evidence in this regard, see Holladay, "Religion in Israel and Judah under the Monarchy," 295–99; Stager, "Toward the Future," 752; and Keel and Uehlinger, *Gods, Goddesses, and Images of God*, 133–40. It should be noted that Uehlinger has significantly revised his judgments expressed in that book, and he now argues that there was considerable anthropomorphic cultic statuary in Iron Age II Palestine and that there was a cultic statue of Yahweh in both northern and southern central sanctuaries ("Anthropomorphic Cult Statuary in Iron Age Palestine"). Similar arguments on other but not firmer evidence are made by other authors in the same volume. It should be noted that much of the evidence marshalled by Uehlinger is not specifically Israelite and Judean, and it is difficult to interpret, though there is certainly anthropomorphic evidence there. He tends to dismiss the contrast between the imageless sanctuary at Arad in Judah and the richly imaged shrine at Horvat Qitmit in Edom, a contrast that Pirhiya Beck and Stager, among others, have noted as suggesting a difference in cultic practice between Edom and Judah. While not over weighting this contrast, there are not sufficient grounds at this point for claiming that a Yahweh statue was a central part of the cult of Yahwism.

Tallay Ornan has contrasted the Mesopotamian tradition of iconography on seals with that of the West Semitic regions, where there is little evidence of anthropomorphic deity representation, especially among Hebrew seals but not only those ("Mesopotamian Influence on West Semitic Inscribed Seals," 71–72).

91. Mettinger, *No Graven Image*, 18–27; cf. his essay, "Israelite Aniconism," 174–75. It should be noted that the aniconism under discussion is specifically the absence or rejection of cult images of the divine. There is much evidence that images of various sorts were abundant in ancient Israel.

92. Mettinger, "Israelite Aniconism," 191–96.

93. Ibid., 184–93. Mettinger seems inclined to regard the bulls as pedestals and thus de facto aniconism, but allows for the possibility that they were divine images, as they later came to be regarded (Hosea).

94. Ibid., 179–80. Miller and Roberts, *Hand of the Lord*, 73–74, argue for dating

this text fairly close to the time of the conflict between the Israelites and the Philistines about which it speaks, though there are others who would date this text much later.

95. See Keel and Uehlinger, *Gods, Goddesses, and Images of God,* 354–67. In his study of iconism versus aniconism in the preexilic Hebrew seals, Benjamin Sass notes that already in the eighth century "the human image and celestial bodies were not widespread on inscribed seals" and by the seventh the tendency is toward purely ornamental seals or seals that were completely imageless. The trend is never total, Sass observes, because even in the seventh century there are one or two examples of anthropomorphic figures on Judean seals ("Pre-Exilic Seals," 243–45).

96. On the significance of these texts for the issue of images of Yahweh, see Toews, *Monarchy and Religious Institution in Israel,* 122–23.

97. In the most thorough survey and presentation of the archaeological evidence for Israelite religion during Iron Age II or the time of the monarchy, Holladay concludes as follows:

> According to the archaeologically witnessed materials, the officially sanctioned religious praxis of Israel and Judah seems to have been basically aniconic during both the united monarchy and the divided monarchy, especially if one exempts the floral motifs of the early chalices and tall stands with their bowls. ("Religion in Israel and Judah under the Monarchy," 295)

98. Cf. below on "Yahweh and his asherah" at Kuntillet 'Ajrud and Khirbet el-Qom. On the question of the history of the aniconic tendency, cf. Mettinger, "Veto on Images and the Aniconic God," 15–29.

99. See Holladay, "Religion in Israel and Judah under the Monarchy," 249–99, especially the summary on pp. 280–81. He notes in detail the greater iconographic tendency in such domestic and extramural sites.

100. Cf. Cross, *Canaanite Myth and Hebrew Epic,* 73 n. 117; Toews, *Monarchy and Religious Institution in Israel,* chap. 3.

101. On this chapter and the symbol of the fire that dominates it, see Miller, *Deuteronomy,* 57–61.

102. Cf. Miller, *Deuteronomy,* 56–57. Note the later explicit indication of this sense of torah's replacement of image in 1 Macc. 3:4: "And they opened the book of the law to inquire into those matters about which the Gentiles consulted the likenesses of their gods."

103. For drawings of the chief examples, see Mettinger, *In Search of God,* 28–30.

104. Hendel, "Social Origins of the Aniconic Tradition," 380. The argument at this point is that of Hendel. It is reinforced by the work of William W. Hallo, "Texts, Statues, and the Cult of the Divine King," 54–66. For further formulation of this interpretation, see Hendel, "Aniconism and Anthropomorphism in Ancient Israel," 224–28.

105. Hendel, "Social Origins of the Aniconic Tradition," 381.

106. Brueggemann, "Old Testament Theology as a Particular Conversation."

107. The Book of the Covenant associates idols and images with silver and gold (Ex. 20:23).

108. See, e.g., Isa. 2:7, 20; 30:22; 31:7; 40:19; 46:6; Jer. 10:4, 8–9; Ezek. 16:17; Hos. 2:8; Hab. 2:19. The female figurines in clay are thus not indicative of affluence, though one cannot assume they belong only to poorer economic units.

109. "Iconic tendencies occur in Israel when there is a social context in which *surplus value* can function with reference to the *location of God as patron*" (Brueggemann, "Old Testament Theology as a Particular Conversation," 131).

110. Holladay, "Religion in Israel under the Monarchy," 295–99.

111. See Miller, "God and the Gods." There are some similarities to this way of looking at Yahweh's relation to the gods and the proposal of Mark Smith to speak of convergence and differentiation, which are his terms for talking about what is indicated here by the gods in Yahweh or integration of the divine world in Yahweh and Yahweh against the gods. He notes that Cross, whose reconstruction is followed below, uses the terms conflation and differentiation. There is more of a tendency in Smith's reconstruction than in what follows below to see convergence (early) and differentiation (later) as historical stages. While there is some justification for indicating that the three modes of relationship between Yahweh and the divine world suggested here took place in a historical sequence, the actuality was probably somewhat more complex, and differentiation was going on even as there was convergence. In the process of the development of Yahweh out of the world of the gods there was at early stages both convergence and differentiation. See M. Smith, *Early History of God*, esp. xxiii and xxxiii n. 12 and the sections of his book referred to there.

112. Cross, *Canaanite Myth and Hebrew Epic*, 3–75. The amount of reconstruction necessary to discern the prehistory of Yahweh is such that any proposal requires a certain amount of speculation and cannot be definitive. Other proposals have been and will be made (e.g., that of de Moor in *Rise of Yahwism*). Most of them, however, share the basic point being made here, that Canaanite religion as we know it from Late Bronze Age texts and clan religion as we can discern it from a study of the patriarchal narratives and Near Eastern sources are the matrix out of which Yahweh and Yahwism came into being. If, therefore, the reconstruction of Cross is not the last word and new data require revision, modification, or alternative reconstruction, it is at least indicative.

113. Cross, *Canaanite Myth and Hebrew Epic*, 6.

114. Ibid., 12.

115. Ibid., 42ff.

116. Note that the parallel Elohistic text, Ex. 3:15, sees Yahweh as a manifestation of the God of the ancestors. The biblical record explicitly identifies the continuities of Yahweh with pre-Yahwistic clan deities and El.

117. Riemann's important work, presented to the Colloquium for Biblical Research (1972), is as yet unpublished. Jacobsen's treatment of the subject appears in his volume of essays, *Toward the Image of Tammuz*, esp. "Mesopotamian Gods and Pantheons" and "Ancient Mesopotamian Religion: The Central Concerns," as well as in his larger work on Mesopotamian religion, *Treasures of Darkness*.

118. Jacobsen, *Toward the Image of Tammuz*, 20–21. Cf. his comment: "With favorite gods, therefore, a trend away from specialization of power developed and endowed such gods with more extensive, or even all-embracing control: either by assumed delegation from other divine potentates or by seeing the favorite god as

sharing in—and equaling—the special competences of major gods" (*Treasures of Darkness*, 236). The development within Mesopotamian religion discussed here is also described by Lambert, "Historical Development of the Mesopotamian Pantheon."

119. The factors discussed here are treated, along with others, in more detail in Riemann's paper.

120. Obviously not every feature of the deities of the ancient world was integrated in Yahweh. Some features, such as theriomorphism, for example, are missing, although the indication that the bulls of Jeroboam were later identified with Yahweh may reflect a tendency toward theriomorphism in heterodox or idolatrous Yahwism.

121. Riemann in the unpublished work referred to in note 117.

122. See Mullen, *Assembly of the Gods*; Miller, "Sovereignty of God"; idem, "Cosmology and World Order"; and Handy, *Among the Host of Heaven*.

123. Miller, "Cosmology and World Order," 74.

124. Ibid., 57–64.

125. Volz, *Dämonische in Jahwe*. Volz speaks of "dieser monotheistischen Aufsaugung, dieser Jahwisierung des Dämonischen," that is, "this monotheistic absorption, this Yahweh-izing of the demonic" (32).

126. On possible demonic elements referred to in the Hebrew Bible, see Jirku, *Dämonen und ihre Abwehr*.

127. A similar suggestion is made by Riemann in the paper referred to in note 117.

128. Miller, "God and the Gods," 55.

129. See Miller and Roberts, *Hand of the Lord*.

130. See chapter 2. Baal elements in personal names were present in the early period as indicated by Gideon's other name, Jerubaal, although he was clearly born into a Yahwistic family. They show up also in northern Israel later in the names on the Samaria Ostraca. The earliest poetry indicates resistance to the claims of other or new gods (e.g., Ex. 15:11; Judg. 5:8; Deut. 32:15–18).

131. Cf. Crüsemann, *Torah*, 126.

132. Miller, "God and the Gods," 56. Cross, *Canaanite Myth and Hebrew Epic*, 194, argues that the rejection of Baal's mode of revelation followed by the oracle to Elijah implies support for the mode of revelation associated with El and the council of El, that is, the prophetic language of the "word" or "judgment" of Yahweh.

133. In some instances, particularly with the South Canaanite tribal and national groups such as Moabites and Ammonites, whose origins somewhat paralleled those of Israel, the data are insufficient to tell us much about goddess worship.

134. An earlier presentation of this proposal may be found in Miller, "Absence of the Goddess in Israelite Religion."

135. Lambert, "Historical Development of the Mesopotamian Pantheon," 197.

136. Jacobsen, *Treasures of Darkness*, 235; Lambert, "Historical Development of the Mesopotamian Pantheon," 198.

137. Lambert, "Historical Development of the Mesopotamian Pantheon," 198. He says of this text that it "has every claim to present Marduk as a monotheistic god."

138. It is worth noting that at this point in our knowledge, we do not know of goddesses alongside the national gods of the Moabites and Ammonites.

139. Both "Yahweh of Samaria" and "Yahweh of Teman" appear in these blessing formulae. Samaria was the capital of the Northern Kingdom; Teman was a region in the south with which Yahweh was closely associated in the early poetry (see above).

140. For detailed discussion of this translation and the reading of the inscription lying behind it, see Miller, "Psalms and Inscriptions," 315–20. The reading of the translation is the result of study of the photographs, the proposed readings of others, especially Lemaire ("Inscriptions de Khirbet el-Qom"), and my own extended study of the actual inscription itself in 1980 at the Israel Museum, courtesy of Miriam Tadmor.

141. For discussion of the biblical texts, see, among others, Reed, *Asherah in the Old Testament*; Olyan, *Asherah and the Cult of Yahweh*; M. Smith, *Early History of God*; Hadley, "Yahweh's Asherah in the Light of Recent Discovery"; Frevel, *Aschera und der Ausschliesslichkeitsanspruch YHWHs*, Band 1.

142. The word *ʾšrt*, "asherah," appears more than once in brief inscriptions from the seventh century found at Tel Miqne, presumably the site of the Philistine city of Ekron. The most important reads *qdš lʾšrt*, "sanctified [or holy] to Asherah." In this instance we may have a clear reference to the goddess Asherah, which is important inasmuch as, until now, there has been "no clear attestation of a goddess Asherah in Canaanite (Phoenician and Punic) texts from the Iron Age" (McCarter, "Aspects of the Religion of the Israelite Monarchy," 144; cf. Koch, "Aschera als Himmelskönigin in Jerusalem," 98). The absence of Asherah in Phoenician and Punic texts of the first millennium may be due to the fact that this goddess was probably identified with Tannit, well known in this period (See Cross, *Canaanite Myth and Hebrew Epic*, 28–33 and Olyan, *Asherah and the Cult of Yahweh*, 58–61).

At Ekron, of course, we are dealing with a Philistine site and so presumably with the remains of Philistine religious practices, though the language of the inscriptions is uncertain. Preliminary reports may be found in Gitin, "Ekron of the Philistines, Part 2"; idem, "Cultic Inscriptions Found in Ekron"; and idem, "Seventh Century B.C.E. Cultic Elements." The fact that the inscriptions are in a Philistine context has led André Lemaire to utter a word of caution about immediate identification of the word *ʾšrt* with the goddess inasmuch as Philistia seems to have been much influenced by Canaanite-Phoenician culture, and in Phoenician, *ʾšrt* is a word commonly designating a sanctuary (see Lemaire, "Déesses et dieux de Syrie-Palestine," 146). Mark Smith has made the same observation and has noted that the association of the epithet *qdš* with Asherah is problematic ("Yahweh and Other Deities in Ancient Israel," 200 n. 20). Cf. Emerton, "Yahweh and His Asherah," 323–24, n. 4. A reference to El and Asherah has been identified in an Aramaic text written in demotic script from the fourth to second century B.C.E. (Kottsieper, "Papyrus Amherst 63.")

143. For some of the literature on the asherah within biblical and inscriptional texts, see, in addition to works cited in notes 141 and 142, the following: Day, "Asherah in the Hebrew Bible"; Freedman, "Yahweh of Samaria and His Asherah"; Keel and Uehlinger, *Gods, Goddesses, and Images of God*, 210–48 (but see Uehlinger's revision of his views in his essay "Anthropomorphic Cult Statuary," 139–55); M. Smith, *Early History of God*, chap. 3; Coogan, "Canaanite Origins and Lineage," esp. 118–20; Hess, "Yahweh and His Asherah?"; Dearman, *Religion and Culture in Ancient Israel*, 78–84; Manfred Dietrich and Oswald Loretz, *"Jahwe und*

seine Aschera"; Hadley, "Yahweh and 'His Asherah,'" together with the extensive bibliography up to that time (1994); Halpern, "Baal (and the Asherah) in Seventh-Century Judah"; Wiggins, *Reassessment of "Asherah"*; Frevel, *Aschera und der Ausschliesslichkeitsanspruch YHWHs*; Kletter, *Judean Pillar-Figurines and the Archaeology of Asherah*; Binger, *Asherah*; and Emerton, "Yahweh and His Asherah."

144. See, e.g., Ex. 34:13; Deut. 12:3; 16:21; 1 Kings 14:23; 2 Kings 17:9–11; 18:4; 23:14, 15; 2 Chron. 31:1; 33:3; 34:3–7; Isa. 17:7–8; 27:9; Jer. 17:2; Micah 5:13.

145. Cf. McCarter, "Aspects of the Religion of the Israelite Monarchy," 144–46, for references and elaboration.

146. Cf. Judg. 2:13; 10:6; 1 Sam. 7:3–4; and 12:10, where the Baals and the Astartes are paired together as worshiped deities. Nowhere else is there reference to worshiping the Baals and the Asherahs. Some of the ancient versions have corrected the text to read "the Astartes." For another approach to the text of Judg. 3:7, see M. Smith, *Early History of God*, 90–91.

147. For discussion, see M. Smith, *Early History of God*, 80, and the bibliography cited in n. 5 there. Not only do the prophets of Asherah play no further part in the story of the Mount Carmel conflict while the prophets of Baal are referred to several times, the phrase is marked with an asterisk in Origen's Hexapla, indicating that it was not an original part of the Septuagint translation.

148. See 2 Kings 17:16; 21:3; 2 Chron. 33:3.

149. One notes further that Astarte, the Phoenician goddess of the first millennium who appears several times in the biblical texts, is *always* identified as goddess, either by explicit reference (1 Kings 11:5, 33; 2 Kings 23:13), by reference to her temple (1 Sam. 31:10), or, more commonly, by verbs for serving, worshiping, and bowing down (Judg. 2:13; 10:6; 1 Sam. 7:3, 4; 12:10; 1 Kings 11:33).

150. For further discussion of the problems in reading the biblical texts as referring to a goddess named Asherah worshiped in Israel, see M. Smith, *Early History of God*, 88–93. He also lists scholars who had taken positions on opposite sides of this question up to 1990 and provides a bibliography where their proposals and arguments may be found. The list on both sides has grown considerably since that time. For a recent review of positions and arguments, see Emerton, "Yahweh and His Asherah."

151. Implicit and explicit references to Asherah or the asherah have been discerned in Hosea, but they are a matter of much debate. For arguments against any such allusions in Hosea, see Olyan, *Asherah and the Cult of Yahweh*, 19–22. For proposals that identify reference to a goddess as the object of worship in alcoholic and sexual rites, see Braulik, "Rejection of the Goddess Asherah," 172–74. For an extended discussion of prophetic texts that may contain references to Asherah or the asherah, see Frevel, *Aschera und der Ausschliesslichkeitsanspruch YHWHs*, Band 1.

152. It must be noted that this argument involves the joining of the silence about any reference to asherah in the detailed account of Jehu's purge and the later indication that the asherah still stood in Samaria.

153. That is, of course, not entirely the case at Kuntillet 'Ajrud because there is another inscription there, apparently hymnic in type, referring to Baal and El. Its relation to the Yahweh inscriptions is not clear, but McCarter has argued that the

references to Baal and El here indicate Yahweh and that the fragmentary text is a piece of early Yahwistic poetry comparable to Deut. 33:2; Judg. 5:4–5; Ps. 68:8–9; and Hab. 3:3, 7. See McCarter, "Origins of Israelite Religion," 119–36.

154. This interpretation, set forth first in 1986 in the author's essay, "Absence of the Goddess in Israelite Religion," is not entirely dissimilar to that of McCarter, "Aspects of the Religion of the Israelite Monarchy." McCarter, however, is convinced that the figures drawn on the pithos where the reference to "Yahweh of Samaria and his asherah" appears are those of Yahweh and his consort, obviously the goddess Asherah. He sees, therefore, a hypostatization of Yahweh's presence in visible form. It was associated with the wooden upright pole called an asherah and then personified and worshiped as a hypostatic personality, that is, as a goddess, probably consort of Yahweh. The assumption that the painted figures at Kuntillet 'Ajrud are Yahweh and Asherah cannot be proven and goes against some weighty evidence to the contrary, presented in some cases by those who would agree with McCarter that the inscription refers to a consort of Yahweh. See McCarter's later reprisal of these views in "The Religious Reforms of Hezekiah and Josiah." For an extended argument in favor of reading the reference to asherah in these inscriptions as a cultic object, see M. Smith, *Early History of God*, 80–94; Tigay, "Israelite Religion," 173–75; and Keel and Uehlinger, *Gods, Goddesses, and Images of God*, 228–40. Keel and Uehlinger conclude their discussion with these words: "In summary, we can assert: the *asherah*s in eighth-century Israel *and* Judah were thought of not as partners of Yahweh but as cult objects in the form of a tree—and thus as a medium that delivered *his* blessing" (240). They later discuss a representation of El and his asherah, a stylized tree, on a cylinder seal from Beth-Shean (312–14).

155. See, e.g., Braulik, "Rejection of the Goddess Asherah"; Dever, "Asherah, Consort of Yahweh?"; and Zevit, "Khirbet el-Qom Inscription Mentioning a Goddess." Among the scholars mentioned in note 143, one may cite Coogan, Freedman, Uehlinger, Dietrich and Loretz, Frevel, Binger, Hadley, and Hess as examples, though the particular interpretation of the inscriptions and the drawings varies considerably among the interpreters of both.

156. For further discussion of the linguistic problems and other difficulties with the goddess/consort interpretation of *wl'šrth*, see Tigay, "Israelite Religion," 173–75 and nn. 89–90; and especially Emerton, "Yahweh and His Asherah," who reviews the various arguments up to 1999 and makes a strong case for reading "his asherah" and not "his Asherah," interpreting the reference to a cultic object, in his judgment a symbol of the goddess but not the goddess herself. Emerton does not rule out the interpretation of the symbol as implying that Asherah was the consort of Yahweh. If it could be clearly established that the figures painted on the Kuntillet 'Ajrud pithos were Asherah and a male god who was not the Egyptian god Bes, as is likely to be the case, then the weight of evidence would shift significantly toward the goddess interpretation. On the iconography surrounding these inscriptions, see Keel and Uehlinger, *Gods, Goddesses, and Images of God*, 210–25.

157. See McCarter, "Origins of Israelite Religion," 124–25; Keel and Uehlinger, *Gods, Goddesses, and Images of God*, 205; and Dearman, "Baal in Israel," 173–91.

158. Keel and Uehlinger, *Gods, Goddesses, and Images of God*, 236. Their interpretation of the stylized tree in relation to Asherah and Yahweh is developed on

the basis of an extensive analysis of the iconographic representations of the tree (232–36). For a more recent and extended treatment of the tree symbol and its relation to goddesses, see Keel, *Goddesses and Trees, New Moon and Yahweh.*

159. With regard to the separation of "Yahweh" and "his asherah" in the Khirbet el-Qom inscription, Keel and Uehlinger interpret it as follows in the light of the iconographic evidence:

> Only one divine power, namely Yahweh, is considered as the active agent who provides freedom from enemies, whereas Yahweh's *asherah* is the medium or entity through which it happens (*Gods, Goddesses, and Images of God*, 240–41).

In reference to the inscriptions from Kuntillet ʿAjrud and Khirbet el-Qom, Keel and Uehlinger conclude as follows:

> [I]t can be stated with confidence that none of the evidence from Kuntillet ʿAjrud (nor from Khirbet el-Qom) offers any compelling reason to argue against the thesis that adoration of Yahweh in Israel during Iron Age IIB was largely monolatrous. There is evidence that speaks *against* the notion that Yahweh was thought of as having a female partner during this time period. (248)

The authors believe that images of Asherah do come into the picture in the Iron IIC period, that is, that there was "a shift toward an anthropomorphic, personalized image for depicting the goddess during Iron Age IIC" and argue that the pillar figurines are probably to be seen as representations of Asherah. Following the conclusion of Schroer (*In Israel gab es Bilder*, 43f.), they see the development as follows:

> The cultic symbol that was associated with Yahweh, subordinate to him to mediate his blessing, and present as a numinous symbol of power within the Israelite cult for centuries, offered . . . a constant means of access to the fertility cults and goddess cults from which it had evolved. (335)

Cf. Maier, *Ašerah,* 172; and Dearman, *Religion and Culture in Ancient Israel*, 79–80.

160. See n. 142.

161. While the asherah was often listed alongside pillar and altar in the biblical texts and, in some instances at least, stood alongside an altar, neither pillar nor altar ever received the separate status that the asherah seems to have had in some times and places.

162. Note that in the tomb inscription of Uriyahu at Khirbet el-Qom (fig. 8), "his asherah" is separated poetically from "Yahweh," so that he is "blessed" by Uriyahu according to one line while in the next line "by his asherah he [i.e., Yahweh] has saved him." The activity is always Yahweh's but, in some fashion, not only blessing, as in the inscriptions from K. ʿAjrud, but also salvation comes by means of Yahweh's asherah. On the poetic parallelism of "Yahweh" and some characteristic of the deity such as "face" or "name," see Miller, "Psalms and Inscriptions," 317. For a

similar interpretation of the biblical and extrabiblical data concerning the asherah, cf. Schroer, *In Israel gab es Bilder*, 21–45.

163. Lemaire, "Who or What Was Yahweh's Asherah?" 51.

164. Cf. Sir. 1:1–10; 24:1–7; Wisd. Sol. 7:22. Mark Smith, noting the number of scholars who have for a long time compared the figure of Wisdom to the Canaanite goddess Asherah, comments: "If the symbolic content of the asherah was in any sense a model for the figure of Wisdom, it may have been due to the influence of the indigenous cult of Yahweh and his asherah" (*Early History of God*, 9. See also his discussion and the bibliography cited there).

165. See excursus 2.

166. Hadley, "Yahweh and His Asherah," 115–16. Cf. Braulik, "Rejection of the Goddess Asherah," 176–78.

167. There is usually one pillar-based figurine to a domestic site. Female figurines have also been found in numbers at two presumed cultic areas, Jerusalem Cave 1 and Samaria Locus E 207. See Holladay, "Religion in Israel and Judah under the Monarchy," 257–60. But a caution must be entered at this point in the light of Kletter's arguments that Jerusalem Cave 1 is not really a cultic site but rather a storage assemblage of artifacts (Kletter, *Judean Pillar-Figurines*, 59, 63). Keel and Uehlinger suggest that because of the presence of cooking, eating, and drinking utensils, both caves were probably "used for the so-called *marzēaḥ* sacral meals, a cultic institution deriving from Canaanite El religion" (*Gods, Goddesses, and Images of God*, 349). On the *marzēaḥ*, see chapter 2 of this book. For an older collection of these and other female figurines, see Pritchard, *Palestinian Figurines in Relation to Certain Goddesses*. More recent listings of finds and collections of examples may be found in Winter, *Frau und Göttin*, 107–9; Holland, "Study of Palestinian Iron Age Baked Clay Figurines"; and Engle, "Pillar Figurines of Iron Age Israel." For discussion of these figurines, cf. Holladay's essay and Hadley, "Yahweh's Asherah in the Light of Recent Discovery," 224–48, as well as Keel and Uehlinger, *Gods, Goddesses, and Images of God*, 325–36. The most recent and comprehensive treatment of the pillar figurines, including full bibliography, the history of research, and a detailed catalog, is that of Kletter, *Judean Pillar-Figurines*.

168. Hadley, "Yahweh's Asherah in the Light of Recent Discovery," 253.

169. Tigay, "Israelite Religion," 193 n. 116, quoting Pritchard, *Palestinian Figurines in Relation to Certain Goddesses*, 86–87. Pritchard, unlike Tigay, regards this as one possibility of interpretation.

170. Holladay, "Religion in Israel and Judah under the Monarchy," 275–78. Holladay's study focuses on four sites and his data on distribution is with regard to two of them, Tell Beit Mirsim and Beer-sheba. He does not indicate the statistics for the other published sites he discusses, Tell en Nasbeh and Hazor. The dominance of the pillar-based figurine, Holladay suggests, "signifies the central figure of the domestic shrines represented by these remains" (278). The more recent and extensive work of Kletter indicates that the Judean pillar figurines were "found, and probably used, in all types of contexts, or at all levels of human activity, and especially in the daily domestic realm" and that they functioned separately and not in groups (*Judean Pillar-Figurines*, 62, 64).

171. On domestic or family religion and the figurines, see also chapter 2. Female figurines appear also in some nondomestic extramural shrines, such as Jerusalem

Cave 1 and Samaria Locus E 207 as well as in graves. It is uncertain, of course, whether the figurines were brought to the cultic site from domestic loci.

172. See Schroer, *In Israel gab es Bilder*, 40–45.

173. See in this regard the analysis of Ackerman, "Queen Mother and the Cult."

174. Woven and embroidered garments were used to cover divine statues in Mesopotamia. See Cogan and Tadmor, *II Kings*, 286 and the reference cited there.

175. It should be noted that in and around the cultic structure at Taanach, near which was found the tenth-century cultic stand with apparent Asherah imagery on it, there were found at least sixty loom weights and numerous spindle whorls, indicating spinning and weaving among the activities taking place there. Also, at Kuntillet 'Ajrud, one of the two sites where there is inscriptional evidence alluding to Yahweh's asherah, as well as pictorial representation of it in the form of a sacred tree, there is evidence of a textile industry. In this case, however, there is not sufficient evidence to suggest that the site was a sanctuary, so the textile production may have been for another purpose altogether. See Lawrence E. Stager and Samuel Wolff, "Production and Commerce in Temple Courtyards," 98. On the cultic stand at Taanach and the asherah imagery at Kuntillet 'Ajrud, see excursus 2.

176. See M. Weippert, "Synkretismus und Monotheismus," 172–73 n. 49.

177. Hadley, "Yahweh's Asherah in the Light of Recent Discovery," 116.

178. For arguments in favor of identifying the Queen of Heaven with Asherah, see Koch, "Aschera als Himmelskönigin." For an identification of her with Astarte, see Olyan, "Some Observations Concerning the Identity of the Queen of Heaven."

179. Note the query of Walther Zimmerli: "Was the entrance to the (inner) temple forecourt, which was later, according to the vision of Ezek 40ff, firmly reserved for the priests, already prohibited to women in the late pre-exilic period?" (*Ezekiel I*, 242).

180. The making of cakes and pouring out of libations for the Queen of Heaven may have been outside the normal temple cultus and more a part of domestic or family religion. It took place in "the cities of Judah and the streets of Jerusalem" (Jer. 44:17) and involved the participation of the family—men, women, and children (Jer. 7:18). For the understanding of these activities as a part of popular piety or religion, see Rose, *Ausschliesslichkeitsanspruch Jahwes*, 213–63. For an interpretation that places the worship of the Queen of Heaven in the Jerusalem temple cultus, see Koch, "Aschera als Himmelskönigin," 108–9.

181. Braulik, "Rejection of the Goddess Asherah," 172–74. Braulik is dependent upon an unpublished paper by Lohfink, "Die, deren Schilde Schande sind." On iconographic grounds, Keel and Uehlinger specifically reject Lohfink's reading and interpretation of this verse (*Gods, Goddesses, and Images of God*, 199 n. 119).

Chapter 2. Types of Religion in Ancient Israel

1. For a preliminary and brief discussion of some of the methodological issues and bibliography, see Miller, "Israelite Religion," 215–18. The recognition of different levels or types of Israelite religion has come into increasing prominence, especially in light of the major work by Albertz, *A History of Israelite Religion in the Old Testament Period*, but reflected also in the work of Manfred Weippert and others (see chapter 1, note 2).

2. To some extent, this type correlates with the "establishment" cultus in Holladay's model, though that model does not specifically identify orthodox and heterodox features ("Religion in Israel and Judah under the Monarchy"). "Established" is not identical with "orthodox" but often overlaps with it. The Arad "Temple," which he attributes to the "established" cultus, included ostraca with priestly names known from the Bible. The Taanach cult stand with the asherah imagery (see chapter 1, excursus 2), however, is also associated with one of his "establishment" sites, which he describes as typically aniconic. Unfortunately, he does not say anything about this stand except to note its discovery. It seems to run contrary to his conclusion about the aniconic character of "established" sites.

The same is true of his "nonconformist" archaeological type and the "heterodox" Yahwism discussed below. His model does assume that the "nonconformist" sites incorporated features of some sorts that were not a part of the "established" sites and were probably open to foreign influences.

3. See Lev. 19:31; 20:6, 27; Deuteronomy 18; 1 Samuel 28; Isa. 8:19; 2 Kings 21:6; Micah 5:11.

4. See the catalog of cultic activities from the eighth-century Northern Kingdom in Amos 5:21–24.

5. While the cultus of the Northern Kingdom came to be regarded by elements in the Southern Kingdom as unorthodox—and a case could be made for that by virtue of the move away from the Jerusalem temple—the establishment of that cultus by Jeroboam was in origin an alternative cult rooted in Israel's ancient traditions and in various respects a parallel to the practices of the Jerusalem cultus. On these matters, see Toews, *Monarchy and Religious Institution in Israel.*

6. Holladay has called attention to the incongruity between the iconographic character of the Jerusalem temple (apart from the representation of the deity) according to the biblical tradition and the aniconic character of most of the shrines belonging to the officially established religion that have been excavated ("Religion in Israel and Judah under the Monarchy," 295–99).

7. Whether cult object or image of a goddess, the asherah was not a part of orthodox Yahwism insofar as the biblical record informs us of that.

8. The centrality of sacrifice and offering is indicated in the cultic calendars of Ex. 23:14–19; 34:18–26; Leviticus 23; Deut. 16:1–17; as well as in 1 Kings 9:25. The eating of food at the shrines as a part of ritual activity is suggested not only by Deuteronomy, with reference to the regulations concerning sacrifice and tithes, but also by the excavation of vessels associated with food preparation, eating, and drinking at cultic locations. See Holladay, "Religion in Israel and Judah under the Monarchy," 281.

9. The festivals are discussed in more detail later in this chapter.

10. Leadership and participation in the formal cultus are discussed more in chapter 5. Cf. chapter 1 for discussion of the peripheral role of women in the cultus.

11. See note 2 above.

12. See McCarter, "Origins of Israelite Religion," 123–28.

13. On these inscriptions, see chapter 1.

14. "His asherah" is associated both with Yahweh of Samaria in the north, and with Yahweh of Teman in the far south. In addition, Khirbet el-Qom places a reference to Yahweh's asherah in central Judah. Biblical references, whether to cult

object or goddess figure, identify asherah veneration in both Northern and Southern Kingdoms (see chapter 1).

15. Note that, according to Uriyahu's inscription, he was "rich" (see chapter 1) and so probably a part of the upper class. The inscriptions at Kuntillet 'Ajrud may attest to economically well-off travelers passing through that site.

16. Arad, Taanach, and Megiddo are three such sites. See Holladay, "Religion in Israel and Judah under the Monarchy," 252–57, 265, and 272; and Lapp, "1963 Excavations at Ta'anek," 35–37. Mettinger, *No Graven Image*, has placed the standing stones within the larger context of West Semitic practice that, in Israelite religion moved from acceptable to unacceptable, particularly in the later period when a programmatic aniconism replaced the de facto aniconism that was represented in the *maṣṣēbôt* or standing stones.

17. Holladay, "Religion in Israel and Judah under the Monarchy," 280. As Holladay notes, this dating is rough and the question of why the changeover happened has not been answered. On the Judean pillar figurines, see Kletter, *Judean Pillar-Figurines*.

18. This is Holladay's term for those sites, mostly extramural, where the more iconographic tendency is present and a large number of figurines and objects have been found.

19. Holladay, "Religion in Israel and Judah under the Monarchy," 280.

20. Ibid., 278.

21. There is considerable literature that seeks to figure out what a *bāmâ* is, its type of structure and its use. Unfortunately, as many references as there are to *bāmôt*, and as many cultic structures as have been discovered or thought to have been discovered in archaeological excavations, there is much that is still unclear about this structure and its use. The most recent monographic treatment of the *bāmâ* is that of Gleis, *Bamah*. Emerton has provided a review of some of the literature and issues in his essay "The Biblical High Place in the Light of Recent Study." Gleis also provides a helpful summary of previous scholarship in his monograph (2–31). Cf. Nakhai, "What's a Bamah?" 19–29.

22. Gleis, *Bamah*, 185, 245, argues that Josiah was the only king who exercised any influence over the high places or *bāmôt*. Apart from Josiah, the kings left these local cult manifestations largely alone. Over against this interpretation, Lowery sees in the Judean high places royal sanctuaries that were a part of the temple system (*Reforming Kings*, 75–80).

23. Cf. the summary statement of M. Smith, *Early History of God*, 126:

> Like the royal religion of the central sanctuaries (Amos 7:13), the high places were staffed with priests (1 Kgs 13:2, 33; 23:20; 2 Kgs 23:8–9) who conducted sacrifice (2 Kgs 18:22; 23:15; Ezek 18:6, 15; 20:28; cf. 2 Kgs 17:11; Ezek 6:3–4). The geographical range of the high places likewise reflects widespread popular support for high places. High places were present in both rural (Ezek 6:13; cf. Hos 4:13) and urban settings (1 Kgs 13:32; 2 Kgs 23:8).
>
> Like the asherah, high places were not specific to Israelite society, but belonged to a broader cultural picture. The Mesha stele (KAI 181:3), Isaiah 15:2; 16:12, and Jeremiah 48:35 indicate that high places were a feature of Moabite religion as well.

24. On divination, see the monograph of Cryer, *Divination in Ancient Israel.*

25. See, e.g., Gen. 31:10–11, 24; 20:3, 6; 28:12; Num. 12:6; Daniel 2; 5:12; and the Joseph story.

26. See, e.g., Jer. 23:23–32; Deut. 13:1ff.

27. See, e.g., Jer. 14:13–14; 23:27, 31; Ezekiel 13.

28. See, for example, the condemnation of prophets for taking money for giving oracles in Micah 3:11 and the indication of divination fees being offered to Balaam by the elders of Midian and Moab (Num. 22:7). Cf. Acts 16:16.

29. Cryer, *Divination in Ancient Israel,* 327, suggests that the Deuteronomic and Priestly strictures against divination were "a means of restricting the practice to those who were 'entitled' to employ it, that is, to the central cult figures who enjoyed the warrants of power, prestige and, not least, education, as at least the 'élite' forms of divination were very much the privilege of the tiny literate stratum in ancient Near Eastern societies."

30. On the practice of necromancy in ancient Israel, see the very different conclusions of Lewis, *Cults of the Dead in Ancient Israel and Judah,* and B. Schmidt, *Israel's Beneficent Dead.* Schmidt regards necromancy as a relatively late phenomenon in Israel arising under Assyrian influence (286ff.) and regards most of the texts generally associated with cults of the dead as dealing with mourning rites, child sacrifice, and the like, but not with the veneration of ancestors. His extended analysis of 1 Samuel 28 leads him to the conclusion that this is a late text (Deuteronomistic or post-Deuteronomistic) and thus not indicative of any necromancy prior to the Assyrian period. On necromancy generally, cf. Tropper, *Nekromantie.* For a strong presentation of the evidence for an Israelite cult of the dead, see also van der Toorn, *Family Religion in Babylonia, Syria and Israel,* chapter 9. A more archaeological approach to the issue of the cult of the dead is found in the monograph of Bloch-Smith, *Judahite Burial Practices and Beliefs about the Dead,* and the paper of Wenning, "Iron Age Tombs and Burial Customs in Judah." Bloch-Smith argues that there was a widespread cult of the dead, while Wenning finds it "difficult to say that we have a cult of the dead in Judah."

31. On this text, see M. Smith, *Early History of God,* 128–29.

32. See Lewis, *Cults of the Dead.*

33. For appropriate prophetic texts, see M. Smith, *Early History of God,* 129; Lewis, *Cults of the Dead,* 128–60; and B. Schmidt, *Israel's Beneficent Dead,* 143–65. For a similar caution about a cult of the dead in ancient Judah prior to Assyrian influence, see Tappy, "Did the Dead Ever Die in Biblical Judah?" a review of Bloch-Smith, *Judahite Burial Practices and Beliefs about the Dead.*

34. With regard to the death cult legislation of the late-eighth and seventh centuries Tappy proposes that such texts may simply "represent the reaction of orthodox Yahwism against the increasing encroachments from those cultures of oracles, incantation, and conjurations relating to the dead. . . . In other words, the appearance of negative legislation in the Bible at this time may reflect more an attempt to keep something out of Israel than it does an effort to control a long-established ideology and its attendant practices" ("Did the Dead Ever Die in Biblical Judah?" 62).

35. On the Mesopotamian and Syrian evidence, see van der Toorn, *Family Religion in Babylonia, Syria and Israel,* chapter 3.

36. Cf. Sir. 30:18.

37. Lewis, *Cults of the Dead*, 118–20. Cf. van der Toorn, *Family Religion in Babylonia, Syria and Israel*, 208.

38. See Miller, "*Mrzḥ* Text." For further discussion, see Greenfield, "The *marzēaḥ* as a Social Institution" and Ackerman, *Under Every Green Tree*.

39. On the *marzēaḥ*, see King, "*Marzeaḥ*."

40. See, e.g., Isa. 57:6–9; 65:4; Sir. 30:18; Tobit 4:17. See also the discussion of these texts in M. Smith, *Early History of God*, 131–32; Lewis, *Cult of the Dead*; and B. Schmidt, *Israel's Beneficent Dead*.

41. On this narrative as reflective of family religion, see below and also van der Toorn, *Family Religion in Babylonia, Syria and Israel*, 246–51.

42. The value of the idol was twenty times what Micah later paid his Levite priest as an annual wage.

43. See van der Toorn, "Nature of the Biblical Teraphim." He writes,

> If the teraphim were indeed symbolic representations of human dead, one is better placed to understand the ambivalent attitude of the biblical writers vis-a-vis this phenomenon. There is no hint of indignation at the presence of teraphim in David's home [1 Sam 19:11–17], nor is the use of ephod and teraphim condemned by itself in Hos 3:4. Judging from Isa 8:19, the populace of Judah considered it quite normal to consult the dead on behalf of the living." (216)

Van der Toorn compares the attitudes of many Israelites toward the dead as "not dissimilar to that of many Catholic believers towards the saints" and notes a similarity also to the presence of saints' images, like the teraphim, in homes and sanctuaries.

The use of teraphim in divination is explicitly indicated in at least three texts (1 Sam. 15:23; Ezek. 21:26[20]; Zech. 10:2) and strongly suggested by 2 Kings 23:24, especially when compared with Deut. 18:11, which speaks about the same unacceptable practices.

44. The story of Gideon's ephod seems to be another case of a Yahwist setting up an image made of gold and silver as a part of the local cultus of Yahweh, though we cannot be sure what the ephod was in this instance.

45. Examples include the figurines in domestic sites and the veneration and cult of the dead.

46. Examples include the use of female figurines and the involvement of women in asherah cults, possibly also in association with teraphim, though not exclusively so (see van der Toorn, "Nature of the Biblical Teraphim," 210, following a note of Wellhausen in his *Prolegomena to the History of Israel*). Note also the involvement of Micah's mother in the construction of his shrine and the woman who conjures up the spirit of the dead Samuel. In this regard, one should take note of the association of women with other more syncretistic practices identified in the next section.

47. Note the comment of M. Smith: "With regard to practices involving the dead, royal and popular religion belonged to the same fabric" (*Early History of God*, 131).

48. That would seem to be the case, for example, in the work of Ahlström, *Aspects of Syncretism in Israelite Religion*; and idem, *Archaeological Picture of Iron Age Religion*.

49. For the actual data on divine names in the Hebrew inscriptions and the virtual absence of deities other than Yahweh, see chapter 1, excursus 1.

50. See also Tigay, "Israelite Religion," 157–94, and *You Shall Have No Other Gods*, 37–41.

51. It may also have been around the goddess Anath, on which see below the discussion of the Queen of Heaven at the Jewish colony at Elephantine. See also Ackerman, *Under Every Green Tree*, chapter 1.

52. Rose has suggested that in such practices as the worship of the Queen of Heaven, which probably came into Judah during the time of Manasseh and under Assyrian domination, we have an example of popular religion, in which the women especially turn to the Queen of Heaven for security in matters of daily life, that is, the provision of food, while not relinquishing the expectation that Yahweh would continue to provide security in the national realm. He sees the time of Manasseh as one of the periods of general security, disrupted in Josiah's time, when the worship of the Queen of Heaven would have been banned along with all other Assyrian religious elements. With the disintegration of daily life in the last days of the Judean kingdom and among the refugees, there was the desire to return to the service of the Queen of Heaven in order to regain the daily provision of food that came with her veneration (*Ausschliesslichkeitsanspruch Jahwes*, 213–68).

53. For a comprehensive treatment of the Phoenician and Punic evidence, see Shelby Brown, *Late Carthaginian Child Sacrifice*. For a general orientation to the biblical data and issues, see M. Smith, *Early History of God*, 132–38.

54. See Lev. 18:21; 20:2–5; 2 Kings 23:10; Jer. 32:35.

55. This position is espoused in the two most recent monographs on the subject, Heider, *Cult of Molek*, and Day, *Molech*. Both of these volumes give a review of the evidence and the various positions taken on the meaning of *mlk* in this context.

56. This position was first set forth in detailed fashion by Otto Eissfeldt in *Molk als Opferbegriff im Pünischen und Hebräischen*. It has been followed by many scholars, most recently by Mosca in his unpublished Harvard dissertation "Child Sacrifice in Canaanite and Israelite Religion," and Stager and Wolff, "Child Sacrifice at Carthage." A quite different position has been espoused by Weinfeld, who argues that there was a syncretistic dedicatory ritual to a deity that involved children but did not include their slaughter or sacrifice. The language "burn" is not to be understood literally but has to do with the ritual handing over of the children, a practice which Weinfeld sees as derivative from Aramean and Assyrian practices ("Molech Cult in Israel and Its Background" and "Worship of Molech and of the Queen of Heaven." Albertz has adopted this understanding of the "molek cult" in his *History of Israelite Religion*, 1:190–93, though in another context he raises the possibility, in the light of Genesis 22, that child sacrifice in extreme emergencies may have been carried out in early family piety. For a critique of Weinfeld and Albertz and a proposal to see the molek sacrifice as belonging to the worship of an astral or heavenly deity, see Koch, "Molek astral."

57. For helpful reviews of the issues and the discussion, see Ackerman, *Under Every Green Tree*, 117–43; and Dearman, "Tophet in Jerusalem."

58. For the question of the identification of these deities, see Heider, *Cult of Molek*, 291–92, and the literature cited there.

59. De Vaux, *Ancient Israel*, 445 (cf. Day, *Molech*, 69). Heider is inclined to see

the cult of Molek as premonarchical and a reflection of general Canaanite influence, but he says this is "on the basis of admittedly slim evidence" (*Cult of Molek*, 402).

60. E.g., Malta and Carthage.

61. On the Isaiah 57 text, see the extended discussion of Ackerman in *Under Every Green Tree*.

62. In Jer. 7:31; 19:5; and 32:35, Yahweh states with reference to child sacrifice, "I did not command, nor did it come into my mind," suggesting that there was an assumption on the part of some that this was permissible in the worship of Yahweh. In Ezek. 23:38–39 and Lev. 20:3, there is mention of the slaughter of children in sacrifice in relation to defiling Yahweh's sanctuary at the same time, again suggesting that this was done alongside other more traditional Yahwistic practices. Child sacrifice is specifically associated with Yahweh in Ezek. 20:25–26 and a rationale is provided.

63. That would be the case also if the story of Jephthah's vow and sacrifice of his daughter were to be regarded as an instance of the practice of child sacrifice in ancient Israel. It seems, however, to be an isolated incident, shocking in character. Note also the shocked reaction of the Israelites at the king of Moab's sacrifice of his firstborn (2 Kings 3:27).

Heider sees the sacrifices to Molek as fulfillment of a vow that had to do with fertility but admits it is "less than clear" how that concern for fertility was enhanced by such a sacrifice (*Cult of Molek*, 406).

64. On the tophet, see Schmitz, "Topheth" and Dearman, "Tophet in Jerusalem."

65. See Cross, "Phoenician Inscription from Idalion," 102–3.

66. On this passage, see Ackerman, *Under Every Green Tree*, chapter 2.

67. Albright interpreted this as a "figured slab" with cultic and mythological scenes like the orthostats that were common in Syria and Assyria from the twelfth to the seventh century (*Archaeology and the Religion of Israel*, 166). The image has often been seen as a statue of the Canaanite goddess Asherah because of the use of similar terminology to refer to the asherah in 2 Chron. 33:7. See, for example, Ackerman, *Under Every Green Tree*, 60–66.

68. See the use of šeqeṣ in Leviticus 11 with reference to such animals. Cf. Zimmerli, *Ezekiel I*, 240.

69. See Albright, *Archaeology and the Religion of Palestine*, 166–67. For other proposals about possible association of these figures with Egyptian deities, see Schroer, *In Israel gab es Bilder*, 71–75. Ackerman interprets the passage as referring to unclean food rather than animals or zoomorphic deities. She would interpret the scene as depicting a ritual banquet or, more specifically, a marzēaḥ (*Under Every Green Tree*, 70–79).

70. "In the cult drama of the death of the god and lament for him, celebrated at the end of spring, the loss of the god, the waning of the power for new life in nature, is counteracted by mourning and lament" (Jacobsen, *Toward the Image of Tammuz*, 100).

71. Albright, *Archaeology and the Religion of Israel*, 167–68; Zimmerli, *Ezekiel I*, 243–44; and M. Smith, *Early History of God*, 114–24. For a broader picture of solar elements in Near Eastern religions and in Yahwism, see M. Smith, *Early History of God*, 114–24; Stähli, *Solare Elemente in Jahweglauben*; Taylor, *Yahweh and the Sun*; and Keel and Uehlinger, *Gods, Goddesses, and Images of God*.

72. See Keel and Uehlinger, *Gods, Goddesses, and Images of God*, 274–81.
73. Cf. Rose, *Ausschliesslichkeitsanspruch Jahwes*, 200–213. For criticism of this position, see Koch, "Aschera als Himmelskönigin in Jerusalem," 112.
74. See, e.g., Koch, "Aschera als Himmelskönigin in Jerusalem," 111–12; Greenberg, *Ezekiel 1–37*, 168; and Ackerman, *Under Every Green Tree*. For problems with that interpretation, see Zimmerli, *Ezekiel 1*, 239.
75. At least it should be noted that there is no other reference to Tammuz in the Bible, though Zechariah preserves the record of a similar mourning ritual for Hadad-rimmon (Zech. 12:11). One might compare the various mourning rites mentioned elsewhere in the Bible and often condemned (e.g., Jer. 16:6; 41:5; 47:5; Hos. 7:14; Lev. 19:28; Deut. 14:1).
76. Albright, *Archaeology and the Religion of Israel*, 173; Porten, *Archives from Elephantine*, 133–50.
77. Kraeling suggests that since the oath by the goddess Sati was demanded and imposed by the court, one cannot conclude that the Yahwist who swore the oath, Mibtahiah, was actually a worshiper of Sati (*Brooklyn Museum Aramaic Papyri*, 87).
78. Porten, *Archives from Elephantine*, 170–79. For arguments in favor of seeing the Queen of Heaven here and in the biblical texts as the goddess Asherah, see Koch, "Aschera als Himmelskönigin in Jerusalem."
79. Albright, *Archaeology and the Religion of Israel*, 174.
80. For a more extended treatment of Jewish religion at Elephantine, see Albright, *Archaeology and the Religion of Israel*, 168–75; Vincent, *La religion des Judeo-Araméens d'Éléphantine*; Porten, *Archives from Elephantine*, 105–86; Kraeling, *Brooklyn Museum Aramaic Papyri*.
81. Cf. Holladay, "Religion in Israel and Judah under the Monarchy," 290 n. 99. Albright's judgment, quoted by Kraeling, that the religion of the Elephantine colony represented "a symbiosis between heretical Yahwism and a syncretistic Aramaean cult, rather than a fusion between the two" may not be wide of the mark (Kraeling, *Brooklyn Museum Aramaic Papyri*, 88). Albright and others have suggested that the worship of the Aramaic god Bethel may have combined with the possibility of employing "Bethel" as a surrogate for "Yahweh" (e.g., Jer. 48:13) to produce the particular form of syncretistic cult at Elephantine. See Albright, *Archaeology and the Religion of Israel*, 168–73; Kraeling, *Brooklyn Museum Aramic Papyri*, 88–90.
82. The typology proposed in this section is in general comparable to those typologies found in M. Weippert, "Synkretismus und Monotheismus," 143–79 (although the reconstruction of Israelite religion in this essay is in many ways quite different from what is described here); Holladay, "Religion in Israel and Judah under the Monarchy," 249–99; Mettinger, "Study of the Gottesbild," 136; van der Toorn, "Domestic Cult at Emar," 48–49; and especially the two-volume work of Albertz, *History of Israelite Religion*. The typology of this chapter was developed before and independent of the publication of the German edition of Albertz's *History* but very much dependent upon his earlier monograph, *Persönliche Frömmigkeit und offizielle Religion*.
Another work of importance and drawn upon in the following presentation is Rose, *Ausschliesslichkeitsanspruch Jahwes*.
83. See van der Toorn, *Family Religion in Babylonia, Syria and Israel*. This study draws also upon an unpublished paper written by van der Toorn some years prior

to the publication of his monograph and which he kindly made available to me, "Family Gods in Mesopotamia, Syria and Israel," a paper presented at the 1992 Annual Meeting of the Society of Biblical Literature. Much of the material in this essay is developed further in the long monograph, but several quotations in the notes that follow draw upon the paper because of the briefer summary formulations it provides. The reader is referred to the monograph for more extended development of the points made in the quotations from van der Toorn's paper. For a broader look at the family in ancient Israel with some brief attention to family religion, see Perdue, et al., *Families in Ancient Israel*. A recent treatment of the family in the postexilic period, less concerned with specific religious features and more with the interaction of social phenomena and theological developments and tending to place various texts as descriptive of family makeup and practices of a much later time than van der Toorn and others have been inclined to do (e.g., Leviticus 18; Joshua 7; Micah 7:5–6) is Fechter, *Familie in der Nachexilszeit*.

84. "All available evidence suggests that the *mishpāḥāh* lived together in the same village or neighborhood" (Gottwald, *Tribes of Yahweh*, 257). Gottwald argues that the *bêt 'āb,* or extended family, "constructed along patrilineal and patriarchal lines of authority, was the primary socioeconomic unit" (315). It may be assumed that this was also the center of family religion, while acknowledging that its practice may have taken place also simply within the single nuclear family household or within the larger social unit of the *mišpāḥâ* made up of a number of extended villages, sometimes comprising whole villages.

85. Note the helpful summary of van der Toorn:

> In pre-exilic Israel, the basic level of religious involvement was that affecting the extended family (*bêt 'āb*), lineage or clan (*mišpāḥâ*). In juridical and ethical matters, the *mišpāḥâ* had a corporate identity (Lev 20:5; 25:10. 41; Num 27:11), which entailed the common celebration of certain religious rites as well (1 Sam 20:6. 29; cf. Ex 12:3. 21 [*bêt 'āb // mišpāḥâ*]; Zech 12:12–14; Est 9:28). Constituted along the lines of patrilineal descent, the joint family consisted primarily of one's parents (and paternal grandparents, if still alive), the paternal uncles, one's brothers and unmarried sisters, one's wife and one's own children (cf. Lev 27:1–11). These people lived in proximity to each other (cf. Deut 25:5; Ps 133:1), judging by the relationships dealt with in the laws against promiscuity (Lev 20:11–21). ("Family Gods in Mesopotamia, Syria and Israel," 69)

For more extended discussion of the various terms for kinship units and particularly *bêt 'āb* and *mišpāḥâ,* see Gottwald, *Tribes of Yahweh*, 239–92; Bendor, *Social Structure of Ancient Israel*; and van der Toorn, *Family Religion in Babylonia, Syria and Israel*, chapter 8 (and bibliography there). For important treatments of archaeological data that tell us about family and domestic life, see Holladay, "Religion in Israel and Judah under the Monarchy," and Stager, "Archaeology of the Family in Ancient Israel."

86. The dating of the Genesis material is difficult and debated, but it is reasonable to suppose that its narratives represent relatively early practices, many of which

would have continued on. Van der Toorn, while acknowledging the problem of the historical reliability of the patriarchal narratives with regard to times, people, and places, says that "their portrait of family religion cannot so easily be dismissed" ("Family Gods in Mesopotamia, Syria and Israel," 58). He is cautious, at least in part, on the basis of the comparative data that he brings into the picture in his essay and in his monograph.

87. Holladay, "Religion in Israel and Judah under the Monarchy," has especially called attention to the varying intensity of religious practice in regard to both family religion and local cults as far as the archaeological evidence is concerned.

88. See the comment of Holladay relative to the sudden bursts of domestic cultic artifacts in the final strata at such sites as Tell Beit Mirsim, Beer-sheba, and Hazor: "That these sudden bursts of popular piety were inspired by the events of the day seems a reasonable assumption" ("Religion in Israel and Judah under the Monarchy," 279).

89. Cf. van der Toorn, *Family Religion in Babylonia, Syria and Israel*, chapter 10.

90. See Ruth 1:15–16.

91. See Gen. 31:42, 53; 49:24.

92. See chapter 1.

93. Cf. van der Toorn, *Family Religion in Babylonia, Syria and Israel*, 240–41. In the two main family stories in Judges, that of Gideon (chaps. 6–8) and that of Micah (chaps. 17–18), the former speaks of "the altar of Baal that belongs to your father," while the latter seems to understand Micah's family god as Yahweh.

It should be noted that tomb inscriptions and cave inscriptions, such as those of Khirbet el-Qom and Khirbet Beit Lei, where one might expect the family god to be invoked or thanked by the deceased or those who have fled or hidden, the deity is always Yahweh. See Dearman, "Baal in Israel."

93a. Holladay, "Religion in Israel and Judah under the Monarchy," 276.

94. See Jer. 19:13; 32:29; Zeph. 1:5. These texts have to do with the host of heaven and other deities. For evidence of sacrifices on rooftops in the Ugaritic texts, see Miller, "Aspects of the Religion of Ugarit," 61.

95. While Holladay argues that all of these kinds of objects were "characteristic furnishings of unquestionable shrines and sanctuaries in countries bordering Israel and Judah" and cannot be passed off as children's playthings or talismans, the use and function of such objects is not at all clear ("Religion in Israel and Judah under the Monarchy," 291 n. 109). Voight has identified five "functional categories" into which "most of the ethnographically documented figurines fall":

> (1) cult figures, or representations of supernatural beings used primar-
> ily as symbols or objects of worship (prayer, musical performances,
> offerings, sacrifice); (2) vehicles of magic, or figurines which are
> manipulated and in many cases disposed of as a key element (simula-
> tion) in rituals intended to produce, prevent or reverse a specific situ-
> ation or state (for example, to insure fertility or healthy children, to
> cause harm to other persons, to protect one's own health or property,
> to prevent natural disasters, to cure illness); (3) didactic or teaching
> figures, for example, figures used to teach values, sexual facts and sex-
> ual mores during initiation ceremonies; (4) toys or figures used for

entertainment; and (5) representations of deceased persons (as well as of people or animals associated with the deceased) used as mortuary furniture. (Voight, "Functional Interpretation: Figurines," 186).

Not all of these are textually or archaeologically documented for the ancient Near East, but none of them is excluded as a possible function of the objects found in Israelite cultic sites.

96. H. Weippert claims that the Taanach "cultic structure" from the tenth century is not really a separate shrine but a domestic site and therefore an indication of a house cult (*Palästina in vorhellenistischer Zeit*, 447; cf. Fowler, "Concerning the 'Cultic' Structure at Taanach"). Holladay thinks that these rooms are storerooms of either a sanctuary or of someone closely connected, perhaps commercially, to a nearby sanctuary, or of "a rather devout household," noting that model shrines—like the famous Taanach cult stand—found at Sarepta and early monarchical Jerusalem seem to be associated with domestic debris rather than sanctuaries ("Religion in Israel and Judah under the Monarchy," 253). The artifactual evidence is ambiguous. A large body of domestic objects (apparently) was found there, but also cultic stands, a figurine mold, and possible standing stones. Again, one has to note, on the one hand, that cultic or offering stands as well as figurines were found in domestic sites as well as clearly identifiable separate shrines while, on the other hand, commercial activities, indicated by the olive press and the loom weights found at the Taanach cult structure, were a part of the activities of sanctuaries.

97. H. Weippert, *Palästina in vorhellenistischer Zeit*, 448; M. Weippert, "Synkretismus und Monotheismus," 154. Cf. Gitin, "Incense Altars from Ekron, Israel and Judah."

98. M. Weippert notes the absence of archaeological evidence for bloody or flesh sacrifices in domestic contexts but speculates that they may have taken place in connection with rites of passage and the Passover celebration ("Synkretismus und Monotheismus," 154).

99. Some such cultic centers were short-lived, such as the Bull Site (see below) and Tell el-Mazar Mound A in the mid-Jordan Valley (Yassine, "Open Sanctuary of the Iron Age I *Tell el-Mazar* Mound A"). Others would have continued over much longer periods. Certainly there is evidence for the tenacity of family groupings and locations over long periods and even in the face of major structural change such as took place with the institution of the monarchy in Israel. Some of the territorial names in the Samaria Ostraca are an indication of this. Cf. Stager, "Archaeology of the Family in Ancient Israel," 24.

100. It needs to be recognized that the line or distinction between cult centers of the *mišpāḥâ*, or extended family, and those of a region may be very fuzzy. We are not always able to distinguish between the cultic center of an extended family that made up a whole village or more and a regional shrine serving a broad area and several clans or tribes.

101. Wenning and Zenger, "Bäuerliches Baal-Heiligtum im samarischen Gebirge."

102. For a plausible hypothesis concerning the antecedents of Jeroboam's bull iconography in the north, see Cross, *Canaanite Myth and Hebrew Epic*, 74–75.

103. Rainey, "Toponyms of Eretz-Israel," 3.

104. Mazar, "Early Israelite Settlement in the Hill Country"; Rosen, "Early Israelite

Cultic Centres in the Hill Country." Cf. van der Toorn, "Family Gods in Mesopotamia, Syria and Israel," 61–62; and idem, *Family Religion in Babylonia, Syria and Israel*, 240–41.

105. So Saul, a firm Yahwist, gave one son a Yahwistic name, Jonathan, but named another son Ishbaal or Eshbaal (1 Chron. 8:33). For some of his sons, David used Yahwistic names, such as Adonijah and Shephatiah, but one son's name is twice given as an "el" name, Eliada (2 Sam. 5:16; 1 Chron. 3:8), and once as a "baal" name, Beeliada (1 Chon. 14:7). Saul's son Jonathan had a son named Merib-baal, who gave his son a Yahwistic name, Micah (1 Chron. 8:34; 9:40). Gideon's father bore the Yahwistic name Joash but is depicted as having set up a Baal altar; he later makes a defense of Yahweh, while Gideon, who sets up an altar to Yahweh and tears down the Baal altar of his father, has a Baal name, Jerubbaal (Judg. 6:32; 7:1; 8:35—see below).

The interchange of theophoric names, such as Eliada = Beeliada (above) or Ahibaal = Ahiyahu, is not uncommon in the early part of Israel's history (cf. Mazar, "Early Israelite Settlement in the Hill Country," 48 nn. 39–40).

106. See Dearman, "Baal in Israel."

107. See Na'aman, "Beth-aven, Bethel and Early Israelite Sanctuaries"; and van der Toorn, "Family Gods in Mesopotamia, Syria and Israel," 64. Cf. van der Toorn, *Family Religion in Babylonia, Syria and Israel*, 251–53.

108. The report of Gideon's call-up of the militia against the Midianites is instructive about family and clan relations and the role of such structures as "protective associations of families" (see Gottwald, *Tribes of Yahweh*, 257ff.). Gideon first calls up his *mišpāḥâ* or extended family, the Abiezrites, and then sends messengers throughout the tribe to which that *mišpāḥâ* belongs, Manasseh, and then seeks help from other tribes contiguous to Manasseh or threatened by the Midianite move to the Valley of Jezreel—that is, Asher, Zebulun, and Naphtali (Judg. 6:33–35; 7:23). It is not clear why Issachar is not included in the call.

109. It is possible that the narrative refers to a single actual family shrine—depicted here as two separate and successive shrines—consisting of altar, asherah (which some would see represented also by the terebinth ['ēlâ] at Ophrah where Gideon met the angel and built the altar [Judg. 6:11, 19]), and ephod. Because the last item is reported also to have been a central item in Micah's shrine (see below) and appears in later accounts of shrine activity, it may have been a standard item in such shrines. It is unfortunate that we are not more sure of its character.

110. Cf. the account of Abimelech, son of Gideon = Jerubbaal, killing his brothers at "his father's house at Ophrah" (Judg. 9:5).

111. Van der Toorn suggests that "the ephod probably denotes an image or a divine throne not unlike the ark (Judg 8:24–27)" ("Family Gods in Mesopotamia, Syria and Israel," 64).

112. See Albright, *Archaeology and the Religion of Israel*, 112. De Vaux thinks the text contains two traditions, an older one showing how the worship of Yahweh replaced a previous cult without any problems and a later one showing Yahwism ousting the cult of Baal forcibly (*Ancient Israel*, 307).

113. Albright, *Archaeology and the Religion of Israel*, 112, notes that the original meaning of Jerubbaal was probably "May Baal give increase."

114. Cf. van der Toorn, "Family Gods in Mesopotamia, Syria and Israel," 65.

115. Van der Toorn has called attention to a similar report of a citizen of Old Babylonian Sippar setting up a sanctuary for his personal god and appointing someone as its priest ("Family Gods in Mesopotamia, Syria and Israel," 63–64; idem, *Family Religion in Babylonia, Syria and Israel*, 250–51).

116. Van der Toorn, "Family Gods in Mesopotamia, Syria and Israel," 64.

117. Note that Gideon's hesitation in tearing down the cultic structure erected by his father is for fear of both his family (*bêt 'āb*) and the townspeople (*'anšê hā'îr*). That most or all of the inhabitants of Ophrah were from the clan of Abiezer is indicated by the reference to "Ophrah of the Abiezrites" (Judg. 8:32).

118. Van der Toorn, "Family Gods in Mesopotamia, Syria and Israel," 64. For analysis of the demographic and family structure reflected in this story, see Gottwald, *Tribes of Yahweh*, 291, and Stager, "Archaeology of the Family in Ancient Israel," 22.

119. The character of this site as a Saulide sanctuary is further indicated by the desire of the Gibeonites that when Saul's sons are to be hanged to expiate for his crime against them, they asked that it be done "at Gibeah of Saul on the Mountain of the Lord" (van der Toorn, "Family Gods in Mesopotamia, Syria and Israel," 66; cf. idem, *Family Religion in Babylonia, Syria and Israel*, 267–71.). For indications from the text that the *bāmâ* or shrine itself was outside Gibeah proper, see Na'aman, "Beth-aven, Bethel and Early Israelite Sanctuaries," 20; and van der Toorn, "Family Gods in Mesopotamia, Syria and Israel," 66.

120. Van der Toorn, "Family Gods in Mesopotamia, Syria and Israel," 66, n. 322.

121. See 1 Sam. 1:1 and 9:5; cf. 1 Chron. 6:11(26).

122. See 1 Sam. 7:17; 9:14.

123. Note references to going up and coming down from the shrine (1 Sam. 9:13–14, 25). Barrick has argued that the *bāmâ* here and in other instances was in the town, a fact disguised by the conflation of two accounts in one story ("What Do We Really Know about 'High-Places'?" Na'aman reads the location of the shrine as near the city gate ("Beth-aven, Bethel and Early Israelite Sanctuaries," 20).

124. Barrick has suggested that this story gives the best indication of what a *bāmâ* or "high place" was like and that the reference to a *liškâ*, a "room" or "hall" always associated with temple or sanctuary architecture, at this *bāmâ* is the chief clue. He summarizes:

> [T]his *bamah*-installation was a sanctuary-complex of some architectural sophistication not too different in its essentials from the sanctuary-complex at Arad or for that matter, the sanctuary-complex in the royal quarter of Jerusalem—which one climbed up *to* and descended from, *within* which cultic acts were performed, which possessed *liškôt* (as well as altars, even an *'ašerah* [2 Kgs 23:6]!), which was "built" and "burned" (and, although the term is not used, was certainly capable of being "torn down"). ("What Do We Really Know about 'High-Places'?" 57).

One notes, with Barrick, that the original text of 1 Sam. 1:18, preserved in the Septuagint but lost by haplography in the MT, told of Hannah going to the *liškâ*, "room/hall" to eat after her prayer in the shrine at Shiloh had been heard. This was probably a room for meals connected to the sanctuary. On the text, see McCarter, *1 Samuel*.

125. Van der Toorn, "Family Gods in Mesopotamia, Syria and Israel," 65; cf. idem, *Family Religion in Babylonia, Syria and Israel*, 212–18.

126. Klein, *1 Samuel*, 89–90. Haran thinks that while the report of this sacrificial feast has some differences from those reported in 1 Samuel 1 and 20 (see below), they all three refer to annual family sacrifices ("*zebaḥ hayyamîm*," 11–20).

127. See van der Toorn, "Family Gods in Mesopotamia, Syria and Israel," 66–68, for the interesting proposal that the family shrine spoken about here was at Kiriath-jearim where an ark/ephod was enshrined, which David then took to Jerusalem in an attempt to move the religious center of his clan to that spot. He thus modeled his cult center after the family sanctuaries of his time, with an ephod/ark divine image or representation and family figures as priests (2 Sam. 8:18). The intent, therefore, would have been more the creation of a private family or royal chapel than a national shrine. Van der Toorn notes that descendants of David at Jerusalem worshiped "the god of [their] father David" there (2 Kings 20:5; cf. 1 Chron. 28:9; 2 Chron. 17:4; 34:3). Cf. *Family Religion in Babylonia, Syria and Israel*, 280.

128. See 1 Sam. 1:21; 2:19; 20:6.

129. See Deut. 12:8–27; 14:22–27; 16:9–17.

130. Dever, "Contribution of Archaeology to the Study of Canaanite and Early Israelite Religion," 233; Holladay, "Religion in Israel and Judah under the Monarchy," 258, 266, 274, and 280.

131. See chapter 1.

132. The Sabbath is recognized in all the legal collections and was known to such prophets as Isaiah, Amos, and Hosea. Its association with the "new moon" celebration (e.g., 2 Kings 4:22; Isa. 1:13; Hos. 2:13; Amos 8:5) has led some to argue that in the preexilic period the Sabbath as a regular celebration was the new moon festival and celebrated in the temple as a part of the official state cultus (see 2 Kings 16:17f.). Later in the exile, this was combined with the family custom of breaking from work every seven days to create the Sabbath festival as a family and all-Israel celebration. The data are sufficiently elusive to make this proposal plausible but difficult to confirm. See Albertz, *History of Israelite Religion*, 2:408–9 and the literature cited there.

133. This may have been in a process of the joining of all–Israel celebration (new moon) and family practice (day of rest). See the previous note.

134. For this and other aspects of the ritual of circumcision, see de Vaux, *Ancient Israel*, 46–48, and Wyatt, "Symbols of Exile," 45–48.

135. See Gen. 17:9–14; 34:14–16; Ex. 12:47–48.

136. See Boling, *Joshua*, 194.

137. See, e.g., Gen. 4:1; 29:32–35; 30:6, 18, 20, 22–24; 1 Sam. 1:20; 4:21.

138. See Tigay, "Israelite Religion," 192–93 n. 116, quoting James B. Pritchard. Tigay points to the concern for fertility and infertility in blessings and curses (e.g., Gen. 49:25; Ex. 23:26; Hos. 9:14).

139. See, e.g., Holladay, "Religion in Israel and Judah under the Monarchy, 277–78. Dever, "Material Remains and the Cult in Ancient Israel," represents a position that combines these two alternatives:

Obvious fertility aspects, usually exaggerated sexual characteristics, connect these figurines with the ancient Near Eastern cult of the "Mother-goddess," but they do not specify the deity further. Since these figurines are found almost without exception in domestic or tomb contexts, they are undoubtedly talismans to aid in conception and childbirth, rather than idols in the true sense, designed for sanctuary usage. (574)

140. On cults of the dead, see the earlier discussion in this chapter; also Lewis, *Cults of the Dead*; Spronk, *Beatific Afterlife in Ancient Israel*; and Pope, *Song of Songs*, 210–29. For specific discussion of the teraphim as ancestor figurines, see Rouillard and Tropper, "TRPYM, rituels de guérison et culte des ancêtres"; van der Toorn, "Nature of the Biblical Teraphim," 203–22; idem, "Family Gods in Mesopotamia, Syria and Israel," 71–73; and idem, *Family Religion in Babylonia, Syria and Israel*, 218–25. For a reserved viewpoint on the possibility of ancestor cults in ancient Israel, see Albertz, *History of Israelite Religion*, 1:34–39. For a more negative judgment, see B. Schmidt, *Israel's Beneficent Dead*.

141. Van der Toorn, "Nature of the Biblical Teraphim," 203–22 (and bibliography); idem, "Family Gods in Mesopotamia, Syria and Israel," 71–73; and idem, *Family Religion in Babylonia, Syria and Israel*, 218–25.

142. As van der Toorn has noted, the Deuteronomic slave law in Deut. 15:17 that is a later version of the one appearing in Ex. 21:1–6 reinterprets the earlier custom, eliminating any reference to bringing the slave near "to the god(s)" at the door, thus divesting the procedure encoded here of any religious significance. Instead of the domestic Elohim or ancestor figures, Deuteronomy provides the Shema at the doorpost for protective purposes (Deut. 6:9; 11:20). Cf. Miller, "Apotropaic Imagery in Proverbs 6:20–22."

In this regard, as with the confessional denial of any sacrifices to the dead in Deut. 26:14, Deuteronomy demonstrates its opposition to some of the practices of family religion. For further such indications, see van der Toorn, "Family Gods in Mesopotamia, Syria and Israel," 74–75. It is also the case, however, that Deuteronomy draws other aspects of family religion and incorporates them into the stream of official national religion and theology that centered around Yahweh's dealings with the people Israel as a community. In this regard, see below and Albertz, *Persönliche Frömmigkeit und offizielle Religion*, 169–78. Rose has shown how Deuteronomy both was opposed to and incorporated dimensions of popular piety, though he does not identify this completely with the social unit of the family (*Ausschliesslichkeitsanspruch Jahwes*).

143. The consultation of the dead spirits is reflected also in the 'ôbôt and the yiddĕ'ōnîm (e.g., Deut. 18:11), whose consultation was expressly forbidden by Deuteronomy, along with the "inquiry of the dead" (v. 11b), as an expression of the national form of religion. Cf. Lust, "On Wizards and Prophecy."

144. See, e.g., Isa. 1:13; 66:23; Ezek. 46:1; Amos 8:5; Judith 8:6. On the relation of new moon and Sabbath, see notes 132–33.

145. Gerstenberger, *Bittende Mensch*; Albertz, *Persönliche Frömmigkeit und offizielle Religion*, 23–49. Gerstenberger and Albertz focus on the laments of the individual in the Psalms and associate them with the clan or family group. Green-

berg, *Biblical Prose Prayer as a Window*, should be mentioned in this connection also, even though he does not deal with the family particularly. Greenberg focuses more on the embedded narrative prayers as an example of popular religion, but he does not associate them with any particular social setting.

146. Albertz has argued with some cogency that the enemies in the individual prayers of the Psalter were often, if not usually, demonic powers that possessed the individual in sickness or some other form. This would have been in distinction from the political powers that are present in the communal laments. Here, of course, Albertz is following Mowinckel and others. See Albertz, *Persönliche Frömmigkeit und offizielle Religion*, 43–48.

147. First Samuel 1 is an important instance of a family prayer that connects with the sanctuary and its priesthood. Its situational impetus was very much the family; its actual setting was the sanctuary, to which Hannah returned for formal thanksgiving and sacrifice.

148. Second Kings 4:18–37 is a particularly interesting example in this instance because of the way that it is thoroughly a family story—note the response of the prophet to the woman hurrying to him: "Are you all right (*hăšālôm lāk*)? Is your husband all right? Is the child all right?" (v. 26)—around a family crisis, the illness and death of a child. The child becomes sick while farming with his father. The father carries him into his mother, who holds him on her lap until he dies. The narrative includes an apparent inquiry of a seer (vv. 22–23), prayer in behalf of the dead child by the prophet (v. 33), and a kind of ritual over the body of the child (vv. 32–35).

149. See 1 Samuel 28; 1 Kings 14; 2 Kings 4; and possibly Gen. 25:22. One should take note in this instance of other kinds of activities associated with magic that are found in the family stories but not necessarily with religious dimensions to them, for example, the mandrakes that Reuben brought to his mother Leah to help her conceive (Gen. 30:14–21) and the rods used by Jacob to improve the breeding of his flocks (Gen. 30:37–43). It should be noted in Leah's case that the use of the mandrakes as a kind of fertility device in no way vitiated her conviction that the family deity had given her a child (Gen. 30:18, 20).

150. See Gen. 48:15–16; 49:24–26. On Gen. 49:24ff. see Freedman, "Who Is Like Thee among the Gods?" 322–27.

151. Examples invoking the deity are found in Gen. 27:28; 28:3–4; 31:49–50; 32:26(?); 48:15–16, 20; 49:22–26; Judg. 17:2; Ruth 2:4, 20. The Kuntillet 'Ajrud inscriptions have several blessings by Yahweh (and his asherah), but the social context of these blessings cannot be determined. Examples of blessing in which the deity is not referred to are found in Gen. 24:60 and 27:39–40.

152. See, e.g., Gen. 24:60; 28:1–5; 31:49–50, 55; Ruth 1:8–9. The parting was often permanent where women were concerned because it involved leaving their father's home to go to the home of their husband (Gen. 24:60; 31:55). The husband's death might or might not mean a return to the woman's family home (Gen. 38:11; Ruth 1).

153. See, e.g., Gen. 27:1–4; 48:8–22 (note v. 21); 49:1–27.

154. See Gen. 24:60; 27:28; 28:3.

155. See Gen. 24:60; 28:4; 48:15–16; 49:25.

156. See Gen. 31:49–50.

157. See Gen. 27:29, 40; 48:17–21; 49:3–12, 26. The blessing of Moses in Deuteronomy 33 is a type of family blessing pronounced over the tribes of Israel and also having to do in part with family or tribal relationship.

158. See Gen. 24:60; 28:1–5; Ruth 4:11–12.

159. See Gen. 24:60; Judg. 17:2.

160. The clearest example of this is Genesis 27.

161. See, e.g., Gen. 27:37, 39–40; 48:19; 49:1.

162. Freedman has argued that the Balaam oracles in their context are a strong statement of Yahwism's early resistance to magic ("Who Is Like Thee among the Gods?" 331–33). That may well be the case, but if so, that resistance is implicit rather than explicit in the texts. The point of the narrative and poems of Numbers 22–24 is Yahweh's power over the magic of the seer and the seer's function as an agent of Yahweh. But that in itself does not tell us much about how magic was regarded in this early period except that it could be used by Yahweh for the deity's own ends, as Num. 22:22–35 suggests quite strongly.

163. In this section, I am particularly indebted to the work of Albertz, *Persönliche Frömmigkeit und offizielle Religion*, especially 92–96. His summary is drawn from a detailed examination of the psalmic laments of the individual, the theophoric personal names, and the stories of the ancestors in Genesis.

164. See Cross, "Kinship and Covenant in Ancient Israel," 6–7, and the theophoric names with elements such as *'āb, 'āḫ,* and the like.

165. See Pss. 22:10–11(9–10); 139:13–16.

166. See Gen. 35:3; 48:15.

167. See Ps. 22:5–6(4–5) and the expressions of trust in the individual laments in general. While Gen. 15:6 may be a more theologically reflective note in the stories of the ancestors, it is an accurate indication of the relationship between deity and family members.

168. Albertz rules out any theophanic or epiphanic dimension to this relation, but the family stories of Genesis suggest otherwise (e.g., Gen. 22:9–19; 28:10–22; 32:21–32).

169. This is suggested in general by the Genesis stories and more particularly by the lack of divine anger toward Abraham and Isaac in the stories of the endangered tribal mother (Gen. 12:17–20; 20:1–17; 26:6–11).

170. Albertz notes the different verbs for the community laments (verbs of rejection) and for the individual laments (verbs of abandonment). The same thing is also indicated by the motif of God's hiding the face, which in the individual laments that are more oriented toward the individual experience in the context of the family is a hiding of abandonment and silence, and in the prophets and communal laments is a hiding of rejection and anger. See Balentine, *Hidden God.* It should be noted that reference to divine anger and rejection is not totally absent from individual laments or prayers for help (e.g., Pss. 27:9; 71:9; 88:6–18. See Miller, *They Cried to the Lord.*

171. Virtually all the family stories in Genesis and elsewhere make this clear.

172. Examples include the presence of God on the holy mountain (Ex. 19:12; 20:18–21; Deut. 5:22–33) or with the ark of the covenant (2 Sam. 6:6–11).

173. See Gen. 26:23–25; 35:3.

174. The stories of the ancestors in Genesis 12–36, of Samson in Judges 13–16, and of the birth of Samuel in 1 Samuel 1–2 are prime indicators of this.

175. See e.g., Gen. 24:27; 35:2–3.

176. See Gen. 26:12; 30:30.

177. See, e.g., 1 Kings 17:17–24; 2 Kings 4:18–37; and the laments of the individual in Psalms that cry for help in the face of sickness.

178. See 1 Kings 16:32; 2 Kings 10:18–24 (*bêt habba'al*).

179. See chapter 1.

180. First Kings 3:2 reports the regular custom of the people to sacrifice at the *bāmôt* before the temple was built.

181. The *bāmâ* at Rama around which the activities of 1 Samuel 9 took place appears to have been a family shrine, but it cannot be excluded that it served as a center of Yahwistic worship for a larger group. The sacrifice and meal that took place there does not seem to have been a family occasion (see the discussion of 1 Samuel 9 above). The "great high place" (*bāmâ gĕdôlâ*) at Gibeon, where Solomon used to offer a thousand sacrifices and which presumably was in existence before the time of Solomon, was certainly more than simply a family shrine, although it is not identified as a center of worship for all Israel.

182. See Barrick, "What Do We Really Know about 'High Places'?"

183. See 1 Kings 14:23.

184. If the high places were open-air shrines originally, which is not the way that the high place at Rama is depicted in 1 Samuel 9, they gained a structural character at this point.

185. See 1 Kings 12:31–32; 13:32; 2 Kings 23:8–9.

186. See Cross, *Canaanite Myth and Hebrew Epic*, 73 n. 114.

187. These include the Bull Shrine already discussed (eleventh century?), a cult structure at Hazor (eleventh–tenth century?), possibly the Migdal Temple at Shechem (twelfth–eleventh century? see Judg. 9:46) and the cultic structure at Taanach (tenth century?), a tenth-century structure at Lachish, the large platform shrine at Dan (ninth century?), the cave structures at Samaria (Locus E 207 [cave?]) and Jerusalem (Cave 1), the Arad temple (tenth–ninth century to seventh–sixth century). Arad is the clearest example of a real temple structure, with its architectural shape and its large courtyard altar as well as other altars. The Arad sanctuary, however, belonged to the system of state religion in Judah (see below). On these sanctuaries, see Zwickel, *Tempelkult in Kanaan und Israel*.

188. Samaria is an interestingly ambiguous case. The biblical record speaks only of a Baal sanctuary and an asherah at Samaria, while the Kuntillet 'Ajrud inscriptions contain a blessing by "Yahweh of Samaria and his asherah." On this expression, see below.

189. See Gen. 35:7.

190. See Amos 8:14 and the Hellenistic Greek and Aramaic inscription found at Dan and inscribed "to the god who is in Dan" or "to the god who is in the district of the Danoi" (so D. Flusser). See Biran, "To the God Who Is in Dan." The nature of the cult at Dan is a matter of some complexity and uncertainty. In the premonarchical era, a shrine is reported there with a priesthood descended from Moses and a sanctuary (*bêt ha'ĕlōhîm*) containing the statue (*pesel*) originally made as an icon for a family shrine by Micah (Judges 17–18). Neither in this context, nor in Amos 8:14, nor in the much later inscription from Dan is the deity worshiped there identified. The image of Micah seems to have been Yahwistic, and if there was a

Mushite priesthood there at an early time, that would also have been the case with its removal to Dan. But the priesthood may well have been established by Jeroboam when he made Dan one of the two national Yahweh shrines of the Northern Kingdom. It is possible that the deity worshiped there was Yahweh from the beginning and that this was an early local cult of Yahweh, at least from the time of the Danite migration. That would have made it easy for Jeroboam to set up his Yahwistic center there. Cross has suggested that the choice of Bethel was tied to its having an ancient association with bull iconography introduced under the authority of Aaron (Exodus 32). See Cross, *Canaanite Myth and Hebrew Epic*, 73–74. He does not say anything about the Dan shrine in this connection, but it is plausible, if speculative, that that sanctuary also had a tradition of bull iconography. The discovery of bull images in recent years at the Manassite Iron I Bull Shrine and at Ashkelon suggests the ubiquity of this image in sacred areas and the reason why Jeroboam may have chosen this particular symbol. It was familiar in the north.

What is important in this context, however, is that early and late, there seems to have been a local cult at the site of Dan. Wolff comments with regard to the references to Dan, Ashimah, and Beer-sheba in Amos 8:14:

> It is not an apostate invocation of some foreign deity that is the primary issue in each case [vis-à-vis Amos 8:14], but rather the emphatic insistence on the deity's localization at a particular sanctuary and on the religious practice of making pilgrimage there. In the fashion of the Canaanite cults, Yahweh has been fragmented into several gods, conceived as patron deities of territorial regions. (*Joel and Amos*, 332)

The formulation "[god/divine name] in [place name]" is characteristic of local cults (see below). M. Weippert suggests that since both Amos and the Hellenistic inscription seem to identify the god worshiped at Dan as "the god of Dan," one must suppose that this deity was not Yahweh and that the identification of the deity at Dan with Yahweh by Jeroboam's action was an innovation that would have slipped away when Dan was lost to Israel ("Synkretismus und Monotheismus," 170 n. 33). Biran interprets the same data as indicating that the deity was so well-known that it was unnecessary to name him, while Flusser believes that the Danites of the inscription and the god they worshiped was so ancient and obscure that the memory of that god's identity was lost but that it was, of course, the God of Israel (Biran, "To the God Who Is in Dan," 147, 149).

191. McCarter, "Aspects of the Religion of the Israelite Monarchy," 139. The following discussion is directly indebted to McCarter's analysis of the inscriptional and biblical material.

192. Ibid., 140.

193. Ibid. McCarter has identified two plausible references to local cults in the Bible and has suggested others. In 2 Sam. 15:7, David's son Absalom says to David, "Let me go fulfill the vow I made to Yahweh-in-Hebron (*yhwh běhebrôn*), for your servant made a vow when I was living in Aram-geshur." It is possible that "in Hebron" modifies the verb for fulfilling the vow, but the most natural syntactical reading is as a modifier of "Yahweh," as McCarter has proposed. The reference to "Dagon in Ashdod" in 1 Sam. 5:5 is another example of an apparent local cult of the Philistine deity in that city. Cf. van der Toorn, "Yahweh," 919.

194. Ibid., 141.

195. See 2 Kings 18:4; 23:8.

196. McCarter views the Deuteronomic movement somewhat differently at this point:

> [T]here is nothing to suggest that the reforming kings viewed the exis-
> tence of local shrines as a threat to the concept of the unity of Yahweh.
> They must have understood the several Yahwehs to be exactly what
> they were, namely, local forms of the national god. Still, we can see
> that their policies, by unifying the worship of Yahweh, had the effect
> of unifying the way in which he was conceived by the worshipers, thus
> eliminating the earlier theology of local manifestation. ("Aspects of the
> Religion of the Israelite Monarchy," 141)

197. For discussion of some of the issues involved in defining official religion in distinction from popular or other modes, see Vrijhof and Waardenburg, *Official and Popular Religion*. While many features of religion in ancient Israel may be called "popular," that term is more difficult to define and its content more amorphous. I have sought to locate the types of religion, as they have to do with the form and character of the cult, in some relation to the social-cultural-political groups that were their matrix. Cf. Albertz, *History of Israelite Religion*, 1:17–21.

198. The term "all Israel" is used to refer to the gathering of the larger sociopolitical entity "Israel" as distinct from a family or tribal unit. It does not presume any particular definition of what smaller units comprised that "Israel" at any particular time.

199. Gottwald, *Tribes of Yahweh*, 90.

200. See Judg. 5:11, 13; 1 Sam. 2:24. Cf. Num. 17:6(16:41); 2 Kings 9:6; 11:17; Ezek. 36:20; Zeph. 2:10; and the expression "people of God" (e.g., Judg. 20:2). The designations "my people," "your people," and "his people" are ubiquitous in the Bible (cf. Ex. 19:5–6; Deut. 7:6; 14:2, 21; 26:19; 27:9; 28:9; 32:8–9; 1 Sam. 12:22).

201. Cf. Mendenhall, "Social Organization in Early Israel"; and Cross, "Kinship and Covenant," 17.

202. See Ex. 23:14–17; Leviticus 23; Deut. 16:1–17.

203. For the view that this was originally and primarily a historical festival, see B. Goldstein and A. Cooper, "Festivals of Israel and Judah," 22.

204. On the reliability of this chapter of Chronicles, see Vaughn, *Theology, History, and Archaeology in the Chronicler's Account of Hezekiah*.

205. Cross, *Canaanite Myth and Hebrew Epic*, 86.

206. Ibid., 88.

207. Ibid., 104–5.

208. Mayes, *Deuteronomy*.

209. Ibid.

210. See, e.g., de Vaux, *Ancient Israel*, 490; but this matter is very uncertain.

211. Cross, *Canaanite Myth and Hebrew Epic*, 105 n. 48.

212. Kraus, *Worship in Israel*, 163.

213. See Deut. 16:13; 31:10; cf. Lev. 23:34; Neh. 8:14–18; Ezra 3:4; 2 Chron. 8:15; Zech. 14:16–19.

214. This would have been, literally, "the first fruits of wheat harvest" (cf. Num. 28:26).

215. The later name "Pentecost," referring to the fiftieth day, comes from the tradition of Lev. 23:15–16, which dates the festival more precisely to the fiftieth day from the Sabbath after the first sheaf was offered.

216. Childs, *Book of Exodus*, 484.

217. The book of Judges subsumes such occasions under a Deuteronomic cycle of apostasy, crying to Yahweh, and deliverance under the leadership of a judge (*šōpēt*) chosen by the deity.

218. See, e.g., Psalms 74, 79, 80; Jer. 14:7–9, 19–22; Lamentations 5. Cf. Joel 2:12–17; Ezra 10:1 (the great assembly when the people gathered to repent of having taken foreign wives).

219. Deuteronomy makes such celebration and rejoicing a regular part of the pilgrimage festivals.

220. Miller, *Divine Warrior in Early Israel*. The battles may not always have involved all twelve tribes, but the obligation of those summoned to "come to the help of the LORD" is clear from Judg. 5:23. For the positive or blessing character of the recital of the tribes in Judg. 5:12–18, see Miller, *Divine Warrior in Early Israel*, 96–97; Cross, *Canaanite Myth and Hebrew Epic*, 235 n. 7; idem, "Epic Traditions of Early Israel," 37 n. 67; and idem, "Reuben, First-Born of Jacob," 54–55 n. 7.

221. See 1 Kings 3:5.

222. See 1 Sam. 14:40–42; Ezra 2:63. Casting by lot is also indicated or may be inferred in Joshua 7 and 1 Sam. 10:20–21.

223. See 1 Sam. 9:9; 10:22; Micah 3:6–7.

224. See Lev. 8:8; Num. 27:21; Deut. 33:8; 1 Sam. 14:36–37; 23:6–13; Ezra 2:63. First Sam. 23:1–13 is an interesting instance in which David first inquires of the Lord about the prospects for victory but without any indicated oracular technique. Shortly after that, when the priest Abiathar comes to join him with an ephod in his hand, David calls for the ephod and uses it in some fashion to consult Yahweh and divine the future. The ephod was, in this instance, a container for the Urim and Thummim, the sacred lots. A similar sequence occurs in 1 Sam. 14:36–42 where Saul first inquires of Yahweh, and when that produces no response, he resorts successfully to the use of the sacred lots.

225. See Cross, "Kinship and Covenant in Ancient Israel."

226. It is likely that Passover was in the earliest period an all-Israel occasion. During the monarchy, prior to Josiah's reform, it was a family celebration (2 Kings 23:21–23). At all times, its association with the exodus seems clear.

227. See Deut. 6:20–24. This text is very Deuteronomic in its character, but it points to one of the roles that the recital of the divine acts in behalf of Israel fulfilled.

228. The theological analysis provided here is indebted to Albertz's careful study of the differences between personal piety and official religion, *Persönliche Frömmigkeit und offizielle Religion*, 92–94.

229. Such differences reach behind the split of the United Monarchy, but they cannot be differentiated in the manner that is possible from the time of the division into two kingdoms.

230. Schunck, "Zentralheiligtum, Grenzheiligtum und 'Hohenheiligtum' in Israel,"

136–37, following the earlier suggestion of Aharoni, "Arad: Its Inscriptions and Temple." Examples of such border sanctuaries, which Schunck thinks corresponded in layout and function very much to the *hêkāl* or temple in Jerusalem but without being bound to a royal palace or functioning as a central sanctuary, were those at Arad, Beer-sheba, Geba, and Mizpah, as well as the northern sanctuaries of Bethel and Dan. For criticism of the border sanctuary proposal with regard to Bethel, see Ahlström, *Royal Administration and National Religion*, 58. Ahlström thinks Jeroboam chose Bethel as a national sanctuary because of its ancient traditions that made it closer to the mainstream of Israelite religion.

231. That David and later kings also began to build up both military and economic means of power is evident from textual and archaeological data. But the cultic undergirding of their kingship was important even in legitimating and justifying those military and economic trends. As Lowery has noted, economically "the monarchy shifted the decentralized subsistence agriculture toward surplus production for the support of the monarchy," while culturally, "the monarchy legitimated its social role through an official cult which presented the king as the divinely chosen earthly representative of Yahweh, the true owner of the land and sovereign of the people" (*Reforming Kings*, 37).

232. Meyers, "David as Temple Builder," 363.

233. For further discussion, see chapter 5.

234. The use of this term in reference to the shrine at Shiloh is probably a projection back from later usage identifying the Shiloh sanctuary as the precursor of the Jerusalem temple (cf. Schunck, "Zentralheiligtum, Grenzheiligtum und 'Hohenheiligtum' in Israel," 134 n. 6). Less likely is his conjecture that the Shiloh shrine was originally called that because it was the central sanctuary of the league and also the place where the judge of Israel resided.

235. Both terms occur in Amos 7:13 on the lips of Amaziah, "priest of Bethel."

236. It should be noted that the transfer of the ark to Jerusalem was accomplished with sacrifices followed by David's distribution of food "among all the people" (2 Sam. 6:17–19). Here a shrewd political act takes place in the context of a religious occasion to cement further the support of the people. It is not unimportant that it was also consistent with the Deuteronomic History's frequent insistence upon the community's eating together at festal and sacrificial occasions as a celebration of Yahweh's provision of blessing. David's act was not the same as the Deuteronomic instruction, but it reflected a similar joining of the people's sacrifice and the sharing of food by all.

237. First Kings 11:1–8; 16:31–34. The very Deuteronomic character of these reports should not inhibit recognition of the fact that non-Israelites in positions of power as wives in the royal court would have been able to exercise that power in significant ways to influence the king's manipulation of the state religion.

238. See Spieckermann, *Juda unter Assur in der Sargonidzeit*.

239. See the discussion of the inscriptional data in chapter 1, excursus 1, as well as Tigay, "Israelite Religion," and idem, *You Shall Have No Other Gods*.

240. See 1 Sam. 22:20–23; 2 Sam. 8:17; 20:25; 1 Kings 1:7–8. Cf. chapter 5.

241. On the history of the priestly families and especially David's move to bind league elements together as a part of his cultic establishment, see Cross, *Canaanite Myth and Hebrew Epic*, 195–215.

242. Toews, *Monarchy and Religious Institution in Israel*, 92 (citing Mazar).

243. Ahlström, *Royal Administration and National Religion*, 80.

244. See, for example, Cross's discussion of Solomon's move to consolidate power and the consequent disappearance from the scene of chief supporters of the cultus of the league (*Canaanite Myth and Hebrew Epic*, 237–38).

245. See Meyers, "David as Temple Builder."

246. Cross, "Priestly Tabernacle in Light of Recent Research," 174–75.

247. Ibid., 175.

248. See Albright, *Archaeology and the Religion of Israel*, 142–55; Holladay, "Religion in Israel and Judah under the Monarchy," 265. Ahlström has contested the association of the plan of the Solomonic temple with the Syrian temple at Tell Ta'yinat (*Royal Administration and National Religion*, 34.) The association of the temple with some Canaanite models does not mean that there was none of that in the design and conceptuality of the previous tent shrine of the league. See Cross, "Priestly Tabernacle," 169–80. Canaanite deities also dwelt in *'ōhel* and *miškān*, as we now know from Late Bronze Age Ugaritic texts.

249. Cross, *Canaanite Myth and Hebrew Epic*, 238. It must be recognized that Solomon's moves were also in some direct continuity with the major efforts on David's part to shift the political structure from tribal confederation to monarchical state.

250. See 1 Kings 9:25.

251. Second Kings 23:21–23 and 2 Chron. 35:18 indicate both the fact of an earlier all-Israel Passover celebration and its disappearance during the monarchy. It is possible that some celebration of the feast of Unleavened Bread was carried on during the monarchy as a pilgrimage festival, but the Josianic note indicates that his act was a revival of an important and long-since defunct cultic practice. It is that act of reinstituting the Passover that stands as a major counterpart to the autumn festival of the royal era. Second Chronicles 30 reports that Hezekiah earlier had reinstituted the Passover. Whether or not that is an accurate report, like the parallel account of Josiah's Passover, the Chronicles text confirms the decline of Passover and the spring festival during the period of the monarchy. Cf. Cross, *Canaanite Myth and Hebrew Epic*, 106 n. 51. On the reliability of 2 Chronicles 30, see Vaughn, *Theology, History, and Archaeology*.

252. See 1 Kings 8:12; 12:32.

253. See 1 Sam. 7:8–16; Pss. 132; 78:68–71 (cf. Kraus, *Worship in Israel*, 179–88, 208–18); Cross, *Canaanite Myth and Hebrew Epic*, 238–39 and n. 85; and Miller, "Israelite Religion," 220–22.

254. See Toews, *Monarchy and Religious Institution in Israel*.

255. See, e.g., Cross, *Canaanite Myth and Hebrew Epic*, 74.

256. For Dan, see Judges 17–18. Cf. M. Weippert, "Synkretismus und Monotheismus," 159.

257. See Genesis 28 and 35, esp. 35:6–7.

258. Bull images associated with sacred sites, well-known from Syrian excavations, have now been discovered in two Palestinian locations, the Bull Shrine excavated by Mazar and the Philistine city of Ashkelon. The Taanach cult stand may contain a bull relief, though it has been argued that it is an equine figure (see chapter 1).

259. Cross, *Canaanite Myth and Hebrew Epic*, 74. On Jeroboam's cultus in gen-

eral, see pp. 73–75 and Toews, *Monarchy and Religious Institution in Israel*, 41–69. For the associations of the bull language and imagery with El, see Miller, "El the Warrior," 411–31.

260. See Ex. 32:4 = 1 Kings 12:28; Hos. 8:4–6.

261. Cf. 1 Kings 8:2.

262. Kraus, *Worship in Israel*, 152. For reservations about this view and discussion of various possible reasons, see Toews, *Monarchy and Religious Institution in Israel*, 100–107.

263. Toews, *Monarchy and Religious Institution in Israel*, 95–100; and Cross, *Canaanite Myth and Hebrew Epic*, 196–99.

264. See Amos 7:10–17.

265. First Kings 12:31a is very terse and its meaning unclear (cf. 1 Kings 13:32b). For discussion, see Toews, *Monarchy and Religious Institution in Israel*, 73–74.

266. On the use of the word *qābāl* as a designation for the postexilic community of Judah, see Blenkinsopp, "Temple and Society in Achaemenid Judah," 44–45; and Weinberg, *Citizen-Temple Community*, 65–66. Both Blenkinsopp and Weinberg identify other terms that were used or may have been used to designate the politico-religious community of Judah.

267. For a critique of the use of the term "community" to refer to the Judean province in the sixth to fourth centuries, see the summary of Frank Crüsemann and the response to his position by Albertz in the latter's *History of Israelite Religion*, 2:448–49.

268. Blenkinsopp, "Temple and Society in Achaemenid Judah," 45.

269. Weinberg, *Citizen-Temple Community*, 58–61; cf. Albertz, *History of Israelite Religion*, 2:447.

270. For the terms and texts identifying these groups and for more detail on the administrative structure, see Albertz, *History of Israelite Religion*, 2:446–47.

271. Washington, *Wealth and Poverty in the Instruction of Amenemope and the Hebrew Proverbs*, 164–65.

272. For a review and critique of the various proposals of Plöger, Hanson, Berquist, and Cook, and the literature wherein these proposals may be found, see Carter, *Emergence of Yehud in the Persian Period*, 316–23. Hanson has offered a more nuanced treatment of early postexilic religion and the group conflicts within it than in his earlier book, *The Dawn of Apocalyptic* (see "Israelite Religion in the Early Postexilic Period"). This essay seems to have been overlooked by Cook and Carter in their critiques of Hanson. See Cook, *Prophecy and Apocalypticism*, 1–9. Williamson has recently entered a cautionary note about the assumption of extensive conflict in the postexilic community and especially with regard to strained relations between the returnees and those who remained behind in Judah. See Williamson, "Exile and After," 255.

273. Note the various terms here to refer to the adversarial groups. On the one hand, "the returned exiles" (*běnê haggôlâ*), "Judah and Benjamin," and "the people of Judah"; on the other hand, "the adversaries of Judah and Benjamin" and "the people of the land," the latter a term that seems to refer to inhabitants of Judah or neighboring provinces, such as Samaria and Idumea, who were not a part of the *gôlâ*, the returnees, and were religiously suspect. See Blenkinsopp, *Ezra and Nehemiah*, 108.

274. Talmon, "Emergence of Jewish Sectarianism." Cf. Carter, *Emergence of Yehud in the Persian Period*, 310–16, for a similar construction.

275. Talmon, "Emergence of Jewish Sectarianism," 598.

276. Ibid.

277. Ibid., 600.

278. See Ezra 9:2–4, where the faithlessness of the "holy seed" (v. 2) is the faithfulness of the "returned exiles" (v. 4).

279. Talmon, "Emergence of Jewish Sectarianism," 599. Smith-Christopher has argued that the Ezra documents testify to the situation of a threatened group whose separation emphasis is not really from foreign elements in the old sense but is a reflection of a later time and of the development of sects within the life of the community differing on what makes a true Jew. See Smith-Christopher, "Mixed Marriage Crisis in Ezra 9–10 and Nehemiah 13," 255–58.

280. Carter, *Emergence of Yehud in the Persian Period*, 313.

281. Talmon, "Emergence of Jewish Sectarianism," 594.

282. Cf. Nehemiah 10 and the covenant renewal ceremony participated in by "all who have separated themselves from the peoples of the lands to adhere to the law of God."

283. For recent discussion of the origin and nature of the synagogue, see L. Levine, "Nature and Origin of the Palestinian Synagogue Reconsidered"; and Binder, *Into the Temple Courts*. Levine sees the roots of the synagogue in the function of the city gate in preexilic and postexilic times (e.g., Ezra 8:1) and does not regard it as arising out of the temple or in competition with the temple and its cult. Binder adopts a "modified version" of Levine's hypothesis, suggesting that the city gate had a more sacred character to it than Levine has recognized (210–20, 482–83).

284. Balentine, "Politics of Religion in the Persian Period," 138–40. Cf. Berquist, *Judaism in Persia's Shadow*, 137–39; and Albertz, *History of Israelite Religion*, 2:467.

285. For detailed discussion of the similarities and differences, see Albertz, *History of Israelite Religion*, 2:458–59.

286. Ibid., 459.

287. Ibid., 461–62. This point is where there is some validity in the "citizen-temple community" model that Weinberg has proposed (*Citizen-Temple Community*). It is likely that the community was not as large as he has suggested and that there was not the clear difference between the political province and the citizen-temple community within it that he has indicated. His recognition of the significance of the "houses of the fathers" in the community structure and the centrality of the temple religiously and economically is borne out by the texts and his analysis of them. While Weinberg's model has been adopted by a number of interpreters of the history and sociology of this period, significant criticisms have been leveled by various scholars who have worked extensively in this period. See, for example, Blenkinsopp, "Temple and Society in Achaemenid Judah"; Williamson, "Judah and the Jews"; idem, "Exile and After," 246–52; and Carter, *Emergence of Yehud in the Persian Period*, 294–307. It should be noted that Williamson has expressed some skepticism about the temple playing a central economic role, pointing to the evidence of Haggai, Malachi, and Nehemiah 10 and 13 that the temple was constantly neglected and neither owned land nor exercised control over title to property by way of membership in its community ("Exile and After," 251).

288. Balentine, "Politics of Religion in the Persian Period," 140. Cf. the extended presentation of examples of such regional temples in other locales in Blenkinsopp, "Temple and Society in Achaemenid Judah," 24–34.

289. Balentine, "Politics of Religion in the Persian Period," 140–43. Balentine concludes that "the catalyst for Yehud's self-definition was as much the Persian imposition of social and political directives as it was the internal convictions of a fervent faith" (143). For a more extended analysis of this dialectic of internal and external factors in the evolution of Judaism in this period, see Berquist, *Judaism in Persia's Shadow*.

290. Balentine, "Politics of Religion in the Persian Period," 142.

291. Albertz, *History of Israelite Religion*, 2:462–64.

292. Mason has suggested that echoes of this move may be found also in Joel 3:1–2(2:28–29) and Zechariah 9–14. See Mason, "Messiah in the Postexilic Old Testament Literature."

293. See Hanson, "Israelite Religion in the Early Postexilic Period," 496–99. Hanson notes with others that the formulations and the use of the term *nāśî'* represent a pro-priestly movement or the decline of the Davidic-royal figure in favor of the priestly leader. He sees reflected in the latest redactional stages of Ezekiel and Zechariah as well as in the later stages of the Chronicler's history "a fifth-century community that has moved—in part because of changed international circumstances—away from a royal Davidic model of community, and even beyond a model of a balanced royal-priestly diarchy, toward an exclusively priestly form of rule most accurately described as a hierocracy. We have entered the era in which the patrons of the Zadokite leaders were no longer the kings and princes of the house of David but the members of the imperial house of Persia" (499). Cf. the discussion of this term in Ezekiel in Joyce, "King and Messiah in Ezekiel," 330–32.

294. Tuell, *Law of the Temple in Ezekiel 40–48*, 115–17.

295. Joyce, "King and Messiah in Ezekiel," 337.

296. Ackroyd, *Chronicler in His Age*, 71; cited by Mason, "Messiah in the Postexilic Old Testament Literature," 363. Mason's examination of the literature from the sixth to fourth centuries leads him to the conclusion: "In summary, then, we have to say how little influence the concept of a renewal of the Davidic line after the exile exercised in the extant postexilic biblical literature" (364).

297. The details of this economic conflict and its significance have been laid out by Albertz, to whom this summary discussion is much indebted. See his *History of Israelite Religion*, 2:493–507.

298. Ibid., 496–97.

299. Ibid., 500–503.

300. Ibid., 503–7. Albertz identifies two positive effects of the social crisis of this era on the history of Israelite religion. One was the raising of the question of the theological legitimation of riches at the level of official Yahweh religion (note the later strong tradition of almsgiving), and the other was that the impulse of Yahwism toward social revolution and support of lower-class religious groups was not lost but demonstrated its capacity for being taken up time and again (507).

301. See, e.g., Plöger, *Theocracy and Eschatology*; and Hanson, *Dawn of Apocalyptic*.

302. See especially Cook, *Prophecy and Apocalypticism*; and Berquist, *Judaism*

under Persia's Shadow, 177–92. In Berquist's analysis, apocalyptic arises from persons in power but out of their frustrations over control, so there is a dimension of deprivation or power versus powerlessness in his analysis also. Cf. the discussion of these different proposals in Carter, *Emergence of Yehud in the Persian Period*, 316–23; and Albertz, *History of Israelite Religion*, 2:564–66.

303. Cross, "Kinship and Covenant in Ancient Israel," 7–11.

304. Ibid., 12.

305. Ibid.

306. Stager, "Archaeology of the Family in Ancient Israel," 24–25. Weinberg has argued that the *battê 'ābôt* that form the basis for the social structure of the Judean community in the sixth to fourth centuries are rooted in the clan structure of the preexilic period, even if significantly altered in the new situation arising out of the destruction of Jerusalem and the exile and return of many citizens. See "The *Bêt 'ābôt* in the Sixth to Fourth Centuries BCE," in Weinberg, *Citizen-Temple Community*, 60–61.

307. On this term in Deuteronomy, see Perlitt, "Ein einzig Volk von Brüdern."

308. See, e.g., Deut. 21:10–21; 22:13–29; 24:1–4; 25:5–12. On these laws, see Pressler, *View of Women Found in the Deuteronomic Family Laws*; and Westbrook, *Property and Family in Biblical Law*.

309. Cross, "Kinship and Covenant in Ancient Israel," 5.

310. See, e.g., Pss. 5:8(7) ("your house" and "your holy temple"); 11:4; 23:6; 27:4.

311. See, e.g., Pss. 3:5(4); 9:12(11); 61:7–8(6–7).

312. See, e.g., Pss. 14:7; 25:22; 28:8–9; 51:20–21(18–19); 131:3. See the summary comment of Albertz:

> In a series of individual laments there are petitions for Israel or Zion; the history of the people is incorporated into some or the personal vow of praise is extended to the community. The confession of confidence on the part of the individual is offered as a basis for the trust of the community; and in some individual laments the difference between personal enemies and the adversaries of Israel becomes blurred. Alongside this, in some songs of thanksgiving it is possible to recognize an extension of the private Toda community to the whole liturgical community. (Albertz, *History of Israelite Religion*, 2:508–9.)

See Albertz's notes for specific references to the Psalms.

313. For *qāhāl* and *'ēdâ* as terms for the assembled cultic community, see Ex. 16:1–2; Lev. 4:13–14, 21; Num. 10:1–10; 14:27; 15:15, 25–26; 17:12(16:47); 21:1–13; 22:22, 29.

314. For a strong case for seeing a larger role of the king in the individual laments, see Eaton, *Kingship and the Psalms*. On the possibility of reading some of the psalms as either the voice of the king or an individual Israelite, see Miller, "Beginning of the Psalter."

Chapter 3. Sacrifice and Offering in Ancient Israel

1. On the scripturalization of sacrifice, see the summary statement of Anderson, "Sacrifice and Sacrificial Offerings (OT)," 882–86; and the more extended study of Fishbane, *Biblical Interpretation in Ancient Israel*.

2. It should be acknowledged that the practice is easier to define than the conceptuality and that, while the latter is inferred from what one knows of the former and the texts about practice, it is not always easy to make that inference. Every conception of sacrifice is something of a conjecture from the evidence of practice.

3. The term *minḥâ* is used in some instances in this broad sense of "gift" or "offering" (e.g., Gen. 4:3–5), while in other instances, notably in the Priestly sacrificial legislation, it means specifically a grain or cereal offering, with P using *qorbān* as the more general term for offering. The specific and generic meanings of *minḥâ* may arise out of the fact that the grain offering would have been the standard gift in an agricultural society, although other gifts, and even tribute, could be called *minḥâ*. The priestly personnel, however, in their responsibility for organizing and regularizing the variety of gifts that would have been brought to the sanctuary, needed more specific categorization and so used the term *minḥâ* to identify specifically the most common "gift," the grain offering, and used the term *qorbān* and its related forms for the more general act of offering. On this kind of distinction between the uses of cultic terms in the general society and their accommodation to the specialized needs of cultic personnel see Anderson, *Sacrifices and Offerings in Ancient Israel*, 27–34. Anderson deals specifically with *minḥâ* but also notes similar kinds of general and specific uses of other cultic terms such as *maś'ēt* and *tēnûpâ*, as well as Phoenician *mtn*, "offering."

4. These categories of orientation have been proposed by B. Levine, *In the Presence of the Lord*, 6–7.

5. B. Levine lists thirty-one different types of sacrifices, falling into one or more of the three categories above (*In the Presence of the Lord*, 6–7, nn. 6–8).

6. On these terms and their history, see the extended study of Rendtorff, *Studien zur Geschichte des Opfers*. For an effort to catalog the Hebrew terms for sacrifice and offering according to the dating of the texts in which the terms appear and to reconstruct the history of sacrifice in light of that dating, see Zwickel, *Tempelkult in Kanaan und Israel*, 285–376. Obviously, such specific dating of these many texts is debatable at many points, but the reader can get some broad perspective about the use of the terms over a chronological spectrum.

7. The burnt offering is known from the Ugaritic texts of the mid to late second millennium, although identified by a different word, as well as among the practice of Canaanite priests of Baal reported in 1 Kings 18. Further, some form of burnt offering seems to have been present in Punic sacrificial practice, as suggested by the sacrificial tariffs of Marseille and Carthage. See *ANET*, 502–3. For a summary indication of the evidence for the burnt offering in the surrounding cultures, see Milgrom, *Leviticus 1–16*, 173–75.

8. The presenters of sacrifice seem to have been primarily males, but there is some debate about the extent to which females could have actually carried out sacrificial activity beyond simply presenting the offering to the priest (see chapter 5). Braulik has argued that Deuteronomic legislation brought women fully into all cultic activity including sacrifice, a point conceded by Phyllis Bird, who generally points to the exclusion of women from regular cultic leadership. She sees a growing weight upon the distinction between priest and laity rather than male and female as the priesthood became more dominant and specialized in the postexilic history of Israel's religion. Both Braulik and Bird would recognize differences

between Deuteronomic and Priestly practice that cannot be simply harmonized into a single practice at all times. See Braulik, "Rejection of the Goddess Asherah in Israel," 178–82; idem, "Haben in Israel auch Frauen geopfert? 19–28; and Bird, "Place of Women in the Israelite Cultus," esp. p. 412 and n. 34. On the ideological and conceptual place of women in relation to sacrifice, see Jay, *Throughout Your Generations Forever.* For discussion of Jay's views in relation to other works on the theory of sacrifice and its relation to the roles of women, see Strenski, "Between Theory and Speciality."

9. Cf. Milgrom, *Leviticus 1–16*, 174.

10. B. Levine, *In the Presence of the Lord*, 22.

11. Levine sees this function of attracting the deity as also evident in the burnt offering of Manoah in Judg. 13:16 and the sacrifice of his son by the king of Moab in 2 Kings 3:26–27.

12. B. Levine, *In the Presence of the Lord*, 26.

13. See Milgrom, *Leviticus 1–16*, 175–77.

14. For a proposal that the apportioning of part of the cereal offering to the priests arose as a polemic against the use of the cereal offering as a private or family offering to other deities, specifically the Queen of Heaven (Jer. 7:18; 44:15–19), see Milgrom, *Leviticus 1–16*, 200–202.

15. See 1 Kings 18:36; 2 Kings 16:15; Ezra 9:4–5; Dan. 9:21; Ps. 141:2. For indications of grain and burnt offerings at both morning and evening hours, see Numbers 28.

16. Milgrom, "Sacrifices and Offerings, OT," 769.

17. As Milgrom has pointed out, when the grain offering appears in a series such as this, it is not easy to tell whether it is a discrete offering or an adjunct to the *ʿōlâ* or the *šelem* sacrifice (*Leviticus 1–16*, 200).

18. For the Rabbinic and Philonic evidence, see Milgrom, *Leviticus 1–16*, 195–96.

19. Oppenheim, *Interpretation of Dreams in the Ancient Near East*, 301.

20. *CAD* 10:331, s.v. *maṣḫatu.* Cited in Milgrom, *Leviticus 1–16*, 196.

21. In Leviticus 5 and 14 there are developed provisions and gradations of sacrificial material to enable the poor to make offerings within their means. The Punic Marseilles Tariff also makes provision for the poor in its sacrificial listings (see *ANET*, 656–57).

22. Anderson, *Sacrifices and Offerings in Ancient Israel*, 31–33.

23. Milgrom, *Leviticus 1–16*, 218.

24. Ibid., 419–20.

25. On sacrifice as an aspect of family religion, see chapter 2 and Albertz, *History of the Israelite Religion*, 1:99–103.

26. The basic work at this point is that of Milgrom, elaborated in detail in his commentary *Leviticus 1–16*, but developed in earlier studies noted in the bibliography to his commentary. Levine has supplied examples of the verb *ḫiṭṭēʾ* used to refer to purification of buildings (Lev. 14:52; Ezek. 45:18), of persons (Num. 19:19; Ps. 51:9), of the altar (Ex. 29:36; Lev. 8:15; Ezek. 43:20, 22–23), and of a sacrificial animal (Lev. 6:19; 9:15). See B. Levine, *In the Presence of the Lord*, 102 n. 123.

27. Milgrom argues that the sin that is forgiven in the ritual is not the inadvertent sin itself but the sin of having contaminated the sanctuary. He argues that the violation itself is cleansed by the fact that it was inadvertent and that the sinner "feels

guilty" (*Leviticus 1–16*, 254, 256). This is the weakest part of Milgrom's argument and depends upon a translation of *wĕ'āšēmû* (Lev. 4:13, 22, 27; 5:2, 4, 17), as "feel/realize guilt" when many would understand the verb as meaning "incur guilt."

28. B. Levine, *In the Presence of the Lord*, 65–66. Levine sees here a development in the usage of the term *kippēr*, customarily translated as "make atonement for" or "make expiation for." In the sacrificial texts, it does not mean the act of granting atonement or expiation but the process of performing rites of expiation that lead to the granting of forgiveness or purification. The outcome is clear but it is not automatic, a distinction he regards as crucial. The forgiveness and cleansing that comes out of the priest performing expiatory rites on behalf of or with respect to something or someone, is that God purifies or forgives. When the text speaks about God's direct expiation or absolution of someone, a different phrase is used than when the text speaks about performing expiation rites in behalf of someone to effect God's forgiveness. The latter, which is what we have in the cultic texts dealing with the *ḥaṭṭā't*, involves *kippēr* + *'al* or *bĕ'ad* as in the cultic texts dealing with the *ḥaṭṭā't*, while the former has the expression *kippēr* + *lĕ*, as in Deut. 21:8 and Ezek. 16:63. In a noncultic text, for example, Moses says to the people who have sinned in making the golden calf: "Perhaps I can make expiation/atonement in behalf of your sin (*kippēr* + *bĕ'ad* + "your sin"—Ex. 32:29). He then prays that God will lift up, that is, forgive the sin of the people (v. 32). His expiatory rite is the act of prayer as the *ḥaṭṭā't* is the act of sacrifice.

29. See, e.g., Albertz, *History of Israelite Religion*, 2:462.

30. See particularly Milgrom, *Leviticus 1–16*, 1067–79. For arguments in behalf of a late postexilic origin, see de Vaux, *Ancient Israel*, 509–10.

31. Milgrom, *Leviticus 1–16*, 1061–63.

32. Wright, "Day of Atonement," 73. Wright goes on to say that "the implication following from this is that were the sanctuary left sullied by these impurities, God's presence, which manifests itself in the tent, could not dwell there and would leave (cf. Ezekiel 8–11)."

33. The ritual as presented in Leviticus 16 also includes a bull that is slaughtered and its blood sprinkled on the ark of the covenant (Lev. 16:14).

34. "Thus the ritual in the sanctuary concerns itself with removing its pollution (also caused by Israel's wrongs . . .); the rite with the Azazel goat, by contrast, focuses not on pollution, the effects of Israel's wrongs, but exclusively on the wrongs themselves" (Milgrom, *Leviticus 1–16*, 1033).

35. Ibid., 1021.

36. For more extended discussion of Azazel and theories about its meaning and background, see Milgrom, *Leviticus 1–16*, 107–79; Wright, "Azazel," 1:563–67; Janowski, "Azazel und der Sündenbock"; and idem, "Azazel."

37. See de Vaux, *Ancient Israel*, 507–8; and Albertz, *History of Israelite Religion*, 2:462–63.

38. For analogous rituals of both purification and elimination among the cultures of the ancient Near East, especially the Mesopotamian world and the culture of the Hittites, see Wright, "Day of Atonement," 74; idem, *Disposal of Impurity*, 31–74; Milgrom, *Leviticus 1–16*, 1067–79; Janowski, "Azazel und der Sündenbock"; and idem, "Azazel."

39. For discussion of this analogy and its implications for the evolution of the Day

of Atonement, see Milgrom, *Leviticus 1–16*, 1044; Wright, "Day of Atonement," 75; and Janowski, "Azazel."

40. For a brief summary of the various views on the nature and character of the *'āšām* offering, see Diether Kellermann, "*'asham*," *TDOT* 1:432.

41. For discussion of the various instances where equivalence in money is to be assumed, see Milgrom, *Leviticus 1–16*, 326–28; and B. Levine, *In the Presence of the Lord*, 95–101.

42. On 1 Samuel 4–6, see Miller and Roberts, *Hand of the Lord*. On the dating of this text, see pp. 73–75.

43. It is not altogether clear whether the process allowed for the conversion of a sacrifice into monetary value or the replacement of the money offering by a sacrifice of equivalent value. The Philistine *'āšām* (see below) and the reference to "the money from the guilt offerings" in 2 Kings 12:17 suggest that the *'āšām* was originally a presentation of money or objects of value which later could be and were converted into an altar sacrifice. The *'āšām* thus moved between the mode of sacrifice as a presentation to the deity that was used in some other manner and the mode of sacrifice in which the presentation was consumed or burnt (in whole or part) on the sacrifice (see below). The possibility that 2 Kings 12:17 is a postexilic addition to the text precludes certainty on these matters.

44. Milgrom, *Cult and Conscience*; idem, *Leviticus 1–16*, 339–78; B. Levine, *In the Presence of the Lord*, 91–101. The term "misappropriation" translates the verb *mā'al*, translated in the NRSV as "commit a trespass" (Lev. 5:14; 5:21[6:2]). Milgrom has presented extended analyses and analogues to make the case for all of the instances of *'āšām* offerings as covering instances of violation or desecration of sacred things. Both interpreters see the unintentionality of the sin as a prerequisite for the possibility of expiation through the ritual of the *'āšām* offering.

45. For a summary discussion of the evidence from Ugarit, see Anderson, *Sacrifices and Offerings in Ancient Israel*, 78–80.

46. Fenn has suggested that it is "the secret of society" to turn desire into devotion and devotion into civic obligation, a process that may be at work not only in tithing and first fruits but in the whole process of sacrifice and its ritual. He suggests further that the urban establishment, civic and religious, may have drawn on a surplus of devotion in order to finance its demands on citizenry for attending to the work of the polis (Fenn's term) and the people, for paying tribute and taxes, and for maintaining public order. See Fenn, *Secularization of Sin*, especially on his analysis of the movement from desire to devotion to obligation (pp. 26–28).

47. Fenn suggests that tithing not only expressed devotion and thanksgiving but was also a means of protection of what one had produced: "If one offers a gift to the gods, whatever one has left will not be taken away—hence the origin of tithing. . . . The obligation to the gods, once settled symbolically, allows one to enjoy the remaining fruits of one's labors." See Fenn, *Secularization of Sin*, 135, quoting Burkert, *Structure and History in Greek Mythology and Ritual*, 53.

48. For further discussion of the thanksgiving prayer and sacrifice, see Miller, *They Cried to the Lord*, 130–33.

49. The fallacy of looking for a single theory of sacrifice has been pointed out in Hendel, "Sacrifice as a Cultural System." On the basis of Ex. 24:3–8, Hendel makes some helpful suggestions about the role of sacrifice in pilgrimage festivals as it rein-

forces social solidarity and unity, and the significance of some of the distinctions in the mode of preparation or cooking the sacrifice as symbolic and ritual indicators of boundaries and distinctions between the human and the divine.

50. The primary influences in this analysis have been Douglas, particularly in her two volumes, *Natural Symbols* and *Purity and Danger*, and Turner, particularly in his work, *Ritual Process*.

51. For a helpful discussion of Israel's "culture map" and various dimensions of anthropological and structuralist approaches to sacrifice, see Nelson, *Raising Up a Faithful Priest*, chapters 2 and 4.

52. Cf. at this point the critique of Rogerson, "Anthropology and the Old Testament," 22–26.

53. The fundamental work on the ordering of the sacrificial system has been done by B. Levine, "Ugaritic Descriptive Rituals"; idem, "Descriptive Tabernacle Texts of the Pentateuch"; and Rainey, "Order of Sacrifices." The discussion here is particularly indebted to Rainey's form-critical analysis.

54. "Throughout this entire *descriptive* passage special attention is paid to the actual conduct of the ritual. The place of slaughter, the disposition of the various parts of the animal, and the type of animal required in various circumstances were all stressed. One might say that the entire section looks like an excerpt from a 'Handbook for Priests.' The treatment seems to follow a didactic principle by which the officiant could learn his job. Details of this nature are best learned by logical association with one another" (Rainey, "Order of Sacrifices," 487).

55. The fact that the listing in Amos—and elsewhere in later texts, such as Josh. 22:23, 29; 1 Kings 8:64 // 2 Chron. 7:7; Jer. 33:18—does not include the two expiation sacrifices could be an indication of their later development. But that argument from silence, particularly for the later texts, is a weak one. We may simply have an ABC didactic listing in which the first three are referred to as a way of speaking about the whole system (see above). Rainey has suggested that in light of the Chronicler's reference to Hezekiah's beginning the cleansing and restoration of the temple with a sin or purification offering, the same may be reflected in the reference to "sacrifices" at the beginning of Solomon's dedication of the temple (1 Kings 8:5). Milgrom challenges this, suggesting that "the purification offering is an offshoot of the *'ōlâ* and, hence, a late development in the history of Israelite sacrifices" though he suggests that some texts "make clear that its origins are preexilic" (e.g., 2 Kings 12:17; Hos. 4:8; Ezek. 40:39; 46:20; 2 Chron. 29:20–24). The "annalistic reference to the purification offering in the Temple during the reign of Joash" (2 Kings 12:17) points Milgrom to a ninth century date (*Leviticus 1–16*, 288–89; cf. 488–89).

56. Rainey, "Order of Sacrifices," 487.

57. See the earlier discussion of the burnt offering as a type.

58. Rainey, "Order of Sacrifices," 498. B. Levine has built upon Rainey's work in the following summary statement about the order of sacrifice:

> Anson Rainey has demonstrated that no sacrifice of an expiatory nature (*'āšām* or *ḥaṭṭā't*) intervened between the *'ōlāh* and the *zebaḥ* in the usual procedures of the cult. The *minḥāh* and libation which often followed the *'ōlāh* in listing the sacrifices were actually accompaniments to the *'ōlāh*, forming with it a unified complex. . . . [T]he type of *ḥaṭṭā't*

which became part of public ritual and which appeared to precede the
'ōlāh and zebaḥ in certain cases, was actually a preliminary rite, which
did not affect the 'ōlāh-zebaḥ or 'ōlāh-šelāmîm dynamic as we have
explained it. The actual approach to the deity began with the 'ōlāh,
whereas the ḥaṭṭā't, in such cases, was a prerequisite to invoking the
deity. This becomes all the more evident when we realize that there
were actually two fairly distinct types of ḥaṭṭā't, one a riddance rite,
patently introductory and preliminary to the celebration, proper, and
the other, a ḥaṭṭā't of the people offered so as to render individual
Israelites and their leaders free of offense, thus ritually fit to engage
in sacrificial activity, public and private. (*In the Presence of the Lord*,
26–27)

59. It is the merit of Nelson's presentation of the sacrificial system in his book
Raising Up a Faithful Priest to have identified in clear fashion not only the clearly
anthropological analyses but other dimensions of the sacrificial system in ancient
Israel.

60. The dating and relationship of the Priestly source and Holiness Code are matters of considerable debate, with dates from the tenth century to the postexilic
period having been proposed and arguments having been made both ways about
the priority of the one over the other. The recent and very important work of Israel
Knohl has opened up the discussion afresh with his detailed arguments for the
chronological priority of the Priestly source (his Priestly Torah = PT) and his analysis of the Holiness Code (his Holiness School = HS) as a later and very powerful
effort "to create a broad, all-inclusive framework of faith and cult, in which the mul-
tifarious values of the religious experience would be combined: it would express
both the reflections of the priests serving in the Sanctuary and the innermost needs
of the people in the fields" (*Sanctuary of Silence*, 198). Knohl makes the following
summary statement about the dating of both sources:

> [T]he Priestly corpus results from a long, multileveled process that
> began with the composition of the various PT strata, continued with the
> various stages in HS's creative activity, and terminated with the final
> editing of the "Priestly source" and the Pentateuch as a whole. Thus,
> the Priestly source—that is, the combined works of PT and HS—is the
> result of literary activity spanning the course of several centuries. (200)

In this context, no explicit presumption is being made about the dating. The con-
cern for proper slaughter of meat and eating the blood with the meat is present in
Deuteronomic and Priestly materials and seems to have been fairly pervasive in
Israelite culture. For a presentation of some of the arguments about the preexilic or
postexilic date of the Priestly source, see Blenkinsopp, "Assessment of the Alleged
Pre-Exilic Date"; and the response by Milgrom, "Antiquity of the Priestly Source."

61. Hallo, "Origins of the Sacrificial Cult." Milgrom has appropriated this data in
his treatment of the theories of sacrifice in ancient Israel. He summarizes Hallo's
Sumerian evidence concisely:

> The Sumerian myth of Lugalbanda relates that its hero, heretofore a
> vegetarian, receives divine approval in a dream to sacrifice whatever

animals he can trap. He invites the four principal deities of the Sumerian pantheon to partake of the ritual meal. "The slaughtering itself is
carried out according to divinely inspired prescriptions. . . , by a
divinely chosen individual, with weapons of rare metals. Presumably,
then we are to understand it as sacred, not profane, slaughter, indeed
as the etiology of the sacrificial cult" (Hallo 1987: 9). (Milgrom, *Leviticus 1–16*, 442)

62. Hallo, "Origins of the Sacrificial Cult," 5. Here he draws specifically on Milgrom's work on the sacrificial cult.

63. Ibid., 7.

64. One notes, however, that the thigh and the breast were traditionally reserved
for the priest and his family or for a person of high status, as is indicated when
Samuel reserved the thigh for Saul on the occasion of Samuel's sacrificial feast at
Ramathaim (1 Sam. 9:24). So there were some ways in which status had its play in
the distribution of the best portions. Note that the presence of a number of bones
belonging to the right foreleg of sheep and goats have been found in a cultic structure from the eleventh century at Tell Qiri (Ben-Tor, "Qiri, Tell," 582).

65. Hallo, "Origins of the Sacrificial Cult," 7, 11. Hallo observes that this was the
ostensible purpose of sacrificial activity but that it was in fact "a thinly disguised
method" for sanctifying meat consumption, the mythic foundation of which is now
recognized in the Sumerian myth of Lugalbanda he discusses in this essay.

66. The story of Bel and the Dragon in Dan. 14:1–22 presents a much later Jewish satirical attack on Mesopotamian practice as a deceit, the disappearance of the
food set before the gods being revealed by Daniel as a ruse by priests, who spir-
ited the food away at night through a hole in the floor and fed their families with
it.

67. Nelson suggests that the notion of sacrifice as food for the deity is also implicit
in the way in which Israelite religion shared with Mesopotamian forms of religion
the sense of the temple as a house for the deity and the priests as the god's courtiers
and ministers who were responsible for serving and providing for the needs of the
deity: food and drink, and incense to provide "a pleasant ambience for the meal"
(*Raising Up a Faithful Priest*, 62).

68. For linguistic and comparative data to support this notion, see Gray, *Sacrifice
in the Old Testament*, 76–81; and Milgrom, *Leviticus 1–16*, 162–63.

69. On the understanding of this text as suggesting a propitiatory sacrifice—not
expiatory, for there is no reference to sin in David's remarks—see Gray, *Sacrifice
in the Old Testament*, 83–84.

70. Gray, *Sacrifice in the Old Testament*, 78; Milgrom, *Leviticus 1–16*, 163. As Gray
points out also, the term "odor pleasing to the Lord" does not seem to have a particular sense of propitiation or expiation in the Priestly Code because it is used primarily with regard to burnt offerings, offerings of well-being, grain offerings, etc.,
and only once in reference to the *ḥaṭṭā't* or purification offering where one might
expect a term that had notions of expiation or purification attached to it. Even that
one usage, Lev. 4:31, Gray regards as intrusive (78–80).

71. The anthropologist Martin Sahlins puts it as follows: "Food dealings are a del-
icate barometer, a ritual statement as it were, of social relations, and food is thus

employed instrumentally as a starting, a sustaining, or a destroying mechanism of sociability." The quotation is from his *Stone Age Economics*, as cited by Halvor Moxnes in his essay, "Meals and the New Community in Luke," 158. The point about food dealings is not confined to the ritual of sacrifice, but it is clearly a part of what happened in that ritual.

72. See Deut. 12:15–19, 26–27; 14:22–29; 15:19–23; 16:1–17.

73. Nelson, *Raising Up a Faithful Priest*, 67–68.

74. Moxnes, "Meals and the New Community in Luke," 161–62.

75. Erhard Gerstenberger has seen in the ritual that accompanied the prayers for help or laments a socioreligious activity whose final goal was the rehabilitation of the individual as a member of his or her small group or primary social sphere, the clan or family, and thus the restoration of communal harmony. See Gerstenberger, *Bittende Mensch,* and the summary presentation in Miller, *Interpreting the Psalms*, 6–7.

76. The notion of sacrifice as gift to the deity is longstanding and not confined to Israelite sacrifice. In modern biblical studies, the most extensive and cogent case has been made by Gray in his *Sacrifice in the Old Testament*, especially pages 1–54. The two contemporary scholars who have given the most continuing attention to sacrifice, B. Levine and Milgrom, have agreed with the claim that sacrifice is best (but not only) conceived of as gift or tribute to the deity. Thus, Levine sees the "organizing principle" as the proposition "that the God of Israel desired the sacrifices of his people as a form of tribute to him as their sovereign" ("Prolegomena," in Gray, *Sacrifice in the Old Testament*, xxxii) and Milgrom writes that the purpose of sacrifice as "a gift to the deity to induce his aid, seems to be the only one that manifests validity in all sacrificial systems" (*Leviticus 1–16*). Note his persuasive translation of the term *'išševh* (e.g., Lev. 1:9, 13, 17; 2:3) as "food gift" rather than the more customary "offering by fire" (161–62).

77. See Ex. 28:38; Deut. 16:17; Ezek. 20:26, 31, 39.

78. See 2 Sam. 8:2, 6; 1 Kings 5:1; 2 Kings 17:3–4 // 1 Chron. 18:2, 6; 2 Chron. 17:5, 11; 26:8; Hos. 10:6; cf. Judg. 3:15. The term can also mean simply "present" or "gift," usually in acknowledgment of the authority or rule of the one to whom the gifts are presented or in order to seek a favor (Gen. 32:14; 33:10; 43:11; Judg. 16:18; 1 Sam. 10:27; 1 Kings 10:25 // 2 Chron. 9:24; 2 Kings 8:8–9; 20:12 // Isa. 39:1; 2 Chron. 32:23; and Ps. 45:13[12]).

79. See "the LORD's offering (*qorbān*)" in Num. 9:7, 13; 31:50.

80. See Milgrom with reference to the verb *hiqrîb* and drawing upon the Hebrew University dissertation of Menahem Paran, "Literary Features of the Priestly Code: Stylistic Patterns, Idioms and Structures" (Hebrew) (Milgrom, *Leviticus 1–16*, 145). B. Levine makes a similar claim:

> Like many names given to sacrifices, the term *minhāh* was appropriated by priestly writers from the administrative vocabulary because it effectively expressed the subservient relationship of the worshiper toward God. At the same time, it conveyed the duty of the worshiper to present gifts to God, often in the form of sacrifices. (*Leviticus*, 9)

81. Milgrom, who sees the character of sacrifice as gift as prominent, has pointed out that the *hattā't*, or purification sacrifice, was never called an *'išševh*, which is also

a term for "gift" offering, because the *ḥaṭṭā't*, as a sacrifice to purge the sanctuary "of the pollution caused by the accumulation of sin . . . can hardly be called a gift" (*Leviticus 1–16*, 162).

82. Taking a cue from the prophetic and psalmic critique of sacrifice, as well as many other texts, Sigrid Brandt has suggested that sacrifice and the cult more generally had as its basic function a response to God's participation in human life and that the memory of God's name and of the gifts, the presence, and the salvation acts effected by that name and the glorifying of that name were what sacrifice sought to effect or to maintain. Her identification of the cultic concern for the nurture of the memory of God's name and all that goes with that is a further contribution to thinking about the meaning and purpose of sacrifice. See Brandt, "Opfer als Gedächtnis." I am indebted to Dr. Brandt for making her *Habilitationsschrift* available to me.

Chapter 4. Holiness and Purity

1. The text, of course, does not tell why the Lord was angry, so any proposal about that, including the one above, is speculative.

2. Cf. Miller and Roberts, *Hand of the Lord*, 58–59.

3. See van der Leeuw, *Religion in Essence and Manifestation*, 1:43–44. Cf. B. Levine, "Language of Holiness."

4. Milgrom, *Leviticus 1–16*, 733.

5. Milgrom sees the weeklong application of the blood of the purification offering on the altar in Leviticus 4 as pointing to the original purpose of the rite. It provided for "repeated coatings of prophylactic blood to protect it against ritual and moral pollutants (originally demonic)" (*Leviticus 1–16*, 279). Cf. the apotropaic blood ritual at the slaughter of the paschal lamb in Ex. 12:21–27.

6. It is worth noting in this regard that the parallelism of "blood" (*dām*) and "life" (*nepeš*) is found not only in Hebrew poetic texts (e.g., Ps. 94:21; cf. Pss. 72:14 and 116:15, where "blood" and "death" occur in the same contexts) but also in Ugaritic and Akkadian texts (Avishur, *Stylistic Studies of Word-Pairs*, 559, 577).

7. See, e.g., Isa. 1:4; 5:16, 19, 24; 10:17, 20; 12:6; 17:7; 29:19, 23; 43:3, 14, 15; 49:7; 60:9; Jer. 50:29; 51:5; Hos. 11:9, 12; Hab. 1:12; cf. Isa. 6:1–6; 8:13.

8. See, e.g., Ezek. 20:39; 36:21; Amos 2:7.

9. Reading with Septuagint and Samaritan versions.

10. See Ezek. 20:41; 28:25; 36:23; 38:16; 39:27.

11. See Num. 20:12; 27:14; Deut. 32:51.

12. Two other priestly responsibilities are included in this list of priestly duties: deciding or judging in difficult cases (see Deut. 17:8–13) and keeping all the laws and statutes regarding the appointed festivals (Ezek. 44:24). One notes that the definition of priestly responsibility as teaching (*yārâ*) the distinction between sacred and common, holy and profane, is the positive counterpart of the negative indictment of the priests for having done violence to "my teaching" (*tôrātî*) when they did not distinguish between the holy and the profane (Ezek. 22:26).

13. In Ugaritic mythology, the gods are called *bn qdš*, "holy ones," and El has an epithet with the word *qdš* in it (*ltpn wqdš*). Baal's voice is called *qdš*. For references, see Müller, "קדשׁ *qdš* holy," 1104–5.

In Mesopotamia, Sumerian gods or goddesses were sometimes called holy, for example, Inanna and An, as were certain body parts of various deities. Purity seems to have been a significant dimension of divine character in Akkadian texts but also a quality that could be lost with consequent negative effects upon performance of divine duties and acts. On the Mesopotamian evidence, see Wilson, *"Holiness" and "Purity" in Mesopotamia*, 30–31, 72–76.

14. See the discussion above on holiness and power.

15. For a broader phenomenological analysis of the realm of the sacred, see van der Leeuw, *Religion in Essence and Manifestation*. For illustration within a specific religion in the Israelite milieu, see Wilson, *"Holiness" and "Purity"* in Mesopotamia, 5–34, 68–78.

16. For a fairly extensive overview of all the kinds of things that were in some fashion understood as holy or sacred, see Wright, "Holiness (OT)," 239–41.

17. See Douglas, *Purity and Danger*; idem, *Implicit Meanings*. Cf. Miller, *Deuteronomy*, 162–63.

18. Jenson, *Graded Holiness*, 85–87, 124–28.

19. Ibid., 86–87.

20. "[T]he anointment 'sanctifies' the high priest by removing him from the realm of the profane and empowering him to operate in the realm of the sacred, namely, to handle the sancta" (Milgrom, *Leviticus 1–16*, 554).

21. Milgrom, *Leviticus 1–16*, 538.

22. Ibid., 566–68.

23. For this tripartite analysis of the ritual of ordination and its indebtedness to Edward Leach, see Wright, "Holiness (OT)," 247. He notes a similar ritual in the Nazirite dedication but one that has some notable differences also, especially the lack of a connection to the larger social aggregate.

24. See the expression *nĕzîr 'ĕlōhîm,* "a nazirite to God" in Judg. 13:5, 7.

25. See Num. 6:1–21; Judg. 13:2–14; 16:4–31; 1 Sam. 1:11; Jeremiah 35; Amos 2:12.

26. Here, as in many other places, the highly male-oriented and dominated character of Israelite religion is exemplified not only in the assignment of the priestly role exclusively to the male line but in the fact that the Levitical law singles out the daughter of the priest as meriting death if she profanes her father by engaging in prostitution (Lev. 21:9).

27. It is important to recognize that there were variations in the ways that these different characteristics or modes of behavior functioned with different types of holy persons. For example, the handling of hair, baldness, locks, and beards varied among different categories of consecrated persons or groups. The Nazirite was the only one forbidden to cut hair altogether, and the abstention from beer and wine that was an obligation for the extent of the time of the Nazirite vow (Num. 6:4) was applicable to the priest only when in the sanctuary (Lev. 10:8–9; Ezek. 44:21).

28. See chapter 2 and Albertz, *History of Israelite Religion*, 2:408–10 for discussion of the possible date and origins of the Sabbath.

29. Cf. Jenson, *Graded Holiness*, 196–97.

30. Cf. Isa. 30:29 ("holy festival"); Joel 1:14; 2:15 ("sanctify a fast").

31. Jenson, *Graded Holiness*, 188. On the *ḥaṭṭā't* sacrifice, see chapter 3.

32. Ibid., 125, 138.

33. Houston has described the priestly concern for order as being expressed in binary oppositions and concentric grades (*Purity and Monotheism*, 221–22, 237).

34. Milgrom, *Leviticus 1–16*, 722. Both Milgrom (722–24) and Jenson (*Graded Holiness*, 146) see a correlation between the three divisions of the human world and the three classes of the animal world (sacrificial, clean, and unclean).

35. See B. Levine, *Numbers 1–20*, 405–32; and Milgrom, *Numbers*, 129–57, 414–23.

36. Cf. Ezek. 44:9–14 and the distinction between the "Levites" (Ezek. 44:10) and the "Levitical priests" (Ezek. 43:19; 44:15), which probably reflects different stages of the composition, Ezek. 44:9–14 being a later reflection of the Priestly tradition in Numbers 16 and the move to subordinate the Levites to temple service rather than service in the inner sanctuary.

37. "In the morning the LORD will make known who is his, and who is holy, and who will be allowed to approach him; *the one* whom he will choose he will allow to approach him. . . . [T]he man whom the LORD chooses shall be the holy one" (Num. 16:5, 7b). The forms in these verses are all singular.

38. For details and texts, see Wright, "Holiness (OT)," 238, 247; and Jenson, *Graded Holiness*, 119–23.

39. Jenson, *Graded Holiness*, 124–28.

40. Ibid., 128–30.

41. See Polk, "Levites in the Davidic-Solomonic Empire."

42. Jenson, *Graded Holiness*, 132–33.

43. The chart is from Jenson, *Graded Holiness*, 90.

44. Wright, "Holiness (OT)," 248. His discussion draws explicitly upon the theoretical work of Jonathan Z. Smith in his book *To Take Place*. Cf. Tuell, *Law of the Temple*, 176–77.

45. Wright, "Holiness (OT)," 248.

46. Ibid. On the way in which this was the case for women, see Bird, "Place of Women in the Israelite Cultus," 403.

47. Wright, "Spectrum of Priestly Impurity," 158. Milgrom has made a similar point in observing that with regard to the four possible states in which a thing or person could exist—holy, common, pure, and impure—one combination of these, holy and impure, was not allowed within the Priestly system, and this precisely because what is impure is a threat to the holy. See Milgrom, *Leviticus 1–16*, 731–32.

48. See, e.g., Frymer-Kensky, "Pollution, Purification, and Purgation in Biblical Israel"; Wright, "Spectrum of Priestly Impurity" and idem, "Unclean and Clean (OT)."

There is clear evidence of a sense of impurity attributed to some of the types of tolerated impurities prior to the Priestly legislation and its schematization and regulation of them. These would include the skin disease that is often, but not correctly, regarded as leprosy (e.g., 2 Sam. 3:29; 2 Kings 7:3–10; 15:5 = 2 Chron. 26:16–21), menstruation (e.g., Isa. 30:22; Ezek. 7:19–20; 36:17), and abnormal sex discharges (e.g., 2 Sam. 3:29). Cf. Wright, "Spectrum of Priestly Impurity," 176 n. 2.

49. Frymer-Kensky, "Pollution, Purification, and Purgation in Biblical Israel," 399–404; Wright, "Unclean and Clean (OT)," 729–35; Jenson, *Graded Holiness*, 225–26. The term "tolerated" is drawn from Wright's analysis in "Spectrum of Priestly Impurity." The choice of "tolerated" over "permitted" is to convey the notion

that any impurity, while allowed, was not necessarily encouraged and was to be generated as infrequently as possible because any impurity threatened the holy and everything that pertained to it. See Wright, "Unclean and Clean (OT)." In that same essay, Wright has sorted the tolerated impurities (major and minor) into four classes: (1) death related impurities (human corpses and animal carcasses), (2) sexual impurities (bodily discharges such as semen and menstrual blood), (3) disease related impurities (such as the ṣāraʿat or skin disease), and (4) cultic impurities (such as the ḥaṭṭāʾt carcass, blood, and the scapegoat [Lev. 16:26–28]).

50. Contrast Milgrom, *Leviticus 1–16*, 667; and Gerstenberger, *Leviticus*, 142.

51. See chapter 3. Wright has laid out the gradation or "spectrum" of impurities relative to the requirement of sacrifice for restoration to a pure state, moving from no sacrifice required to individual sacrifices required to communal sacrifices required to the Day of Atonement sacrifices required. This gradation of sacrifice he correlates with the locus of pollution (person, outer altar and person, etc.) and with a gradation in the restriction or exclusion of the impurity (from the sacred, from sacred and profane, permanent exclusion or *kārēt*, on which see below). See Wright, "Spectrum of Priestly Impurity," 164–65.

52. Wright's terminology of "prohibited" focuses attention on the distinction between the permissible and the impermissible. Frymer-Kensky's terminology of "danger beliefs" focuses on the distinction between contagion and danger. Both distinctions are significant in understanding the category of purity as a feature of Israelite religion. There are some differences in their categorization in that Frymer-Kensky sees all "danger beliefs" as guilt bearing because they are prohibitions—in distinction from the major and minor pollutions that are tolerated—and incapable of amelioration, while Wright distinguishes between unintentional prohibited pollutions, which are guilt bearing but can be ameliorated, and intentional prohibited pollutions, which are guilt bearing but cannot be ameliorated.

53. Wright, "Spectrum of Priestly Impurity," 163.

54. Frymer-Kensky, "Pollution, Purification, and Purgation in Biblical Israel," 404–5.

55. As Milgrom puts it, "[B]etween them God and man will terminate the criminal: man will put him to death and God will extirpate his line and/or deny him life in the hereafter" (*Leviticus 1–16*, 460). Frymer-Kensky notes that the violation was expected to result in direct intervention of God without social action. "This belief in automatic retribution protects the realm of the sacred by deterring acts which would encroach upon it" ("Pollution, Purification, and Purgation in Biblical Israel" 405).

56. For a complete listing of all the instances where the Priestly legislation calls for the penalty of *kārēt*, see Milgrom, *Leviticus 1–16*, 458.

57. Note the comment of Milgrom: "[T]he holiness of God is associated with his moral attributes (cf. Exod 34:6–7). It therefore follows that the commandments, Israel's ladder to holiness, must contain moral rungs. It is then no wonder that the quintessential program for achieving holiness, Leviticus chapter 19, is a combination of moral as well as ritual injunctions. Conversely, impurity, the opposing doctrine to holiness, cannot be expected to consist solely of physical characteristics. It must *ipso facto* impinge on the moral realm" ("Rationale for Cultic Law," 106).

58. Frymer-Kensky, "Pollution, Purification, and Purgation in Biblical Israel," 407.

59. Douglas, *Purity and Danger*; cf. Sawyer, ed., *Reading Leviticus*. For a helpful survey of Douglas's work and some of its respondents, see Budd, "Holiness and Cult," 282–89. An extensive description and critique of the explanations of Douglas and others is offered by Walter Houston in his monograph, *Purity and Monotheism*, chapter 3. The reader is referred to that excellent discussion for the history and categorization of the range of explanatory possibilities and the difficulties with each of the proposals.

60. See, e.g., Ex. 22:30(31); 23:19; 34:26.

61. There is a distinction between Deuteronomy 14 and Leviticus 11 with regard to the winged insects, the former excluding all of them and the latter allowing for the eating of those that "walk upon all fours" and have leg joints or knees (Lev. 11:20–21; Deut. 14:19). For the rationale for viewing the exceptions of Leviticus as prior to and lying behind the more exclusive Deuteronomic text, see Milgrom, *Leviticus 1–16*, 665, 702.

62. Milgrom, "Rationale for Cultic Law," 105.

63. Wright, "Observations on the Ethical Foundations," 195. In similar fashion but more nuanced, Houston suggests that two different cultural currents merged in the Levitical and Deuteronomic texts having to do with clean and unclean animals: "(1) a formal, organizing thrust, whether expressed in classification and systematization and the development of the criteria, or in theology and exhortation, and (2) common dietary customs that at several points appear to be independent of the formal aspect" (*Purity and Monotheism*, 66; cf. 234ff.).

64. Ibid., 196.

65. For the following analysis, I am indebted to the careful work of Bryan Bibb in his unpublished thesis, "Religious Language and Social Norms," as well as to the more extended studies of Milgrom, *Leviticus 1–16* and "Changing Concept of Holiness"; and Knohl, *Sanctuary of Silence*. Cf. Wright, "Holiness in Leviticus and Beyond."

66. For an extended discussion of the incorporation of the moral and the social into the sphere of the sacred in the Holiness Code in distinction from the Priestly source, see Knohl, *Sanctuary of Silence*, 175–86. Milgrom has succinctly summarized the way in which the Holiness Code (H) is different from the Priestly source's (P) understanding of holiness:

> H introduces three radical changes regarding P's notion of holiness. First, it breaks down the barrier between the priesthood and the laity. The attribute of holy is accessible to all Israel. Secondly, holiness is not just a matter of adhering to a regimen of prohibitive commandments, taboos; it embraces positive, performative commandments that are ethical in nature. Thirdly, Israel as a whole, priests included, enhances or diminishes its holiness in proportion to its observance of all of God's commandments. ("Changing Concept of Holiness," 67)

67. See, e.g., Milgrom, *Leviticus 1–16*, 48.

68. Eilberg-Schwartz has used these categories to describe differences between priestly communities in Judaism and the early Christian communities with regard to status in the community and purity. See *Savage in Judaism*, 195–216. Eilberg-

Schwartz includes references to the earlier work of Ralph Linton, Talcott Parsons, and Edward Shils in developing these categories.

69. Milgrom, *Leviticus 1–16*, 48.

70. Ibid., 48–49.

71. Houston, *Purity and Monotheism*, 224–25. The second perspective set forth by Houston seems to refer to the Deuteronomists, but it is applicable also to the Holiness Code, which has affinities with Deuteronomy.

72. Cf. chapter 1.

73. Weinfeld, *Deuteronomy and the Deuteronomic School*, 191–243.

74. For more extended discussion, see Miller, *Deuteronomy*, 54–57.

75. Lohfink, "Opfer und Säkularisierung im Deuteronomium." An earlier criticism of the "secularizing" thesis was offered by Milgrom, "The Alleged 'Demythologization and Secularization' in Deuteronomy." Both Milgrom and Lohfink have noted how much of Weinfeld's argument is an argument from silence, a point noted above with regard to the demythologizing argument about the ark.

76. Lohfink, "Opfer und Säkularisierung im Deuteronomium," 35–36. Lohfink proposes that the Deuteronomic ritual of holiness is not found in sacrifice and purification or sanctification rites but in the pilgrimage festivals to the central sanctuary, "before the LORD your God," where the unity of Israel is symbolically realized—its oneness as a people holy to the Lord and chosen out of all the other nations as the Lord's special possession.

77. While some would make a fairly sharp distinction between Deuteronomy's (D) assertion of Israel's holiness and the Holiness Code's (H) view of the holiness of the people not as a given but as conditional upon obedience, Knohl is surely correct in seeing more similarity than difference at this point. In one case (D), holiness is the reason for the regulations, while in the other (H), the regulations are the means to holiness (*Sanctuary of Silence*, 183 n. 43).

78. Knohl gives examples of specific regulations that show the difference between H and D and those that show how H expressed the wider view of holiness in the whole community. With regard to the former, he suggests that the tradition of the Holiness Code avoided such formulations as "you are a people holy to the LORD your God" (e.g., Deut. 7:6) in order to preserve the difference between the holiness of the priests and the holiness of all Israelites. Deuteronomy does not mention holiness in regard to priests and Levites, while H does assume the special holiness of the priests. Knohl suggests that this explains the difference between D and H with respect to the prohibition against eating animal carcasses. In D it applies to all Israelites because of their holiness (Deut. 14:21). The same is true of the Book of the Covenant (Ex. 22:30[31]). In H, however, this prohibition applies only to the priests, who are especially holy (compare Lev. 22:8–9 with 17:15).

Knohl summarizes the model of holiness in H as follows:

> All Israel is separated from the nations, and consecrated by the sanctity of the commandments, which include both the ceremonial and the cultic realms (Lev 11:44–45; 19:2; 20:7–8, 24–26; Num 15:40). The Levites are separated from the Israelites and dedicated to the service of the tabernacle, in order to prevent the Israelites from entering the worship

and to atone for them (Num 8:14–19; 16:9–10; 18:2–4, 6). The priests, Aaron and his sons, were elected to serve before the Lord—to guard מִשְׁמֶרֶת הַקֹּדֶשׁ, the holy enclosure—and the altar and to offer the bread of God. This election endows them with the highest grade of holiness, that emanating from the cult, in which Israelites and Levites may not participate (Exod 29:44; Lev 21:6, 8; Num 16:5–11; 17:20–23; 18:1, 5, 7). (*Sanctuary of Silence*, 192; see 183 n. 43 and 189–92)

Recognizing as others have before him that Numbers 15 has affinities with the Holiness Code, Knohl attributes that chapter to the Holiness School and sees in the law of fringes in Num. 15:37–41 an example of the way in which a specific regulation serves the purpose of extending the domain of holiness beyond the confines of the sanctuary and the priesthood. In those verses, the main purpose of the fringes is "to remind the people of all God's commandments and the requirement that they be observed." The repeated reference to remembering *all* of the commandments is because for the Holiness School all commandments are of equal status. In verse 40 the point is made that Israel is consecrated to God through obedience to the commandments (cf. Num. 16:3). See Knohl, *Sanctuary of Silence*, 53, 90, 186.

79. Milgrom has argued that both the Holiness Code and Deuteronomy differed sharply from the earlier JE tradition: "The epic tradition had also proposed that Israel could become a holy people, but only if it would accept the covenantal obligations of the Decalogue (Exod 19:6), the two distinctive elements of which are the rejection of idolatry and the observance of the Sabbath (Exod 20:3–11). This tradition also added abstention from *ṭĕrēpâ* 'torn flesh [by prey]' as a holiness requirement (Exod 22:31; Heb. v. 30). These three injunctions, abstention from idolatry, sabbath labor and torn flesh, are therefore JE's prescription for holiness" ("Changing Concept of Holiness," 68). The texts cited, however, suggest continuity of understanding more than they do difference. Exodus 19:6 has its closest analogues in the three texts from Deuteronomy, already cited, that have to do with Israel as a treasured possession and a holy people (Deut. 7:6; 14:2, 21; 26:18–19). Furthermore, there is no reason to single out idolatry and Sabbath from the rest of the commandments, the dating of which, in their present form at least, is rather late. In that respect, Exodus 19–24 is similar to the Holiness Code and Deuteronomy. Finally, the regulation about torn flesh in Ex. 22:30(31) is at least analogous to Deuteronomy's regulation about not eating the carcass of an animal that dies of itself, which is one of the specific Deuteronomic statutes tied to the identification of the people as holy (Deut. 14:21). Both statutes have to do with eating the carcass of an animal. In various ways, therefore, the presumedly earlier material of Exodus 19–24—and the literary analysis and dating of this pericope is much debated—is congruent also with the Deuteronomic and Holiness Codes—and also prophetic—understanding of Israel's holiness.

80. Milgrom regards the affinities of Lev. 11:43–45, which betray the same understanding of holiness as discussed above, with the Holiness Code as one of the strong arguments for seeing the Priestly material as prior to the Holiness Code and subsequently redacted or edited in part by the Holiness Code (*Leviticus 1–16*, 695–96). In any event, these verses serve to bring the Priestly presentation of holiness

into some conformity, albeit a somewhat contradictory one, with the other traditions that equate the sphere of holiness with the whole people.

81. Eilberg-Schwarz, *Savage in Judaism*, 199–216.

Chapter 5. Leadership and Participation in Israelite Religion

1. While Zadok and Abiathar are obvious examples in the time of the United Monarchy, the priest Amaziah, who is spoken about only briefly in Amos 7, was clearly chief priest at Bethel, the national shrine of the Northern Kingdom.

2. Milgrom, *Leviticus 1–16*, 554. Some would see the office of the high priest and the anointing of priests—high priest and the priestly family—as a late development, the anointing of the priest coming from the prior anointing of kings (see Noth, "Office and Vocation in the Old Testament," 237–38). The question of when the high priest became a regularized priestly office is still much debated, some continuing to argue for it as a postexilic development (see Nelson, *Raising Up a Faithful Priest*, 13), while others seeing the high priestly office as a relatively early preexilic phenomenon (e.g., Milgrom, *Leviticus 1–16*, 554). It is less likely that the priest's anointing was derivative from the anointing of kings or that the high priest took over royal functions (Nelson). The priestly activities of the kings that are attested were most often associated with the establishment of cultic centers, though that is not entirely the case (see below).

On the basis of comparative materials and analysis of the biblical texts, Daniel Fleming has suggested that the very different procedures for anointing the high priest and for anointing the other priests reflect "two separate priestly heritages that are subsumed into one tale of origins. . . . Where the anointing of Aaron suggests a natural origin in the Jerusalem Temple heritage of the Priestly Torah, the anointing of his sons may have roots in a more widespread practice from the old towns, villages, and shrines of the countryside." This last can only be a suggestion but would be consistent with the typology of religions suggested in chapter 2 of this volume. See Fleming, "Biblical Tradition of Anointing Priests." On the differences between the anointing of Aaron or the high priest and the anointing of the other priests, see Fleming and also Milgrom, *Leviticus 1–16*, 554–55.

3. See, for example, the Levite whom Micah recruits as priest for his "house," providing him a living to do so (Judg. 17:7–13).

4. For a brief indication of how these responsibilities may have changed in the course of the history of the priesthood, see Nelson, *Raising Up a Faithful Priest*, 11–14.

5. See Miller, *They Cried to the Lord*, 294–99.

6. On the Urim and Thummim, see Kitz, "Plural Form of *'ûrîm* and *tummîm*," and the literature cited there, as well as van Dam, *Urim and Thummim*. Van Dam reads with the MT instead of the LXX on the important text in 1 Sam. 14:41 (see below) and does not see the Urim and Thummim as functioning as a form of lot oracle. For discussion of some of the older literature, see Cryer, *Divination in Ancient Israel*. Cryer is skeptical about the existence of priestly divination and oracle giving in ancient Israel. He is correct in noting that this is an area that shows the absence of a sharp line between priestly and prophetic responsibilities. Prophets also divined and gave oracles. In other respects, however, one may note different roles for these two religious specialists without claiming the kind of sharp,

even contradictory distinctions that are often made between priest and prophet. In the oracles of a prophet like Jeremiah, the prophets are condemned with as much vigor as the priests, but one notes a significant difference in that the error of the prophets has most to do with oracles that are not true while the sin of the priests is in their failure to instruct the people in the torah.

7. For the most recent discussion of the ephod and various interpretations of its character and function, see van Dam, *Urim and Thummim*, 140–53, and Meyers, "Ephod."

8. Cf. Huffmon, "Priestly Divination in Israel"; and Long, "Effect of Divination on Israelite Literature." Long makes a distinction between priestly and prophetic forms of divination. One can clearly argue both distinction and similarity, depending upon where one places the weight.

9. The full text of this passage is gotten at only through careful examination of the LXX along with the MT. See McCarter, *1 Samuel,* 241–50.

10. Huffmon, "Priestly Divination in Israel," 355–56.

11. Ibid., 355.

12. Park, "Divination and Its Social Contexts," 240.

13. Huffmon, "Priestly Divination in Israel," 357.

14. Park, "Divination and Its Social Contexts, 241.

15. Huffmon, "Priestly Divination in Israel," 358.

16. The involvement of the priests in the divine response is not explicit in this text. It is inferred from their role as the lamenters for the people (v. 17).

17. The basic study of the priestly oracle of salvation remains that of Begrich, "Priesterliche Heilsorakel"; cf. Raitt, *Theology of Exile,* 152–54. For an extended discussion of the oracle of salvation citing most of the possible examples together with analogues from the ancient Near East, see Miller, *They Cried to the Lord*, chapter 4.

18. See Long, "Effect of Divination on Israelite Literature," 96–97.

19. See, for example, Cody, *History of Old Testament Priesthood*, 116.

20. In 2 Kings 17:27–28, the king of Assyria sends back to the province of Samaria one of the exiled northern priests to teach "the law of the god of the land" to the deportees who had been brought into the province from other countries. This is then described in verse 28 as teaching them "how they should fear/worship the LORD."

21. On the priestly torah, see Begrich, "Priesterliche Tora"; and Gunnar Östborn, *Tōrā in the Old Testament,* chapter 4.

22. "Making distinctions and drawing boundaries was the essence of torah teaching. This is clearest in regard to what meat was clean food and what was unclean (Lev 11:47; 20:25). Such distinctions were made in order to influence the behavior of the people. The goal was to reduce the incidence of impurity in the community and to keep holy what was supposed to be holy. The torah of the priests was intended for the benefit of the entire community:

> You shall separate the children of Israel from their uncleanness so that they might not die through their uncleanness by polluting my sanctuary which is in their midst. (Lev 15:31) (Nelson, *Raising Up a Faithful Priest,* 43)

Nelson's study is the best and most accessible comprehensive treatment of Israelite priesthood in recent times. Cf. Blenkinsopp, *Sage, Priest, Prophet*, chapter 2; and Grabbe, *Priests, Prophets, Diviners, Sages*, chapter 3.

23. It is possible that Hosea's accusation against the priests for "feeding on the sin of my people" (Hos. 4:8) refers to the priests profiting from sacrificial practices that were inappropriate in the worship of Yahweh of Israel.

24. Hutton, *Charisma and Authority in Israelite Society*, 147. There were numerous other sources of priestly revenue, which Hutton lists. These included regular tithes of produce and livestock, including those associated with the major festivals (Ex. 23:19; 34:19–23, 26; Num. 18:21–32; Deut. 14:28–29; 16:10–17), temple revenue generated by periodic census taxes (Ex. 30:11–16), private gifts, vows, dedications, and redemptions (Ex. 28:38; Lev. 27:1–34; Deut. 23:21), booty secured through warfare (Num. 31:28–30, 54), and fines and forfeitures (Lev. 5:16; Num. 5:8; Deut. 22:9). "The priesthood, therefore, enjoyed marked stability based on its economic resources, material holdings, and favors granted it through royal patronage" (149).

25. The Priestly text assumes already the secondary status of the Levites in this instance, as already indicated in Numbers 3 and 8, but the story of Korah's rebellion against the priestly leadership of Moses and Aaron serves to undergird and reinforce the distinction. The rebellion is understood explicitly as an effort to "seek the priesthood as well" (Num. 16:10).

26. See Nelson, *Raising Up a Faithful Priest*, 4.

27. Stager, "Archaeology of the Family in Ancient Israel," 27–28; cf. Albright, *Archaeology and the Religion of Israel*, 109.

28. Stager, "Archaeology of the Family in Ancient Israel." Cf. Polk, "Levites in the Davidic-Solomonic Empire," 4.

29. Cross, *Canaanite Myth and Hebrew Epic*, 195–215.

30. White, "Elohistic Depiction of Aaron," 150–51.

31. Tuell, *Law of the Temple*, 124–32. Cf. Nelson, *Raising Up a Faithful Priest*, 8–10, for a different but related suggestion about the complexity of the Levite-priest relation in the preexilic period.

32. See Deut. 10:6; 17:12; 26:3; 2 Kings 11:9–10, 15; 16:10–11, 15; 22:10, 12, 14; 25:18. These references do not use the later Priestly designation "high priest" (*hakkōhēn haggādôl*).

33. See 2 Kings 19:2.

34. See 2 Kings 12:10; 22:4; 23:4; and 25:18. As Tuell notes, they are to guard the entrance into the inner court where the altar is, and they are to collect the contributions of the people for the upkeep of the temple.

35. See 2 Kings 23:4; 25:18.

36. See Deut. 10:8; 31:9, 25; 1 Sam. 6:15 (a textually debatable occurrence); 2 Sam. 15:20; and 1 Kings 8:4. See Tuell's discussion of these texts on the way in which the carrying of the ark is a priestly service whether done by "Levites" or "priests" (*Law of the Temple*, 127–29).

37. See Deut. 21:1–9.

38. See Deut. 21:5.

39. See Deut. 24:8. The quotation is from Tuell, *Law of the Temple*, 131.

40. For a proposal about the increasing conflict between the Zadokite priesthood and the Levites around different programs or views of the future of a restored Israel, see Hanson, *Dawn of Apocalyptic*.

41. Tuell, *Law of the Temple*, 133–41.

42. For a more extended discussion of these various functions and the texts alluding to them, see Blenkinsopp, *Sage, Priest, Prophet*, 94–98. The increasing complexity and hierarchization of the priestly responsibilities in the second temple period is well attested in Chronicles, Ezra, and Nehemiah. Especially to be noted is the class of *nětînîm* or "temple servants," who seem to have served the Levites (Ezra 8:20). Nehemiah 10:29(28) identifies five classes of temple officials among the postexilic community: priests, Levites, gatekeepers, singers, and temple servants. Whether or not these were distinguishable from one another is not altogether clear inasmuch as Levites had responsibilities for gatekeeping and music. But the list of returned exiles in Ezra 2 identifies three primary groups: priests, Levites, and temple servants. Blenkinsopp concludes:

> In sum, the Second Temple was the focus of a more or less rigidly organized and self-enclosed hierarchical community, exclusively male, constituting perhaps as much as 10 percent of the population of the province. This was the immediate social context for the role playing of priest and Levite, though the impact on the province and beyond was profound and long-lasting. (98)

43. On the possible Canaanite background of the association of prophecy with music, see Albright, *Yahweh and the Gods of Canaan*, 187–89. On the way in which music was and is used to alter states of consciousness or achieve mental dissociation, see the brief discussion in Blenkinsopp, *Sage, Priest, Prophet*, 131, and the references there.

44. In all of these instances, the text describes the divinatory activity of the prophet by the term *qāsam/qesem*. Such activity is a part of the list of proscribed magical activities in Deut. 18:10. The Micah text does not seem to regard the activity of divining by the prophet as itself unacceptable but the avaricious misuse of it. This is a further indication that some of the proscription of divination in the Deuteronomic definition of orthodoxy may have been more a protection of access to divine revelation than objection to a type of religious practice (see chapter 2).

45. The word "war" in the Micah text may be simply a poetic way of expressing a negative alternative to *šālôm*, but the latter was probably a specific response to inquiry of the prophet as well as to the priest. Cf. 1 Sam. 1:17.

46. It is not clear that all of these oracles can be specifically connected to the prophets Isaiah, Jeremiah, and the prophet in exilic Babylon, but they demonstrate prophetic use of priestly forms in any event.

47. As a positive word about the future, the oracle of salvation could take various forms, for example, the conveyance formula in response to an inquiry about whether to go into battle or what will be the fate of king or people against an enemy, commonly in the form, "I will give the enemy into your hand" (e.g., 1 Kings 20:13, 28; 22:6, 12, 15; 2 Kings 3:18); or the assurance of peace (*šālôm*) as uttered by the priest Eli to Hannah (1 Sam. 1:17) and by the prophets of Jeremiah's time (Jer. 6:14; 8:11; 14:13; 23:17; 28:9; cf. 8:15; 14:19; 16:5; and Ps. 85:9[8]); or the basic assurance, "do not be afraid," together with divine first-person reasons for the assurance as in 2 Kings 19:4; Jer. 42:11–12, the oracles of Deutero-Isaiah (e.g., Isa.

41:8–13, 14–16), and often elsewhere; or an oracle against one of the nations, as evidenced often in the writing prophets, such as Isaiah 13–23; Jeremiah 46–51; Ezekiel 25–32; Amos 1:3–2:5; Obad. 1–14; and Nahum 1–3. For more extended discussion of the oracle of salvation in its various forms, see Westermann, *Prophetic Oracles of Salvation*; and Miller, *They Cried to the Lord*, chapter 4. The latter includes a number of oracles of salvation from extrabiblical sources.

48. For a review of the literature dealing with this question in the past century, see Wilson, *Prophecy and Society in Ancient Israel*, 8–10; Blenkinsopp, *History of Prophecy in Israel*, 16–26; and Tucker, "Prophecy and the Prophetic Literature," 348–50.

49. Zechariah 7:3 has been seen as attesting also to the combination of priests and prophets in the temple, but the evidence here is ambiguous at best and may mean to distinguish the prophets from the priests functioning in the temple.

50. See Blenkinsopp, *History of Prophecy in Israel*, 121–28; and Murray, "Prophecy and the Cult," 201.

51. A number of psalms are ascribed to Asaph or the Asaphites, who are mentioned as prophesying in 1 Chronicles 25 (Pss. 50, 73–83). The prophets Nathan and Gad are assumed by the tradition to have had to do with the establishment of the Levitical musicians in the temple. On the possible association of Gad with cultic musical groups who may have manifested prophetic frenzy, see Huffmon, "Origins of Prophecy," 180; and Johnson, *Cultic Prophet in Ancient Israel*, 69ff.

52. Wilson, *Prophecy and Society in Ancient Israel*, 69. For further discussion, see his chapter 2. Cf. Grabbe, *Priests, Prophets, Diviners, Sages*, 107; Blenkinsopp, *History of Prophecy in Israel*, 34; and Hutton, *Charisma and Authority in Israelite Society*, chapter 5. Wilson's use of this term is because it well covers prophecy and other societal functionaries, such as shaman, diviner, and medium. He does not use it to refer to the priest, because there are priestly functions that are unique. He acknowledges much overlap, however, between priest and prophet, and there is no reason why the term does not apply to the priest, albeit in frequently different ways.

53. A concise survey of the Near Eastern material is presented by Huffmon, "Prophecy (ANE)." For further discussion and bibliography, see Miller, "World and Message of the Prophets," 109–10 n. 3.

54. One perhaps should include the medium consulted by Saul inasmuch as there was considerable overlap between the divinatory activities of mediums and so-called magicians and the oracular activity of prophets (1 Samuel 28).

55. The plausibility of the designation of Miriam as a prophet is questionable. There is no indication even in later tradition that she engaged in typical prophetic activity (but see Num. 12:2). The association of Miriam with prophecy occurs in connection with her singing, playing instruments, and dancing (Ex. 15:20), activities elsewhere associated with prophecy and spirit possession (1 Sam. 10:5; 2 Kings 3:15). Deborah is called a "prophetess" (Judg. 4:4) and is depicted as giving an oracular command to Barak that is very similar to what the prophets give to Jehoshaphat and the king of Israel in 1 Kings 22:6, 12, and 15.

56. See Neh. 6:14.

57. Bowen, "Daughters of Your People."

58. In Hebrew, the verbal forms seem to be denominative from the noun, occurring in Niphal and Hithpael forms. But the verbal root is a more generally Semitic root.

59. Fleming, "Etymological Origins of the Hebrew *nābî'*."

60. See Hutton, *Charisma and Authority in Israelite Society*, 116.

61. For hypotheses about the possible social location of the prophetic bands, see Blenkinsopp, *Sage, Priest, Prophet*, 134–38. The data for determining this are scant, and conclusions, therefore, remain quite uncertain and broad in nature.

62. See Wilson's discussion of the Elisha traditions in *Prophecy and Society in Ancient Israel*, 202–6.

63. Ibid., 201.

64. Ibid., 266–70; cf. Kselman, "Social World of the Israelite Prophets," 124.

65. See Long, "Prophetic Authority and Social Reality."

66. The way in which the call narratives identify themes and motifs that are prominent within the prophetic book, for example, in the case of Isaiah 6 and Jeremiah 1, tends to support the notion that the call stories preserved in the prophetic books are to be seen in primary connection with the book rather than the actual career of the prophet.

67. See, for example, the analysis of the conflict between Jeremiah and Hananiah by Burke O. Long as a conflict of political policies represented by various individuals and groups, specifically the conflict between the nationalist group insisting on serious resistance to Babylonian encroachment (Hananiah) and those elements supporting capitulation and coexistence (Jeremiah) ("Social Dimensions of Prophetic Conflict"). The significance of this political conflict is well identified in Brueggemann, *Commentary on Jeremiah*; and in the monograph by Seitz, *Theology in Conflict*.

68. The significance of the call experience as pointing to the self-transcendence of the prophet has been pointed out by Martin Buss, who notes that the call locates the prophet's message in a source outside himself. He comments: "In referring to a reality (or to a group of realities) which is ultimate, one finds a center of orientation outside of oneself. . . . From the perspective of such an ultimate reference point the action of an individual or a group can be evaluated so that a framework is given for self-evaluation including self-criticism." This quotation is excerpted from the discussion of Buss's work in Kselman, "Social World of the Israelite Prophets," 126. Cf. Buss, "Anthropological Perspective upon Prophetic Call Narratives."

69. The same was true for prophecy generally in the ancient Near East.

70. On the social dimensions of prophetic conflict, see Long, "Social Dimensions of Prophetic Conflict"; and Hutton, *Charisma and Authority in Israelite Society*, 130–37. The discussion above parts company from the claim that Hutton makes, citing Long, to the effect that prophetic conflict "has less to do with ideological and theological differences than with social and political dynamics" (133).

71. The classic example is the conflict between Jeremiah and Hananiah, both of whom give oracles that begin, "Thus says the LORD . . ." (Jeremiah 28).

72. At the conclusion of the vision of the deity calling for a lying spirit to enter into the mouth of the prophets, Micaiah says, "See now (*wĕ'attâ hinnēh*) . . . the LORD has spoken doom for you" (v. 23), indicating the conclusion that the king is to draw from the vision.

73. On this issue, see Grabbe, *Priests, Prophets, Diviners, Sages*, 145–48, where the case is argued for the general overlap of dreams and prophecy.

74. This analysis is dependent upon Malamat, "Forerunner of Biblical Prophecy," 33–35.

75. Hutton, *Charisma and Authority in Israelite Society*, 111.

76. Hutton speaks of this distinction as one between divinatory and prophetic or mediumistic modes of securing information from the deity.

77. The hithpael form of the verb *nābā'* clearly describes ecstatic prophecy in such places as 1 Sam. 10:5–6, 10, 13; 19:20, 21, 23–24; 1 Kings 18:29; cf. 1 Sam. 18:10; Num. 11:24–30. Note the distinction in 1 Kings 22 between the "prophesying" (hithpael) that seems to be an ecstatic or frenzied state (v. 10) and the "prophesying" (niphal) that is a verbal communication (v. 12). For the distinction between trance, "a psycho-physiological state marked by disassociation," and possession, "a cultural theory that explains how contact takes place between the supernatural and natural worlds," see Wilson, *Prophecy and Society in Ancient Israel*, 34.

78. On the place of ecstasy and trance in the revelatory mechanisms of prophecy, see Wilson, *Prophecy and Society in Ancient Israel*; and Grabbe, *Priests, Prophets, Diviners, Sages*, 108–12.

79. Cross, *Canaanite Myth and Hebrew Epic*, 228–29.

80. For the way in which the transition from primary address to the king to address to the larger community (a transition that seems to have taken place in the ninth century if the Elijah stories are at all a reflection of prophetic activity in that century) correlates with changes in Assyrian political policy and statecraft, see Holladay, "Assyrian Statecraft and the Prophets of Israel."

81. Jeremiah's reference to the "prophets" healing "the wound of my people lightly" may arise out of the prophetic activity of announcing life or death and indeed of healing persons (Jer. 8:11, 15; 14:19). The association of prophets with healing acts should not be too surprising in light of the way in which shamans and other intermediaries have traditionally combined divinatory and healing activities. See in this regard the case studies in Overholt, *Prophecy in Cross-Cultural Perspective*.

82. Hutton, *Charisma and Authority in Israelite Society*, 121–22. Hutton properly notes a supporting text from the New Testament, where a blind man is healed by Jesus and responds by saying, "He is a prophet!" (John 9:17).

83. For a more extended discussion of the intercessory role of prophets, see Miller, *They Cried to the Lord*, chapter 8.

84. Second Samuel 7:1–16 is important in this regard for the way in which it combines perspectives on the relationship between deity, king, and sanctuary. As it stands in its present form, which is in various ways quite Deuteronomistic, it is "primarily a political text that justifies the Davidic monarchy" and ties together "house of David" and "house of Yahweh" (see below), but the text includes an old oracle that opposes the building of a permanent temple in favor of the older combination of tent and ark that was central to the cultus of the Israelite confederation. Cross has suggested that this opposition "was directed against the Canaanite ideology of kingship of the sort which developed immediately in fact, with the building of the Temple" (*Canaanite Myth and Hebrew Epic*, 243).

85. See in this regard Lowery, *Reforming Kings*, 37, 211.

86. Whitelam, "Israelite Kingship," 130.

87. Cross, *Canaanite Myth and Hebrew Epic*, 222–23, 260, 264.

88. Toews, *Monarchy and Religious Institution*, 80.

89. Cross, *Canaanite Myth and Hebrew Epic*, 239. For the development of the typology of the royal ideology generally, see 219–73.

90. See Ahlström, *Royal Administration and National Religion*, 61. Ahlström believes that Tirzah, as a capital, would have had a sanctuary also.

91. See Toews, *Monarchy and Religious Institution*, 80–86.

92. See the summary comment of Lowery: "The king built sanctuaries, instituted and ultimately controlled religiously legitimated taxes, used the temple treasuries as political events dictated, appointed and deposed priests, erected and demolished cult objects, and defined priestly roles. Though he probably held no cultic office, the king was the single most important figure in the cultic life of Judah" (*Reforming Kings*, 119). For a detailed examination of Jeroboam's activities in establishing a cultus in the Northern Kingdom, see Toews, *Monarchy and Religious Institution*. Walter Rast has sought to show how the cultic structure at Taanach and those at other tenth-century sites "show a new type of uniformity in the management of cultic *realia*, which is expressive of a more controlled society emerging under the developing monarchy" ("Priestly Families and the Cultic Structure at Taanach," 363).

93. On the evaluation of the Kings account with regard to what measures Jeroboam took in installing a new official cult, see Toews, *Monarchy and Religious Institution*; and Gleis, *Die Bamah*, 121–26. Cf. Albertz, *History of Israelite Religion*, 1:143–46; and Talmon, "Cult and Calendar Reform of Jeroboam I."

94. On the ideology of kingship in the ancient Near East, see the classic work of Frankfort, *Kingship and the Gods*. For a recent and helpful analysis of Mesopotamian and Israelite kingship with particular attention to the role of deity and people in the choice of the king, see Dietrich and Dietrich, "Zwischen Gott und Volk." (One notes that the reported trigger event that led to rule by kings in ancient Israel was the request of the elders to Samuel to "appoint for us, then, a king to govern us, *like other nations*" [1 Sam. 8:5].)

95. See Miller, "Prophetic Critique of Kings."

96. For detailed discussion of the texts, see Dietrich and Dietrich, "Zwischen Gott und Volk," 247–58.

97. Cross, *Canaanite Myth and Hebrew Epic*, 222–23, 260; Toews, *Monarchy and Religious Institution*, 79–80.

98. For a brief discussion of some of these sanctuary sites, see Miller, "Israelite Religion," 227. On the Arad sanctuary, see Ahlström, *Royal Administration and National Religion*, 40–41, where he notes various indicators that this was an official sanctuary, possibly tied directly to the Levitical priesthood. Certainly the ostracon referring to the "house of Yahweh," which is either the Jerusalem temple or the Arad temple, tends to confirm this (see Aharoni, *Arad Inscriptions*, nn. 18, 35–38.) Ahlström shows how Arad "provides an excellent example of the relationship between royal administration and national religion" (40).

99. See Rainey, "Hezekiah's Reform and the Altars." Cf. Albertz, *History of Israelite Religion*, 1:180–81; and the judgment of Lowery: "The Hezekian reform, as it is reported in Kings, is more plausible as history than as fiction" (*Reforming Kings*, 149). Lowery, however, does not think that Hezekiah's removal of the high places (2 Kings 18:4) meant destruction of these cultic centers. Instead, he believes it was a temporary reform as a part of resistance to Assyrian domination by cutting off the possibility of Yahweh cult objects being captured by the Assyrian army or stored up taxes being confiscated from the cult centers.

100. Rainey, "Hezekiah's Reform and the Altars," 333.

101. On the archaeological data confirming the practices that Josiah sought to suppress or eliminate, see Dever, "Silence of the Text." On Josiah's reform generally—or the Deuteronomic reform as may be more accurately the case—see for summary purposes Albertz, *History of Israelite Religion*, 1:195–231.

102. Albertz, *History of Israelite Religion*, 1:199. Albertz has rightly noted that the reform is not to be ascribed simply to Josiah's efforts. Other elements in the community, for example, the *'am hā'āreṣ* and priestly groups in Jerusalem together with prophets, may have helped push and give impetus to the reform measures described in 2 Kings 23.

103. On these issues, see Lowery, *Reforming Kings*.

104. Lowery, *Reforming Kings*, 111. See his extensive discussion of this tax.

105. Ibid., 138. Cf. Spieckermann, *Juda unter Assur*.

106. Miller, "Aspects of the Religion of Ugarit," 60–62; and Tsumura, "Kings and Cults in Ancient Ugarit."

107. On this text and the general question of the relation of the high priesthood to the king, see Rooke, "Kingship as Priesthood."

108. Because of the conflict of this statement with the assumption that the priesthood was hereditary and confined to the tribe of Levi at this time, some have emended the text with some of the versions. But the principle of *lectio difficilior* makes that highly unlikely. See McCarter, *II Samuel*, 254–55. Cf. Grabbe, *Priests, Prophets, Diviners, Sages*, 23. McCarter has suggested that there were probably special priests assigned to the royal household and that members of the royal family might serve in this capacity (257). As we have indicated above, it cannot be presumed that the priesthood was always hereditary and Levitical. Persons may have come into the Levitical order from outside.

109. McCarter, *II Samuel*, 180–82. Miller and Roberts have compared this ritual procession to the ritual of the return of a divine statue to its sanctuary after it had been captured by an enemy. The analogy offered by McCarter is even closer but both are indicators of what is going on in this one-time event. In the case of Assurbanipal's return of Marduk to Babylon, sacrifices were offered every double mile from the quay of Assur to the quay of Babylon, very much like David's offering of sacrifices every six steps on the procession of the ark into Jerusalem. See Miller and Roberts, *Hand of the Lord*, 15–17.

110. McCarter, *II Samuel*, 181.

111. Ibid., 182.

112. Ibid.

113. Much of this discussion is drawn from the author's essay, "Israelite Religion," 220–22.

114. Kraus, *Worship in Israel*, 179–88.

115. See Weiser, "Zur Frage nach den Beziehungen der Psalmen zum Kult"; and idem, *Psalms*.

116. Mowinckel, *Psalms in Israel's Worship*, chapter 5.

117. Cross, *Canaanite Myth and Hebrew Epic*, 91–111.

118. On the sage and the wise generally, see especially Blenkinsopp, *Sage, Priest, Prophet*, 9–65; and Grabbe, *Priests, Prophets, Diviners, Sages*, 152–80. On the scribe, see Saldarini, "Scribes"; and Fishbane, *Biblical Interpretation in Ancient Israel*, 23–37. Fishbane gives attention to the relation of scribe and sage. A wide-ranging

collection of essays on the sage in the ancient Near East and in the history of Israel and early Judaism is to be found in Gammie and Perdue, eds., *Sage in Israel and the Ancient Near East*.

119. Blenkinsopp, *Sage, Priest, Prophet*, 30.

120. See the description of David's uncle, Jonathan, as "an advisor, a man of understanding, and a scribe" (1 Chron. 27:32), or the description of Ahiqar in the Aramaic Ahiqar text as "a wise and skilled scribe who gave advice." Ezra is depicted as a "skilled" scribe. In light of that skill being manifest in his knowledge of the law, this is more than a technical literary or writing skill.

121. Fishbane, along with many others, sees in the Jeremiah text an indication that the scribes referred to there were identical with the sages or the followers of the wisdom tradition (*Biblical Interpretation in Ancient Israel*, 35).

122. See Stone, "Ideal Figures and Social Context," 576–78.

123. This may have something to do with the fact that Ezra is described as both priest and scribe. By the fifth century, the responsibility for preserving and teaching the Torah was surely a shared duty. Indeed, that seems to have been the case much earlier, but the identification of both roles around the handling of the Torah is especially the case in the postexilic period. Note an anticipation of this in the way that the account of the discovery of the law book in the temple in 2 Kings 22 involves both the high priest Hilkiah and the scribe Shaphan. The priest found the law book and gave it to the scribe, who reported this to the king and then read the law book to the king.

124. Ibid., 23.

125. See, for example, the correction by one scribe of a mistake by another scribe in the transmission of Isa. 40:7–8 in the great Isaiah scroll from Qumran.

126. See Talmon commenting on the postexilic "need for a replacement of personal inspiration as a principle of public guidance, by more rational and controllable forms of instruction," a move that produced what he calls "new classes of spiritual leaders," that is, the scribes and sages ("Emergence of Jewish Sectarianism," 594).

127. For other instances of this Persian imperial practice, see Fishbane, *Biblical Interpretation in Ancient Israel*, 37 n. 53 and 107. Fishbane suggests that the prominent role of sage-scribes in relation to the Torah in Jeremiah's time may reflect their taking "advantage of a cultural vacuum created by the renewal of Judaean independence after Assyria's collapse, and the cultic elevation of Jerusalem as the dominant national-royal shrine after the fall of Samaria, to propagate their adjustment of old Wisdom traditions to the ancient, sacred teachings of Moses," but he acknowledges that this can only be speculation (35–36).

128. Fishbane's great work on biblical interpretation is aimed at showing in some detail how that happened. Cf. his essay "From Scribalism to Rabbinism."

129. While these regulations, together with other ones (e.g., 16:16; 20:1–9), seem to have in mind the adult males of the community, there are other places where Deuteronomy speaks of the "whole assembly" and has in mind the full community, including women and children (e.g., 5:22; 31:30; cf. 29:10–11; 31:10–13).

130. See Tigay, *Deuteronomy*, 210.

131. "In banning people from the Temple, Deuteronomy would undoubtedly have called it 'the place which the Lord your God has chosen'; 'assembly,' or

'congregation,' does not refer to a sanctuary in Deuteronomy or anywhere else in the Bible" (Tigay, *Deuteronomy*, 479).

132. See Cohen, "From the Bible to the Talmud."

133. Tigay, *Deuteronomy*, 479. For a careful analysis of the way in which the Ezra text represents an exegetical elaboration and extension of Deut. 7:1–3, joined with features of Deut. 23:4–9 to reinterpret the Deuteronomy text specifically with regard to intermarriage in the later situation, see Fishbane, *Biblical Interpretation in Ancient Israel*, 114–29.

134. Christine Hayes has recently argued that the older restrictions against intermarriage as reflected in Deuteronomy were for moral-religious reasons—the danger of being tempted to idolatry—and so did not necessarily effect a universal rule, while Ezra's rationale, that intermarriage would profane the holy seed of Israel (Ezra 9:1–2) made intermarriage a universally prohibited act ("Intermarriage and Impurity in Ancient Jewish Sources").

135. On some of the sociological dimensions of the tension between these different voices in postexilic Judah, see Hanson, *Dawn of Apocalyptic*. See also the discussion of community religion in chapter 2 of this book.

136. On the place and status of the *gēr,* see van Houten, *Alien in Israelite Law*; Ramirez Kidd, *Alterity and Identity*; and Milgrom, *Numbers*, 398–402.

137. Milgrom, *Numbers*, 399.

138. Ibid.; and Ramirez Kidd, *Alterity and Identity*, 71.

139. See the decree of Antiochus III calling for fines for any foreigner who entered the Israelite court of the temple.

140. See especially out of earlier discussions Peritz, "Women in the Ancient Hebrew Cult." More recently, the best treatments (with discussion of earlier literature) are Bird, "Place of Women in the Israelite Cultus"; and Winter, *Frau und Göttin*. Cf. Gruber, "Women in the Cult"; van der Toorn, *From Her Cradle to Her Grave*; Henshaw, *Female and Male*; Vos, *Woman in Old Testament Worship*; Braulik, "Rejection of the Goddess Asherah"; idem, "Haben in Israel auch Frauen geopfert?"; idem, "Durften auch Frauen in Israel opfern?; and Reuter, *Kultzentralisation*.

141. This is well indicated by the absence of women from the "important cultic officials" that Henshaw lists in chapter 1 of *Female and Male*.

142. Bird, "Place of Women in the Israelite Cultures," 405–8. The discussion at this point is heavily indebted to Bird's excellent study but draws upon some other materials, including the review of the issues and the history of scholarship by Winter, *Frau und Göttin*, chapter 1.

143. See Bird, "Place of Women in the Israelite Cultures," 406 and nn. 36–38 for the inferential grounds for these suggestions.

144. On the later temple musicians depicted as "prophesying" with musical instruments, see 1 Chron. 25:1.

145. On the women as singers, dancers, and instrumentalists in the cultus, see Peritz, "Women in the Ancient Hebrew Cult," 147–48, who calls attention to women singers in the assembly that returned from Babylon in the sixth and fifth century (Ezra 2:65; Neh. 7:67; cf. Gruber, "Women in the Cult," 39); and Henshaw, *Female and Male*, 116–24. Marc Brettler has questioned whether the women singers referred to in Ezra and Nehemiah would have been cultic singers and does not see

any positive evidence for the participation of women in the cult in some role connected to singing psalms ("Women and Psalms," 40). For the preexilic period there is iconographic evidence in support of the picture in Psalm 68 in the form of the several figurines of a woman with a tambourine, which Keel and Uehlinger argue do not represent a goddess but a female participant in the cult (see *Gods, Goddesses, and Images of God*, 166–67).

146. On women's prayers, see Miller, "Things Too Wonderful."

147. Bird, "Place of Women in the Israelite Cultures," 405–6, 408, and n. 34; Winter, *Frau und Göttin*, 38–40.

148. Bird, "Place of Women in the Israelite Cultures," 415–16 n. 34.

149. See the references in note 140.

150. On the textual differences between the MT (where Hannah is the dominant figure) and the LXX (where Hannah is not mentioned in the slaughtering or sacrificial act), see Braulik, "Durften auch Frauen in Israel opfern?" 230 n. 27; and Walters, "Hannah and Anna." Walters points out that the Greek and Hebrew texts represent two quite different accounts of the event and cannot be used to correct or harmonize with one another.

151. Braulik, "Rejection of the Goddess Asherah," 180–81. Braulik argues that Deut. 16:16–17, with its reference to the appearing of all the "males" three times a year, represents pre-Deuteronomic legislation. There is clearly a tension in the text, but Braulik is correct to insist that 16:16–17 not control the data so that the other texts are not brought into play, including other parts of Deuteronomy 14, specifically vv. 10–11 and 14.

152. For this list, see Braulik, "Durften auch Frauen in Israel opfern?" 246.

153. Gruber, "Women in the Cult," 39. Gruber notes the way in which Num. 5:5–7 uses both *nepeš* and *'ādām* and specifically identifies the subject of the legislation as "a man or a woman." Cf. Milgrom, *Leviticus 1–16*, 178–79.

154. See Gruber, "Women in the Cult," 39.

155. The expression occurs again in the MT of 1 Sam. 2:22, but it is missing from the LXX and 4QSam[a]. For discussion, see McCarter, *I Samuel*, 81; and Cross, *Canaanite Myth and Hebrew Epic*, 202–3 n. 34.

156. For discussion, see Bird, "Place of Women in the Israelite Cultus," 406 and n. 40; Winter, *Frau und Göttin*, 58–65; and Wacker, "'Religionsgeschichte Israels' oder 'Theologie des Alten Testaments.'"

157. Görg, "Spiegeldienst der Frauen."

158. Winter, *Frau und Göttin*, 58–65.

159. Phyllis Bird has argued that the masculine term is a Deuteronomic or Deuteronomistic construction derived from the feminine noun, to which it is appended as a complement. She finds "no historical evidence for the existence in Israel/Judah of male hierodules, or cult prostitutes, known as *qdš(ym)*, either as a legitimate class of cultic servants or as devotees of a Canaanite cult" ("End of the Male Cult Prostitute," 74–75).

160. I am indebted to Eric Elnes for much careful research on this topic. Among those recent works that best present the various voices in the debate and draw judicious conclusions in the light of the data, one may cite—in addition to the various essays by Phyllis Bird cited here—Henshaw, *Female and Male*; Oden, *Bible without*

Theology, 131–53; and Westenholz, "Tamar, *Qĕdēšā, Qadištu,* and Sacred Prostitution." The most recent extensive bibliography is to be found at the end of Bird's essay, "End of the Male Cult Prostitute."

161. See, for example, the discussion in Henshaw, *Female and Male,* 226–28; and Oden, *Bible without Theology,* 144–46.

162. Phyllis Bird's summary comment is cogent and to the point:

> *Zônôt* are defined by their sexual activity; *qĕdēšôt* by their cultic association. It is impossible to determine the nature of their cultic service from the biblical sources, which are too fragmentary and polemical. It is clear, however, from the limited Old Testament references that the Israelite authors understood their role to include some form of sexual activity, which they identified with prostitution. Through juxtaposition with *zônâ* the term *qĕdēšâ* acquired the sense of "sacred prostitution." Neither the assumption of sexual activity, however, nor its equation with prostitution can be taken at face value. Since Israel appears to have recognized no legitimate role for women as cult functionaries during the period in which *qĕdēšôt* are attested, it would be easy for Israelites to assume that the presence of women at a sanctuary involved sexual activity. It is possible then that the charge of "sacred prostitution" has no base in cultic sex, but is rather a false inference. It is also possible to understand the charge as a polemical misrepresentation of a cultic role that did involve some form of sexual activity, but was not understood by the practitioners as prostitution. . . . A final possibility is that the isolated biblical references to *qĕdēšôt* represent a perverted remnant of an earlier Israelite or Canaanite cult, perpetuated in a perverted Israelite cult. ("To Play the Harlot," 87)

163. This is the suggestion of Westenholz, "Tamar, *Qĕdēšâ, Qadištu,* and Sacred Prostitution," 250. More recently, Phyllis Bird has suggested something similar: "I believe we must reconstruct a class of female attendants at the rural shrines representing a form of cultic service on the part of women that may once have had a recognized place in Israelite worship, but was ultimately rejected. One might see an earlier attestation of the class in the references to women serving at the entrance to the tent of meeting or in the role of Miriam leading the praise of YHWH at the sea" ("End of the Male Cult Prostitute," 46–47).

164. The reference to the "house" in this verse probably means the sanctuary or temple.

Bibliography

Ackerman, Susan. "The Queen Mother and the Cult in Ancient Israel." *JBL* 112 (1993): 385–401.

_____. *Under Every Green Tree: Popular Religion in Sixth-Century Judah.* HSM 46. Atlanta: Scholars Press, 1992.

Ackroyd, Peter R. *The Chronicler in His Age.* JSOTSup 101. Sheffield: JSOT Press, 1991.

Aharoni, Yohanan. *Arad Inscriptions.* Jerusalem: Israel Exploration Society, 1981.

_____. "Arad: Its Inscriptions and Temple." *BA* 31 (1968): 2–32.

Ahlström, Gösta. *An Archaeological Picture of Iron Age Religion in Ancient Palestine.* StudOr 55:3. Helsinki: Societas Orientalis Lennica, 1984.

_____. *Aspects of Syncretism in Israelite Religion.* Translated by Eric Sharpe. Horae Soederblomianae 5. Lund: C. W. K. Gleerup, 1963.

_____. *Royal Administration and National Religion in Ancient Palestine.* Studies in the History of the Ancient Near East 1. Leiden: E. J. Brill, 1982.

Albertz, Rainer. "Biblische oder nicht-biblische Religionsgeschichte Israels? Ein Gespräch mit Oswald Loretz." In *"Und Mose schrieb dieses Lied auf": Studien zum Alten Testament und zum Alten Orient: Festschrift für Oswald Loretz zur Vollendung seines 70. Lebensjahres mit Beiträgen von Freunden, Schülern und Kollegen,* edited by Manfried Dietrich and Ingo Kottsieper. AOAT 250. Münster: Ugarit-Verlag, 1998.

_____. *A History of Israelite Religion in the Old Testament Period.* Translated by John Bowden. 2 vols. OTL. Louisville, Ky.: Westminster John Knox Press, 1994.

_____. *Persönliche Frömmigkeit und offizielle Religion: Religionsinterner Pluralismus in Israel und Babylon.* Calwer Theologische Monographien 9. Stuttgart: Calwer Verlag, 1978.

Albright, William F. *Archaeology and the Religion of Israel.* 3d ed. Baltimore: Johns Hopkins University Press, 1953.

_____. *Yahweh and the Gods of Canaan: A Historical Analysis of Two Contrasting Faiths.* Jordan Lectures in Comparative Religion 7. London: Athlone, 1968.

Anderson, Gary A. *Sacrifices and Offerings in Ancient Israel: Studies in Their Social and Political Importance.* HSM 41. Atlanta: Scholars Press, 1987.

_____. "Sacrifice and Sacrificial Offerings (OT)." *The Anchor Bible Dictionary,* edited by David N. Freedman, 5:870–86. New York: Doubleday, 1992.

Arnold, Bill T. "Religion in Ancient Israel." Pages 391–420 in *The Face of Old Testament Studies: A Survey of Contemporary Approaches,* edited by David W. Baker and Bill T. Arnold. Grand Rapids: Baker Book House, 1999.

Avishur, Yitshak. *Stylistic Studies of Word-Pairs in Biblical and Ancient Semitic Literatures*. AOAT 210. Neukirchen-Vluyn: Neukirchener Verlag, 1984.

Baker, David W., and Bill T. Arnold, eds. *The Face of Old Testament Studies: A Survey of Contemporary Approaches*. Grand Rapids: Baker Book House, 1999.

Balentine, Samuel E. *The Hidden God: The Hiding of the Face of God in the Old Testament*. Oxford: Oxford University Press, 1983.

———. "The Politics of Religion in the Persian Period." Pages 129–46 in *After the Exile: Essays in Honour of Rex Mason*, edited by John Barton and David J. Reimer. Macon, Ga.: Mercer University Press, 1996.

Baltzer, Klaus. *The Covenant Formulary*. Philadelphia: Fortress Press, 1971.

Barkay, Gabriel. *Ketef Hinnom: A Treasure Facing Jerusalem's Walls*. The Israel Museum Catalogue 274. Jerusalem: Israel Museum, summer 1986.

Barrick, W. Boyd. "What Do We Really Know about 'High-Places'?" *SEÅ* 45 (1980): 50–57.

Begrich, Joachim. "Die priesterliche Heilsorakel." Pages 217–31 in *Gesammelte Studien zum Alten Testament*. TBü 21. Munich: C. Kaiser, 1964.

———. "Die priesterliche Tora." Pages 232–60 in *Gesammelte Studien zum Alten Testament*. TBü 21. Munich: C. Kaiser, 1964.

Bendor, Shunya. *The Social Structure of Ancient Israel: The Institution of the Family* (beit 'ab) *from the Settlement to the End of the Monarchy*. Jerusalem Biblical Studies 7. Jerusalem: Simor, 1996.

Ben-Tor, Amnon. "Qiri, Tell." *The Anchor Bible Dictionary*, edited by David N. Freedman, 5:581–82. New York: Doubleday, 1992.

Berlejung, Anjelika. "Die Macht der Bilder." *Jahrbuch für Biblische Theologie* 13 (1998).

———. *Die Theologie der Bilder: Herstellung und Einweihung von Kultbildern in Mesopotamien und die alttestamentliche Bilderpolemik*. OBO 162. Freiburg: Universitätsverlag, 1998.

Berlinerblau, Jacques. "Preliminary Remarks for the Sociological Study of Israelite 'Official Religion.'" Pages 153–70 in *Ki Baruch Hu: Ancient Near Eastern, Biblical, and Judaic Studies in Honor of Baruch A. Levine*. Winona Lake, Ind.: Eisenbrauns, 1995.

Berquist, Jon L. *Judaism in Persia's Shadow: A Social and Historical Approach*. Minneapolis: Fortress Press, 1995.

Bibb, Bryan D. "Religious Language and Social Norms: Holiness in Leviticus 17–27," Master's thesis, Princeton Theological Seminary, 1996.

Binder, Donald D. *Into the Temple Courts: The Place of the Synagogues in the Second Temple Period*. SBLDS 169. Atlanta: Scholars Press, 1999.

Binger, Tilde. *Asherah: Goddesses in Ugarit, Israel and the Old Testament*. JSOTSup 232. Sheffield: Sheffield Academic Press, 1997.

Biran, Avraham, ed. *Temples and High Places in Biblical Times: Proceedings of the Colloquium in Honor of the Centennial of the Hebrew Union College–Jewish Institute of Religion, Jerusalem, 14–16 March 1977*. Jerusalem: Nelson Glueck School of Biblical Archaeology, 1981.

Biran, Avraham. "To the God Who Is in Dan." Pages 142–51 in *Temples and High Places in Biblical Times: Proceedings of the Colloquium in Honor of the Centennial of the Hebrew Union College-Jewish Institute of Religion, Jerusalem, 14–16 March 1977*. Jerusalem: Nelson Glueck School of Biblical Archaeology, 1981.

Bird, Phyllis. "The End of the Male Cult Prostitute: A Literary-Historical and Socio-logical Analysis of Hebrew *qādēš-qĕdēšîm*." Pages 37–80 in *Congress Volume, Cambridge 1995,* edited by John A. Emerton. VTSup 66. E. J. Brill: Leiden, 1997.

_____. "The Place of Women in the Israelite Cultus." Pages 397–419 in *Ancient Israelite Religion: Essays in Honor of Frank Moore Cross,* edited by Patrick D. Miller, Jr., Paul D. Hanson, and S. Dean McBride. Philadelphia: Fortress Press, 1987. Repr. pages 81–102 in *Missing Persons and Mistaken Identities: Women and Gender in Ancient Israel.* OBT. Minneapolis: Fortress Press, 1997.

_____. "To Play the Harlot: An Inquiry into an Old Testament Metaphor." Pages 75–94 in *Gender and Difference in Ancient Israel,* edited by Peggy L. Day. Min-neapolis: Fortress Press, 1989. Repr. pages 219–36 in *Missing Persons and Mis-taken Identities: Women and Gender in Ancient Israel.* OBT. Minneapolis: Fortress Press, 1997.

Blenkinsopp, Joseph. "An Assessment of the Alleged Pre-Exilic Date of the Priestly Material in the Pentateuch." *ZAW* 108 (1996): 495–518.

_____. *Ezra and Nehemiah.* OTL. Philadelphia: Westminster Press, 1988.

_____. *A History of Prophecy in Israel.* Rev. and enlarged ed. Louisville, Ky.: West-minster John Knox Press, 1996.

_____. *Sage, Priest, Prophet: Religious and Intellectual Leadership in Ancient Israel.* Library of Ancient Israel. Louisville, Ky.: Westminster John Knox Press, 1995.

_____. "Temple and Society in Achaemenid Judah." Pages 22–53 In *Second Tem-ple Studies 1: Persian Period,* edited by Philip R. Davies. JSOTSup 117. Sheffield: JSOT Press, 1991.

Bloch-Smith, Elizabeth. *Judahite Burial Practices and Beliefs about the Dead.* JSOTSup 123. Sheffield: JSOT Press, 1992.

Boling, Robert. *Joshua: A New Translation with Notes and Commentary.* AB 6. Gar-den City, N.Y.: Doubleday, 1982.

Bordreuil, Pierre, Felice Israel, and Dennis Pardee. "Deux ostraca paléo-hébreux de la Collection Sh. Moussaieff." *Sem* 46 (1996): 49–76.

Bowen, Nancy. "The Daughters of Your People: Female Prophets in Ezekiel 13:17–23," *JBL* 118 (1999): 417–33.

Brandt, Sigrid. "Opfer als Gedächtnis: Zur Kritik und Neukonturierung theologischer Rede von Opfer." Habilitationsschrift, Evangelisch-Theologische Fakultät der Ruprecht-Karls-Universität Heidelberg, 1997.

Braulik, Georg. "Durften auch Frauen in Israel opfern? Beobachtungen zur Sinn- und Festgestalt des Opfers im Deuteronomium." *Liturgisches Jahrbuch* 48 (1998): 222–48.

_____. "Haben in Israel auch Frauen geopfert? Beobachtungen am Deuteronomium." Pages 19–28 in *Zur aktualität des Alten Testaments: Festschrift für Georg Sauer zum 65. Geburtstag,* edited by Siegfried Kreuzer and Kurt Lüthi. Frankfurt am Main: P. Lang, 1991.

_____. "The Rejection of the Goddess Asherah in Israel: Was the Rejection as Late as Deuteronomistic and Did It Further the Oppression of Women in Israel?" Pages 165–82 in *The Theology of Deuteronomy: Collected Essays by Georg Braulik, O.S.B.* North Richland Hills, Tex.: BIBAL Press, 1994.

Brettler, Marc. "Women and Psalms: Toward an Understanding of the Role of Women's Prayer in the Israelite Cult." Pages 25–56 in *Gender and Law in the Hebrew Bible and the Ancient Near East.* JSOTSup 262. Sheffield: JSOT Press, 1998.

Brown, Shelby. *Late Carthaginian Child Sacrifice and Sacrificial Monuments in Their Mediterranean Context.* JSOT/ASOR Monograph Series 3. Sheffield: JSOT Press, 1991.

Brueggemann, Walter. *A Commentary on Jeremiah: Exile and Homecoming.* Grand Rapids: Wm. B. Eerdmans Publishing Co., 1998.

_____. "Old Testament Theology as a Particular Conversation: Adjudication of Israel's Socio-Theological Alternatives." Pages 118–49 in *Old Testament Theology: Essays in Structure, Theme and Text,* edited by Patrick D. Miller. Philadelphia: Fortress Press, 1992.

_____. "The Social Significance of Solomon as a Patron of Wisdom." Pages 117–32 in *The Sage in Israel and the Ancient Near East,* edited by John G. Gammie and Leo G. Perdue. Winona Lake, Ind.: Eisenbrauns, 1990.

Budd, Philip J. "Holiness and Cult." Pages 275–98 in *The Social World of Ancient Israel,* edited by Ronald J. Clements. Cambridge: Cambridge University Press, 1989.

Burkert, Walther. *Structure and History in Greek Mythology and Ritual.* Berkeley: University of California Press, 1979.

Buss, Martin. "An Anthropological Perspective upon Prophetic Call Narratives." *Semeia* 21 (1981): 9–30.

_____. "The Social Psychology of Prophecy." Pages 1–11 in *Prophecy: Essays Presented to Georg Fohrer on his Sixty-fifth Birthday 6 Sept 1980,* edited by John A. Emerton. BZAW 150. Berlin: Walter de Gruyter, 1979.

Carter, Charles E. *The Emergence of Yehud in the Persian Period: A Social and Demographic Study.* JSOTSup 294. Sheffield: Sheffield Academic Press, 1999.

Childs, Brevard S. *The Book of Exodus: A Critical, Theological Commentary.* OTL. Philadelphia: Westminster Press, 1974.

Cody, Aelred. *A History of Old Testament Priesthood.* AnBib 35. Rome: Pontifical Biblical Institute, 1969.

Cogan, Mordechai, and Hayim Tadmor. *II Kings.* AB 11. Garden City, N.Y.: Doubleday, 1988.

Cohen, Shaye J. D. "From the Bible to the Talmud: The Prohibition of Intermarriage." *HAR* 7 (1983): 23–39.

Coogan, Michael D. "Canaanite Origins and Lineage: Reflections on the Religion of Ancient Israel." Pages 115–24 in *Ancient Israelite Religion: Essays in Honor of Frank Moore Cross,* edited by Patrick D. Miller, Paul D. Hanson, and S. Dean McBride. Philadelphia: Fortress Press, 1987.

Coogan, Michael D., J. Cheryl Exum, and Lawrence E. Stager, eds. *Scripture and Other Artifacts: Essays on the Bible and Archaeology in Honor of Philip J. King.* Louisville, Ky.: Westminster John Knox Press, 1994.

Cook, Stephen L. *Prophecy and Apocalypticism: The Postexilic Social Setting.* Minneapolis: Fortress Press, 1995.

Cross, Frank M. *Canaanite Myth and Hebrew Epic: Essays in the History of the Religion of Israel.* Cambridge, Mass.: Harvard University Press, 1973.

_____. "The Epic Traditions of Early Israel: Epic Narrative and the Reconstruction of Early Israelite Institutions." Pages 13–39 in *The Poet and the Historian: Essays in Literary and Historical Biblical Criticism,* edited by Richard E. Friedman. Chico, Calif.: Scholars Press, 1983.

_____. *From Epic to Canon: History and Literature in Ancient Israel.* Baltimore: Johns Hopkins University Press, 1998.

_____. "Kinship and Covenant in Ancient Israel." Pages 3–21 in *From Epic to Canon: History and Literature in Ancient Israel.* Baltimore: Johns Hopkins University Press, 1998.

_____. "A Phoenician Inscription from Idalion: Some Old and New Texts Relating to Child Sacrifice." Pages 93–107 in *Scripture and Other Artifacts: Essays on the Bible and Archaeology in Honor of Philip J. King,* edited by Michael D. Coogan, J. Cheryl Exum, and Lawrence E. Stager. Louisville, Ky.: Westminster John Knox Press, 1994.

_____. "The Priestly Tabernacle in Light of Recent Research." Pages 169–80 in *Temples and High Places in Biblical Times: Proceedings of the Colloquium in Honor of the Centennial of the Hebrew Union College–Jewish Institute of Religion, Jerusalem, 14–16 March 1977,* edited by Avraham Biran. Jerusalem: Nelson Glueck School of Biblical Archaeology, 1981.

_____. "Reuben, First-Born of Jacob." *ZAW* 100 (1988): 46–65. Repr. pages 53–70 in *From Epic to Canon: History and Literature in Ancient Israel.* Baltimore: Johns Hopkins University Press, 1998.

Cross, Frank M., Werner E. Lemke, and Patrick D. Miller, eds. *Magnalia Dei, the Mighty Acts of God: Essays on the Bible and Archaeology in Memory of G. Ernest Wright.* Garden City, N.Y.: Doubleday, 1976.

Crüsemann, Frank. *The Torah: Theology and Social History of Old Testament Law.* Minneapolis: Fortress Press, 1996.

Cryer, Frederick H. *Divination in Ancient Israel and its Near Eastern Environment.* JSOTSup 142. Sheffield: JSOT Press, 1994.

Dalley, Stephanie. "Yahweh in Hamath in the 8th Century BC: Cuneiform Material and Historical Deductions." *VT* 40 (1990): 21–32.

Dam, Cornelis van. *The Urim and Thummim: A Means of Revelation in Ancient Israel.* Winona Lake, Ind.: Eisenbrauns, 1997.

Davies, Graham I. *Ancient Hebrew Inscriptions.* Cambridge: Cambridge University Press, 1991.

Day, John. "Asherah in the Hebrew Bible and Northwest Semitic Literature." *JBL* 105 (1986): 385–408.

_____. *King and Messiah in Israel and the Ancient Near East: Proceedings of the Oxford Old Testament Seminar.* JSOTSup 270. Sheffield: Sheffield Academic Press, 1998.

_____. *Molech: A God of Human Sacrifice in the Old Testament.* University of Cambridge Oriental Publications 41. Cambridge: Cambridge University Press, 1989.

Dearman, J. Andrew. "Baal in Israel: The Contribution of Some Place Names and Personal Names to an Understanding of Early Israelite Religion." Pages 173–91 in *History and Interpretation: Essays in Honour of John H. Hayes,* edited by Matt Graham, William P. Brown, and Jeffrey K. Kuan. JSOTSup 173. Sheffield: JSOT Press, 1993.

_____. *Religion and Culture in Ancient Israel.* Peabody, Mass.: Hendrickson Publishers, 1992.

_____. "The Tophet in Jerusalem: Archaeology and Cultural Profile." *JNSL* 22 (1996): 59–71.

Dentan, Robert C. "The Literary Affinities of Exodus XXXIV 6f." *VT* 13 (1963): 34–51.

Dever, William. "Asherah, Consort of Yahweh? New Evidence from Kuntillet 'Ajrud." *BASOR* 255 (1984): 21–37.

———. "The Contribution of Archaeology to the Study of Canaanite and Early Israelite Religion." Pages 209–47 in *Ancient Israelite Religion: Essays in Honor of Frank Moore Cross*, edited by Patrick D. Miller, Jr., Paul D. Hanson, and S. Dean McBride. Philadelphia: Fortress Press, 1987.

———. "Material Remains and the Cult in Ancient Israel: An Essay in Archaeological Systematics." Pages 571–87 in *The Word of the Lord Shall Go Forth: Essays in Honor of David Noel Freedman in Celebration of His Sixtieth Birthday*, edited by Carol L. Meyers and Michael O'Connor. Philadelphia: American Schools of Oriental Research, 1983.

———. "The Silence of the Text: An Archaeological Commentary on 2 Kings 23." Pages 143–68 in *Scripture and Other Artifacts: Essays on the Bible and Archaeology in Honor of Philip J. King*, edited by Michael D. Coogan, J. Cheryl Exum, and Lawrence E. Stager. Louisville, Ky.: Westminster John Knox Press, 1994.

Dick, Michael B. *Born in Heaven, Made on Earth: The Making of the Cult Image in the Ancient Near East*. Winona Lake, Ind.: Eisenbrauns, 1999.

Dietrich, Manfred, and Walter Dietrich. "Zwischen Gott und Volk: Einführung des Königtums und Auswahl des Königs nach mesopotamischer und israelitischer Anschauung." Pages 215–64 in *"Und Mose schrieb dieses Lied auf": Studien zum Alten Testament und zum Alten Orient: Festschrift für Oswald Loretz zur Vollendung seines 70. Lebensjahres mit Beiträgen von Freunden, Schülern und Kollegen*, edited by Manfred Dietrich and Ingo Kottsieper. AOAT 250. Münster: Ugarit-Verlag, 1998.

Dietrich, Manfred, and Ingo Kottsieper, eds. *"Und Mose schrieb dieses Lied auf": Studien zum Alten Testament und zum Alten Orient: Festschrift für Oswald Loretz zur Vollendung seines 70. Lebensjahres mit Beiträgen von Freunden, Schülern und Kollegen*. AOAT 250. Münster: Ugarit-Verlag, 1998.

Dietrich, Manfred, and Oswald Loretz. *"Jahwe und seine Aschera": Anthropomorphes Kultbild in Mesopotamien, Ugarit und Israel, Das biblische Bildverbot*. Ugaritische-biblische Literatur 9. Münster: Ugarit-Verlag, 1992.

Dietrich, Walter, and Martin A. Klopfenstein, eds. *Ein Gott allein? JHWH-Verehrung und biblischer Monotheismus im Kontext der israelitischen und altorientalischen Religionsgeschichte*. OBO 139. Freiburg: Universitätsverlag, 1994.

Dohmen, Christoph. *Das Bildverbot: Seine Entstehung und seine Entwicklung im Alten Testament*. BBB 62. Frankfurt: Peter Hanstein Verlag, 1985.

Douglas, Mary. *Implicit Meanings*. London: Routledge & Kegan Paul, 1975.

———. *Natural Symbols: Explorations in Cosmology*. New York: Penguin Books, 1973.

———. *Purity and Danger: An Analysis of the Concepts of Pollution and Taboo*. London: Routledge & Kegan Paul, 1969.

Dozeman, Thomas B. "Inner-Biblical Interpretation of Yahweh's Gracious and Compassionate Character." *JBL* 108 (1989): 207–23.

Eaton, John H. *Kingship and the Psalms*. 2d. ed. Sheffield: JSOT Press, 1986.

Eilberg-Schwartz, Howard. *The Savage in Judaism: An Anthropology of Israelite Religion and Ancient Judaism*. Bloomington, Ind.: Indiana University Press, 1990.

Eissfeldt, Otto. *Molk als Opferbegriff im Pünischen und Hebräischen und das Ende des Gott Moloch.* Beiträge zur Religionsgeschichte des Altertums 3. Halle: Max Niemeyer, 1935.

Emerton, John A. "The Biblical High Place in the Light of Recent Study," *PEQ* 129 (1997): 116–32.

_____. "New Light on Israelite Religion: The Implications of the Inscriptions from Kuntillet 'Ajrud." *ZAW* 94 (1982): 2–24.

_____. "'Yahweh and His Asherah': The Goddess or Her Symbol?" *VT* 49 (1999): 315–37.

Engle, James R. "Pillar Figurines of Iron Age Israel and Asherah/Asherim." Ph.D. diss., University of Pittsburgh, 1979.

Everson, Joseph A. "The Days of Yahweh." *JBL* 93 (1974): 329–37.

Fechter, Friedrich. *Die Familie in der Nachexilszeit: Untersuchungen zur Bedeutung der Verwandtschaft in ausgewählten Texten des Alten Testaments.* BZAW 264. Berlin: Walter de Gruyter, 1999.

Fenn, Richard. *The Secularization of Sin.* Louisville, Ky.: Westminster John Knox Press, 1991.

Fishbane, Michael L. *Biblical Interpretation in Ancient Israel.* Oxford: Clarendon Press, 1985.

_____. "Form and Reformulation of the Biblical Priestly Blessing." *JAOS* 103 (1983): 115–21.

_____. "From Scribalism to Rabbinism: Perspectives on the Emergence of Classical Judaism." Pages 439–56 in *The Sage in Israel and the Ancient Near East,* edited by John G. Gammie and Leo G. Perdue. Winona Lake, Ind.: Eisenbrauns, 1990.

_____. "Revelation and Tradition: Aspects of Inner-Biblical Exegesis." *JBL* 99 (1980): 343–61.

_____. "Torah and Tradition." Pages 275–300 in *Tradition and Theology in the Old Testament,* edited by Douglas A. Knight. Philadelphia: Fortress Press, 1977.

Fleming, Daniel. "The Biblical Tradition of Anointing Priests." *JBL* 117 (1998): 401–14.

_____. "The Etymological Origins of the Hebrew *nābî'*: The One Who Invokes God," *CBQ* 55 (1993): 217–24.

Fowler, Jeaneane D. *Theophoric Personal Names in Ancient Hebrew: A Comparative Study.* JSOTSup 49. Sheffield: JSOT Press, 1988.

Fowler, Mervyn D. "Concerning the 'Cultic' Structure at Taanach." *ZDPV* 100 (1984): 30–34.

Frankfort, Henri. *Kingship and the Gods: A Study of Ancient Near Eastern Religion as the Integration of Society and Nature.* Chicago: University of Chicago Press, 1948.

Freedman, David N. Review of Mark Smith, *The Early History of God. JBL* 110 (1991): 693–98.

_____. "'Who Is Like Thee among the Gods?' The Religion of Early Israel." Pages 314–35 in *Ancient Israelite Religion: Essays in Honor of Frank Moore Cross,* edited by Patrick D. Miller, Jr., Paul D. Hanson, and S. Dean McBride. Philadelphia: Fortress Press, 1987.

_____. "Yahweh of Samaria and His Asherah." *BA* 50 (1987): 241–49.

Frevel, Christian. *Aschera und der Ausschliesslichkeitsanspruch YHWHs: Beiträge zu literarischen, religionsgeschichtlichen und ikonographischen Aspekten der Ascheradiskussion.* 2 vols. BBB 94. Weinheim: Beltz Athenäum, 1995.

Frymer-Kensky, Tikva. "Pollution, Purification, and Purgation in Biblical Israel." Pages 399–414 in *The Word of the Lord Shall Go Forth: Essays in Honor of David Noel Freedman in Celebration of his Sixtieth Birthday*, edited by Carol L. Meyers and Michael O'Connor. Winona Lake, Ind.: Eisenbrauns, 1983.

Gammie, John G., and Leo G. Perdue, eds. *The Sage in Israel and the Ancient Near East*. Winona Lake, Ind.: Eisenbrauns, 1990.

Gerstenberger, Erhard. *Der bittende Mensch: Bittritual and Klagelied des Einzelnen im Alten Testament*. WMANT 51. Neukirchen-Vluyn: Neukirchener Verlag, 1980.

_____. *Leviticus: A Commentary*. OTL. Louisville, Ky.: Westminster John Knox Press, 1996.

Gitin, Seymour. "Cultic Inscriptions Found in Ekron." *BA* 53 (1990): 232.

_____. "Ekron of the Philistines, Part 2: Olive-Oil Suppliers to the World." *BARev* 16/2 (1990): 33–42, 59.

_____. "Incense Altars from Ekron, Israel and Judah: Context and Typology." *ErIsr* 20 (1989): 52*–67*.

_____. "Seventh Century B.C.E. Cultic Elements at Ekron." Pages 248–58 in *Biblical Archaeology Today, 1990: Proceedings of the Second International Congress on Biblical Archaeology, Jerusalem, June–July 1990*, edited by Avraham Biran. Jerusalem: Israel Exploration Society, 1993.

Gleis, Matthias. *Die Bamah*. BZAW 251. Berlin: Walter de Gruyter, 1997.

Gnuse, Robert. *No Other Gods: Emergent Monotheism in Israel*. JSOTSup 241. Sheffield: JSOT Press, 1997.

Goldstein, Bernard R., and Allan Cooper. "The Festivals of Israel and Judah and the Literary History of the Pentateuch." *JAOS* 110 (1990): 19–31.

Görg, Manfred. "Der Spiegeldienst der Frauen (Ex 38,8). *BN* 23 (1984): 9–13.

Gottwald, Norman K. *The Tribes of Yahweh*. Maryknoll, N.Y.: Orbis Books, 1979.

Grabbe, Lester L. *Priests, Prophets, Diviners, Sages: A Socio-Historical Study of Religious Specialists in Ancient Israel*. Valley Forge, Pa.: Trinity Press International, 1995.

Gray, George B. *Sacrifice in the Old Testament: Its Theory and Practice*. Library of Biblical Studies. New York: KTAV Publishing House, 1971.

Greenberg, Moshe. *Biblical Prose Prayer as a Window to the Popular Religion of Ancient Israel*. Taubman Lectures in Jewish Studies 6. Berkeley: University of California Press, 1983.

_____. *Ezekiel 1–37: A New Translation with Introduction and Commentary*. AB 22–22A. Garden City, N.Y.: Doubleday, 1983.

Greenfield, Jonas C. "The *marzēaḥ* as a Social Institution." *Acta Antiqua* 22 (1974): 451–55.

Gruber, Mayer I. "Women in the Cult according to the Priestly Code." Pages 35–48 in *Judaic Perspectives on Ancient Israel*, edited by Jacob Neusner, Baruch A. Levine, and Ernest S. Frerichs. Philadelphia: Fortress Press, 1987).

Hadley, Judith M. "Chasing Shadows? The Quest for the Historical Goddess." Pages 169–84 in *Congress Volume, Cambridge 1995*, edited by John A. Emerton. VTSup 66. Leiden: E. J. Brill, 1997).

_____. "The De-deification of Deities in Deuteronomy." Paper presented at the Congress meeting of the International Organization for the Study of the Old Testament, Oslo, Norway, August 1998.

_____. "The Fertility of the Flock? The De-Personalization of Astarte in the Old Testament." Pages 114–33 in *On Reading Prophetic Texts: Gender-Specific and Related Studies in Memory of Fokkelien van Dijk-Hemmes,* edited by Bob Becking and Meindert Dijkstra. BibInt 18. Leiden: E. J. Brill, 1996).

_____. "Yahweh and 'His Asherah': Archaeological and Textual Evidence for the Cult of the Goddess." Pages 235–68 in *Ein Gott allein? JHWH-Verehrung und biblischer Monotheismus im Kontext der israelitischen und altorientalischen Religionsgeschichte,* edited by Walter Dietrich and Martin A. Klopfenstein. OBO 139. Freiburg: Universitätsverlag, 1994.

_____. "Yahweh's Asherah in the Light of Recent Discovery." Ph.D. diss., University of Cambridge, 1989.

Hallo, William W. "The Origins of the Sacrificial Cult: New Evidence from Mesopotamia and Israel." Pages 3–13 in *Ancient Israelite Religion: Essays in Honor of Frank Moore Cross,* edited by Patrick D. Miller, Jr., Paul D. Hanson, and S. Dean McBride. Philadelphia: Fortress Press, 1987.

_____. "Texts, Statues, and the Cult of the Divine King." Pages 54–66 in *Congress Volume, Jerusalem 1986,* edited by John A. Emerton. VTSup 40. Leiden: E. J. Brill, 1988.

Halpern, Baruch. "The Baal (and the Asherah) in Seventh-Century Judah: YHWH's Retainers Retired." Pages 115–54 in *Konsequente Traditionsgeschichte: Festschrift für Klaus Baltzer zum 65. Geburtstag,* edited by Rüdiger Bartelmus, Thomas Krüger, and Helmut Utzschneider. OBO 126. Freiburg: Universitätsverlag, 1993.

Handy, Lowell K. *Among the Host of Heaven: The Syro-Palestinian Pantheon as Bureaucracy.* Winona Lake, Ind.: Eisenbrauns, 1994.

Hanson, Paul D. *The Dawn of Apocalyptic: The Historical and Sociological Roots of Jewish Apocalyptic Eschatology.* 2d ed. Philadelphia: Fortress Press, 1979.

_____. "Israelite Religion in the Early Postexilic Period." Pages 485–508 in *Ancient Israelite Religion: Essays in Honor of Frank Moore Cross,* edited by Patrick D. Miller, Jr., Paul D. Hanson, and S. Dean McBride. Philadelphia: Fortress Press, 1987.

_____. *The People Called: The Growth of Community in the Bible.* San Francisco: Harper & Row, 1986.

_____. "The Song of Heshbon and David's *Nîr.*" *HTR* 61 (1968): 297–320.

Haran, Manahem. "*zebaḥ hayyamîm.*" *VT* 19 (1969): 11–22.

Hayes, Christine. "Intermarriage and Impurity in Ancient Jewish Sources." *HTR* 92 (1999): 3–36.

Heider, George C. *The Cult of Molek: A Reassessment.* JSOTSup 43. Sheffield: JSOT Press, 1985.

Hendel, Ronald S. "Aniconism and Anthropomorphism in Ancient Israel." Pages 205–28 in *The Image and the Book: Iconic Cults, Aniconism, and the Rise of Book Religion in Israel and the Ancient Near East,* edited by Karel van der Toorn. Louvain: Peeters, 1997.

_____. "Sacrifice as a Cultural System: The Ritual Symbolism of Exodus 24, 3–8." *ZAW* 101 (1989): 366–90.

_____. "The Social Origins of the Aniconic Tradition in Early Israel." *CBQ* 50 (1988): 365–82.

Henshaw, Richard A. *Female and Male: The Cultic Personnel: The Bible and the Rest of the Ancient Near East.* Princeton Theological Monograph Series 31. Allison Park, Pa.: Pickwick Publications, 1994.

Hess, Richard. "Yahweh and His Asherah? Epigraphic Evidence for Religious Pluralism in Old Testament Times." Pages 13–42 in *One God, One Lord: Christianity in a World of Religious Pluralism,* edited by Andrew D. Clarke and Bruce W. Winter. Grand Rapids: Baker Book House, 1992.

Hestrin, Ruth. "Understanding Asherah: Exploring Semitic Iconography." *BARev* 17 (Sept./Oct. 1991): 50–59.

Hillers, Delbert. *Covenant: The History of an Idea.* Baltimore: Johns Hopkins University Press, 1969.

———. *Treaty Curses and the Old Testament Prophets.* BibOr 16. Rome: Pontifical Biblical Institute Press, 1964.

Holladay, John S. "Assyrian Statecraft and the Prophets of Israel." *HTR* 63 (1970): 29–51. Repr. pages 122–43 in *Prophecy in Israel,* edited by David L. Petersen. IRT 10. Philadelphia: Fortress Press, 1987.

———. "Religion in Israel and Judah under the Monarchy." Pages 249–99 in *Ancient Israelite Religion: Essays in Honor of Frank Moore Cross,* edited by Patrick D. Miller, Jr., Paul D. Hanson, and S. Dean McBride. Philadelphia: Fortress Press, 1987.

Holland, Thomas A. "A Study of Palestinian Iron Age Baked Clay Figurines, with Special Reference to Jerusalem: Cave 1." *Levant* 9 (1977): 121–55.

Houston, Walter. *Purity and Monotheism: Clean and Unclean Animals in Biblical Law.* JSOTSup 140. Sheffield: JSOT Press, 1993.

Houten, Christiana van. *The Alien in Israelite Law.* JSOTSup 107. Sheffield: JSOT Press, 1991.

Huffmon, Herbert. "The Origins of Prophecy." Pages 171–86 in *Magnalia Dei, the Mighty Acts of God: Essays on the Bible and Archaeology in Memory of G. Ernest Wright,* edited by Frank M. Cross, Werner E. Lemke, and Patrick D. Miller, Jr. Garden City, N.Y.: Doubleday, 1976.

———. "Priestly Divination in Israel." Pages 355–59 in *The Word of the Lord Shall Go Forth: Essays in Honor of David Noel Freedman in Celebration of his Sixtieth Birthday,* edited by Carol L. Meyers and Michael O'Connor. Winona Lake, Ind.: Eisenbrauns, 1983.

———. "Prophecy (ANE)." *The Anchor Bible Dictionary,* edited by David N. Freedman, 5:477–82. New York: Doubleday, 1992.

Hutton, Rodney. *Charisma and Authority in Israelite Society.* Minneapolis: Fortress Press, 1994.

Jacobsen, Thorkild. "The Graven Image" Pages 15–32 in *Ancient Israelite Religion: Essays in Honor of Frank Moore Cross,* edited by Patrick D. Miller, Jr., Paul D. Hanson, and S. Dean McBride. Philadelphia: Fortress Press, 1987.

———. *The Harab Myth.* Sources from the Ancient Near East 2/3. Malibu: Undena Publications, 1984.

———. *Toward the Image of Tammuz,* edited by William L. Moran. Cambridge, Mass.: Harvard University Press, 1970.

———. *The Treasures of Darkness: A History of Mesopotamian Religion.* New Haven, Conn.: Yale University Press, 1976.

Jahrbuch für Biblische Theologie 10 (1995). "Religionsgeschichte Israels oder Theologie des Alten Testaments?"

Jahrbuch für Biblische Theologie 13 (1998). "Die Macht der Bilder."

Janowski, Bernd. "Azazel." Pages 128–31 in *Dictionary of Deities and Demons in the Bible*, 2d rev. ed., edited by Karel van der Toorn, Bob Becking, and Pieter Willem van der Horst. Leiden: E. J. Brill, 1999.

———. "Azazel und der Sündenbock: Zur Religionsgeschichte von Leviticus 16, 10.21f." Pages 303–26 in *Gottes Gegenwart in Israel: Beiträge zur Theologie des Alten Testaments* (Neukirchen-Vluyn: Neukirchener Verlag, 1993).

Jaroš, Karl. "Die Motive der heiligen Bäume und der Schlange in Gen 2–3." *ZAW* 92 (1970): 204–15.

Jay, Nancy. *Throughout Your Generations Forever: Sacrifice, Religion and Paternity.* Chicago: University of Chicago Press, 1992.

Jenson, Philip Peter. *Graded Holiness.* JSOTSup 106. Sheffield: JSOT Press, 1992.

Jirku, Anton. *Die Dämonen und ihre Abwehr im Alten Testament.* Leipzig: A. Deichert, 1912.

Johnson, Aubrey R. *The Cultic Prophet in Ancient Israel.* 2d ed. Cardiff: University of Wales Press, 1962.

Joyce, Paul. "King and Messiah in Ezekiel." Pages 322–37 in *King and Messiah in Israel and the Ancient Near East: Proceedings of the Oxford Old Testament Seminar*, edited by John Day. JSOTSup 270. Sheffield: Sheffield Academic Press, 1998.

Kang, Sa-Moon. *Divine War in the Old Testament and the Ancient Near East.* BZAW 177. Berlin: Walter de Gruyter, 1989.

Keel, Othmar. *Goddesses and Trees, New Moon and Yahweh: Ancient Near Eastern Art and the Hebrew Bible.* JSOTSup 261. Sheffield: Sheffield Academic Press, 1998.

———. *Monotheismus im alten Israel und seiner Umwelt.* Fribourg: Verlag Schweizerisches Katholisches Bibelwerk, 1980.

Keel, Othmar, and Christoph Uehlinger. *Gods, Goddesses, and Images of God in Ancient Israel.* Minneapolis: Fortress Press, 1998.

King, Philip J. "The *Marzeaḥ*: Textual and Archaeological Evidence," *ErIsr* 20 (1998): 98*–106*.

Kitz, Anne Marie. "The Plural Form of *'ûrîm* and *tummîm*." *JBL* 116 (1997): 401–10.

Klein, Ralph. *1 Samuel.* WBC 10. Waco: Word Books, 1983.

Kletter, Raz. *The Judean Pillar-Figurines and the Archaeology of Asherah.* Oxford: Tempus Reparatum, 1996.

Knight, Douglas A., and Gene M. Tucker. *Hebrew Bible and Its Modern Interpreters.* Philadelphia: Fortress Press; Atlanta: Scholars Press, 1985.

Knohl, Israel. *The Sanctuary of Silence: The Priestly Torah and the Holiness School.* Minneapolis: Fortress Press, 1995.

Koch, Klaus. "Aschera als Himmelskönigin in Jerusalem." *UF* 20 (1988): 97–120.

———. "Molek astral." Pages 29–50 in *Mythos im Alten Testament und seiner Umwelt: Festschrift für Hans-Peter Müller zum 65. Geburtstag*, edited by Armin Lange, Hermann Lichtenberger, and Diethard Römheld. BZAW 278. Berlin: Walter de Gruyter, 1999.

Korpel, Marjo C. A. "The Poetic Structure of the Priestly Blessing." *JSOT* 45 (1989): 3–13.

———. *A Rift in the Clouds: Ugaritic and Hebrew Descriptions of the Divine.* Münster: Ugarit-Verlag, 1990.

Kottsieper, Ingo. "Papyrus Amherst 63: Einführung, Text und Übersetzung vom 12,11–12." Pages 55–75 in *Die Königpsalmen* 1, edited by Otto Loretz. Münster: Ugarit-Verlag, 1988.

Kraeling, Emil G. *The Brooklyn Museum Aramaic Papyri: New Documents of the Fifth Century B.C. from the Jewish Colony at Elephantine.* New Haven, Conn.: Yale University Press, 1953.

Kraus, Hans-J. *Worship in Israel: A Cultic History of the Old Testament.* Richmond, Va.: John Knox Press, 1966.

Kselman, John. "The Social World of the Israelite Prophets." *RelSRev* 11 (1985): 120–29.

Lambert, W. G. "The Historical Development of the Mesopotamian Pantheon: A Study in Sophisticated Polytheism." Pages 191–200 in *Unity and Diversity: Essays in the History, Literature, and Religion of the Ancient Near East,* edited by Hans Goedicke and J. J. M. Roberts. Baltimore: Johns Hopkins University Press, 1975.

Lang, Bernhard. *Monotheism and the Prophetic Minority.* Sheffield: JSOT Press, 1983.

Lapp, Paul W. "The 1963 Excavations at Ta'anek." *BASOR* 173 (1964): 4–44.

Leeuw, Gerhardus van der. *Religion in Essence and Manifestation: A Study in Phenomenology.* 2 vols. New York: Harper & Row, 1963.

Lemaire, André. "Déesses et dieux de Syrie-Palestine d'après les inscriptions (c. 1000–500 av. n. é.)." Pages 127–58 in *Ein Gott allein? JHWH-Verehrung und biblischer Monotheismus im Kontext der israelitischen und altorientalischen Religionsgeschichte,* edited by Walter Dietrich and Martin A. Klopfenstein. OBO 139. Freiburg: Universitätsverlag, 1994.

————. "Les inscriptions de Khirbet el-Qom et l'asherah de YHWH." *RB* 84 (1977): 595–608.

————. "Who or What Was Yahweh's Asherah?" *BARev* 10/6 (1984): 42–51.

Levine, Baruch A. "The Descriptive Tabernacle Texts of the Pentateuch." *JAOS* 85 (1965): 307–18.

————. *In the Presence of the Lord.* SJLA 5. Leiden: E. J. Brill, 1974.

————. "The Language of Holiness: Perceptions of the Sacred in the Hebrew Bible." Pages 241–55 in *Backgrounds for the Bible,* edited by Michael P. O'Connor and David N. Freedman. Winona Lake, Ind.: Eisenbrauns, 1987.

————. *Leviticus: The Traditional Hebrew Text with the New JPS Translation.* JPS Torah Commentary. Philadelphia: Jewish Publication Society, 1989.

————. *Numbers 1–20.* AB 4. New York: Doubleday, 1993.

————. "Ugaritic Descriptive Rituals." *JCS* 17 (1963): 105–11.

Levine, Lee I. "The Nature and Origin of the Palestinian Synagogue Reconsidered." *JBL* 115 (1996): 425–48.

Lewis, Theodore J. *Cults of the Dead in Ancient Israel and Judah.* HSM 39. Atlanta: Scholars Press, 1989.

————. "Divine Images and Aniconism in Ancient Israel." *JAOS* 118 (1998): 36–53.

Liebreich, Leon J. "Psalms 34 and 145 in the Light of Their Key Words." *HUCA* 27 (1956): 181–92.

————. "The Songs of Ascents and the Priestly Blessing." *JBL* 74 (1955): 33–36.

Lohfink, Norbert. "'Die, deren Schilde Schande sind' (Hos 4,18). Hat Jahwe im Hoseabuch eine göttliche Gegenspielerin?" Unpublished paper.

_____. "Opfer und Säkularisierung im Deuteronomium." Pages 15–43 in *Studien zu Opfer und Kult im Alten Testament*, edited by Adrian Schenker. Tübingen: J. C. B. Mohr, 1992.

Long, Burke O. "The Effect of Divination on Israelite Literature." *JBL* 92 (1973): 489–97.

_____. "Prophetic Authority and Social Reality." Pages 3–20 in *Canon and Authority: Essays in Old Testament Religion and Theology*, edited by George W. Coats and Burke O. Long. Philadelphia: Fortress Press, 1977.

_____. "Social Dimensions of Prophetic Conflict." *Semeia* 21 (1981): 30–53.

Lowery, Robert H. *The Reforming Kings: Cults and Society in First Temple Judah*. JSOTSup 120. Sheffield: JSOT Press, 1991.

Lust, Johan. "On Wizards and Prophecy." Pages 133–42 in *Studies on Prophecy*. VTSup 26. Leiden: E. J. Brill, 1974.

Maier, Walter A. *AŠERAH: Extrabiblical Evidence*. HSM 37. Atlanta: Scholars Press, 1986.

Malamat, Abraham. "A Forerunner of Biblical Prophecy: The Mari Documents." Pages 33–52 in *Ancient Israelite Religion: Essays in Honor of Frank Moore Cross*, edited by Patrick D. Miller, Jr., Paul D. Hanson, and S. Dean McBride. Philadelphia: Fortress Press, 1987.

Mann, Michael. *The Social Sources of Power*, vol 1: *A History of Power from the Beginning to A.D. 1760*. Cambridge: Cambridge University Press, 1986.

Mason, Rex. "The Messiah in the Postexilic Old Testament Literature." Pages 338–64 in *King and Messiah in Israel and the Ancient Near East: Proceedings of the Oxford Old Testament Seminar*, edited by John Day. JSOTSup 270. Sheffield: Sheffield Academic Press, 1998.

Mayes, A. D. H. *Deuteronomy: Based on the Revised Standard Version*. NCB. Grand Rapids: Wm. B. Eerdmans Publishing Co., 1981.

Mazar, Benjamin. "The Early Israelite Settlement in the Hill Country." Pages 35–48 in *The Early Biblical Period: Historical Studies*, edited by Shmuel Ahituv and Baruch A. Levine. Jerusalem: Israel Exploration Society, 1986. First appeared in *BASOR* 241 (1981): 75–85.

McCarter, P. Kyle. *I Samuel: A New Translation with Introduction, Notes, and Commentary*. AB 8. Garden City, N.Y.: Doubleday, 1980.

_____. *II Samuel: A New Translation with Introduction, Notes and Commentary*. AB 9. Garden City, N.Y.: Doubleday, 1984.

_____. "Aspects of the Religion of the Israelite Monarchy: Biblical and Epigraphic Data." Pages 137–55 in *Ancient Israelite Religion: Essays in Honor of Frank Moore Cross*, edited by Patrick D. Miller, Jr., Paul D. Hanson, and S. Dean McBride. Philadelphia: Fortress Press, 1987.

_____. "The Origins of Israelite Religion." Pages 118–41 in *The Rise of Ancient Israel*, edited by Hershel Shanks. Washington, D.C.: Biblical Archaeology Society, 1992.

_____. "The Religious Reforms of Hezekiah and Josiah." Pages 57–80 in *Aspects of Monotheism: How God Is One; Symposium at the Smithsonian Institution, October 19, 1996, Sponsored by the Resident Associate Program*, edited by Hershel Shanks and Jack Meinhardt. Washington, D.C.: Biblical Archaeology Society, 1997.

McCarthy, Dennis J. *Old Testament Covenant: A Survey of Current Opinions.* Richmond: John Knox Press, 1972.

———. *Treaty and Covenant: A Study in Form in the Ancient Oriental Documents and in the Old Testament.* 2d ed. AnBib 21A. Rome: Pontifical Biblical Institute Press, 1978.

Mendenhall, George. *Law and Covenant in the Old Testament.* Pittsburgh: Biblical Colloquium, 1955.

———. "Social Organization in Early Israel." Pages 132–51 in *Magnalia Dei, the Mighty Acts of God: Essays on the Bible and Archaeology in Memory of G. Ernest Wright,* edited by Frank M. Cross, Werner E. Lemke, and Patrick D. Miller, Jr. Garden City, N.Y.: Doubleday, 1976.

Mettinger, Tryggve. "Aniconism—A West Semitic Context for the Israelite Phenomenon?" Pages 159–78 in *Ein Gott allein? JHWH-Verehrung und biblischer Monotheismus im Kontext der israelitischen und altorientalischen Religionsgeschichte,* edited by Walter Dietrich and Martin A. Klopfenstein. OBO 139. Freiburg: Universitätsverlag, 1994.

———. *In Search of God: The Meaning and Message of the Everlasting Names.* Philadelphia: Fortress Press, 1988.

———. "Israelite Aniconism: Developments and Origins." Pages 173–204 in *The Image and the Book: Iconic Cults, Aniconism, and the Rise of Book Religion in Israel and the Ancient Near East,* edited by Karel van der Toorn. Louvain: Peeters, 1997.

———. *No Graven Image? Israelite Aniconism in Its Ancient Near Eastern Context.* ConBOT 42. Stockholm: Almqvist & Wiksell, 1995.

———. "The Study of the Gottesbild—Problems and Suggestions." *SEÅ* 54 (1988): 135–45.

———. "The Veto on Images and the Aniconic God in Ancient Israel." Pages 15–29 in *Religious Symbols and Their Functions,* edited by Harald Biezais. Stockholm: Almqvist & Wiksell, 1979.

Meyers, Carol. "David as Temple Builder." Pages 357–76 in *Ancient Israelite Religion: Essays in Honor of Frank Moore Cross,* edited by Patrick D. Miller, Jr., Paul D. Hanson, and S. Dean McBride. Philadelphia: Fortress Press, 1987.

———. "Ephod." *The Anchor Bible Dictionary,* edited by David N. Freedman, 2:550. New York: Doubleday, 1992.

Meyers, Carol L., and Michael O'Connor, eds. *The Word of the Lord Shall Go Forth: Essays in Honor of David Noel Freedman in Celebration of His Sixtieth Birthday.* Philadelphia: American Schools of Oriental Research, 1983.

Milgrom, Jacob. "The Alleged 'Demythologization and Secularization' in Deuteronomy (Review Article)." *IEJ* 23 (1973): 156–61.

———. "The Antiquity of the Priestly Source: A Reply to Joseph Blenkinsopp." *ZAW* 111 (1999): 10–22.

———. *Cult and Conscience: The ASHAM and the Priestly Doctrine of Repentance.* Leiden: E. J. Brill, 1976.

———. *Leviticus 1–16: A New Translation with Introduction and Commentary.* AB 3. New York: Doubleday, 1991.

———. "The Changing Concept of Holiness in the Pentateuchal Codes, with Emphasis on Leviticus 19." Pages 65–75 in *Reading Leviticus: A Conversation with Mary Douglas*, edited by John Sawyer. JSOTSup 227. Sheffield: JSOT Press, 1996.

_____. *Numbers: The Traditional Hebrew Text with the New JPS Translation*. JPS Torah Commentary. Philadelphia: Jewish Publication Society, 1990.

_____. "Rationale for Cultic Law: The Case of Impurity." *Semeia* 45 (1989): 103–9.

_____. "Sacrifices and Offerings, OT." Pages 763–71 in *The Interpreter's Dictionary of the Bible, Supplementary Volume*. Nashville: Abingdon Press, 1976.

Miller, Patrick D. "The Absence of the Goddess in Israelite Religion." *HAR* 10 (1986): 239–48.

_____. "Apotropaic Imagery in Proverbs 6:20–22." *JNES* 29 (1970): 129–30.

_____. "Aspects of the Religion of Ugarit." Pages 53–66 in *Ancient Israelite Religion: Essays in Honor of Frank Moore Cross*, edited by Patrick D. Miller, Jr., Paul D. Hanson, and S. Dean McBride. Philadelphia: Fortress Press, 1987.

_____. "The Beginning of the Psalter." Pages 83–92 in *The Shape and Shaping of the Psalter*, edited by J. Clinton McCann. JSOTSup 159. Sheffield: JSOT Press, 1993.

_____. "Cosmology and World Order in the Old Testament: The Divine Council as Cosmic-Political Symbol." *HBT* 9 (1987): 53–78.

_____. *Deuteronomy*. IBC. Louisville, Ky.: John Knox Press, 1990.

_____. "Deuteronomy and Psalms: Evoking a Biblical Conversation." *JBL* 118 (1999): 3–18.

_____. "The Divine Council and the Prophetic Call to War." *VT* 18 (1968): 100–107.

_____. *The Divine Warrior in Early Israel*. Cambridge, Mass.: Harvard University Press, 1973.

_____. "El, Creator of Earth." *BASOR* 239 (1980): 43–46.

_____. "El the Warrior" *HTR* 60 (1967): 411–31.

_____. "Eridu, Dunnu, and Babel: A Study in Comparative Mythology." *HAR* 9 (1985): 227–51. Repr. pages 143–68 in *I Studied Inscriptions from Before the Flood: Ancient Near Eastern, Literary, and Linguistic Approaches to Genesis 1–11*, edited by Richard A. Hess and David Tsumura. Sources for Biblical and Theological Study 4. Winona Lake, Ind.: Eisenbrauns, 1994.

_____. "Faith and Ideology in the Old Testament." Pages 464–79 in *Magnalia Dei, the Mighty Acts of God: Essays on the Bible and Archaeology in Memory of G. Ernest Wright*, edited by Frank M. Cross, Werner E. Lemke, and Patrick D. Miller, Jr. Garden City, N.Y.: Doubleday, 1976.

_____. "God and the Gods: History of Religion as an Approach and Context for Bible and Theology." *Affirmation* 1/5 (Sept. 1973): 37–62.

_____. *Interpreting the Psalms*. Philadelphia: Fortress Press, 1986.

_____. "Israelite Religion." Pages 201–37 in *The Hebrew Bible and Its Modern Interpreters*, edited by Douglas A. Knight and Gene M. Tucker. Philadelphia: Fortress Press; Atlanta: Scholars Press, 1985.

_____. "The *Mrzḥ* Text." Pages 37–49 in *The Claremont Ras Shamra Tablets*. AnOr 48. Rome: Pontifical Biblical Institute, 1971.

_____. "The Prophetic Critique of Kings." *Ex Auditu* 2 (1986): 82–95.

_____. "Psalms and Inscriptions." Pages 311–32 in *Congress Volume, Vienna 1980*, edited by John A. Emerton. VTSup 32. Leiden: E. J. Brill, 1981.

_____. "The Sovereignty of God." Pages 129–44 in *The Hermeneutical Quest:*

Essays in Honor of James Luther Mays on His Sixty-fifth Birthday, edited by Donald G. Miller. Allison Park, Pa.: Pickwick Publications, 1986.

_____. *They Cried to the Lord: The Form and Theology of Biblical Prayer.* Minneapolis: Fortress Press, 1994.

_____. "'Things Too Wonderful': Prayers of Women in the Old Testament." Pages 237–51 in *Biblische Theologie und Gesellschaftlicher Wandel: Für Norbert Lohfink, S.J.,* edited by Georg Braulik O.S.B., Walter Gross, and Sean McEvenue. Freiburg: Herder, 1993. Repr. in revised form as chapter 6 of Patrick D. Miller, *They Cried to the Lord: The Form and Theology of Biblical Prayer.* Minneapolis: Fortress Press, 1994.

_____. "Two Critical Notes on Psalm 68 and Deuteronomy 33." *HTR* 57 (1964): 240–43.

_____. "The World and Message of the Prophets." Pages 97–112 in *Old Testament Interpretation: Past, Present, and Future: Essays in Honor of Gene M. Tucker,* edited by James L. Mays, David L. Petersen, and Kent H. Richards. Nashville: Abingdon Press, 1995.

Miller, Patrick D., Jr., Paul D. Hanson, and S. Dean McBride, eds. *Ancient Israelite Religion: Essays in Honor of Frank Moore Cross.* Philadelphia: Fortress Press, 1987.

Miller, Patrick D., Jr., and J. J. M. Roberts. *The Hand of the Lord: A Reassessment of the "Ark Narrative" of 1 Samuel.* Baltimore: Johns Hopkins University Press, 1977.

Moor, Johannes C. de. *The Rise of Yahwism: The Roots of Israelite Monotheism.* Louvain: Leuven University Press, 1990.

Moran, William L. "The Ancient Near Eastern Background of the Love of God in Deuteronomy." *CBQ* 25 (1963): 77–87.

Mosca, Paul. "Child Sacrifice in Canaanite and Israelite Religion: A Study in *Mulk* and *mlk.*" Ph.D. diss., Harvard University, 1975.

Mowinckel, Sigmund. *The Psalms in Israel's Worship.* Oxford: Basil Blackwell Publisher, 1962.

Moxnes, Halvor. "Meals and the New Community in Luke." *SEÅ* 51–52 (1986): 158–67.

Mullen, E. Theodore. *The Assembly of the Gods: The Divine Council in Canaanite and Early Hebrew Literature.* HSM 24. Cambridge, Mass.: Harvard University Press, 1980.

Müller, Hans-P. "קדשׁ *qdš* holy." *Theological Lexicon of the Old Testament,* edited by Ernst Jenni and Claus Westermann, 3:1003–18. Peabody, Mass.: Hendrickson Publishers, 1997.

Murray, Robert. "Prophecy and the Cult." Pages 200–216 in *Israel's Prophetic Tradition: Essays in Honour of Peter R. Ackroyd,* edited by Richard Coggins, Anthony Phillips, and Michael Knibb. Cambridge: Cambridge University Press, 1982.

Na'aman, Nadav. "Beth-aven, Bethel and Early Israelite Sanctuaries." *ZDPV* 103 (1987): 13–21.

Nakhai, Beth Alpert. "What's a Bamah? How Sacred Space Functioned in Ancient Israel." *BARev* 20/3 (May/June 1994): 18–29, 77–78.

Negbi, Ora. *Canaanite Gods in Metal.* Tel Aviv: Tel Aviv University, 1976.

Nelson, Richard D. *Raising Up a Faithful Priest: Community and Priesthood in Biblical Theology.* Louisville, Ky.: Westminster John Knox Press, 1993.

Nicholson, Ernest W. *God and His People.* Oxford: Clarendon Press, 1986.

Niditch, Susan. *Ancient Israelite Religion*. New York: Oxford University Press, 1997.

Niehr, Herbert. "In Search of Yahweh's Cult Statue in the First Temple." Pages 73–95 in *The Image and the Book: Iconic Cults, Aniconism, and the Rise of Book Religion in Israel and the Ancient Near East*, edited by Karel van der Toorn. Louvain: Peeters, 1997.

Norin, Stig. "Onomastik zwischen Linguistik und Geschichte." Paper presented at the Congress of the International Organization for the Study of the Old Testament, Oslo, Norway, August 1998. Forthcoming in the proceedings of the Congress in a volume of VTSup.

Noth, Martin. "Office and Vocation in the Old Testament." In *The Laws of the Pentateuch and Other Essays*. Philadelphia: Fortress Press, 1967.

Oden, Robert A. *The Bible without Theology: The Theological Tradition and Alternatives to It*. San Francisco: Harper & Row, 1987.

Olyan, Saul. *Asherah and the Cult of Yahweh in Israel*. SBLMS 34. Atlanta: Scholars Press, 1988.

_____. "Some Observations Concerning the Identity of the Queen of Heaven." *UF* 19 (1987): 161–74.

Oppenheim, A. Leo. *The Interpretation of Dreams in the Ancient Near East, with a Translation of an Assyrian Dream-book*. Transactions of the American Philosophical Society 46. Philadelphia: American Philosophical Society, 1956.

Ornan, Tallay. "The Mesopotamian Influence on West Semitic Inscribed Seals: A Preference for the Depiction of Mortals." Pages 52–73 in *Studies in the Iconography of Northwest Semitic Inscribed Seals*. OBO 125. Fribourg: Universitätverlag, 1993.

Östborn, Gunnar. *Tōrā in the Old Testament: A Semantic Study*. Lund: Håkan Ohlssons Boktryckeri, 1945.

Overholt, Thomas W. *Prophecy in Cross-Cultural Perspective: A Sourcebook for Biblical Researchers*. SBLSBS 17. Atlanta: Scholars Press, 1986.

Park, George. "Divination and Its Social Contexts." Pages 233–54 in *Magic, Witchcraft, and Curing*, edited by John Middleton. American Museum Sourcebooks in Anthropology. Garden City, N.Y.: Natural History Press, 1967.

Perdue, Leo G., et al. *Families in Ancient Israel*. Family, Religion, and Culture. Louisville, Ky.: Westminster John Knox Press, 1997.

Peritz, Ismar. "Women in the Ancient Hebrew Cult." *JBL* 17 (1898): 111–48.

Perlitt, Lothar. *Bundestheologie im Alten Testament*. WMANT 36. Neukirchen-Vluyn: Neukirchener Verlag, 1969.

_____. "'Ein einzig Volk von Brüdern': Zur deuteronomischen Herkunft der biblischen Bezeichnung 'Bruder.'" Pages 50–73 in *Deuteronomium-Studien*. Forschungen zum Alten Testament 9. Tübingen: J. C. B. Mohr, 1994.

Plöger, Otto. *Theocracy and Eschatology*. Richmond: John Knox Press, 1968.

Polk, Timothy. "The Levites in the Davidic-Solomonic Empire." *Studia Biblica et Theologia* 9 (1979): 3–22.

Pope, Marvin. *Song of Songs*. AB 7C. Garden City, N.Y.; Doubleday, 1977.

Porten, Bezalel. *Archives from Elephantine: The Life of an Ancient Jewish Military Colony*. Berkeley, Calif.: University of California Press, 1968.

Pressler, Carolyn. *The View of Women Found in the Deuteronomic Family Laws*. BZAW 216. Berlin: Walter de Gruyter, 1993.

Pritchard, James B. *Ancient Near Eastern Texts Relating to the Old Testament.* 3d ed. Princeton, N.J.: Princeton University Press, 1969.

_____. *Palestinian Figurines in Relation to Certain Goddesses Known through Literature.* AOS 24. New Haven, Conn.: American Oriental Society, 1943.

Rad, Gerhard von. *Holy War in Ancient Israel.* Grand Rapids: Wm. B. Eerdmans Publishing Co., 1991.

_____. "The Origin of the Concept of the Day of the Lord." *JSS* 4 (1959): 97–108.

Rainey, Anson F. "Hezekiah's Reform and the Altars at Beer-sheba and Arad." Pages 333–54 in *Scripture and Other Artifacts: Essays on the Bible and Archaeology in Honor of Philip J. King,* edited by Michael D. Coogan, J. Cheryl Exum, and Lawrence E. Stager. Louisville, Ky.: Westminster John Knox Press, 1994.

_____. "The Order of Sacrifices in Old Testament Ritual Texts." *Bib* 51 (1970): 485–98.

_____. "The Toponyms of Eretz-Israel." *BASOR* 231 (1978): 1–17.

Raitt, Thomas. *A Theology of Exile: Judgment and Deliverance in Jeremiah and Ezekiel.* Philadelphia: Fortress Press, 1977.

Ramirez Kidd, José E. *Alterity and Identity: The* ger *in the Old Testament.* BZAW 283. Berlin: Walter de Gruyter, 1999.

Rast, Walter. "Priestly Families and the Cultic Structure at Taanach." Pages 355–65 in *Scripture and Other Artifacts: Essays on the Bible and Archaeology in Honor of Philip J. King,* edited by Michael D. Coogan, J. Cheryl Exum, and Lawrence E. Stager. Louisville, Ky.: Westminster John Knox Press, 1994.

Reed, William L. *The Asherah in the Old Testament.* Fort Worth, Tex.: Texas Christian University Press, 1949.

Rendtorff, Rolf. *The Covenant Formula: An Exegetical and Theological Investigation.* Old Testament Studies. Edinburgh: T. & T. Clark, 1998.

_____. *Studien zur Geschichte des Opfers im Alten Israel.* WMANT 24. Neukirchen-Vluyn: Neukirchener Verlag, 1967.

Reuter, Eleonore. *Kultzentralisation: Entstehung und Theologie von Dtn 12.* BBB 87. Frankfurt: Anton Hain, 1993.

Riesner, Rainer. "Der Priestersegen aus dem Hinnom-Tal." *TBei* 18 (1987): 104–8.

Roberts, J. J. M. *The Earliest Semitic Pantheon: A Study of the Semitic Deities Attested in Mesopotamia before Ur III.* Baltimore: Johns Hopkins University Press, 1972.

_____. "In Defense of the Monarchy: The Contribution of Israelite Kingship to Biblical Theology." Pages 377–96 in *Ancient Israelite Religion: Essays in Honor of Frank Moore Cross,* edited by Patrick D. Miller, Jr., Paul D. Hanson, and S. Dean McBride. Philadelphia: Fortress Press, 1987.

_____. "Zion in the Theology of the Davidic-Solomonic Empire." Pages 93–108 in *Studies in the Period of David and Solomon and Other Essays: Papers Read at the International Symposium for Biblical Studies, Tokyo, 5–7 December 1979,* edited by Tomoo Ishida. Winona Lake, Ind.: Eisenbrauns, 1982.

Rogerson, John. "Anthropology and the Old Testament." Pages 17–37 in *The World of Ancient Israel,* edited by Ronald E. Clements. Cambridge: University of Cambridge Press, 1991.

Rooke, Deborah W. "Kingship as Priesthood: The Relationship between the High Priesthood and the Monarchy." Pages 187–208 in *King and Messiah in Israel and the Ancient Near East: Proceedings of the Oxford Old Testament Seminar,* edited by John Day. JSOTSup 270. Sheffield: Sheffield Academic Press, 1998.

Rose, Martin. *Der Ausschliesslichkeitsanspruch Jahwes: Deuteronomische Schultheologie und die Volksfrömmigkeit in der späten Königszeit.* BWANT 106. Berlin: Walter de Gruyter, 1975.

———. "Yahweh in Israel—Qaus in Edom?" *JSOT* 4 (1977): 28–34.

Rösel, Hartmut N. "Zur Formulierung des aaronitischen Segens auf den Amuletten von Ketef Hinnom." *BN* 35 (1986): 30–36.

Rosen, Baruch. "Early Israelite Cultic Centres in the Hill Country." *VT* 38 (1988): 114–17.

Rouillard, Hedwige, and Josef Tropper, "TRPYM, rituels de guérison et culte des ancêtres d'après 1 Samuel XIX 11–17 et les textes parallèles d'Assur et de Nuzi." *VT* 37 (1987): 340–61.

Runciman, Walter G. *A Treatise on Social Theory,* vol. 2: Substantive Social Theory. Cambridge: Cambridge University Press, 1989.

Sakenfeld, Katharine. *The Meaning of Hesed in the Hebrew Bible: A New Inquiry.* HSM 17. Missoula, Mont.: Scholars Press, 1978.

Saldarini, Anthony J. "Scribes." *The Anchor Bible Dictionary,* edited by David N. Freedman, 5:1012–16. New York: Doubleday, 1992.

Sass, Benjamin. "The Pre-Exilic Seals: Iconism vs. Aniconism." Pages 194–246 in *Studies in the Iconography of Northwest Semitic Inscribed Seals.* OBO 125. Fribourg: Universitätsverlag, 1993.

Sawyer, John F. A., ed. *Reading Leviticus: A Conversation with Mary Douglas.* JSOT-Sup 227. Sheffield: JSOT Press, 1996.

Scharbert, Josef. "Formgeschichte und Exegese von Ex. 34, 6f und seiner Parallelen." *Bib* 38 (1957): 130–50.

Schmid, Hans H. *Gerechtigkeit als Weltordnung: Hintergrund und Geschichte der alttestamentlichen Gerechtigkeitsbegriffes.* BHT 40. Tübingen: Mohr/Siebeck, 1968.

Schmidt, Brian B. "The Aniconic Tradition: On Reading Images and Viewing Texts." Pages 75–105 in *The Triumph of Elohim: From Yahwisms to Judaisms,* edited by Diana Edelman. Grand Rapids: Wm. B. Eerdmans Publishing Co., 1996.

———. *Israel's Beneficent Dead: Ancestor Cult and Necromancy in Ancient Israelite Religion and Tradition.* Winona Lake, Ind.: Eisenbrauns, 1994.

Schmidt, Leo. *"De Deo": Studien zur Literarkritik und Theologie des Buches Jona, des Gesprächs zwischen Abraham und Jahwe in Gen 18, 22ff. und von Hi 1.* BZAW 143. Berlin: Walter de Gruyter, 1976.

Schmidt, Werner. *Königtum Gottes in Ugarit und Israel.* BZAW 80. Berlin: Walter de Gruyter, 1961.

Schmitz, Philip C. "Topheth." *The Anchor Bible Dictionary,* edited by David N. Freedman, 6:600–601. New York: Doubleday, 1992.

Schroer, Silva. *In Israel gab es Bilder: Nachrichten von darstellender Kunst im Alten Testament.* OBO 74. Fribourg: Universitätsverlag, 1987.

Schunck, Klaus D. "Zentralheiligtum, Grenzheiligtum und 'Hohenheiligtum' in Israel." *Numen* 18 (1971): 132–40.

Seitz, Christopher. *Theology in Conflict: Reactions to the Exile in the Book of Jeremiah.* Berlin: Walter de Gruyter, 1989.

Shanks, Hershel. "Three Shekels for the Lord: Ancient Inscription Records Gift to Solomon's Temple." *BARev* 23 (1997): 28–32.

Shanks, Hershel, and Jack Meinhardt, eds. *Aspects of Monotheism: How God Is One: Symposium at the Smithsonian Institution, October 19, 1996, Sponsored by the*

Resident Associate Program. Washington, D.C.: Biblical Archaeology Society, 1997.

Smith, Jonathan Z. *To Take Place: Toward Theory in Ritual.* Chicago: University of Chicago Press, 1987.

Smith, Mark S. *The Early History of God: Yahweh and the Other Deities in Ancient Israel.* San Francisco: Harper & Row, 1990.

——. "The Near Eastern Background of Solar Language for Yahweh." *JBL* 109 (1990): 29–39.

——. "Yahweh and Other Deities in Ancient Israel: Observations on Old Problems and Recent Trends." Pages 197–234 in *Ein Gott allein? JHWH-Verehrung und biblischer Monotheismus im Kontext der israelitischen und altorientalischen Religionsgeschichte*, edited by Walter Dietrich and Martin A. Klopfenstein. OBO 139. Freiburg: Universitätsverlag, 1994.

Smith-Christopher, Daniel. "The Mixed Marriage Crisis in Ezra 9–10 and Nehemiah 13: A Study of the Sociology of the Post-Exilic Judaean Community." Pages 243–65 in *Second Temple Studies 2: Temple Community in the Persian Period*, edited by Tamara C. Eskenazi and Kent H. Richards. JSOTSup 175. Sheffield: JSOT Press, 1994.

Spieckermann, Hermann. "Barmherzig und gnädig ist der Herr . . ." *ZAW* 102 (1990): 1–18.

——. *Juda unter Assur in der Sargonidzeit.* FRLANT 129. Göttingen: Vandenhoeck & Ruprecht, 1982.

Spronk, Klaas. *Beatific Afterlife in Ancient Israel and in the Ancient Near East.* AOAT 219. Neukirchen-Vluyn: Neukirchener Verlag, 1986.

Stager, Lawrence E. "The Archaeology of the Family in Ancient Israel." *BASOR* 260 (1985): 1–35.

——. "Toward the Future: It's Just a Matter of Time." Pages 746–55 in *Biblical Archaeology Today, 1990.* Jerusalem: Israel Exploration Society, 1993.

Stager, Lawrence E., and Samuel Wolff. "Child Sacrifice at Carthage—Religious Rite or Population Control?" *BARev* 10/1 (Jan./Feb. 1984): 30–51.

——. "Production and Commerce in Temple Courtyards: An Olive Press in the Sacred Precinct at Tel Dan." *BASOR* 243 (1981): 95–102.

Stähli, Hans-Peter. *Solare Elemente im Jahweglauben des Alten Testaments.* OBO 66. Freiburg: Universitätsverlag, 1985.

Stone, Michael E. "Ideal Figures and Social Context: Priest and Sage in the Early Second Temple Age." Pages 575–86 in *Ancient Israelite Religion: Essays in Honor of Frank Moore Cross*, edited by Patrick D. Miller, Jr., Paul D. Hanson, and S. Dean McBride. Philadelphia: Fortress Press, 1987.

Strenski, Ivan. "Between Theory and Speciality: Sacrifice in the 90s." *RSR* 22 (1996): 10–20.

Talmon, Shemaryahu. "The Cult and Calendar Reform of Jeroboam I." In *King, Cult and Calendar in Ancient Israel.* Jerusalem: Magnes Press, 1986.

——. "The Emergence of Jewish Sectarianism in the Early Second Temple Period." Pages 587–616 in *Ancient Israelite Religion: Essays in Honor of Frank Moore Cross*, edited by Patrick D. Miller, Jr., Paul D. Hanson, and S. Dean McBride. Philadelphia: Fortress Press, 1987.

Tappy, Ron. "Did the Dead Ever Die in Biblical Judah?" (review of Elizabeth Bloch-

Smith, *Judahite Burial Practices and Beliefs about the Dead.*) *BASOR* 298 (1995): 59–68.

Taylor, J. Glen. "The Two Earliest Known Representations of Yahweh." Pages 557–66 in *Ascribe to the Lord: Biblical and Other Studies in Memory of Peter C. Craigie,* edited by Lyle M. Eslinger and J. Glen Taylor. JSOTSup 67. Sheffield: Sheffield Academic Press, 1988.

———. *Yahweh and the Sun: Biblical and Archaeological Evidence for Sun Worship in Ancient Israel.* JSOTSup 111. Sheffield: JSOT Press, 1993.

Tigay, Jeffrey. *Deuteronomy: The Traditional Hebrew Text with the New JPS Translation.* JPS Torah Commentary. Philadelphia: Jewish Publication Society, 1996.

———. "Israelite Religion: The Onomastic and Epigraphic Evidence." Pages 157–94 in *Ancient Israelite Religion: Essays in Honor of Frank Moore Cross,* edited by Patrick D. Miller, Jr., Paul D. Hanson, and S. Dean McBride. Philadelphia: Fortress Press, 1987.

———. *You Shall Have No Other Gods: Israelite Religion in the Light of Hebrew Inscriptions.* Atlanta: Scholars Press, 1986.

Toews, Wesley I. *Monarchy and Religious Institution in Israel under Jeroboam I.* SBLMS 47. Atlanta: Scholars Press, 1993.

Toorn, Karel van der. "The Babylonian New Year Festival: New Insights from the Cuneiform Texts and Their Bearing on Old Testament Study." Pages 331–4 in *Congress Volume, Leuven 1989,* edited by John A. Emerton. VTSup 43. Leiden: E. J. Brill, 1991.

———. "Currents in the Study of Israelite Religion." *Currents in Research: Biblical Studies* 6 (1998): 9–30.

———. "The Domestic Cult at Emar." *JCS* 47 (1995): 35–49.

———. "Family Gods in Mesopotamia, Syria and Israel." Paper presented at the Annual Meeting of the Society of Biblical Literature, 1992.

———. *Family Religion in Babylonia, Syria and Israel: Continuity and Change in the Forms of Religious Life.* Studies in the History and Culture of the Ancient Near East 7. Leiden: E. J. Brill, 1996.

———. *From Her Cradle to Her Grave: The Role of Religion in the Life of the Israelite and the Babylonian Woman.* Biblical Seminar 23. Sheffield: JSOT Press, 1994.

———, ed. *The Image and the Book: Iconic Cults, Aniconism, and the Rise of Book Religion in Israel and the Ancient Near East.* Contributions to Biblical Exegesis and Theology 21. Louvain: Peeters, 1997.

———. "The Nature of the Biblical Teraphim in the Light of the Cuneiform Evidence." *CBQ* 52 (1990): 202–23.

———. "Yahweh." Pages 910–19 in *Dictionary of Deities and Demons in the Bible.* 2d rev. ed., edited by Karel van der Toorn, Bob Becking, and Pieter Willem van der Horst. Leiden: E. J. Brill, 1999.

Toorn, Karel van der, Bob Becking, and Pieter Willem van der Horst, eds. *Dictionary of Deities and Demons in the Bible.* 2d rev. ed. Leiden: E. J. Brill, 1999.

Tropper, Josef. *Nekromantie: Totenbefragung im Alten Orient und Alten Testament.* AOAT 223. Neukirchen-Vluyn: Neukirchener Verlag, 1989.

Tsumura, David T. "Kings and Cults in Ancient Ugarit." Pages 215–38 in *Priests and Officials in the Ancient Near East: Papers of the Second Colloquium on the Ancient Near East—the City and its Life; held at the Middle Eastern Culture*

Center in Japan (Mitaka, Tokyo), March 22–24, 1996, edited by Kazuko Watanabe. Heidelberg: Universitätsverlag C. Winter, 1999.

Tucker, Gene M. "Prophecy and the Prophetic Literature." Pages 325–68 in *The Hebrew Bible and Its Modern Interpreters,* edited by Douglas A. Knight and Gene M. Tucker. Philadelphia: Fortress Press; Atlanta: Scholars Press, 1985.

Tuell, Steven S. *The Law of the Temple in Ezekiel 40–48.* HSM 49. Atlanta: Scholars Press, 1992.

Turner, Victor. *The Ritual Process: Structure and Antistructure.* Symbol, Myth, and Ritual Series. Chicago: Aldine Publishing Co., 1969.

Uehlinger, Christoph. "Anthropomorphic Cult Statuary in Iron Age Palestine and the Search for Yahweh's Cult Images." Pages 97–155 in *The Image and the Book: Iconic Cults, Aniconism, and the Rise of Book Religion in Israel and the Ancient Near East,* edited by Karel van der Toorn. Louvain: Peeters, 1997.

Ussishkin, David. "Fresh Examination of Old Excavations: Sanctuaries in the First Temple Period." Pages 67–85 in *Biblical Archaeology Today, 1990: Proceedings of the Second International Congress on Biblical Archaeology, Jerusalem, June–July 1990,* edited by Avraham Biran. Jerusalem: Israel Exploration Society, 1993.

Vaughn, Andrew. *Theology, History, and Archaeology in the Chronicler's Account of Hezekiah.* Archaeology and Biblical Studies 4. Atlanta: Scholars Press, 1999.

Vaux, Roland de. *Ancient Israel: Its Life and Institutions.* London: Darton, Longman & Todd, 1961.

Vincent, A. Léopold. *La religion des Judeo-Araméens d'Éléphantine.* Paris: P. Geuthner, 1937.

Voight, Mary M. *Hajji Firuz Tepe, Iran: The Neolithic Settlement.* Edited by Richard H. Dyson Jr. Hasanlu Excavation Reports 1. University Museum Monographs 50. Philadelphia: University Museum, University of Pennsylvania, 1984.

Volz, Paul. *Das Dämonische in Jahwe.* Tübingen: J. C. B. Mohr, 1924.

Vos, Clarence J. *Woman in Old Testament Worship.* Delft: Judels & Brinkman, 1968.

Vrijhof, P. J., and Jean Jacques Waardenburg. *Official and Popular Religion: Analysis of a Theme for Religious Studies.* Religion and Society 19. The Hague: Mouton, 1979.

Wacker, Marie-Theres. " 'Religionsgeschichte Israels' oder 'Theologie des Alten Testaments'—(k)eine Alternative? Anmerkungen aus feministisch-exegetischer Sicht." *Jahrbuch für Biblische Theologie* 10 (1995): 142–55.

Walters, Stanley D. "Hannah and Anna: The Greek and Hebrew Texts of Samuel 1." *JBL* 107 (1988): 385–412.

Washington, Harold C. *Wealth and Poverty in the Instruction of Amenemope and the Hebrew Proverbs.* SBLDS 142. Atlanta: Scholars Press, 1994.

Weinberg, Joel P. *The Citizen-Temple Community.* JSOTSup 151. Sheffield: JSOT Press, 1992.

Weinfeld, Moshe. *Deuteronomy and the Deuteronomic School.* Oxford: Clarendon Press, 1972.

———. "The Molech Cult in Israel and Its Background." Pages 133–54 in *Proceedings of the Fifth World Congress of Jewish Studies, the Hebrew University, Mount Scopus-Givat Ram, Jerusalem, 3–11 August 1969,* edited by Pinchas Peli. Jerusalem: World Union of Jewish Studies, 1969.

———. "The Tribal League of Sinai." Pages 303–14 in *Ancient Israelite Religion:*

Essays in Honor of Frank Moore Cross, edited by Patrick D. Miller, Jr., Paul D. Hanson, and S. Dean McBride. Philadelphia: Fortress Press, 1987.

_____. "The Worship of Molech and of the Queen of Heaven and Its Background." *UF* 4 (1972): 133–54.

_____. "Zion and Jerusalem as Religious and Political Capital: Ideology and Utopia." Pages 75–115 in *The Poet and the Historian: Essays in Literary and Historical Biblical Criticism*, edited by Richard E. Friedman. Chico, Calif.: Scholars Press, 1983.

Weippert, Helga. *Palästina in vorhellenistischer Zeit*. Handbuch der Archäologie 2/1. Munich: C. H. Beck, 1988.

Weippert, Manfred. "'Heiliger Krieg' in Israel und Assyrien: Kritischen Anmerkungen zu Gerhard von Rads Konzept des 'Heiligen Krieges im alten Israel.'" *ZAW* 84 (1972): 460–93.

_____. "Synkretismus und Monotheismus: Religionsinterne Konfliktbewaltigung im alten Israel." Pages 143–79 in *Kultur und Konflikt*, edited by Jan Assmann and Dietrich Harth. Frankfurt: Suhrkamp, 1990.

Weiser, Artur. *The Psalms: A Commentary*. OTL. Philadelphia: Westminster Press, 1962.

_____. "Zur Frage nach den Beziehungen der Psalmen zum Kult: Die Darstellung der Theophanie in den Psalmen und im Festkult." Pages 513–31 in *Festschrift Alfred Bertholet zum 80.*, edited by Walter Baumgartner et al. Tübingen: J. C. B. Mohr, 1950.

Wellhausen, Julius. *Prolegomena to the History of Israel*. Scholars Press Reprints and Translations Series. Altanta: Scholars Press, 1994.

Wenning, Robert. "Iron Age Tombs and Burial Customs in Judah: New Approaches." Paper presented to the Annual Meeting of the American Schools of Oriental Research, Chicago, November 21, 1994.

Wenning, Robert, and E. Zenger, "Ein bäuerliches Baal-Heiligtum im samarischen Gebirge aus der Zeit der Anfänge Israels." *ZDPV* 102 (1986): 75–86.

Westbrook, Raymond. *Property and Family in Biblical Law*. JSOTSup 113. Sheffield: JSOT Press, 1991.

Westenholz, Joan Goodnick. "Tamar, *Qĕdēšâ, Qadištu,* and Sacred Prostitution in Mesopotamia." *HTR* 82 (1989): 245–65.

Westermann, Claus. *Prophetic Oracles of Salvation in the Old Testament*. Louisville, Ky.: Westminster/John Knox Press, 1991.

White, Marsha. "The Elohistic Depiction of Aaron: A Study in the Levite-Zadokite Controversy." Pages 149–59 in *Studies in the Pentateuch*. VTSup 41. Leiden: E. J. Brill, 1990.

Whitelam, Keith W. "Israelite Kingship: The Royal Ideology and Its Opponents." Pages 119–39 in *The World of Ancient Israel*, edited by Ronald E. Clements. Cambridge: Cambridge University Press, 1991.

Wiggins, Steve A. *A Reassessment of "Asherah": A Study according to the Textual Sources of the First Two Millenia* [sic] *B.C.E.* AOAT 235. Neukirchen-Vluyn: Neukirchener Verlag, 1993.

Williamson, H. G. M. "Exile and After: Historical Study." Pages 236–65 in *The Face of Old Testament Studies: A Survey of Contemporary Approaches,* edited by David W. Baker and Bill T. Arnold. Grand Rapids: Baker Book House, 1999.

_____. "Judah and the Jews." Pages 145–63 in *Achaemenid History*, vol. 11: *Studies in Persian History: Essays in Memory of David M. Lewis*, edited by Maria Brosius and Amélie Kuhrt. Leiden: Nederlands Instituut van het Nabije Oosten, 1998.

Wilson, E. Jan. *"Holiness" and "Purity" in Mesopotamia*. AOAT 237. Neukirchen-Vluyn: Neukirchener Verlag, 1994.

Wilson, Robert R. *Prophecy and Society in Ancient Israel*. Philadelphia: Fortress Press, 1980.

Winter, Urs. *Frau und Göttin: Exegetische und ikonographische Studien zum weiblichen Gottesbild im Alten Israel und in dessen Umwelt*. OBO 53. Freiburg: Universitätsverlag, 1983.

Wolff, Hans W. *Joel and Amos: Commentary on the Books of the Prophets Joel and Amos*. Translated by Waldemar Janzen, S. Dean McBride, and Charles A. Muenchow. Hermeneia. Philadelphia: Fortress Press, 1977.

Wright, David P. "Azazel." *The Anchor Bible Dictionary*. Edited by David N. Freedman, 1:536–37. New York: Doubleday, 1992.

_____. "Day of Atonement." *The Anchor Bible Dictionary*, edited by David N. Freedman, 2:72–76. New York: Doubleday, 1992.

_____. *The Disposal of Impurity: Elimination Rites in the Bible and in Hittite and Mesopotamian Literature*. SBLDS 101. Atlanta: Scholars Press, 1987.

_____. "Holiness in Leviticus and Beyond: Differing Perspectives." *Int* 55 (1999): 351–64.

_____. "Holiness (OT)." *The Anchor Bible Dictionary*, edited by David N. Freedman, 3:237–49. New York: Doubleday, 1992.

_____. "Observations on the Ethical Foundations of the Biblical Dietary Laws: A Response to Jacob Milgrom." Page 193–98 in *Religion and Law: Biblical, Jewish, and Islamic Perspectives,* edited by Edwin Firmage, John Welch, and Bernard Weiss. Winona Lake, Ind.: Eisenbrauns, 1990.

_____. "The Spectrum of Priestly Impurity." Pages 150–81 in *Priesthood and Cult in Ancient Israel,* edited by Gary A. Anderson and Saul M. Olyan. JSOTSup 125. Sheffield: JSOT Press, 1991.

_____. "Unclean and Clean (OT)." *The Anchor Bible Dictionary*, edited by David N. Freedman, 6:729–41. New York: Doubleday, 1992.

Wyatt, Nick. "Symbols of Exile." *SEÅ* 55 (1990): 39–58.

Yardeni, Ada. "Remarks on the Priestly Blessing on Two Ancient Amulets from Jerusalem." *VT* 41 (1991): 176–85.

Yassine, Khari. "The Open Sanctuary of the Iron Age I *Tell el-Mazar* Mound A." *ZDPV* 100 (1984): 108–18.

Zevit, Ziony. "The Khirbet el-Qom Inscription Mentioning a Goddess." *BASOR* 255 (1984): 39–47.

Zimmerli, Walther. *Ezekiel I*. Hermeneia. Philadelphia: Fortress Press, 1979.

_____. "The History of Israelite Religion." Pages 251–84 in *Tradition and Interpretation*, edited by George W. Anderson. Oxford: Clarendon Press, 1979.

Zwickel, Wolfgang. *Der Tempelkult in Kanaan und Israel: Studien zur Kultgeschichte Palästinas von der Mittelbronzezeit bis zum Untergang Judas*. Forschungen zum Alten Testament 10. Tübingen: J. C. B. Mohr, 1994.

Sources of the Illustrations

The following sources are referred to in the credits for figures and plates:

ANEP, *The Ancient Near East in Pictures Relating to the Old Testament* (Princeton, N.J.: Princeton University Press, 1954). (Pages 3, 4, 15, 17, 21, 58)

Beck, Pirhiya, *Tel Aviv* 9 (1982), figs. 3 and 4. (Pages 32, 104)

Biran, Avraham, ed., *Temples and High Places in Biblical Times: Proceedings of the Colloquium in Honor of the Centennial of Hebrew Union College–Jewish Institute of Religion, Jerusalem, 14–16 March 1977*, p. 146, fig. 4 and pl. 20, no. 4. (Page 78)

Collection of the Israel Antiquities Authority. (Pages 18, 22, 38, 49, 65, 164, 166)

Dever, William G., et al., *Gezer II: Report of the 1967–70 seasons in fields I and II* (Jerusalem: Hebrew Union College/Nelson Glueck School of Biblical Archaeology, 1974), pls. 41 and 75. (Page 19)

Gitin, Seymour, "Incense Altars from Ekron, Israel and Judah: Context and Typology," *Eretz Israel* 20 (1989): 53*. (Page 64)

Hadley, Judith M., *Vetus Testamentum* 37 (1987): 52. (Page 31)

Hendel, Ronald S. *The Image and the Book: Iconic Cults, Aniconism, and the Rise of Book Religion in Israel and the Ancient Near East,* ed. Karel van der Toorn (Louvain: Peeters, 1997). (Page 18)

Taylor, J. Glen, *Yahweh and the Sun: Biblical and Archaeological Evidence for Sun Worship in Ancient Israel.* JSOT Supplement 111. Sheffield: JSOT Press, 1993, pl. 7 and fig. 9. (Page 53)

Wright, G. Ernest, *Biblical Archaeology* (Philadelphia: Westminster Press, 1957), p. 138, fig. 92. (Page 91)

Index of Biblical Passages and Ancient Sources

Index of Subjects

Ahaz, 193–94
altars, 50
aniconism, 16–17, 20–23, 225 n.89
apocalyptic, 101–2
Arad temple, 235 n.2
Aram, 220 n.53
ark, 16, 21, 50, 87–88, 89, 90, 117, 132–34, 137, 158, 194–95, 217 n.38, 255 n.236
asherah, 37–40, 225 n.89, 229 n.141, 231 nn.154, 156; 232 n.162
   See also goddess, Asherah; Yahweh, and Asherah
atonement, 263 n.28
   day of, 99, 115, 167
Azazel, 116–17

Baal, 43, 57–58, 91–92
   See also Yahweh, and Baal
ban, 149
bet 'ab, 62, 68, 242 n.84
Bethel, 191
blood, 134–35
Book of the Covenant, 140, 160
boundaries, 97
bronze serpent, 19, 52
bull imagery, 256 n.258
   Bull Site, 64

Christianity, 209
circumcision, 70–71
conflict, postexilic, 96, 100–101, 257 n.273
covenant, 4–6

cult
   ad hoc, 85–86
   community, 94–102
   family center, 64–76
   foreigners, 199–201
   heavenly bodies, 60–61
   "holy to Yahweh," 132
   household shrine, 63
   Israelite confederation, 80–87
   and king, 88
   leadership, 50–51
   male leadership, 202, 270 n.27
   musicians, 202, 280 n.51
   objects, 52, 63–64, 243 n.95
   postexilic, 95–102, 200–201, 258 n.287
   regional centers, 76–79, 244 n.100
   resident alien, 200–201
   restrictions, 14, 206–7
   state religion of Israel, 93–94
   state religion of Judah, 87–93
   sun, 60
   and women, 201–6, 261 n.8, 286 n.145

Dan, 251 n.190
David, 87–88, 89, 194, 247 n.127, 255 n.236
death, 71–72
Deborah, 280 n.55
demons, 27–28
dietary laws, 153–55, 160, 273 n.61
divination, 54
   See also inquiry of deity; priests, divination; prophets, divination

331